*Divine discourse* comprises Nicholas Wolterstorff's philosophical reflections on the claim that God speaks. This claim figures large in the canonical texts and traditions of Judaism, Christianity, and Islam, but there has been remarkably little philosophical reflection on it, in good measure (so Professor Wolterstorff argues) because philosophers have mistakenly assimilated divine speech to divine revelation. He embraces contemporary speech-action theory as his basic approach to language; and after expanding the theory beyond its usual applications, concludes that the claim that God performs illocutionary actions is coherent and entails no obvious falsehoods. Moving on to issues of interpretation, he considers how one would interpret a text if one wanted to find out what God was saying thereby. Prominent features of this part of the discussion are his defense, against Ricoeur and Derrida, of the legitimacy of interpreting a text to find out what its author said, and his analysis of the double hermeneutic involved when the discourse of one person is appropriated into the discourse of another person. The book closes with a discussion of the epistemological question of whether we are ever entitled to believe that God speaks.

Derived from the Wilde Lectures, delivered by the author at the University of Oxford in 1993, *Divine discourse* is noteworthy for the breadth of the sources it brings to bear on the issues it discusses. The speech-act theory of J. L. Austin, Oxford philosophy, Continental hermeneutic philosophy, Protestant theology, and St. Augustine's *Confessions* are all included. This innovative treatment of a major issue in religious studies makes a significant contribution to philosophical and theological debate, and will be of interest to readers in a number of fields.

# DIVINE DISCOURSE

# DIVINE DISCOURSE

*Philosophical reflections on the claim that God speaks*

NICHOLAS WOLTERSTORFF

*Noah Porter Professor of Philosophical Theology, Yale University*

CAMBRIDGE
UNIVERSITY PRESS

Published by the Press Syndicate of the University of Cambridge
The Pitt Building, Trumpington Street, Cambridge CB2 1RP
40 West 20th Street, New York, NY 10011–4211, USA
10 Stamford Road, Oakleigh, Melbourne 3166, Australia

First published 1995
Transferred to digital printing 1998

Printed in the United Kingdom by
Antony Rowe Ltd, Chippenham, Wiltshire

*A catalogue record for this book is available from the British Library*

*Library of Congress Cataloguing in publication data*
Wolterstorff, Nicholas.
Divine discourse: philosophical reflections on the claim that
God speaks / Nicholas Wolterstorff.
p.      cm.
Includes bibliographical references and index.
ISBN 0 521 47539 2 (hardback). – ISBN 0 521 47557 0 (paperback).
1. Word of God (Theology)
2. Direct discourse in the Bible.
3. Language and languages – Religious aspects—Christianity.
4. Speech acts (Linguistics)   I. Title.
BT180.w67w65   1995
231'.014 – dc20 94 – 42264 CIP

ISBN 0 521 47539 2 hardback
ISBN 0 521 47557 0 paperback

# Contents

Contents

# *Preface*

That strange but rivetting declaration, both unsettling and consoling if true, introduced most emphatically into our human odyssey by Judaism, that God speaks to us on our way, and that, accordingly, our calling as human beings is to listen to that speech from beyond and "hear" – I knew almost at once after receiving the invitation to be Wilde Lecturer at Oxford University during Michaelmas Term 1993 that this was what I wanted to discuss. I realized, of course, that most of my philosophical colleagues would regard the topic as "off the wall" for a philosopher – or something one would have to be slightly mad to take seriously. But now, as the twentieth century draws to its close, the conviction is slowly emerging in many quarters that perhaps the hostility of us moderns to the religious traditions which brought us forth and have so long nourished us has been ill-advised and self-defeating. And deep in the traditions of Judaism, Christianity, and Islam, is the attribution of speech to God. To excise those attributions from those religions would be to have only shards left.

So "off the wall" or not – that was my topic. Might it be the case that contemporary philosophy is at a place where it is possible to reflect in fresh ways on the declaration: "And God said ..." Central in the philosophical thought of our century has been the topic of language. Might it be that in addition to *homo linguisticus*, on which we have focused our attention, there is *deus loquens*? The ultimate possibility for our language-preoccupied century to consider: might it be that God is a member of the community of speakers?

To the University of Oxford, I hereby express my appreciation for the honor extended me of being invited to give the Wilde Lectures – from which approximately half of the chapters that follow originated. To Oriel College and its Provost, Ernest Nicholson, my gratitude for their making me a visiting fellow of the College during my term in Oxford. To a large number of philosophers and theologians at Oxford, but especially to Professor Richard Swinburne, my deep appreciation for their hospitality and discussions. To various people at Yale, especially Marilyn and Robert Adams, my thanks for suggestions they made in discussions on the manuscript; likewise my thanks for comments on the manuscript to William P. Alston, Steve Evans, and Eleonore Stump. To my former colleagues in the philosophy department at Calvin College, my thanks for discussions beginning already twenty-five years ago on some of these issues. And finally, my gratitude to the Evangelical Scholarship Initiative, funded by the Pew Charitable Trust, for the financial support which made much of my work on this topic possible.

# *Locating our topic*

My project is to reflect philosophically on the claim that God speaks. In this opening chapter I will situate these reflections within various on-going contemporary discussions. But before I do that, let's have in hand some examples – or purported examples – of the phenomenon we will be discussing.

## *Examples of God speaking*

In the year 386 there took place in the northern Italian city of Milan a conversation which was as fateful for religion in the West as any which has ever taken place. The participants were Augustine, his friend Alypius, and Ponticianus, a fellow countryman from North Africa who held a high position in the Emperor's household. The conversation was initiated by Ponticianus paying a visit to Augustine and Alypius at the villa in which they were staying along with Augustine's mother. Ponticianus, says Augustine in his narration of the episode, "had some request to make of us and we sat down to talk" (*Confessions* VIII, 6). Though Ponticianus eventually completed his business (VIII, 7), what is important to us is not the business transacted – we don't even know what it was – but the fateful crisis Ponticianus triggered in Augustine before they ever got around to discussing business.

Shortly after sitting down, Ponticianus picked up a book lying on a game-table near by. He expected something from Augustine's profession as a teacher of rhetoric; instead it was a copy of St. Paul's epistles. Ponticianus smiled – he himself was a Christian – and remarked how glad and surprised he was to find this book there; it was, in fact, the only book in sight. Augustine replied that he had been studying Paul's writings "with the greatest attention." That led Ponticianus into some remarks about the life of Antony, the Egyptian monk. When it became clear that Augustine and Alypius had never heard of Antony, Ponticianus went farther into the story of Antony's founding of the monastic movement in Egypt. And that, in turn, led him on into some personal reminiscences concerning monasticism.

One afternoon, while on a trip to Trêves as a member of the emperor's entourage, he and three companions went strolling in the gardens near the city wall while the emperor attended the games. At a certain point, Ponticianus and one of his companions parted ways from the other two. While separated, the other pair happened on a modest cottage in which they found a book containing the life of Antony. One of them began reading it, "and was so fascinated and thrilled by the story that even before he had finished reading he conceived the idea of taking upon himself the same kind of life and abandoning his career in the world – both he and his friend were officials in the service of the State – in order to become [God's] servant. All at once he was filled with the love of holiness. Angry with himself and full of remorse, he looked at his friend and said, 'What do we hope to gain by all the efforts we make? What are we looking for? What is our purpose in serving the State? Can we hope for anything better at Court than to be the Emperor's friends? Even so, surely our position would be precarious and exposed to much danger. We shall meet it at every turn, only to reach another danger which is greater still. And how long is it to be before we reach it? But if I wish, I can become the friend of God at this very moment' "(viii, 6). He read on, "his heart leaping and turning in his breast"; by the time he had finished, his resolve was firm. Turning to his companion he said, "I have torn myself free from all our ambitions and have decided to serve God ... If you will not follow my lead do not stand in my way." His companion answered that he would "stand by his comrade, for such service was glorious and the reward was great."

Dusk was falling; and Ponticianus and his comrade had been looking for the pair. Just at this moment they discovered them, there in the cottage. The pair told of the resolution they had made, and invited Ponticianus and his comrade to join them – or if they chose not to join them, at least not to place obstacles in their way. Ponticianus and his comrade replied that they themselves were not ready to change their way of life so drastically; but "in all reverence they congratulated the others and commended themselves to their prayers. Then they went back to the palace, burdened with hearts that were bound to this earth; but the others remained in the house and their hearts were fixed upon heaven."

Ponticianus could not have anticipated the effect of these reminiscences on Augustine. Augustine was a person in torment; and his torment had everything to do with the alternative modes of life faced by those four men standing in the dusk there in that cottage, story of Antony in hand. Those very modes of life were locked in a bitter struggle for dominance within Augustine, with this difference: the mode of life battling it out with asceticism in Augustine's inner self was not a life devoted to political success but a life in the grip of "worldliness." Augustine and Alypius happened not to know anything of monastic asceticism until Ponticianus told them about it; but they were already familiar with other forms of the ascetic life shaped by the love of God. Augustine, in fact, desired intensely to live such a life. But he could not free himself from habits of lust and ambition. The rhetoric of his narrative becomes rich with metaphors of incarceration at this point: "The enemy held my will in his power and from it he had made a chain and shackled me ... [The] links which together formed what I have called my chain ... held me fast in the duress of servitude" (VIII, 5).

To describe the shattering effect on him of Ponticianus' conversation, Augustine uses the extraordinary image of having placed himself behind his own back and God now turning him around to look at himself: "while he was speaking, O Lord, you were turning me around to look at myself. For I had placed myself behind my own back, refusing to see myself. You were setting me before my own eyes so that I could see how sordid I was, how deformed and squalid, how tainted with ulcers and sores. I saw it all and stood aghast, but there was no place where I could escape from myself. If I tried to turn my eyes away they fell on Ponticianus, still telling his tale, and in this way you brought me face to face with myself once more, forcing me upon my own sight so that I should see my wickedness and loathe it ... I stood naked before my own eyes ... " (VIII, 7).

After Ponticianus left, Augustine, in torment, went out into the garden, Alypius on his heels. "I was beside myself with madness that would bring me sanity," he says in retrospect, "I was dying a death that would bring me life ... I was frantic, overcome by violent anger with myself for not accepting [God's] will and entering into [God's] covenant. Yet in my bones I knew that this was what I ought to do" (VIII, 8). "In my heart I kept saying 'Let it be now, let it be now!', and merely by saying this I was on the point of making the resolution. I was on the point of making it, but I did not succeed. Yet I did not fall back into my old state. I stood on the brink of resolution, waiting to take fresh breath. I tried again and came a little nearer to my goal, and then a little nearer still, so that I could almost reach out and grasp it. But I did not reach it. I could not reach out to it or grasp it, because I held back from the step by which I should die to death and become alive to life ... And the closer I came to the moment which was to mark the great change in me, the more I shrank from it in horror. But it did not drive me back or turn me from my purpose: it merely left me hanging in suspense" (VIII, 11).

Augustine broke down in a "deluge of tears." "I stood up," he says, "and left Alypius so that I might weep and cry to my heart's content, for it occurred to me that tears were best shed in solitude." Throwing himself down under a fig tree, he cried out in misery, over and over, tears flowing, "How long shall I go on saying 'tomorrow, tomorrow'? Why not now?"

Now the part of the story which we all know and which is important for my purposes:

I was asking myself these questions, weeping all the while with the most bitter sorrow in my heart, when all at once I heard the sing-song voice of a child in a nearby house. Whether it was the voice of a boy or a girl I cannot say, but again and again it repeated the refrain "Take it and read, take it and read". At this I looked up, thinking hard whether there was any kind of game in which children used to chant words like these, but I could not remember ever hearing them before. I stemmed my flood of tears and stood up, telling myself that this could only be a divine command to open my book of Scripture and read the first passage on which my eyes should fall. For I had heard the story of Antony, and I remembered how he had happened to go into a church while the Gospel was being read and had taken it as a counsel addressed to himself when he heard the words *Go home and sell all that belongs to you. Give it to the poor, and so the treasure you have shall be in heaven; then come back and follow me.* By this divine pronouncement he had at once been converted to you.

So I hurried back to the place where Alypius was sitting, for when I stood up to move away I had put down the book containing Paul's Epistles. I seized it and opened it, and in silence I read the first passage on which my eyes fell: *Not in revelling and drunkenness, not in lust and wantonness, not in quarrels and rivalries. Rather, arm yourselves with the Lord Jesus Christ; spend no more thought on nature and nature's appetites.* I had no wish to read more and no need to do so. For in an instant, as I came to the end of the sentence, it was as though the light of confidence flooded into my heart and all the darkness of doubt was dispelled. (VIII, 12).

The language of *decision* has disappeared from the account. Earlier in the text, when Augustine was describing his state of mind before the final turning, will was central: "When I was trying to reach a decision about serving the Lord my God, as I had long intended to do, it was I who willed to take this course and again it was I who willed not to take it ... But I neither willed to do it nor refused to do it with my full will" (VIII, 10). Now, when Augustine is describing the actual moment of turning, there is not a word about will, not a word about decision, not a word about resolution; just this: "as I came to the end of the sentence, ... the light of confidence flooded into my heart ... " The language is now the language of *being overcome*: Rejecting his former way of life and embracing the new way was not something he *decided to do* but something he *found himself doing*.

*Tolle lege, tolle lege*; take and read, take and read: the most famous words any child has ever uttered. They were indeed uttered by a child. Though Augustine couldn't tell whether the chanter was a boy or girl, it never crossed his mind to doubt that it was a child. And after the briefest reflection, he had no doubt that by way of the child chanting these words, *God* was then and there saying something, performing a speech action; specifically, an action of *commanding*. The command was not addressed to some collectivity of human beings but addressed specifically to him: God was commanding *him* to open *his* book of Scripture and read the first passage on which *his* eye should fall. Perhaps the child was doing no more than uttering words – over and over for the sake of the sound of them. Or perhaps the child was also performing a speech action. If so, presumably that action was also an action of *commanding* or *requesting*. The content of the command would have been different, however, from the content of God's command. For the child was not commanding *Augustine* to open *his* copy of scripture and read the first thing on which *his* eye should fall; the child didn't know Augustine, and hence couldn't issue such a command. Either way, two agents: the divine agent saying something by way of the human agent either just uttering words, or saying something by way of uttering words.

Augustine describes the case of Alypius differently: Alypius, he says, *applied* an "admonition" found in scripture to himself. Augustine does not tell us whether he construed the admonition in question as issued only by Paul, or as issued by God by way of what Paul said. One guesses the latter. But in any case, the idea here is not that God was then and there issuing a command to Alypius, but that Alypius was applying to himself a command issued more than three centuries earlier.

Why did Augustine believe that God was then and there speaking to him? Long before he stumbled out into the garden, Augustine believed that God was a speaking God – that God says things to human beings. That belonged to his background beliefs. Now in his misery he hears the strange phenomenon of a child chanting over and over, "*tolle lege, tolle lege.*" He can think of only one thing in human affairs which would lead a child to chant in this fashion: a game. But he can recall no game involving this chant. Then the story he has just heard comes to mind, of Antony addressed by God through a reading of scripture which he just happens to hear. That's it: background belief that God speaks, inexplicable uncanny chanting, sudden intimation of the possibility, and relevance to his own life, of God saying *take and read.* The quick train of thought eventuates in Augustine saying to himself: "this could only be a divine command to open my book of Scripture and read the first passage on which my eyes should fall." If one is looking for it, perhaps one can spot in the process a quick calculation of probabilities; but if so, what a careless job of collecting evidence! No careful research into children's games. No hurdling the wall to ask the child why he or she was chanting these words. And – let it be noted – no miracles! Just a few quick thoughts resulting in Augustine finding himself saying to himself that this could only be God speaking to him. Neither then nor later did anything come to mind or happen to him which led him to doubt this interpretation. Quite the contrary: the light of confidence flooded into his heart and all the darkness of doubt was dispelled.

Augustine obeyed the divine imperative. On the page to which his copy of Paul's letters happened to fall open, he read silently the first lines which happened to catch his eye. And then, by way of his doing this, God spoke to him a second time. Admittedly Augustine does not, in his narration of the episode, offer this interpretation of what happened. He just cites the words he read, and says that as he finished the sentence, it was as though the light of confidence flooded into his heart and all the darkness of doubt was dispelled. But at the beginning of the next book of the *Confessions* Augustine says, addressing God, "all that you asked of me was to deny my own will and accept yours"; I understand him to be referring here to the episode he has just described, of reading those words from Paul. So I think we can safely infer that Augustine interpreted the situation as God speaking to him a second time, instructing him to arm himself with the Lord Jesus Christ and spend no more thought on nature and nature's appetites.

Now Paul regarded himself as an apostle, an *apostolos*, commissioned by Jesus Christ to speak on behalf of God in being his witness. He introduces his letter to the Roman Christians, from which Augustine happened to read, with the words: "Paul, a servant of Jesus Christ, called to be an apostle, set apart for the gospel of God." So if we accept Paul's self-understanding, the structure of the situation was that by way of Paul's saying certain things to the Christians in Rome, *God* was saying certain things – at some points saying the same things Paul was saying, perhaps at other points different things, saying them of course to the Roman Christians, but perhaps addressing a vastly broader range of human beings as well. It's possible, then, that Augustine interpreted what happened to him along the following lines: back several centuries God had said, by way of Paul's writing his letter to the Roman Christians: arm yourselves with the Lord Jesus Christ and spend no more thought on nature and nature's appetites; and he, Augustine, recognized this command as addressed (or applying) also to himself, and found himself obeying it.[1] It appears to me more likely, however, that Augustine interpreted what happened to him along the following, more striking, lines: by way of his now reading those words from Paul's letter, God was *here and now* saying to him: Augustine, arm yourself with the Lord Jesus Christ and spend no more thought on nature and nature's appetites.

Antony's situation was significantly different. The passage Antony heard read in church was from the narrative entitled "The Gospel according to Matthew." In this passage, it was reported that Jesus said to a young man with many possessions, "Go home and sell all that belongs to you. Give it to the poor, and so the treasure you have shall be in heaven; then come back and follow me." Augustine describes Antony as persuaded that, by way of the reader reading those words which the gospel of Matthew reports as addressed by Jesus to a rich young man, God was then and there issuing a counsel to him, Antony, a man of many possessions. The event of a human being standing in a church reading another human being's report of how yet another human being once told a rich young man to give his possessions to the poor and become a disciple: by way of that event, God then and there said to Antony: Antony, give your possessions to the poor and become a disciple of Jesus.

Three episodes of God speaking to someone – or at least, of a person believing that God was speaking to him. In one of them, God spoke by way of a child's casual sing-songing; in two of them, God spoke by way of what the addressees regarded as a sacred text. In one of these latter,

God spoke by way of the addressee's reading the text silently; in the other, God spoke by way of the combination of someone reading the text aloud and the addressee's hearing it. In one of the cases, certainly, and probably in a second as well, the addressee wasn't on the lookout for divine discourse. In the third case, that of Augustine reading what his eye happened to fall on, probably the addressee was on the lookout.

### *Why has the topic been so little discussed?*

Augustine was, of course, not at all eccentric in speaking of God as speaking. It was characteristic of Jews and Christians then, and it remains characteristic of them now, to speak of God as commanding, promising, blessing, forgiving, exhorting, assuring, asserting, and so forth. To these we must add the adherents of Islam, who in Augustine's day were not yet on the scene. Not only are such attributions characteristic of Jews, Christians, and Muslims; they are *fundamental* in the religious thought of these communities and in the theological reflections of their scholars – the most important reason for that being that reports of God speaking are fundamental in the sacred texts of these communities. What would Judaism, Christianity, and Islam look like if no one spoke of God commanding, no one, of God promising, no one, of God telling?

Audacious. Only the glaze of familiarity conceals from us how extraordinarily audacious it is to claim that by way of the sing-song voice of a child the Master of the Universe would tell me to open a book, and that by way of my opening that book and reading, the Creator of heaven and earth would command me to turn away from lust. This quality of audaciousness is noted, and something of it captured, by Emmanuel Levinas when, writing about revelation in the Jewish tradition, he remarks that "Our world lies before us, enabling us, in its coherence and constancy, to perceive it, enjoy it (*jouissance*), and think about it; it offers us its reflections, metaphors and signs to interpret and study. Within this world, it appears that the opening of certain books can cause the abrupt invasion of truths from outside ...!"[2] He continues:

How can we make sense of the "exteriority" of the truths and signs of the Revelation which strike the human faculty known as reason? It is a faculty which, despite its "interiority," is equal to whatever the world confronts it with. But how can these truths and signs strike our reason if they are not even of this world?

These questions are indeed urgent ones for us today, and they confront anyone who may still be responsible to these truths and signs but who is troubled to some degree – as a modern person – by the news of the end of metaphysics, by the triumphs of psychoanalysis, sociology and political economy; someone who has learnt from linguistics that meaning is produced by signs without signifieds and who, confronted with all these intellectual splendours – or shadows – sometimes wonders if he is not witnessing the magnificent funeral celebrations held in honour of a dead god[3]

Audacious, but common: the attribution of speech to God. Yet it has received little attention from philosophers. In no anthology or textbook on philosophy of religion will you find a section on divine discourse. The philosopher who wants to discuss it doesn't have many conversation partners. In the first half of this century there was a great deal of talk among *theologians* about "the Word of God." That talk, so far as I can tell, has withered on the vine in recent years; but even when it flourished, many if not most of the questions that a philosopher would want to deal with went unmentioned.

Why has the topic received so little attention from philosophers? Is it because of the strong preference among philosophers, when doing philosophy of religion, for speaking about some generalized thing called "theism" rather than about the particularities of any one religious tradition? Perhaps. But the attribution of speech to God isn't all that "particular"; and in any case, recent years have seen a surge of philosophical interest in various particularities of the religions. Is it because of the strong preference among philosophers, when doing philosophy of religion, for dealing with those aspects of God which seem to have some chance of being established for all rational comers? Perhaps. But as Richard Swinburne makes clear in his recent book, *Revelation,* there's more to be done by way of giving reasons for the conclusion that God reveals than has commonly been supposed. Is it because to philosophers it just seems bizarre to speak of God speaking – a remnant of the childhood of the race, before man had come of age? No doubt that's true for a good many contemporary philosophers. But that too can't be the whole of it; because, to the best of my knowledge, one also doesn't find any medieval philosopher devoting a section in his philosophical theology to the topic of God speaking. So once again: why the neglect among philosophers of the topic of divine discourse, given the prominence of attributions of speech to God in the three great religious traditions which have shaped the West and the near East?

I think in good measure it is because it has been widely thought that divine speech is reducible to divine revelation – which *has* received a great deal of attention from philosophers. George Mavrodes, in his recent book, *Revelation in Religious Belief*, breaks with this assumption of reducibility by construing divine speech as a *species of* divine revelation.[4] I view that as a gain in one respect and a loss in another. A gain, in that divine speech at least becomes visible when it is treated as a distinct species of revelation; a loss in that, as I will argue in my next lecture, it's plausible so to treat it only if one stretches the concept of *revelation* beyond recognition.

The traditional assumption that divine speech is reducible to divine revelation was not just fortuitous error; an interesting reason was sometimes offered. Since God has no vocal cords with which to utter words, and no hands with which to write them down, God cannot literally speak, cannot literally be a participant in a linguistic community. Accordingly, attributions of speech to God, if not judged bizarrely false, must be taken as metaphorical. But if so taken, what is *the fact of the matter* to which the metaphor points? The answer customarily given was that *divine revelation* is the fact of the matter. Divine speech disappeared into divine revelation because speaking of God speaking was taken to be a metaphorical way of attributing revelation to God. Here, for example, is what the medieval Jewish philosopher–theologian Moses Maimonides said about the attribution of speech to God in his *Guide of the Perplexed*:

Since ... all these acts are only performed by means of bodily organs, all these organs are figuratively ascribed to Him: those by means of which local motion takes place – I mean the feet and their soles; those by means of which hearing, seeing, and smelling come about – that is, the ear, the eye, and the nose; those by means of which speech and the matter of speech are produced – that is, the mouth, the tongue, and the voice ... To sum up all this: God, may He be exalted above every deficiency, has had bodily organs ascribed to Him in order that His acts should be indicated by this means. And those particular acts are figuratively ascribed to Him in order to indicate a certain perfection, which is not identical with the particular act mentioned ... Action and speech are ascribed to God so that an overflow proceeding from Him should thereby be indicated ... organs of speech [are] mentioned with a view to indicating the overflow of the intellect toward the prophets ...[5]

And here, to leap over some eight centuries, is what Sandra M. Schneider says in her recent book, *The Revelatory Text*:

Despite the widespread insistence to the contrary that biblical fundamentalism represents, it seems evident that word of God or divine discourse cannot be taken literally. First, words ... are the intelligible physical sounds emitted by the vocal apparatus (or some substitute for that apparatus) of a rational creature or, by extension, some auditory or visual representation of those utterances. Language, in other words, is a human phenomenon rooted in our corporeality as well as in our discursive mode of intellection and as such cannot be literally predicated of pure spirit ...[6]

One response to this argument of Maimonides and Schneider is that they have just overlooked some things – overlooked, for example, the possibility that God might cause soundings-out or inscribings of words even though God has no body. But what I want to do in the chapters which follow is pursue what seems to me a much more interesting line of thought, one suggested by that position in contemporary philosophy of language commonly known as speech-action theory.

### Why discuss the topic today?

Before I indicate what that line of thought is, let me bring the topic in hand to a conclusion. I observed that there aren't many conversation partners for the philosopher who wants to discuss divine discourse; and I went on to speculate why that is. It hasn't been recognized as a topic distinct from divine revelation. To which one obvious response is this: Why not leave it undiscussed? Why bother to start up a philosophical conversation on this topic? One answer is: because it's there – there to be talked about. But perhaps there's more to say than this!

Those rather haunting words of Levinas will speak to some of us. These questions, he said, are "urgent ones for us today, and they confront anyone who may still be responsible to these truths and signs but who is troubled to some degree" – and then he goes on to cite various developments in contemporary philosophy which are troubling to the person who feels "responsible to these truths and signs" which speak of God speaking.

But it is not only the troubled heart and mind of the believer which invites consideration of our topic; various developments within the field of philosophy do so as well. Philosophical reflections on some area of human society or culture do not, in my view, consist of discovering and offering answers to some eternal "problems of philosophy" whose history is no more than the history of their discovery and of successive attempts at solution. Philosophy is not what the Aristotelian tradition called a "science," a "*scientia*"; it is instead a social practice, in Alisdair MacIntyre's sense: a long-enduring tradition of reflection in which new goals and lines of thought and criteria of excellence emerge, in which old goals and lines of thought and criteria die out, and in which always there is "contest" between the new and the old and among the new. Philosophical problems do not *enter history* but *are historical*. Likewise the domains of culture and society on which philosophers reflect, in their various "philosophy of . . . " enterprises, are historical, ever-changing, phenomena – which is not to say that nothing abides. This historicity of philosophy, on the one hand, and of domains of society and culture, on the other, has as its consequence that the issues discussed in a particular age within some "philosophy of . . . " enterprise are those which arise when philosophers at that stage in the practice of philosophy reflect on some domain of society or culture as that finds itself at that stage in its career. The issues emerge in the intellectual space created by the engagement with each other of two long enduring practices at a particular stage in the career of each. Thus it is, for example, that philosophers of art – while by no means forgetting the writings of their predecessors – nonetheless discuss different issues today from those discussed fifty years ago and discuss issues that are more or less the same in different ways. Philosophy has changed, and art and art criticism have changed; and the combination of those changes makes the discussion in philosophy of art very different. Not entirely different; but still, *very* different. The conversation which constitutes philosophy of art is a historically *situated* conversation.

So too for philosophy of religion; this conversation is also historically situated. Nowadays there are many anthologies and textbooks which purport to introduce the student to certain timeless problems in philosophy of religion and to an assortment of attempts to solve these timeless problems. The whole picture is an illusion. It is in that *particular* intellectual space created by the engagement with each other of these two long enduring phenomena, philosophy and religion, at a *particular* stage in the ever-changing career of each, that the conversation of philosophy of religion takes place. Which is not to deny, of course, that some things in philosophy and some things in religion endure, nor that some of the questions discussed in one such intellectual space are similar to those discussed in another, nor that the questions discussed in a previous space are sometimes of interest to those who occupy a later space without being the questions they themselves ask.

Let me, then, point to some of the recent developments in philosophy which give interest and relevance to a philosophical address to the topic of divine discourse and suggest some of the questions to be considered. Begin by recalling our mention of contemporary philosophy of language. When one thinks about speaking in the context of so-called speech-action theory, initiated some forty years ago by J. L. Austin, then the argument of Maimonides and Schneider against God speaking appears patently fallacious. Fundamental to that theory is the distinction between *locutionary acts* and *illocutionary acts*. Locutionary acts are acts of uttering or inscribing words. *Il*-locutionary acts are acts performed *by way of* locutionary acts, acts such as asking, asserting, commanding, promising, and so forth. Once illocutionary acts are thus distinguished from locutionary acts, then it immediately occurs to one that though of course such actions as asking, asserting, commanding, and promising, can be performed by way of uttering or inscribing sentences, they can be performed in many other ways as well. One can say something by producing a blaze, or smoke, or a sequence of light-flashes. Even more interesting: one can tell somebody something by deputizing someone else to speak on one's behalf. In short, contemporary speech-action theory opens up the possibility of a whole new way of thinking about God speaking: perhaps the attribution of speech to God by Jews, Christians, and Muslims, should be understood as the attribution to God of *illocutionary actions*, leaving it open how God performs those actions – maybe by bringing about the sounds or characters of some natural language, maybe not.

Of course, rejecting the Maimonides–Schneider line of argument leaves open the possibility that divine discourse is nonetheless reducible to divine revelation. So it's to this issue that I devote the following chapter, arguing that divine speech and divine revelation are distinct phenomena, each calling for philosophical reflection. My own decision has been to reflect on divine discourse rather than divine revelation, partly because it has received so little attention from philosophers, partly – I do admit – because I find the claim that God speaks a more arresting topic to reflect on!

Secondly, recent developments in epistemology also call for placing the topic of divine discourse on the philosophical agenda and suggest certain approaches and questions. The last twenty-five years or so have seen one of the most luxuriant flowerings of epistemology, including the epistemology of religious belief, in the entire history of philosophy. I know, of course, that Richard Rorty and others, acting as self-appointed coroners, have pronounced epistemology dead. But what

Rorty calls "epistemology" is only one species of epistemology, viz., classically foundationalist epistemology.

An important feature of the contemporary discussions on religious epistemology is the fact that evidentialist lines of thought long taken for granted within the philosophical community have been subjected to powerful attack from various angles. The Wittgensteinian philosophers of religion launched one such attack – much discussed some thirty years ago when it first appeared. I think it safe to say that the line of attack on evidentialism most discussed today is that launched by the so-called "Reformed epistemologists" – among whom I number myself; at the center of their program has been the contention that often it is entirely right and proper for persons to believe things about God without doing so on the basis of propositional evidence. Beliefs about God which are *basic* in a person's belief-system may nonetheless be *proper*.

The most profound, rigorous, and elaborate development of religious epistemology within this particular anti-evidentialist tradition which has thus far appeared is that by William P. Alston in his recent publication, *Perceiving God*. Alston's epistemology of religious belief focuses on the mode and circumstances of a belief's formation. In that regard, it resembles recent general epistemology: it is now widely assumed among epistemologists that whether a person's believing of a certain proposition possesses or lacks some doxastic merit depends, in good measure, on the mode and circumstances of the belief's formation and sustenance. More particularly, Alston focuses on beliefs emergent from, and based on, religious experience; and within the domain of religious experience, he focuses especially on that special mode of experience which he analyses as the "perception" of God.

Now it is of course true that religious experience occupies an important place in the total picture of how religious beliefs are formed. But what strikes one, when considering the abundance of recent discussions on religious epistemology, including then Alston's book, is how little attention has been paid to that particular mode of religious belief formation which is most common among adherents of the three "religions of the book." Most of their convictions about God are not formed in them by experiences of God, nor by abstract reasoning, but by explication of sacred scripture and meditation on the results thereof. And many if not most Jews, Christians, and Muslims, if asked to explain why they allow Scripture to form their beliefs – if they do – would say, sooner or later, that they do so because it is the *word* of God or the *revelation* of God. So a discussion of divine discourse, along with a discussion of divine revelation, belongs on the agenda of the epistemologist. And as for myself, I will be wanting to ask what a *non-evidentialist* epistemology of beliefs grounded on divine discourse might look like.

Our discussion of Augustine reminds us, though, that scripture is not regarded by the adherents of the "religions of the book" as the sole instrument of divine discourse and revelation. Accordingly, though the present state of the epistemological discussion makes particularly urgent a discussion of God speaking and revealing by way of sacred scripture, we will want to keep in mind the more general phenomenon of which that is a special type.

Thirdly, the field of philosophical theology has been the scene in recent years of a great deal of activity and creativity; and developments there also invite placing our topic on the agenda. Up for grabs, in recent years, has been the classical Western concept of God. Is it true, as the tradition claimed, that God is eternal, that God is everlasting, that God is immutable, that God is omniscient, that God is impassible? To these we must add the questions: Is it true that God speaks? What would God have to be like to speak? Is God like that? *Could* God speak?

The philosophical disciplines at whose confluence our topic lies include a fourth, namely, philosophical hermeneutics. Reflecting on how one interprets Scripture so as to discern divine discourse obviously requires addressing some fundamental issues in the theory of interpretation. But something quite different has to be said about the relation of contemporary hermeneutics to our topic from what was said about the relation of philosophy of language, epistemology, and philosophical theology to it. Contemporary hermeneutics doesn't invite placing this topic on its agenda; it *resists* it. A pervasive theme in contemporary hermeneutics is that there is something deeply misguided about reading texts to find out what someone might have been saying thereby. But that is exactly what one does if one reads Scripture to discern what God might have said or be saying thereby. So we shall have to consider whether that near-consensus is correct. Perhaps I have given the impression that what transpires in that intellectual space where philosophy and some domain of society or culture interact at some stage in their careers is that the philosopher both asks and answers all the questions. But that's by no means how it always goes. Sometimes science, art, politics, religion, and so on pose questions to the philosopher which the philosopher never dreamt of asking; and sometimes they give answers to the philosopher's questions that undo the philosopher. So it is here. The practice of interpreting for divine discourse poses a challenge to the hermeneutical consensus among philosophers which, so I will argue, the consensus will not be able to meet. The theory must bend and give in the face of the facts.

## Convergences

The common, though nonetheless audacious, claim that God speaks: I have imagined someone asking why bother talking about that. I have answered by pointing to some dynamics in contemporary philosophy which invite placing this topic on the agenda and suggest fresh new ways of addressing it. Let me close by calling attention to a fascinating and important convergence between the practice of interpreting Scripture for divine discourse and two other modes of Scripture interpretation which have emerged in recent years.

For some two centuries now, the most culturally influential form of biblical scholarship has been that which Robert Alter, in his recent book, *The World of Biblical Literature*, calls "excavative" scholarship. Scholars have attempted to find out all sorts of things about the origin of the Bible: who composed these various books, when and where, for whom, with what pre-existing texts in hand, with what traditional genres as patterns, with which historical events in mind, to make which "ideological" points, and so forth, on and on. The dominance of such scholarship is now threatened by persistent questioning of some of its assumptions and by the emergence of various modes of Scripture interpretation which, each for its own reasons, attends to the text itself rather than to that which lies behind the text. They converge around the text.

One such alternative practice is that of so-called "biblical theology": One interprets the text with the aim in mind of finding out the theology expressed by those who wrote or edited the text. Another, arising more recently, is the new-wave literary studies of the biblical text, particularly of its narrative sections: one interprets the text with the aim in mind of discerning its literary qualities. Let me say just a bit about this latter, newly emergent, practice.

For millennia now it has been assumed that the biblical books in general, and the biblical narratives in particular, have little by way of admirable literary qualities. The categories and strategies of literary analysis available to the readers of late antiquity yielded the conclusion that the bulk of the biblical writings were, if not uncouth, at least inept.

That attitude endured, with minor exceptions, until recently. It's true that throughout our century there have been books and academic courses on "the Bible as literature." But the evident earnestness of the practitioners abetted rather than quelled the feeling that if it is literary qualities one wants, one would be well-advised not to linger long over the Bible – certainly not over its narrative passages.

Now everything looks different. The new-wave literary interpretations of the biblical text make clear that what was lacking all the while was not admirable literary qualities in the biblical writings themselves but the critical categories and strategies, insights and imagination, needed for revealing those qualities – and in particular, for revealing them in the narratives. Let me quote Alter:

> virtually every utterance of biblical narrative reveals the presence of writers who relished the words and the materials of storytelling with which they worked, who delighted, because after all they were writers, in pleasing cadences and surprising deflections of syntax, in complex echoing effects among words, in the kind of speech they could fashion for the characters, and in the way in which the self-same words could be ingeniously transformed as they were passed from narrator to character or from one character to another ... there is evidence of [literary style] in almost every line of biblical narrative, and though the biblical writers are, of course, concerned with conveying "messages" – creedal, moral, historical, ideological – the lively inventiveness with which they constantly deploy the resources of their narrative medium repeatedly exceeds the needs of the message, though it often also deepens and complicates the message.[7]

Reading the Bible to discern what God said or is saying by way of the text is obviously different both from reading it to discern the literary qualities of the text and from reading it to discern the theology of the biblical writers – different in such a way as would make the academy feel acutely uncomfortable were it to practice the former, whereas it feels no discomfort whatever in practicing the latter two. Commitments of a quite different order are required. Nonetheless, these interpretative practices share in common their focus on the text itself – the text we have.

The person who engages in the practice of interpreting Scripture for theological content, and the person who engages in the practice of interpreting Scripture for literary qualities, each looks around for allies in the attempt to resist the hegemony of excavative scholarship. What they see first is each other. But if they continue looking, eventually they'll spy another practice of Scripture interpretation which also requires close attention to the text, a practice far more ancient and enduring than either of theirs – the practice of interpreting Scripture for divine discourse. It's unlikely that they will spy the practice at work in the modern academy; they'll have to look at the workings of Scripture interpretation in homiletical and devotional settings – and in the academies of the ancient and medieval and Reformation worlds. Once spied, though, the question comes naturally: is this practice also acceptable?

It remains a part of the liturgy of many branches of the Christian church for the listeners to respond to the public reading of Scripture with some such words as, "This is the Word of the Lord." There, in that response, is my topic. What is one saying in saying that? How would one go about interpreting the words read to discover what God said? And is it rationally acceptable to say, and mean it, that when sitting one morning in St. Mary's church, or one evening in Oriel chapel, one heard something God had said – or something God was saying?

CHAPTER 2

# *Speaking is not revealing*

When I mentioned to various friends and acquaintances that I had resolved to reflect and write on the topic of divine discourse, further conversation almost always revealed that they assumed my topic was divine revelation, and that my conversation partners would be a sampling from that vast number of thinkers who have written on the topic of revelation. "Is there anything new to be said on revelation?" a rather skeptical theologian friend remarked. I replied that my topic was divine *discourse*, not divine *revelation*. His response was like that of almost everyone else: "What's the difference?"

So I judge that our topic will not have been adequately located until it has been established that divine discourse differs from divine revelation. If we assume that illocutionary actions, such as asserting, commanding, promising, and asking, are a species of revelation, they will elude our grasp. It's true that in promising someone something, one reveals various things about oneself. But the promising does not itself consist of revealing something – does not itself consist of making the unknown known.

My case will not really be complete until, in Chapter 5, I discuss what constitutes speaking. Here I will have to be content with taking various examples of discourse and holding them up against revealing, trusting that the reader has a sufficiently developed intuitive sense of what goes into such cases to recognize that there's not a fit. That makes it sound quite tentative. But I'll have to trust in the presence of the same "sufficiently developed intuitive sense" when later I offer my positive account of what constitutes discourse; how else would the reader know that the account was correct – or incorrect?

## *A first look at why speaking is not revealing*

Augustine assigned central importance in his life to three episodes of what he interpreted as God speaking – two of them, episodes in his own life, one, an episode in St. Antony's life. Let us suppose for the time being that he was correct in his interpretation of these episodes. That is to say: let us suppose that God did command Augustine to open his copy of Paul's letters and read the first passage that his eye might fall on, that God did command him to leave his life of worldliness, and that God did command Antony to give his wealth to the poor and follow Jesus. Did those commandings consist of God revealing something?

Any attempt to analyse them thus will at least have to acknowledge that what was revealed was not that which was commanded. What God commanded Augustine, in one of the three episodes, was to open his book. But it makes no sense to suppose that God revealed to Augustine *to open his book.* If someone commands me to leave the room, it makes no sense to suppose that he revealed to me *to leave the room.* The response will be forthcoming that its nothing more than a grammatical infelicity to say that God revealed to Augustine to open his book. But in fact the undoubted grammatical infelicity points to something deeper.

Recall the distinction, fundamental to speech-action theory, which I introduced in the preceding chapter, between *locutionary* and *illocutionary* actions. Let us then analyze God's illocutionary act of commanding, into *propositional content* and *illocutionary act,* yielding these two components: the propositional content, *that Augustine sometime soon opens his book,* and the illocutionary act, of commanding Augustine *to do what would make that proposition true.* Now the content, *that Augustine sometime soon opens his book,* was in fact true; and since God would have foreknown it, it was, so far forth, a candidate for divine revelation – to Alypius, let's say. But obviously God's *commanding* Augustine to do what would make that content true, is not to be identified with God's *revealing* its truth to Augustine; nor is that act of revealing in any way involved in the act of commanding.

It does sometimes happen that what is revealed is *that some act of commanding occurred.* But then the act of commanding – or the fact that it occurred – is the *content* of the revealing rather than being the revealing itself. The point is worth developing for the Augustine case.

Two quite different possibilities have to be distinguished. Suppose that God had earlier issued some commands of which Antony and Augustine were ignorant. God could then have dispelled their ignorance by revealing to them that He had issued those commands; the fact of the occurrence of the earlier commandings would be the content of the revelation. But that is not the situation as Augustine describes it. God was not dispelling their ignorance concerning something God had already done; God was then and there doing a new thing, namely, commanding. When Antony was standing in that Coptic church – it was *then* that God issued a command to him. When Augustine was thrashing about in the garden of that Milanese villa – it was *then* that God issued those commands to him.

The possibility to be considered, then, is that God was then and there *revealing* to Augustine and Antony that He was then and there issuing those commands. And this may have been how it went; or at least, how Augustine understood it as having gone. Of course the acts *by way of which* God issued those commands wouldn't have been revealed; they were acts of which Antony and Augustine, by the use of their normal human capacities, were fully aware: a lector's reading aloud from the Gospel of Matthew, a child's chanting "*tolle lege, tolle lege*," Augustine's reading a passage from Paul's letters. But the acts of commanding which God issued *by way of* those perceptible events: perhaps those were revealed to them. Perhaps the speech acts had what may be called a *revelational correlate,* consisting of God revealing that He was performing the act. Such a construal goes beyond what Augustine actually says; all he *says* is that he and Antony came to believe that God was speaking to them. But I think it likely that Augustine did regard the episodes of his coming to believe that God was speaking to him as the direct effect of God's action on him. And such episodes – as we shall see in some detail later in this chapter – can be regarded as episodes of revelation. But notice once again: the fact of the occurrence of the commandings would then have been the *content* of the revelation rather than identical with the revelation. God would have revealed to Augustine *that He was commanding Augustine to abandon his life of worldliness.* And only if God was somehow independently performing the act of issuing that command, could God reveal the fact of His issuing it.

With these preliminary points in mind, here is our question: might it be that to command something is to reveal something – not that *same* something which was commanded, but something else? Well, what might that something else be? The usual thought is that it is something about the agent himself. And the most common suggestion along these lines is that for an agent to command that something be done, is for the agent to reveal that he or she *wants* that thing to be done.

But clearly this won't do, for the reason that one might command someone to do something without wanting that person to do it.

Sometimes we command someone to do something so as to test their loyalty and obedience, or their moral character; and sometimes, in such cases, we don't want them actually to do the thing commanded. We may, for example, plan to intervene at the appropriate point to stop them from doing it; God's commanding Abraham to sacrifice his son is a case in point.

The reply might be forthcoming that though God did not want Abraham to sacrifice Isaac, he did want Abraham to *set about the project* of sacrificing Isaac; or to back up even farther, *to form the intention* of doing that. But in a trial sort of situation, one might command someone to do something while hoping that they won't even *form the intention* of doing so – as one might when unwittingly commanding someone to do something, or when issuing a command while under duress.

What, then, about a recasting of Paul Grice's view of speech and meaning, to this effect: commanding some action consists of uttering some words with the primary intention of impelling one's addressee to perform that action, and with the secondary intention of revealing that primary intention to him by one's utterance so that his recognition of that primary intention will be a reason for his performance of the action? This represents a giant leap forwards in sophistication; but it suffers from the same defect: one might command someone to do something without intending to impel her to do it.

It's also worth noticing the converse: one might reveal that one wants someone to do something without asking or commanding or requesting that person to do that. To ask is to impose a certain obligation; and one might hope that the other's *love* or *respect* for one would be sufficient to motivate her doing that which one reveals one wants her to do. One might be disappointed to learn that it was not sufficient, that one had to *ask*!

### *What is revelation?*

For many readers, this quick look will have been too quick, and the considerations adduced, too thin, to generate much conviction. Furthermore, the possibility remains open that what is true of commanding is not true of speech actions in general. What is needed is the situating of the considerations I have adduced within an articulated understanding of revelation. So let us turn to that for a while; and then come back.

Revelation occurs when ignorance is dispelled – or when something is done which *would* dispel ignorance if attention and interpretative skills were adequate. Sometimes there is no agent of the revealing, only a subject revealed to. "Suddenly the significance of all my conflicts with my father was revealed to me." Call such revelation, *agentless* revelation. Obviously speech actions are not a species of agentless revelation. Accordingly, for our purposes here we can set such revelation off to the side and concentrate entirely on *agent* revelation – that is, on revelation in which someone is doing the revealing.

There is a certain form of agent revelation which we can also set off to the side. Suppose that the chairman of the board pushes aside the canvas to reveal the painting to be dedicated to his predecessor and instead reveals, to the horror of everyone, that someone had broken in during the night and stolen it. That would be an example of revelation. But neither what the chairman intended to reveal, namely, the painting, nor what he did reveal, namely, the fact that the painting had been stolen, was an aspect or item of knowledge of himself. What occurred might be called *other*-revelation rather than *self*-revelation. For our purposes we can also set other-revelation off to the side; since, if performing speech actions is a species of revealing, what is revealed will presumably be an aspect or item of knowledge of the agent. Agent revelation, and more particularly, agent self-revelation, will be the focus of our attention.

It is the habit of the analytic philosopher to proceed by starting with such observations as I have already made and then advancing by adding qualifications to cope with counter-examples, eliminating metaphors, resolving ambiguities, dispelling unclarities, and so forth, until finally he arrives at a clear and unambiguous formulation of necessary and sufficient conditions for correctly calling some action "revelation." It is my judgment that indulging this habit on this occasion would be insufferably boring and almost certainly futile. For it would miss something fundamental in our concept of revelation. Revelation is not dispelling just any sort of ignorance. Telling you that I left the keys on the counter is not, in normal circumstances, *revealing* to you the location of the keys – even though it does dispel your ignorance. Dispelling ignorance becomes *revelation* when it has, to some degree and in some way, the character of unveiling the veiled, of uncovering the covered, of exposing the obscured to view. The counterpart of the revealed is the hidden. The difference between just telling somebody something and revealing it, is that telling becomes revealing when, to some degree and in some way, it discloses the hidden.[1] Often, though, to speak or think of what is revealed as something once *hidden* is to speak or think metaphorically. What underlies our use of the concept of revelation, in cases of agent self-revelation, is in good measure the metaphor of the hidden self.

We in our culture are all in the habit of thinking of much about ourselves as hidden from view: thoughts, feelings, beliefs, knowledge, worries, anxieties, and so forth. Of course, what is hidden from the view of one person may be exposed to the view of another. Charles Taylor, in his recent book, *Sources of the Self*, argues that our habit of thinking of human beings as having an inward self and an outward self, along with its corollary habit of thinking of that inward self and its "contents" as hidden from all but the person herself, is to be traced back to Augustine. It is, Taylor remarks, "hardly an exaggeration to say that it was Augustine who introduced the inwardness of radical reflexivity and bequeathed it to the Western tradition of thought"[2] Perhaps Taylor is right about that. But to me it seems likely that even before people operated with an inward self/outward self contrast, they were in the habit of thinking of much about their fellow human beings as not only unknown to them but "hidden" from them. If so, then the introduction of Augustinian conceptuality did not initiate this habit but reinforced it.

In any case, it is those aspects of the self which we appropriately think of as hidden that are candidates for being revealed. And they are revealed only if the act of making the unknown known is appropriately thought of as uncovering the covered or unveiling the veiled. Again, metaphors guide the application. Sometimes we come to know something about another person without either that person or ourselves doing anything which could be thought of as uncovering the hidden; rather than anybody revealing it, we *discover* it. Of course, I may both discover something about you and you may reveal it to me; two different paths may lead to knowledge of the same thing by the same person. But consider one of those paths: if it is a path of discovery by me, then it is not a path of revelation by you; if it is a path of revelation by you, then it is not a path of discovery by me. Self-revelation enters the picture only when the agent, instead of sitting back passively, waiting for the hidden in himself to be discovered, actively discloses the hidden.

Suppose that Aquinas' natural theological arguments for God's simplicity actually satisfy the logical and epistemological requirements that he laid down for such arguments. Suppose further that God's simplicity had not been hidden from us; *unknown* until that time, but not hidden. (Whether that supposition is correct is, of course, a good question!) Then Aquinas, by those arguments, would have *discovered* that God is eternal – without God revealing it. By contrast, if Moses came to know that God wanted to be called "I Am Who I Am" in the way described in the book of *Exodus,* then Moses did not discover that but God revealed it to him.

I said that the phenomenon which I picked out as "agent self-revelation" consists of revealing some aspect or *item of knowledge* of oneself. Let me explain, with an example, why I made a point of adding, "or item of knowledge." Imagine a case in which someone reveals, under threat of torture, where in the garden he had hidden the jewels when the enemy was knocking at the gates. What is then primarily revealed is *the location of the jewels*; and that is not an aspect of the agent. Yet it is not simply unconnected with the agent, in the way in which the slashing of the painting was unconnected with the Board Chairman. Secondarily, or derivatively, the person revealed *his knowledge* of that. What connects *the location of the jewels* to the agent, and makes it possible for him to reveal it, is that it is the content of one of his items of knowledge.

## Types of agent self-revelation

Let us move on, now, to highlight some of the more important distinctions among examples of agent self-revelation. (Some of the following distinctions apply also to agentless revelation, and to agent other-revelation; but I will frame them as they apply to agent self-revelation.) For one thing, it's important to distinguish between *intended* revelation and *non-intended* revelation. Sometimes revealing takes the form of the agent forming and implementing an intention, an action-plan, to disclose what had been hidden. For an example, change somewhat the hidden-jewels example. Suppose that, unbeknownst to the rest of the family, the paterfamilias had hidden the jewels at the beginning of the war, that the war has subsided without his betraying the location, and that now, after assembling the family, he tells them that the jewels were not seized as booty by the enemy but remain where he had hidden them in the far northwest corner of the garden. That would be an example of revelation; and the disclosing of what had been hidden from the others, namely, the location of the jewels, or alternatively, his knowledge as to the location of the jewels, comes about by the paterfamilias forming and acting on the intention to disclose what he had thus far concealed from them. It's a case of *intended* revelation.

Contrast that with the example of a husband revealing his anxiety by unintentionally snapping at his wife; he did not form and act on the intention of disclosing to his wife what had been hidden from her, namely, his anxiety. Nonetheless, his actions do function to disclose that – or if they don't, they *would* if his wife were a bit more perceptive. So it's a case of *non-intended* revelation. Notice that the husband may have revealed his anxiety even though he wasn't aware of it. Alternatively, he may have been aware of it and even have formed the intention of *not* revealing it. It is especially cases of revealing what one not only did not intend to reveal, but intended not to reveal, that are appropriately described as cases of *betraying* that which one revealed. The husband may have *betrayed* his anxiety by snapping at his wife.

Cases of non-intended revelation all fall, so far as I can tell, under the concept of *showing*, or *manifesting*. His behavior *shows* that he is nervous; her speech *manifests* that she knows English; his speech *shows* that he doesn't know the difference in meaning between "fewer" and "less." But we must not jump from that observation to the conclusion that the intended/non-intended distinction coincides with the non-manifesting/manifesting distinction. Though apparently all non-intended revelation is manifestational in character, the converse does not hold. Not all intended revelation is non-manifestational in character. A person might, for example, intentionally *manifest* her grief – intentionally display it, or show it.

What does this distinction between manifestational revelation and non-manifestational revelation come to then? And for a while yet, I'll have to make do with this clumsy phrase, "non-manifestational." The prominence of the distinction in contemporary theological disputes makes the question worth trying to answer. The distinction would seem to be a difference in the *means* of revelation. To find out whether that appearance is veridical, we must ask, *which* difference?

Given the examples with which I have been working, the thought which comes first to mind is that *non-manifestational* revelation is revealing that P by asserting that P, whereas manifestational revelation is revealing that P by some means other than assertion. The old man asserted that he had buried the jewels in the far northwest corner of the garden; that's a case of non-manifestational revelation. The husband revealed his anxiety by snapping at his wife rather than by asserting that he was anxious; that's a case of manifestational revelation. Non-manifestational revelation is *assertoric* revelation; manifestational revelation is *non-assertoric* revelation. That's the thought.

But attractive though this view may be on first sight, it won't do, for the reason that non-manifestational revelation is not necessarily assertoric. Indeed, exactly this sort of case has been prominent in traditional reflections on the nature of divine revelation: revelation which isn't accomplished by assertion and does not take the form of *showing* or *manifesting*. John Locke's picture of original divine revelation was that of God directly transmitting some item of knowledge or true belief to a person. Such a case is obviously not that of God just manifesting something about God's self; but neither is it a case of God asserting something. Yet it seems clearly to be a case of revelation.

We needn't go back into the seventeenth century for examples. In his recent book *Revelation*[3] Richard Swinburne also uses *intended revelation* of the *non-manifestation* sort as his general model for thinking about divine revelation. He describes divine revelation as consisting of God's conveying or communicating messages; and he exhibits no tendency to identify this, in turn, with God's asserting things. Indeed, he seldom speaks of God as speaking. The picture he paints is that of us human beings, being the sort of creatures we are and related to God as we are, needing "to have some information available as to what life is worth living, and how to take steps to live that life"(71); and of God, as one important means of providing such information, bringing about speech and texts such that if we perform the right operations of interpretation on those texts, the requisite information will be conveyed from God's mind to ours.

Swinburne does, here and there, equate conveying or communicating messages with communicating claims that something is so (*passim,* already on p. 1), a claim being, I take it, an assertion. But the equation is always unemphatic; so I doubt that much should be made of it. And even if the equation were correct, we would still have to distinguish between *making claims* and *communicating claims made*.

In any case, I take it to be sufficiently clear that non-manifesting (intended) revelation is not confined to, or need not be confined to, revealing by asserting. Some non-manifesting revelation is assertoric in its means; some is not. And non-assertoric divine revelation can occur in various ways: God directly bringing about a true conviction in a person, God bringing about a text which, when properly interpreted, transmits knowledge from God to us, God planting in a person – or in all persons – some disposition which, when activated, yields true conviction.

So we're back to the question we were considering: if the difference between revelation which is manifestation and revelation which is not manifestation is located in a difference of *means*, what is that difference? The difference, as I see it, is this: in manifestational revelation, the means of the revelation is always a *natural sign* of the actuality revealed. The husband's snapping at his wife is a natural sign (indicator, symptom) of his anxiety. When a speaker manifests that he doesn't know the difference in usage between "fewer" and "less," something in his speech is a natural sign of that. Non-manifestational revelation, then, is revelation in which the means is not a natural sign of the actuality revealed.

To which it's worth adding that non-manifestational revelation always goes through the knowledge of the revealer; that's always a component. The actuality revealed is the actuality corresponding to some *thought* of the revealer, that is, to some proposition entertained by the revealer – and not just entertained but known. *Assertion* of that proposition may then be the specific means of revelation – assertion being a "non-natural sign" of sorts. The paterfamilias knows *that he buried the jewels in the far northwest corner of the garden*; and he now asserts that proposition, in the hope and expectation that his doing so will have the effect of evoking in his hearers knowledge of the fact of *the jewels' being buried in the far northwest corner of the garden*. But as we saw, neither assertion nor any other "non-natural sign" is required: God may directly transmit to the prophet knowledge of something.[4]

I already mentioned that the distinction between manifesting and non-manifesting revelation has been prominent in theological debates of our century; in those debates, non-manifesting revelation has regularly been called *propositional* revelation. If what I have just said is correct, that description is apt. It will be convenient if henceforth we also call it "propositional revelation," most of the time. We saw that non-manifesting revelation is not necessarily *assertoric* revelation; it can occur without assertions being made. But it cannot occur without propositions being entertained and transmitted. (Shortly, I will take note of a species of revelation, distinct from what I have had in view thus far, for which transmission is not necessary.) Though it should be noted that *mere transmission* of a proposition is not sufficient. Suppose that, as the result of some remark by the paterfamilias, members of the family form the thought *that the jewels are buried in the far northwest corner of the garden.* The proposition has then been transmitted from the old man to the family; but revelation hasn't yet occurred. For propositional revelation to occur, the state of *knowing that proposition* (or of justifiedly believing it) has to be transmitted. Just the *thought* that the jewels are buried there won't do it. Propositional revelation is *knowledge-transmitting* revelation (or true-belief-transmitting revelation).

In the course of the theological debates of our century it has often been said or assumed that a peculiarity of manifesting revelation is that it requires *interpretation* on the part of the recipients if the revelation is to go through.[5] This claim or assumption points to a real difference; but it cannot be got at in quite so blunt a fashion. It's true that the husband's manifestation of his anxiety hasn't been picked up by his wife if she doesn't interpret his actions as the behavior of an anxious person; and it's true that the speaker's manifestation of his not knowing the difference in usage between "fewer" and "less" hasn't been picked up by his listeners if they don't interpret his speech as that of someone who doesn't know the difference. But it's also true that the family has to interpret the old man's uttering of words as his asserting that he had buried the jewels in the garden. However, if they do this, and if they believe that he knows what he asserts, so that they believe what he asserts, then and thereby they are accepting *his* construal, *his* interpretation, of the facts about the jewels. Therein lies the difference which the theological debates can be construed as having tried to get at.

Though interpretation is typically involved in the reception of propositional revelation as well as in the reception of manifesting revelation, there's less of it. The revealer has already interpreted the actuality revealed, by way of formulating the proposition; now all we have to do is interpret what he does as the assertion of that proposition. In manifestation, everything needs interpreting, both sign and signified; we are, as it were, confronted with reality raw. That which is the sign we have to interpret as a sign, that which is the fact revealed we have to interpret as that fact, and then we have to interpret that sign as signifying that fact. We can't, so as to get at the manifested fact, take over the revealer's interpretation lodged in the proposition which he knows; we're on our own. We have to do our own interpreting. If the husband reveals the fact of his anxiety by saying to his wife that he feels anxious, then his revealing incorporates his interpretation of his feelings. If he just reveals his anxiety by acting anxiously, then his wife is left to interpret both his behavior and his feelings. If God says that out of love for Israel He led the Israelites through the Red Sea, then we have God's interpretation of those baffling facts – though we are still left with having to interpret some events as God's saying that. If all we have is those baffling events themselves, then it is left to us – perhaps under "the guidance of the Spirit" – to interpret those happenings as God's leading Israel through the Red Sea out of love for this people.[6]

A couple of times now, in laying out the distinction between manifesting and propositional revelation, I have referred to disputes in contemporary theology. Perhaps it will assist the reader in seeing the import of the distinctions I have been making if I take just a moment to go beyond merely referring to those disputes and offer a quick glimpse of the main dispute. I can best do so by citing a lucid and very interesting contribution to the dispute, viz., James Barr's article, "Revelation through History in the Old Testament and in Modern Theology" (*Interpretation*, Vol. 17, 1963).[7] That mode of divine revelation which I characterized above as *intended manifestational revelation*, Barr calls "revelation through history." He claims it to be a near-consensus among contemporary theologians that all divine revelation is of that sort, viz., revelation through history.[8] And the argument of his paper is that this thesis conflicts in various ways with the Old Testament text itself. The most stark point of conflict is with those many passages which present God as engaging in propositional revelation (or more precisely, on my view, as engaging in *speaking*). "Far from representing the divine acts as the basis of all knowledge of God and all communication with him," says Barr, the Old Testament texts "represent God as communicating freely with men, and particularly with Moses, before, during, and after these events. Far from the incident at the burning bush being an 'interpretation' of the divine acts, it is a direct communication from God to Moses of his purposes and intentions. This conversation, instead of being represented as an interpretation of the divine act, is a precondition of it. If God had not told Moses what he did, the Israelites would not have demanded their escape from Egypt, and the deliverance at the Sea of Reeds would not have taken place" (p. 197).[9]

I have drawn attention to two important distinctions among examples of (agent self-)revelation, the distinction between intended and non-intended revelation, and the distinction between manifesting and non-manifesting. I offered an analysis of the latter distinction, arguing that non-manifestational revelation essentially involves known (or true and believed) propositions as the entities revealed. And I argued that the intended/non-intended distinction is not only different in concept from the manifestational/propositional distinction, but that the two distinctions do not coincide in their application. Though it may be the case that all non-intended revelation is of the manifestational sort, intended revelation clearly comes in both sorts, manifestational and propositional: if one intends to reveal something about oneself, one sometimes has the choice of doing so by showing or manifesting that aspect of oneself, or of doing so by communicating knowledge of that aspect from oneself to another person.

Let me now conclude this discussion of revelation by pointing to one more distinction among episodes of revelation; it too has played a large role in contemporary theological discussions, and is worth making for that reason, along with others. In those discussions it has been much debated whether divine revelation of some proposition $P$, or of some actuality $A$, has truly occurred if no one comes to believe $P$ or to know $A$ by means of that revelation. The dispute mixes a verbal issue with a theological issue. Our verb "to reveal" has two different senses (alternatively, we have two different verbs, "to reveal"). According to one of these, a condition of properly predicating "has revealed X" of some agent is that someone actually have come to know X by means of the agent's disclosing it; according to the other, what's necessary is only that the agent make X *knowable* to appropriately qualified observers, not that anyone actually have come to know it by means of the disclosure. Let me label this distinction as that between *transitive* and *intransitive* revelation. That was the verbal issue.[10] The theological issue can be formulated by using the concept of intransitive revelation: Would God ever reveal X without also seeing to it that someone comes to know or believe X by means of that revelation?

### A second look at why speaking is not revealing

Enough about revelation! Let us return to the question which led us into these distinctions and analyses. We saw at the beginning of our discussion that such a speech action as commanding cannot be assimilated to revelation. That insight had a certain superficiality about it, however; it wasn't situated in the context of reflections on the nature and varieties of revelation and discourse. Reflection on the nature and varieties of discourse still awaits us; but after these reflections on revelation, our initial insight can be given a bit more depth.

If speaking is a species of revelation, it will be a species of agent self-revelation; and more particularly, a species of propositional rather than manifestational revelation. If among the species of revelation we are to find speaking, that is where we will have to look. Such revelation, as we have just seen, comes in two sorts, transitive and intransitive; let us consider the two sorts separately.

Begin with transitive. Transitive propositional revelation consists in the transmission, the communication, of knowledge (or true belief) from one person to another. The question then is whether illocutionary actions such as commanding, promising, and asserting are a species of communication. The answer is clearly that they are not. The point is fundamental. Speaking is not communication; it doesn't even require communication. It is a fundamentally different sort of action from communication. One way to see this is to note that such paradigmatic illocutionary actions as asserting, commanding, promising, and asking, all pass what may be called "the hereby-test," whereas communication fails it. What I have in mind is this: in standard English, I can assert that the car will be repaired by uttering, with characteristic inflection, the sentence,

(Ia) The car will be repaired.

But I can also do so by uttering the following sentence with characteristic inflection:

(Ib) I hereby assert that the car will be repaired.

Likewise, I can request or command that the car be repaired by uttering, with characteristic inflection, the sentence,

(IIa) Repair the car.

But I can also do so by uttering with characteristic inflection the sentence,

(IIb) I hereby request that the car be repaired.

Similar points hold for the pair "I will repair the car" and "I hereby promise that I will repair the car"; and for the pair "Will the car be repaired?" and "I hereby ask whether the car will be repaired."

These "hereby" sentences are peculiar in the following way: if a person is in the position to perform the act of Ø-ing, and if by uttering the sentence "I hereby Ø that the car will be repaired" she genuinely says that she thereby Ø's that the car will be repaired, then it *follows* that she has Ø'd that the car will be repaired. For example: one can of course utter the sentence "I hereby promise that the car will be repaired" in all sorts of ways – dreamily, trying it out for sound, and so forth. And one can claim to promise to repair the car when one is not in a position to make that promise. But suppose that one is in the position to make that promise, and suppose further that by uttering the "hereby" sentence one says that one thereby promises that the car will be repaired. Then it *follows* that one has promised that the car will be repaired. This explains what I mean by saying that such speech actions as asserting, commanding, promising, and asking, pass the "hereby" test.

By contrast, transitive propositional revelation, that is, communication of knowledge (or true belief) fails the test. Suppose that when I am in a position to reveal to you that I will repair the car I utter the sentence, "I hereby reveal (communicate) to you that I will repair the car," and thereby say that I do so. It doesn't *follow* that I have done so. The reason it doesn't follow is that success in communication of knowledge is out of the hands of the agent in a way in which success in asserting, commanding, promising, and asking is not. In order for me to communicate an item of knowledge to you, I must produce in you some knowledge which either you now lack or which you had achieved independently of my communication; and no act on my part constitutes the insuring of this effect.

Those familiar with Austinian speech-act theory will at once recognize the difference here as an example of the difference between illocutionary acts and perlocutionary acts. Acts of asserting, commanding, promising, and asking (when brought about by locutionary acts) are all *il*locutionary acts; by contrast, acts of communicating knowledge, when brought about by illocutionary acts, are all *per*locutionary acts. It was by uttering the words "the jewels are buried in the garden" that the old man asserted that the jewels are buried in the garden; his uttering those words, which is the locutionary act in this case, *counts as* his asserting that proposition, this latter being the illocutionary act. In turn, it was by asserting that the jewels are buried in the garden, and by his addressees realizing that he was doing that, that he communicated the knowledge that the jewels were buried in the garden; his asserting that proposition, which is the illocutionary act, *causally* contributed to their coming to know that the jewels were buried in the garden. Illocutionary acts are related to locutionary acts by way of the *counting as* relation; perlocutionary acts are related to illocutionary acts by causality. Asserting, commanding, promising, and asking do not *consist in* the transmission of knowledge.

Intransitive propositional revelation is a different matter, however; in not requiring for its instantiation the transmission of knowledge, it is, so far forth, like illocutionary actions such as asserting, commanding, and promising. So may it be that these are a species of *intransitive* revelation? Intransitive propositional revelation can be thought of as the *expression* of an item of knowledge (or true belief), in contrast to the *communication* of an item of knowledge; whether the expression yields communication depends on whether the recipient "picks up on" what is expressed. And that looks rather like whether an addressee "picks up on" what was commanded, promised, asserted.

But this too will not do, for the reasons noted at the beginning of this chapter: the attempt to find something with whose expression illocutionary actions could be identified winds up in failure. I suggested that God's command to Augustine could be analyzed into the content, *that Augustine sometime soon opens his book*, and the illocutionary act of *commanding Augustine to do what would make that proposition true*. Now that content was in fact true, and God could have known it; thus God could in principle have expressed His knowledge of it. But God's act of *commanding* Augustine to do what would make that proposition true is obviously not the same as God's *expressing* God's knowledge of it. And as to the alternative suggestion, that commanding something is expressing (one's knowledge) that one *wants* it done, we saw at the beginning of our discussion that that too will not do.

Similar points require to be made concerning promising. Suppose God promised Augustine to grant him peace of heart. Such an action could be analyzed into the propositional content, *that Augustine sometime enjoys peace of heart*, and the illocutionary action of *promising to do what would make that proposition true*. Now that content, that Augustine sometime enjoys peace of heart, was in fact true, and God would have known it; so God could have *expressed* God's knowledge of it. But God's *promising* Augustine to bring it about that he sometime enjoys peace of heart is obviously not identical with God's *expressing God's knowledge* that Augustine sometime enjoys peace of heart. (Though, given that it is God who is doing the promising, one could *infer* the truth of that proposition from the promise.) And the alternative suggestion, that promising something consists of expressing (one's knowledge of) one's *intention* to do it, has difficulties like those that confront the counterpart suggestion for commanding: one can promise to do something without intending to do it (and conversely, one can intend to do it without promising to do it; one can even *reveal one's intention to do* it without promising to do it: "I fully intend to do it, but I'm not going to promise").

What promising introduces is the (*prima facie*) right of the addressee to hold the speaker to it; what commanding introduces is the (*prima facie*) right of the speaker to hold the addressee to it. That is the clue which I will be developing in my chapter on the nature of discourse. Speaking consists not in communicating or expressing knowledge (or true belief) but in taking up a certain sort of *normative stance*, as I shall call it. The attempt to treat discourse as a species of revelation – which is, incidentally, an attempt definitive of the Romantic family of theories of discourse – founders on the inherently *normative* character of discourse. The conclusion toward which we are forced is that the phenomenon of discourse, be it divine or human, is fundamentally distinct from that of revelation.

It's worth noting, however, that the relation of *assertion* to propositional revelation is closer than that of commanding and promising to such revelation. It might well be that if God wished to reveal to Augustine the truth that his agony of soul will be relieved if he makes the decision to abandon his "worldliness," God would do so by asserting it – in which case the very same truth that God wished to reveal would be that which he asserted. Not something else; that very same thing. Acts of promising and commanding will always reveal something or other about the agent; what I have been emphasizing is that what they reveal about the agent is not that which the agent promised or commanded. Neither is it the point of the promising or commanding to reveal something about oneself. By contrast, what I assert may be what I reveal; and I may assert it so as to reveal it.

Assertion and propositional revelation do remain distinct phenomena. As we saw earlier, propositional revelation can occur without assertion being its medium. To assert is to *make a claim*; and that, on the analysis I will be offering, is to take up a certain normative stance. Thus an account of divine revelation does not yet give one an account of what it is for God to *assert* things. Nevertheless, divine assertion is one of the media of divine revelation; whereas divine commanding and promising are not. The intended function of promising and commanding is not to inform us of what we don't know but to take on duties *toward* us and to require things *of* us; trust and obedience are the appropriate responses. By contrast, the intended function of assertion sometimes is to inform us of what we don't know. In a discussion of propositional revelation, assertion will turn up as one of the media thereof; commanding and promising, if they turn up at all, will turn up only when the discussion gets around to the *content* of the revelation.

Perhaps somewhere in these facts is to be found an explanation (in addition to the one offered in the last chapter) of why philosophers and philosophically minded theologians have devoted so much more attention to the topic of divine revelation than to the topic of divine discourse. Philosophy has always played an important role in the shaping of theology in the West. In turn, philosophy in the West has always been preoccupied with epistemological questions. That preoccupation may have reached the point of pathology in the modern world; but it was already present in the philosophy of antiquity and of the middle ages. Thus most systematic theologians in the West have felt it incumbent on themselves to address the question of the epistemological basis of what they say about God. In principle, one could place the epistemological discussion at the end of one's discourse; in fact most of them have placed it at the beginning. And almost all have claimed, in their answer, that much of what they were going to say about God was based on God's having revealed it. Some have gone so far as to claim that everything they were going to say about God was based on God's having revealed it! Thus it is that the topic of revelation has assumed looming, structural significance in the theologies of the West. And philosophers, preoccupied with epistemology, have found those theological discussions on revelation irresistibly attractive as material for reflection.[11]

## CHAPTER 3

# *The many modes of discourse*

When we think of someone promising, asking, or asserting something, the image which comes most naturally to mind is that of someone using her mouth and tongue and vocal cords to make the sounds of some language, or using her hands to inscribe the characters of some language. So much are we in the grip of this as the paradigm for discourse that, as noted in our first chapter, a good many theologians, upon hearing talk of God speaking, have concluded immediately that this is metaphor if not nonsense, on the ground that God has neither mouth nor tongue, vocal cords nor hands. Whether the attribution of speech to God is in fact either metaphor or nonsense is a topic I will address in a subsequent chapter. As preliminary for that, I propose to reflect here on the many modes of discourse. There are many ways of saying things other than by making sounds with one's vocal apparatus or inscribing marks with one's limbs.

A terminological point is worth emphasizing: by "saying" and "speaking" and "discoursing," I will never have in mind what Austin called *locutionary* actions, that is, actions of uttering or inscribing words, but only such actions as can be what he called *illocutionary* actions – commanding, promising, asserting, and so on. I say: "such actions as *can be* illocutionary actions." The concept of an *illocutionary* action is a functional concept; an action is an illocutionary action on a certain occasion if it is related in a certain way to a *locutionary* action. But it will be abundantly clear by the end of this chapter that often the very same action which can be related to a locutionary action in such a way as to be an illocutionary action can be performed without the use of words – in which case it's not functioning as an illocutionary action. So what I have in mind by a *speech action* is an action which *can* function as an illocutionary action. (An implication is that speech actions are to be distinguished not only from *locutionary* actions but also from actions capable of functioning as what Austin called *perlocutionary* actions.)

Let us dispense quickly with the most obvious point here: the *media* we use for saying things extend far beyond words. The authors of field guides to flora and fauna use drawings and photographs to assert that the fringed gentian looks like this and the ruby-throated flycatcher like that. Once upon a time Morse Code was used for saying things at a distance, and semaphores, for communicating between ships. And we all know of the sign language used by and for those who are deaf. Actually all of us use conventional gestures of various sorts to say things: winks, nudges, shrugs, nods, and so forth. The media of divine discourse are even more diverse, or so at least the biblical writers claim. Words, yes; but beyond that, happenings of all sorts: dreams, visions, apparitions, burning bushes, illnesses, national calamities, national deliverances, droughts – on and on. When reflecting on discourse, be it human or divine, it's important to keep in mind this diversity of media – especially important to keep in mind that one doesn't need words to say things.

Nevertheless, in what follows I will focus on the diversity of ways of saying things *with words*, mainly since I wish later to consider how to go about reading a text to find out what God might have said or be saying with that text. For the same reason, I will focus my attention on cases in which one person says something with words which he himself hasn't uttered or inscribed. Cases of *double agency*, we might call them.

## Double agency discourse

Someone somewhere in the President's suite of offices prepares an official document; upon completion, he hands it to the President and the President signs it. Thereby the text produced by the secretary becomes the medium of the President's declaration. Examples which fit this description are relatively uncommon, since few of us are presidents; but the phenomenon, of which the species is uncommon, is itself common. Secretaries produce documents on typewriters or word-processors, their superiors sign them, and thereby those documents become the medium of those superiors saying various things. Secretaries in such cases represent the continuation in the modern world of the practice in pre-modern societies of having one's scribe or amanuensis produce the text which is the medium of one's saying something.

The role of the discourser in the production of the text varies. Sometimes the secretary "takes dictation," just as the scribe or amanuensis would have done. But that's by no means how it always goes. Sometimes the superior merely indicates to the secretary the substance of what she wants to say and leaves it to the secretary to find the appropriate words. Presumably the relation of "ghost writers" to authors lies somewhere between these two poles. The ghost writer doesn't take dictation; on the other hand, the author does more to guide the ghost writer's inscribings than merely indicate the substance of what she wants to say. Or so, at least, we who read the resultant book suppose!

The direct role of the discourser in the production of the text may be attenuated even beyond the discourser's merely indicating the substance of what she wants to say. The secretary may continue to compose letters while the executive is out of the office for several weeks – traveling, ill, attending to family matters, or whatever. Without the executive even doing so much as communicating to the secretary the substance of what she wants to say, the secretary may *know* what the executive wants to say to one and another person, and compose letters accordingly. The crucial thing is that the secretary "know the mind" of his superior. Upon the return of the executive, the secretary may then hand the batch of letters to the executive for signing.[1]

Or he may not. Often executives authorize secretaries to sign letters "for" them. Sometimes the letter signed by the secretary "for" the executive will have been dictated by the executive. But again, that's not necessary. In principle, the executive, without even so much as explicitly indicating the substance of what she wants to say, may both ask the secretary to compose letters in her absence and authorize the secretary to sign them "for" her. In such a case, the surface relationship of text-producer to discourser is very thinned out indeed! In all but unusual emergency cases, however, the relationship beneath the surface will not be at all thin; the secretary will "know the mind" of the executive on the matters at hand.

The transition which I made in the discussion just preceding, from secretaries preparing letters for the signature of their executives, to secretaries signing letters "for" their executives, looks insignificant on the face of it. In fact something quite new enters the picture at that point. But before I say what that is, let us take just a moment to look from the opposite perspective at examples of the sort I have been citing. We have been looking at them from the perspective of the discourser, taking note of the various ways in which texts become available as the medium of one's discourse – in addition to being produced by oneself. But we can also look at them from the perspective of the inscriber. Then one sees something of the variety of ways in which one can produce texts without oneself performing any illocutionary actions thereby.

Obviously one way to inscribe without discoursing is to "just write words down." Nothing so casual as that is going on in the cases we have considered. Nonetheless, the people who prepare copies of position papers for the President to sign are not themselves performing the speech actions that the President performs by signing these papers. Some of what he says by signing, they may disagree with; much of what he says by signing, they lack the authority necessary for being in a position to say. In general, those who compose documents for presidential signature are themselves not performing any speech actions at all by producing those texts. So too the secretary, by producing a text, is not performing the speech actions that the executive performs by attaching her signature. Normally the secretary isn't performing any speech actions at all by producing those texts. In none of these cases is double-speaking going on. In none of them is one person speaking by way of another person speaking – that is, in none is one person performing an illocutionary act by way of another person performing an illocutionary act.

A somewhat similar thing can happen even when the split between text-producer and discourser, illustrated by all these examples, is absent – when the inscriber is the discourser. Poets typically go through drafts of their poems, writers of academic papers typically go through drafts of their papers, and writers of letters sometimes go through drafts of their letters. Compare then a final version of some letter with an early draft thereof which is significantly different. Was the writer, in producing that early draft, asserting various things and then later changing his mind on whether to assert them? Or was he not actually asserting anything until he signed that final version? Were his preliminary drafts mere inscriptions whose production enabled him to arrive at that last version which he finally, then, used to say something? Though often it won't be clear one way or the other how this question should be answered, sometimes it is clear that in producing drafts the author was not saying things which later he retracted, but attempting *to arrive at* a text which is to be counted as the medium of his saying something – that is, as the medium of his performance of various illocutionary actions.

Let us end this brief side-trip and put ourselves back in the perspective of the discourser. I have cited a range of cases in which texts serve as the medium of a person's discourse even though the person has not himself or herself produced that text. Looking back over those cases, we can discern two quite different phenomena coming to light. There is, for one thing, the phenomenon of variations in *degree and mode of superintendence*. On one end of the degree-of-superintendence continuum are those cases which on this occasion I rushed right past: cases in which the discourser herself produces the text. Right next to those are the cases with which we began, cases in which the discourser "dictates" to a scribe or secretary the words to be inscribed. Further along the continuum are those cases in which the discourser merely indicates to the secretary the substance of what she wishes to say. Yet further along are those cases in which the secretary knows what the executive wants to say without the executive explicitly telling him or her even the substance of that – knows it by virtue of "knowing the mind" of the executive on such matters and knowing what the situation calls for to be said by a person of such "mind."

And if we keep going in this direction, what do we find at the end of this continuum? Presumably cases of a sort which I haven't even cited up to this point: cases in which the degree of supervision by discourser over inscriber is nil, not even involving the inscribers "knowing the mind" of the discourser. Now and then one comes across an inscription of a sentence over whose production one had no supervision whatsoever but which contains an attractive potential for saying something; by then doing one thing or another with that inscription one brings it about that the inscription becomes the medium of one's own discourse. One comes across an interesting "fortune" in a fortune cookie, glues it on a piece of stationery, adds one's signature, and sends the whole thing off to a friend. One finds a witty birthday card in a shop, signs it, and sends it off. The examples are many – many more than one would at first have thought!

The second phenomenon is *authorization* – and more specifically, variations in mode of authorization. In one or another way the discourser *authorizes* the text – that is, does one thing or another to the text such that her doing that *counts as* her performing some illocutionary acts, with the consequence that that text becomes the *medium* of those illocutionary acts. To authorize a text is in effect to declare: let this text serve as medium of my discoursing. In several of the examples I cited, the authorizing act consisted of the discourser attaching her signature to an inscription of the text. In the case of ghost-written manuscripts, the authorizing act presumably consists of some such thing as the author signing the letter of transmittal which accompanies the manuscript produced by the ghost writer. As we will see in a subsequent chapter, authorization, or something very much like it, underlies all speaking, all discoursing. In most discourse, though, nothing so official as attaching a signature occurs. We turn in or hand over or send off the manuscript we have written. Or we just talk – in which case the authorization resides in our participating in a situation of utterings counting as speakings.

The executive holds in her own person the right, the authority, the "power" to authorize the text – to do something so as to bring it about that it become a medium of discourse on her part. As we have just seen, there are many ways of exercising this authority. Executives in the modern world regularly exercise this authority, for letters typed out by their secretaries, by *signing* these letters; until the executive signs the letter, it's not a medium of discourse by her or anyone else. And normally an executive *signs* a letter by producing an inscription of his or her signature. But the executive may instruct the secretary to sign the letters *for* her, *on her behalf,* thus deputizing to the secretary the authority to sign. The secretary typically accomplishes this by producing an inscription of the executive's name. The secretary's doing that then counts as the executive's signing it; and the executive's signing it brings it about, in turn, that the text of the letter is authorized by the executive as her medium of discourse.

It should be noted that to deputize to someone else some authority that one has in one's own person is not to surrender that authority and hand it over to that other person; it is to bring it about that one exercises that authority by way of actions performed by that other person acting as one's deputy. That's what happens when the executive deputizes the secretary to sign the letters "for" her. The act which generates the executive's authorizing signing, and which thereby generates the executive's discourse, is the secretary's act of producing an inscription of the executive's name.

### Deputized discourse

To be deputized to inscribe the name of some person at the end of a document, so that thereby that person "signs" that document, and then to do that, is not the same as saying things in the name of that person, since signing is not a species of saying. But when the executive both instructs her secretary to compose a letter and also deputizes the secretary to sign the letter "for" her, then the secretary, to all intents and purposes, is saying things in the name of the executive. This phenomenon, of *speaking in the name of*, is of central importance in the case of God's speech; let us, accordingly, take time to look at other, somewhat more paradigmatic, examples of the phenomenon. And let us, for a while, shift over from cases of inscribing to cases of uttering.

Consider the phenomenon of an ambassador speaking in the name of his head of state. To do so, the person who is ambassador must have been deputized to do so; he can't just undertake to do so. And the deputation will always have a more or less limited scope; only if the ambassador's speech falls within that scope will he be speaking in the name of his head of state. The deputation need not, however, take the form of the ambassador's being given *the very words* he is to utter. To be appointed ambassador is to be commissioned to represent one's state. That commissioning includes deputation to perform various actions on behalf of one's state; and the things that fall within the scope of that deputation are mainly specified by citing categories or types of actions. So too when the ambassador is deputized to say something in the name of his head of state. The deputation will often take the form of deputation to say something *of a certain sort* – and then only if certain events take place, or certain conditions arise. Not only can one read aloud the text of a person's discourse without thereby speaking in the name of that person; one can, conversely, speak in the name of some person without the words one utters having been specified by that person.

Perhaps we should dwell just a moment on this last point. One person may request or commission a second person to communicate a message to a third person: "Tell her that I'll be home in time for dinner." "Tell her that I'm asking her to bring the salad." "Tell her that I promise to rake the leaves this weekend." The first person has performed some speech action, often in that very requesting. That speech action has some particular person as addressee – the assertion is addressed *to* someone, the request made *of* someone, the promise made *to* someone. And the first person asks the second to communicate to the addressee the information that the speech action in question has been performed. If all goes well, the second person asserts, to the addressee of the first person's speech action, that the first person has done that, and thereby performs the perlocutionary action of informing that person of that. Of course, if the first person writes down his assertion, his request, his command, or whatever, the second can communicate it to the addressee by simply handing the inscription to the third person. And sometimes we transmit some message of a person to its addressee without being requested or commissioned to do so.

Being asked to communicate a message from someone is not the same as being deputized to speak in the name of someone. The deputy has, as it were, power of attorney; it's by way of the deputy's doing one thing and another that the deputizer acquires the rights and responsibilities of having issued such and such a threat, made such and such a promise, and so on. In the communication case, by contrast, the threat or promise must already have been made if it is to be delivered. In practice, these two cases shade into each other; the more the deputizer specifies the details of what he wants his deputy to say, the more similar becomes the action of the deputy to the action of a person communicating a message.[2]

The fact that speaking as someone's deputy does not require being given the words to speak has important implications. Should George Kennan, speaking in the name of Truman, issue a warning to Stalin about Berlin, then it is *Truman* who has issued a warning to Stalin. Kennan has not done so; Truman has done so. Nonetheless, the warning may well be phrased in Kennan's words rather than Truman's. What is of significance, then, is not the exact words used but whether *the warning* was issued – the warning whose issuance was deputized by Truman. Kennan may in fact express the warning rather differently from how Truman would have expressed it: more elegantly, with more sensitivity to Russian fears, in Russian rather than English, and so forth. Indeed, Kennan may express the warning in words which Truman, if he were issuing the warning in his own person, would resist using. Using only words which Truman himself would use is not a condition of Kennan's issuing the warning in the name of Truman. Kennan may even disagree with the issuance of this warning; that too does not prevent his issuing it, not even if he parenthetically indicates to Stalin that he himself disagrees. In short, Kennan's personality may be evident in the words used, while at the same time Truman's steely determination may be evident in the warning. In cases such as this one finds a peculiarly fascinating blend of two personalities. Naturally this will often yield ambiguities as to what is to be ascribed to which person.

It follows from the above that not only may an ambassador speak in the name of his head of state without the head of state being aware, in detail, of the words used; the head of state may not even know at the time that the speaking-in-the-name-of is taking place – or may never know. And just as deputations vary in the degree to which the verbal detail of the message is specified, so also they vary in the explicitness of the deputation. Thus doubts and controversies can arise both over whether the ambassador really was deputized to speak in the name of his head of state, and, if he was, over whether he really was deputized to say what he did say in the name of his head of state.

If the ambassador was deputized to say what he did say in the name of his head of state, then the head of state speaks (discourses) by way of the utterings of the ambassador; locutionary acts of the ambassador count as illocutionary acts of the head of state. Correspondingly, the listener is presented not merely with locutionary acts of the ambassador but with locutionary acts which *count as* illocutionary acts performed by the ambassador's head of state. Confronted with Kennan's claim to be issuing a warning in the name of Truman, Stalin will naturally want to be assured that Kennan is in fact deputized to say this in the name of Truman. But if Kennan is so deputized, then, upon hearing Kennan's utterances, Stalin is confronted with what counts as Truman's warning – whether he, Stalin, acknowledges that or not.

Does double-speaking take place in the case of an ambassadorially delivered warning? The head of state performs illocutionary acts by way of the ambassador performing locutionary acts. But does the ambassador himself perform illocutionary acts by way of his locutionary acts? Does he speak, discourse, in his own voice? Well, he needn't. But he might. That is, it might sometimes be the case that the very same utterings count both as the performance of speech actions by the ambassador and as the performance of speech actions by his head of state; these might be the very same speech actions, or somewhat different. Probably the most common occurrence, though, is that in the course of issuing the warning, the ambassador moves back and forth between speaking in the name of his head of state and speaking in his own voice; and sometimes part of what he does when speaking in his own voice consists of communicating a message from his head of state.

Biblical prophecy, as recorded for us in the prophetic books of the Old Testament, regularly moves back and forth in just this way between the prophet speaking in the name of God by virtue of having been deputized to do so, the prophet speaking in his own voice but delivering a message from God, and the prophet speaking in his own voice and not delivering a message from God. As to the first two modes, we usually have both of those at once – for reasons that will shortly become clear. Here, by way of illustration, is an example from the book of Hosea:

> Ephraim's glory shall fly away like a bird –
> > no birth, no pregnancy, no conception!
> Even if they bring up children,
> > I will bereave them until no one is left.
> Woe to them indeed when I depart from them! ...
> Give them, O Lord –
> > what will you give?
> Give them a miscarrying womb and dry breasts.
> Every evil of theirs began at Gilgal;
> > there I came to hate them.
> Because of the wickedness of their deeds
> > I will drive them out of my house.
> I will love them no more;
> > all their officials are rebels.
> Ephraim is stricken,
> > their root is dried up,
> > they shall bear no fruit.
> Even though they give birth,
> > I will kill the cherished offspring of their womb.
> Because they have not listened to him,
> > my God will reject them ...                    (9:11–17).

How are we to construe the opening five lines, including "I will bereave them until no one is left"? The "I" in question is clearly God. But is Hosea here speaking in the name of God, or is he speaking in his own voice but communicating a message from God, perhaps by direct quotation? Are we to place quotation marks around the lines? I think the best answer is probably that what God says by way of the deputized speech of Hosea is that very thing which God spoke to Hosea in the course of commissioning him to convey that to Israel. First God said privately to Hosea something meant for Israel which he commissioned Hosea to communicate to them, and then God said that very same thing by way of the public speech of Hosea functioning as God's deputy. Hosea is *commissioned* to communicate a message from God to Israel, and *deputized* so that, by communicating that message, God is then and there once again saying that very same thing, this time in public.

By contrast, lines 6–8,

> Give them, O Lord –
> what will you give?
> Give them a miscarrying womb and dry breasts,

are clearly lines spoken by Hosea in his own voice and not communicating a message from God. (As are the last two lines.) But what about

> Ephraim is stricken,
> their root is dried up,
> they shall bear no fruit?

This could be Hosea speaking in his own voice and not delivering a message from God; but it could also be the blending of the other two possibilities.

My citation of prophecy at this point will have led the reader to surmise, and rightly so, that some of the points I made earlier about modes of discourse were made with an eye on the biblical notion of *prophet*. So let us, for a while, reflect explicitly on that notion. The interplay of *superintendence* and *authorization* will once again come into view, with the former taking the form of God "putting words in the mouth" of the prophet and appointing him to communicate those to the people, and the latter taking the form of God deputizing the prophet to speak "in the name of" God. The *locus classicus* for the biblical concept of a prophet is found in Deuteronomy 18. Moses is speaking to Israel:

"The Lord your God will raise up for you a prophet like me from among you, from your brethren – him you shall heed – just as you desired of the Lord your God at Horeb on the day of the assembly, when you said, 'Let me not hear again the voice of the Lord my God, or see this great fire any more, lest I die.' And the Lord said to me, 'They have rightly said all that they have spoken. I will raise up for them a prophet like you from among their brethren; and I will put my words in his mouth, and he shall speak to them all that I command him. And whoever will not give heed to my words which he shall speak in my name, I myself will require it of him. But the prophet who presumes to speak a word in my name which I have not commanded him to speak, or who speaks in the name of other gods, that same prophet shall die.' And if you say in your heart, 'How may we know the word which the Lord has not spoken?' – when a prophet speaks in the name of the Lord, if the word does not come to pass or come true, that is a word which the Lord has not spoken."

Several things in this passage are worth noting. The prophet is one who speaks *in the name of* God. As a consequence, those who hear the prophet speaking, when he is speaking in his prophetic capacity, are confronted with that which counts as God speaking; the utterances of the prophet are the medium of God's discourse. Speaking in the name of God is not something that a person just undertakes to do; God will "raise up" the prophet, as God raised up Moses. To be a prophet requires being deputized to speak in God's name. In addition, God will tell the prophet what he is to say, putting words in his mouth; the prophet does not devise the words by himself. The prophet is commissioned to communicate a message from God, and God will give that message to the prophet.

Let us add immediately, to forestall a totally mechanical picture of the situation, that nothing at all is said as to how God gives to the prophet the words he is to speak – how God "puts words in the mouth" of the prophet. It may have been by way of the prophet having an experience of hearing God speak to him. But it needn't have been like that. It may have involved far more activity on the part of the prophet than is the case when the experience befalls one of hearing God speak. Though even then it should be noted that when a Hebrew-speaking person has the experience of God speaking to him, what he experiences is God speaking to him in Hebrew!

In any case, the biblical notion of the prophet blends the concept of one who is commissioned to communicate a message from someone, with the concept of one who is deputized to speak in the name of someone. The prophet, speaking in the name of God, communicates a message from God. Hence it's true for a double reason that hearers are confronted with "the word which the Lord has spoken." It's true for a double reason that obedience to the message of the prophet is not a matter of obeying the prophet but a matter of obeying God. "Whoever will not give heed to my words which [the prophet] shall speak in my name, I myself," says God, "will require it of him."

Lastly, the passage addresses the profoundly human anxiety of how to tell which persons are in fact delivering a message from God in speaking on behalf of God, from among all those who claim to do so.

The passage from Deuteronomy describes the prophet abstractly and from above: the description is formulated as a description of *The* Prophet, and is placed in God's mouth. In the book of Jeremiah we find an extraordinarily vivid and concrete description of the prophet from below, but using the same conceptuality. Jeremiah begins at the beginning, with a description of his awareness that God intended to commission him as a prophet:

> Now the word of the Lord came to me saying,
> "Before I formed you in the womb I knew you,
> and before you were born I consecrated you;
> I appointed you a prophet to the nations."

Jeremiah protests:

Then I said, "Ah, Lord God! Behold, I do not know how to speak, for I am only a youth."

God brushes aside his protest:

> But the Lord said to me,
> "Do not say, 'I am only a youth';
> for to all to whom I send you you shall go,
> and whatever I command you you shall speak.
> Be not afraid of them,
> for I am with you to deliver you, says the Lord."

And so, in spite of Jeremiah's protests, the commissioning takes place:

> Then the Lord put forth his hand and touched my mouth;
> and the Lord said to me,
> "Behold, I have put my words in your mouth.
> See, I have set you this day over nations and over kingdoms,
> to pluck up and to break down,
> to destroy and to overthrow,
> to build and to plant."

Jeremiah's existential "prophetic consciousness" has the structure described abstractly in Deuteronomy. He is convinced that he has been commissioned to deliver a message from God: "I have put my words in your mouth," says God. And he is convinced that he has been deputized by God to speak in the name of God, so that God speaks by way of Jeremiah's uttering words: "You shall be as my mouth," says God.

Jeremiah puts the same understanding of the nature of the prophetic calling to use in his running polemic with the false prophets. The false prophet is one who, though he claims to speak in the name of God, has neither been so deputized, nor been given any message to be communicated. His message has been devised from his own heart or taken from a dream. "And the Lord said to me, 'The prophets are prophesying lies in my name, I did not send them, nor did I command them or speak to them. They are prophesying to you a lying vision, worthless divination, and the deceit of their own minds" (14: 14; *cf.* 23: 25ff., 27: 14ff., 29: 9).

This same conceptuality of the prophet is carried over into the New Testament, though with the emphasis now more on the deputation to speak in the name of God than on the commission to communicate a message from God. In Matthew 1: 22 it says, "All this took place to fulfill what the Lord had spoken by the prophet ..." In Luke 1: 70 we find, "as he spoke by the mouth of his holy prophets from of old ..." In Romans 1: 1–2 Paul speaks of the gospel of God "which he promised beforehand through his prophets in the Holy Scriptures." And in Hebrews 1: 1 we read: "In many and various ways God spoke of old to our fathers by the prophets ..."[3]

More interesting, though, than the *fact* that the *concept* of prophet is carried over into the New Testament writings is the *question* whether the New Testament writings regard *the line of the prophets* as continued in the apostles.[4] Jesus was of course understood as a prophet. But were the apostles understood as prophets – albeit, prophets of a special sort, viz., prophets whose core message was that Jesus is the Christ and who were eyewitnesses of him in his resurrected life?

It's not decisively clear. What initially makes one wonder is that they are never called prophets. By itself, that is not decisive; we must look at what an *apostolos* was understood to be. The core of the concept was that of someone sent forth as a commissioned representative. "Truly, truly, I say to you, a servant is not greater than his master, nor is he who is sent (*apostolos*) greater than he who sent him" (John 13: 16). That a person is an apostle of Jesus Christ only if *commissioned* as such, that one cannot become an apostle just by deciding to go into apostling, is especially clear from Paul's writings. Paul was challenged by some of the Christians in Galatia as to the authority with which he was speaking. He replied that he was "an apostle – not from men nor through man, but through Jesus Christ and God the Father, who raised him from the dead" (Gal. 1: 1). He makes the same claim, with only slight variations, in several of his other letters.[5]

So divine commissioning was central to the concept of an apostle. But was an apostle commissioned to deliver a message? And was an apostle deputized to speak in the name of God, so that by way of the apostle uttering or inscribing words, God would speak? Certainly the former – provided we remember that being given a message to deliver from God probably does not require having an experience of God speaking those very words. But whether the apostles were deputized to speak in the name of God is less clear. I know of no place in which the New Testament actually describes the apostle thus; so we have to assemble evidence and judge probabilities. In Luke 10 Jesus is reported as sending out seventy disciples, two by two, into the neighboring towns, commissioning them with instructions as to what to do and what to say, and pronouncing that "He who hears you hears me, and he who rejects you rejects me, and he who rejects me rejects him who sent me." (*Cf.* the saying of Jesus in Matthew 10: 40, set in a different context, "He who receives you receives me, and he who receives me receives him who sent me.") It would be rather surprising if those seventy had been understood as deputized to speak in God's name whereas the apostles were not. On the other hand, though the New Testament speaks of the apostles as commissioned to do such things as disciple the nations, baptize, teach, and witness (Matt. 28: 16ff., Luke 24: 46ff.), it never speaks of them as commissioned to *speak in the name of God*. Such remarks of Paul as "Now concerning virgins, I have no command of the Lord, but I give my opinion as one who by the Lord's mercy is trustworthy," suggest strongly that Paul saw himself as commissioned to deliver a message from God; but they suggest much less strongly – in fact, they don't suggest at all – that Paul saw himself as deputized to speak in the name of God.

## Appropriated discourse

I will have more to say on this matter in my final chapter.[6] In the meanwhile, let us suppose – for the sake of the argument – that the apostles were understood as continuing the line of the prophets. Suppose further – admittedly a controversial assumption – that the New Testament books were all either authorized by an apostle or express the mind of an apostle. And suppose, lastly, that the prophetic books of the Old Testament are fairly accurate expressions of actual prophetic discourse. It remains the case that the biblical writings cannot in general be regarded as record or expression of prophetic discourse. The narrative books, the wisdom writings, but especially the Psalms: the very structure of these prohibits us from taking them as that. The structure of the psalms is that of human beings addressing God, not that of God addressing human beings. So how can these be understood as media of divine discourse? Can they be?

Paul Ricoeur, in his discussion of these matters in his essay, "Toward a Hermeneutic of the Idea of Revelation," concludes that these parts of the Bible cannot be thus understood; some other category is required, he asserts. He himself proposes the category of revelation, understood as manifestation. But his inference is fallacious; a text need not be the residue of prophetic discourse to be an instrument of God's discourse. To see that, let us now take note of yet another way, quite different from any we have thus far considered, in which one person's speaking may depend on another person's use of language.

Sometimes one person says something and another remarks, "I agree with that" or "She speaks for me too" or "Those are also my convictions" or "I share those commitments," or words to that effect. Or one person quotes from another with some such words as, "As de Tocqueville so perceptively remarked ..." Or a person says, in a parliamentary session, "I second the motion." In all such cases, one is not just appropriating *the text* of the first person as the medium of one's own discourse; one is appropriating *the discourse* of that other person. One's own discourse is a function of that other person's discourse. What the second person says is determined, in good measure, by what the first person said.

What decisively distinguishes these cases from the cases we have just been considering is that no deputizing, no speaking-in-the-name of, is involved – though all deputized speech will also in a way be appropriated speech. As to supervision, it may or may not be involved. Earlier we saw that one may appropriate, as the medium of one's own discourse, sentential-inscriptions that one just comes across, sentential-inscriptions whose production one hasn't in any way supervised. Some of the present cases of appropriated discourse resemble those cases, in that no supervision is involved. But even so, there remains the difference that what is appropriated in these new cases is not the text produced by someone else but *the speech of someone else* – this, even though the speech may not been supervised and will not have been deputized by oneself. In the case of the ambassador, the deputy, the prophet – that is, in the case of deputized, in-the-name-of, speech – there may or may not be double-discourse. Here there is inherently double-discourse.

Usually it won't be the case, however, that the content of the appropriating speech is simply identical with the content of the appropriated speech. One senator, call him "Joe," says, "I commit myself to bringing down the deficit." Another, call him Michael, says, "I share that commitment." Joe, in saying what he did, committed himself, that is, committed Joe, to bringing down the deficit. But Michael, in saying "I share that commitment," wasn't doing that. He wasn't committing Joe to bringing down the deficit. He was instead committing himself, Michael, to bringing down the deficit. In addition, there may be various things said or suggested in the appropriated discourse of which the appropriator doesn't want to say even some equivalent. He wants to embrace the main point but not all the incidentals. Thus to get from the propositional content of the appropriated discourse to that of the appropriating discourse requires subtlety and sensitivity of interpretation. In appropriating, we re-fashion, not always, but often.

Likewise for illocutionary stance. The appropriating discourse need not take over all, or even any, of the illocutionary stances of the appropriated discourse. I may cite some person's narration of what supposedly happened to him as a suggestive parable of our human condition. If so, I am then not joining that other person in claiming that the story gives what happened. The story functions in my discourse as a piece of fiction; what I claim is not that the story happened but that it is a suggestive parable of our human condition.

It is sometimes said that the Bible – be it now the Hebrew Bible or the Christian Bible – that the Bible is God's book. By which is not meant that the Bible is *a collection* of books by God, God's *opera omnia* – consisting of approximately thirty-nine volumes if it be the Hebrew Bible one has in mind, precise number depending on what exactly one counts as one book, or of sixty-six plus volumes if it be the Christian Bible one has in mind, precise number depending on which canon one embraces. What is meant is that, whatever its subdivisions, the Bible is *one* book of God. I suggest that the most natural way of understanding this claim is to understand it in terms of divinely appropriated human discourse.

It's not very plausible to understand it as God just taking some text, however produced, and doing something so as to bring it about that those words serve as the medium of divine discourse. For what the writers *said* matters, that is, it matters what illocutionary acts they performed: what they were referring to, where they were speaking literally and where metaphorically, what cosmological picture served as background to their discourse, and so forth. And though some of the text is plausibly regarded as the record of prophetic utterance, we saw above that to regard all of it thus would be to force square pegs into round holes. That leaves, as the most natural way of understanding the claim that as a whole this is God's book, understanding it in terms of appropriated discourse. Some of the discourse appropriated will itself be divine discourse; that will be true for those passages which are a record of prophetic utterance.[7] Some or all of the rest, though not a record of utterances in the name of God, may nonetheless have been produced under a unique form of divine supervision – inspiration, let us say. But not even that need be true of a given part for it to belong to God's book.[8] All that is necessary for the whole to be God's book is that all the human discourse it contains have been appropriated by God, as one single book, for God's discourse. If it is the Christian Bible we are speaking of, the event which *counts as* God's appropriating this totality as the medium of God's own discourse is presumably that rather drawn out event consisting of the Church's settling on this totality as its canon.

If the Bible is indeed God's book, and if that claim is understood in the way I have just suggested it is most naturally understood, then two of the most salient facts to be faced as one makes the interpretative move from appropriated discourse to appropriating discourse are the fact that God is the agent of the appropriating discourse whereas, with the exception of the record of prophecy, human beings are the agents of the appropriated discourse, and the fact that these writings which saw the day as a sizable number of independent books, and still retain that separate identity, are all together appropriated into a text which is one single book. Later in our discussion, when our topic is interpretation, I will probe some of the implications of these salient facts.

### *Addressees; and presentational vs. authorial discourse*

Two interconnected issues remain before we can bring these reflections on the many modes of discourse to a close. Many, though not all, speech acts have what one might call an *addressee*. The concept can be introduced, well enough for our purposes, by example rather than definition. One makes a promise to *someone*, one asks *someone* to do something, one asks *someone* a question, one tells *someone* something, one addresses one's remarks to *someone*; and so forth. All these are examples of discourse having an addressee.

Often persons other than the addressee of one's discourse will hear or read one's text. All who do hear or read it (with some degree of understanding) might be called the *audience* of one's discourse. Some of these may "overhear" what one says. But some may be such that one *intended* that they, and perhaps others as well, would hear or read one's text with some understanding; thus we can introduce the concept of an *intended audience*. In turn, one's intent might take two quite different forms. Some persons may be such that it is true of them that one intended that they would be in one's audience. Alternatively, one's intent may take the form of intending that anyone who is of a certain sort would be among the audience of one's text. Thus there is a number of somewhat different concepts of *audience*. The concept of *addressee*, though, remains distinct from all of them.

It's obvious that a single illocutionary act may have more than one addressee; one may address one's remarks to a number of people. What's not so obvious is that by way of a single locutionary act one may say different things to different addressees. At the family meal in the evening the mother may assertively utter, "Only two more days till Christmas." To her children she may have said just what the sentence means, that there are only two more days till Christmas. To her husband she may have said, in a rather arch and allusive way, that he must stop delaying and get his shopping done. One locutionary act, several illocutionary acts, different ones for different addressees[9]

That phenomenon is in turn worth distinguishing from the phenomenon of a person using a given text *on different occasions* to say different things to the same or different addressees – or indeed, to re-say the same thing to the same or different addressees. After being at a loss for some time as to how to make a certain point effectively to one of one's children, one might hit on the device of writing a story to make the point to them; later one might give the same story to one of one's friends to make quite a different point to them. The distinction here which it is important to keep in mind is that between saying something by *authoring* a text and saying something by *presenting* a text to someone, be it a text that one has oneself authored, or one that someone else authored.

These points are rich with potential for application to divine discourse. I have suggested that it is not decisively clear that the writers of the New Testament regarded apostles as prophets of a special sort. But suppose, for a moment, that St. Paul was deputized to speak in the name of God, and that, when he wrote his letter to

the Christians in Rome and made it available to them, he was acting
in his "capacity" of prophet. Then by way of Paul's doing those
things, God would have been saying various things to those Christians
in Rome. Possibly all the things God said to any of them, God said to
all of them; then again, perhaps with some passages in the text God
said one thing to some of them and something different to others of
them. Furthermore, it may be that by Paul's doing those things, God
was addressing not only those Christians then in Rome but other
human beings as well. Even you and me, perhaps. If so, it seems likely
that God was, with at least some passages of the text, saying
something different to you and me from what God was saying to
them. Alternatively, perhaps God's saying something to you and me
by way of Paul's letter to the Roman Christians awaited the Church's
inclusion of that letter in its canon, in which it has the status of part
of a much larger work, the Bible; and perhaps what God says to you
and me by way of *that part* of the Bible which originated as Paul's
letter to the ancient Roman Christians is rather different from what
God said to those ancient Roman Christians when they received that
letter as an independent writing.

One more possibility, an application of a distinction made above:
apart from what God might have said back in antiquity, whether by
way of Paul writing and sending off that letter or by way of that letter
becoming a part of that book which is the Bible, and whether only to
people then or to people down through the ages, it may be that God
*now speaks to us* by way of our now being *presented* in some fashion with
that text. That is to say, it may not only be the case that this text was a
medium of divine discourse which occurred back in antiquity – when
Paul wrote it and sent it off, or when it became part of that single book
which is the Bible. It may be a medium of *contemporary* divine discourse,
a medium of God's *here and now* addressing you and me, the generating
event being some such thing as our now being confronted with the text
or *God's* now presenting the text to us. It appears to me that it was
along these lines that Augustine interpreted what happened to him in
the garden and what happened to Antony in the Coptic church. By
way of Antony's being presented with those words from the Gospel of
Matthew, God *then and there* addressed Antony. By way of Augustine's
being presented with those words from Paul's letter, God *then and there*
addressed Augustine.

Let it be noted, however, that what God said or says through the
medium of a certain text may be relevant to me even if God did not

then and does not now address me, neither me individually nor me as member of some group. Perhaps some of the things God said then to the Roman Christians are of such scope and generality as to apply to me as well as them; or perhaps some of the things *implied by* what God said to them then are of such scope and generality as to apply to both of us. Or perhaps there are clear analogues between them in their situation, to which God spoke, and me in my situation.

CHAPTER 4

# *Divine discourse in the hands of theologians*

With one eye constantly on the claim that God speaks, I reflected in my last chapter on the many modes of human discourse. My assumption was and is that if it is coherent to suppose that God speaks, then here and there among the many modes of human discourse will be some that can be used to illuminate how God speaks. We must now reflect on the nature of speech as such. But I propose postponing that topic for one chapter. We have looked at divine discourse from the perspective of the many modes of human discourse. Let us also look at it from the perspective of reflections by theologians on the modes and means of divine discourse. We must be selective though. Here is not the place to introduce a history of theological reflections on the Word of God. It was Karl Barth who, of all contemporary theologians, spoke most insistently and persistently, and I might add, provocatively, about God speaking. So let us look at the structure of Barth's thought. With one addendum. Let us preface our study of Barth with a glance at Paul Ricoeur's essay (to which I already referred in my preceding chapter), "Toward a Hermeneutic of the Idea of Revelation."

## *Ricoeur's account of divine revelation*

Ricoeur's account of divine speech and divine revelation is especially instructive for our purposes here because it situates a rather close look at the biblical text in the context of general reflections on the nature of language. In establishing such reflections as the context for his account, Ricoeur's approach resembles mine. It differs in the aspect of language brought to the fore. Whereas speech actions are central in my discussion, texts and the "worlds" they "project" are central in Ricoeur's. But the main point I wish to establish here is that Ricoeur develops his thought in such fashion that, by the time he has finished, divine speech has disappeared from view and only revelation of the manifestation sort is left. One more example of divine speech being absorbed into divine revelation!

Ricoeur is not interested in the role played in theology by the concept of revelation, nor by the attributions of revelation to God made by theologians. Theology, he says, is "second degree discourse"(90),[1] "derived and subordinate" (74). "A hermeneutic of revelation must give priority to those modalities of discourse that are most originary within the language of a community of faith; consequently, those expressions by means of which the members of that community first interpret their experience for themselves and for others" (90).

Given this description of his project, one naturally expects Ricoeur to consider how the concept of revelation, along with attributions of revelation, function in the "originary ... language of a community of faith." That is not what he does. He does not ask how the concept of revelation functions in the religious lives of Jews and Christians; he does not even ask how it functions in the sacred writings of Jews and Christians. Instead, working *de facto* as a theologian of the Christian community with deep sympathies for Judaism, he looks for that concept of revelation which, to his mind, best fits the Hebrew and the Christian Bibles. He himself describes the concept which emerges as "pluralistic, polysemic, and at most analogical in form" (75). I shall contend that, on close scrutiny, it proves not to be that. Though the concept emerges by Ricoeur's pursuit of certain analogies, the concept that emerges is not itself analogical.

Ricoeur moves successively through five genres of biblical text: prophetic discourse, narrative discourse, prescriptive discourse, wisdom discourse, and hymnic discourse. Since prophetic discourse "is the original nucleus of the traditional idea of revelation," he takes this as his "basic axis of inquiry" (75); then, each time that he moves to a new genre of biblical discourse, he asks what there is in it which is analogous to what was identified as revelation in the preceding discourses. At the end he arrives, so he claims, "at a polysemic and polyphonic concept of revelation" (92).

We start, then, with prophetic discourse. "There revelation signifies inspiration from a first person to a first person. The word prophet implies the notion of a person who is driven by God to speak and who does speak to the people about God's name and in God's name" (92). From there we move on to the narrative genre: this, rather than confronting us with "the double voice of the prophet," invites us to "displace onto the recounted events that revealing light that proceeds from their founding value and their instituting function. The narrator is a prophet, but only inasmuch as the generative meaningful events are brought to language." Moving on again from there, we find that in "a similar manner, the nuances of revelation that are derived from the prescriptive force of instruction, the illuminating capacity of the wisdom saying, and the quality of lyrical *pathos* in the hymn, are connected to these forms of discourse."

In all these latter cases, inspiration "designates the coming to language of the prescriptive force, this illuminating capacity, and this lyric *pathos*, but only as analogous to one another" (92–93). Accordingly, we "over-psychologize revelation if we fall back on the notion of scripture as dictated in a literal fashion. Rather it is the force of what is said that moves the writer. That something requires to be said is what the Nicene Creed analogically signifies by the expression, 'We believe in the Holy Spirit who spoke through the prophets'" (92–93).

Having thus articulated the modes of revelation characteristic of each of the biblical genres of discourse, Ricoeur then articulates what he calls "The Response of a Hermeneutic Philosophy." Here he briefly spells out a "philosophical poetics," as he calls it; that finished, he applies this poetics to the biblical writings.

Texts that function poetically, he says, are "removed from the finite intentional horizon of the author"(99). Likewise they are removed from "the ordinary referential function" – which Ricoeur identifies with "the capacity to describe familiar objects of perception or the objects which science alone determines by means of its standards of measurement. Poetic discourse suspends this descriptive function" (100). But rather than turning in on itself, "poetic language alone restores to us that participation-in or belonging-to an order of things which precedes our capacity to oppose ourselves to things taken as objects opposed to a subject. Hence the function of poetic discourse is to bring about this emergence of a depth-structure of belonging-to amid the ruins of descriptive discourse ... [T]his poetic function conceals a dimension of revelation where revelation is to be understood in a nonreligious, nontheistic, and nonbiblical sense of the word – but one capable of entering into resonance with one or the other of the aspects of biblical revelation ... [By means of the poetic function there] emerges the Atlantis submerged in the network of objects submitted to the domination of our preoccupations. It is this primordial ground of our existence, of the originary horizon of our being-there, that is the

revelatory function which is coextensive with the poetic function ...
What shows itself is in each instance a proposed world, a world I may
inhabit and wherein I can project my ownmost possibilities. It is in this
sense of manifestation that language in its poetic function is a vehicle of
revelation" (101–2).

And now, the application of this general doctrine of the poetic
function to the specific case of the biblical writings. Two threads of
analogy, says Ricoeur, guided his earlier analysis of revelation in the
biblical texts. One was the thread of *inspiration*. Beginning with
"prophetic discourse, with its implication of another voice behind the
prophet's voice," this "first analogue was communicated to all the
other modes of discourse to the extent that they could be said to be
inspired" (103). We have already seen that Ricoeur takes inspiration to
be the writer's being moved by the force of what is said. The impelled
coming to language of the generative historical event, of the prescriptive force, of the illuminating capacity, of the lyric *pathos* – that is
inspiration.

The second thread of analogy which guided the analysis is *manifestation*. The "philosophical concept of revelation leads us back," says
Ricoeur, to "the primacy of what is said over the inspiration of the
narrator by means of a second analogy that is no longer that of
inspiration, but that of manifestation" (103).

This new analogy invites us to place the originary expressions of biblical faith
under the sign of the poetic function of language ... Religious discourse is
poetic in all the senses we have named ... [T]he intended implicit reference of
each text opens onto a world, the biblical world, or rather the multiple worlds
unfolded before the book by its narration, prophecy, prescriptions, wisdom,
and hymns. The proposed world that in biblical language is called a new
creation, a new Covenant, the Kingdom of God, is the "issue" of the biblical
text unfolded in front of this text ... Just as the world of poetic texts opens its
way across the ruins of the intraworldly objects of everyday existence and of
science, so too the new being projected by the biblical text opens its way
across the world of ordinary experience and in spite of the closed nature of
that experience. The power to project this new world is the power of breaking
through and of an opening. (103–4)

Ricoeur closes his argument by insisting that "this areligious sense of
revelation helps us to restore the concept of biblical revelation to its full
dignity. It delivers us from psychologizing interpretations of the
inspiration of the scriptures in the sense of an insufflation of their words
into the writers' ears. If the Bible may be said to be revealed this must

refer to what it says, to the new being it unfolds before us. Revelation, in short, is a feature of the biblical world proposed by the text" (103–4).

Contrary to what Ricoeur himself claims, there can be little doubt that the concept at which he has arrived by the end of his discussion is not multivocal but univocal: revelation in all its forms is manifestation, and inspiration consists of being moved by the manifested to bespeak the manifested. Analogy does not inhabit the *concept* of revelation; rather, analogies hold among the different *manifestata* that the distinct genres of biblical writing bring to speech. And among those and the *manifestata* that poetic texts in general bring to speech.

And what has happened to the speech of God? We began with that, in looking at prophetic discourse. Dire warnings were then sounded against allowing divine speech to serve as the model of revelation in general; that would subjectivize revelation, psychologize it, treat it as "opaque and authoritarian" rather than as the "nonviolent appeal" (95) which it is. At the end of the discussion, God's speech has entirely disappeared from view, completely absorbed by manifestation; and it is not even clear that the manifestation brought to speech in biblical discourse is God's self-manifestation, as opposed to agentless manifestation.

Of course Ricoeur is right to resist assimilating divine revelation to divine speech; I defended the same position in the second chapter. But I did so in such a way as to show that it is equally mistaken to assimilate divine speech to divine revelation. A striking feature of Ricoeur's discussion is his complete neglect of the fact that attributions of speech to God pervade all the discourse-genres of the Bible: narrative, prescriptive, hymnic, even wisdom. In all of them, speech is attributed to God. To use Ricoeur's conceptuality: an aspect of the world projected by all these texts is that of God speaking. Ricoeur has resisted the "imprisonment" (76) of revelation within the divine-speech model in such a way as to imprison divine speech within the manifestation model.

Two things misled Ricoeur. In the first place, a simplistic understanding of prophetic discourse. The prophet, he says, "presents himself as not speaking in his own name, but in the name of another, in the name of Yahweh. So here the idea of revelation appears as identified with the idea of a double author of speech and writing. Revelation is the speech of another behind the speech of the prophet . . . When extended to all the other forms of biblical discourse . . . this concept of revelation, taken as a synonym for revelation in general, leads to the idea of scripture as dictated, as something whispered in someone's ear" (75–76). But as we saw in our last chapter, the diplomat can speak on behalf of his head of state without that head of state whispering things in the diplomat's ear; why should it be different in the case of the prophet? Why must supervision take this form?

Nonetheless, I agree with Ricoeur that the structure of much of the biblical writings militates against their being construed as inscriptions of prophetic utterances. So the second thing which misled Ricoeur was his lack of any alternative model for divine discourse. The model of discourse which *appropriates* – as I have called it – other discourse, eludes Ricoeur's attention completely.

### Barth on the Word of God

In Barth, God's speaking is center-stage. Barth's discussion of divine discourse is extremely discursive and expansive, covering hundreds of pages in the first two volumes of his *Church Dogmatics*, and extraordinarily rich in its details. But he never wavers in what he sees as the fundamental structure of divine discourse. He is famous for speaking of the "threefold form" of the Word of God: The Word of God preached in the Church, the Word of God written in Scripture, and the Word of God revealed in Jesus Christ. I shall defend the thesis that though it was indeed appropriate for Barth, given his views, to predicate "is the Word of God" alike of church proclamation, Scripture, and Jesus Christ, in each case meaning something different though analogous by the "is," nevertheless it was in fact his own view that divine discourse occurs in just two structurally different, though inter-related, ways – not three. Having established that, I shall then argue that, upon close scrutiny, one of these two ways is not really a way of speaking at all. When we arrive at the end of the maze, we find just *one* mode of divine discourse – not three!

One form of divine discourse occurs in God's speaking by way of the dwelling among us of the person, Jesus Christ. This mode of God speaking, and this alone, Barth calls *revelation*: "God's revelation is Jesus Christ, the Son of God" (1/1,137). The other (putative) form of divine discourse occurs when one person proclaims to another concerning that revelatory speech of God in Jesus Christ, and God uses that proclamation as an occasion to effectively communicate to that second person what God said by way of Jesus Christ. The "Word of God preached means human talk about God which by God's own judgment . . . is for us not just human willing and doing characterized in some way but also and primarily and decisively ... God's own speech ... The Word of God preached means ... man's talk about God in which and through which God speaks about Himself" (1/1,93,95). It is because this second (putative) mode of divine discourse comes in two species, that Barth can speak of "the threefold form" of the Word of God.

The two basic modes of divine discourse stand to each other as God's *original* speech and God's *derivative* speech: "revelation is originally and directly what the Bible and Church proclamation are derivatively and indirectly, i.e., God's Word" (1/1,117). In turn, God's derivative speech is a complex interplay of three, distinctly different, events or actions. First, that of God's *revelatory* speaking by way of Jesus Christ; second, that of some human being's *proclaiming* that revelatory speaking, be it in the mode of witness or in the mode of contemporary proclaimer[2]; and third, that of God's effectively *communicating* to some person the content of God's revelatory speech on the occasion of that person's being confronted with a proclaimer of that revelatory speech. If we can uncover Barth's thoughts concerning each of these three actions, and then concerning their inter-relationship, we will have understood Barth on the two basic modes of divine discourse.

The fact that Scripture is cited by Barth as one of the forms of God's Word, but that I have made no reference to it in my formulation of Barth's model for God's derivative speech, is significant. As we will see, certain situations are such that, for human beings in those situations, Scripture must in fact play a certain role for them if God's derivative speech is to occur on the occasion of some speaking of theirs. But sometimes God's derivative speech occurs without Scripture playing any role at all. And in any case, Scripture is not *intrinsically* a medium of divine discourse.

Let us begin by looking at some of what Barth says concerning divine speech qua revelation. Barth's insistence that divine revelation occurs only in Jesus Christ has evoked approximately equal proportions of puzzlement and angry protest. I think the clue to understanding him on this point is to realize that he is the most relentlessly Chalcedonian of all Christian theologians: Jesus Christ is God among us, one person both divine and human in nature. There may be many things said in many different places, and many things occurring in many different places, which manifest one thing and another *about* God. But in Jesus Christ, *God* is revealed. Not something *about* God, or some aspect *of* God; but *God*. "In the death of [Jesus], in Him the Crucified, [God] reveals not only the work done, but in and with this Himself, His divine person, His divine essence, in distinction from the nature of divinity in general or the divine forms in which this is seen and reverenced. God Himself is needed to reveal this work, and especially to reveal Himself, His divine person and essence. Who but God could or would reveal God?" (iv/3.1, p. 412). It's like the difference between, on the one hand, my anxiety being revealed by something I do or by something someone says, and, on the other hand, my revealing myself by stepping out from some curtain which had been concealing me. "Revelation . . . means the unveiling of what is veiled" (i/1,118–19). The analogue, of unveiling a person, is misleading, though. On the Chalcedonian understanding, that person who is Jesus Christ did not have to be *unveiled* so that revelation of God could occur. That person *is* the revelation. "[R]evelation is no more and no less than the life of God Himself turned to us . . ." (i/2,483). Of course, that *person* who is Jesus Christ must *have come into being* if there was to be this divine revelation; but nothing *else* had to happen. "Above this act there is nothing other or higher on which it might be based or from which it might be derived unless it was from the transcendence of the eternal Word of God that it came forth in revelation" (i/1,118)[3]

We must distinguish, though, between *revelation per se* and *revelation to someone* – between the intransitive and the transitive concept of revelation. The fact that God is revealed in Jesus Christ does not imply that God is revealed *to me*, or *to you*, in Jesus Christ. For transitive revelation of God to you and me – who never saw Jesus Christ in the flesh – to occur, some medium, some instrumentality, is required. "We know it only indirectly, from Scripture and proclamation. The direct Word of God meets us only in this twofold mediacy" (i/1,121). But if Scripture and proclamation do present Jesus Christ to us and we do become acquainted with him, then God is revealed to us – or more strictly, we become acquainted with God's revelation, or with God revealed.

It's the next step Barth takes which makes what he says directly relevant to our discussion of divine discourse. Divine revelation is a case of God's speaking: God speaks by revealing. In becoming Jesus Christ, God speaks, God says something. Barth insists at this point that "we have no reason not to take the concept of God's Word primarily in its literal sense. God's Word means that God speaks. Speaking is not a 'symbol' (as P. Tillich . . . thinks). It is not a designation and description which on the basis of his own assessment of its symbolic force man has chosen for something very different from and quite alien to this expression ... [T]he concept of the Word of God ... means originally and irrevocably that God speaks" (I/1,132–33). Furthermore, God's revelation is *intrinsically* God's Word. "We have said of Church proclamation," says Barth, that it must continually become God's Word. And we have said the same of the Bible: It must continually become God's Word ... But this cannot be said about revelation. When we speak about revelation we are confronted by the divine act [of speaking] itself and as such ..." (I/1, 117). We will see shortly what Barth has in mind when he says that Scripture and proclamation are not intrinsically God's speech but must become that.

And what does God say in and by the revelation of God's self in Jesus Christ? Barth does not beg off by saying that we can't say what God says, that we can't put it into words. " 'God with us' is how we stated generally the content of God's Word," says Barth (I/1,160). Barth characteristically speaks of promise and of command at this point. Promise: "The promise given to the Church in this Word is the promise of God's mercy which is uttered in the person of Him who is very God and very Man and which takes up our cause when we could not help ourselves at all because of our enmity against God. The promise of this Word is thus Immanuel, God with us ..." (I/1,107–8).[4] And command: "God's Word means in this context God's positive command ... which lifts us up and controls us as a command that goes forth in a way we cannot foresee, and to which ... we can only take up an attitude by repeating it as we think we have heard it and by trying to conform to it as well or badly as we can ... [It is] God's own direction" (I/1,90).

Let us move on from this discussion of God's speaking by revealing to Barth's discussion of human beings proclaiming (bespeaking) that revelatory speech of God. The present-day preacher must be understood as standing in a line of succession with the ancient prophets and apostles; all proclaim Jesus Christ. What makes the succession possible is Holy Scripture, which is "the deposit of what was once proclamation by human lips" (I/1,102). Thus, internal to the line of succession of proclaimers is a distinction between the *primary* and the *secondary*: the proclamation of the contemporary preacher is dependent on, and governed by, that of the ancient prophets and apostles as known to us in scripture. They were witnesses to the revelation; that is why their function is primary. Nonetheless, it must be kept in mind that the witnesses and the present-day preacher are to "be set initially under a single genus ... Jeremiah and Paul at the beginning and the modern preacher of the Gospel at the end of one and the same series" (1/1,102).[5] In addition to God's speaking by revealing, there is, in Barth's view, only one other mode of divine discourse: God speaking by way of human proclamation.

Start with that species of the genus of proclamation which is *witnessing*. "Witnessing," says Barth, "means pointing in a specific direction beyond the self and on to another. Witnessing is thus service to this other in which the witness vouches for the truth of the other, the service which consists in referring to this other. This service is constitutive for the concept of the prophet and also for that of the apostle" (1/1,111). Specifically, the prophets and apostles are witnesses to revelation, that is, to that revelatory speech of God which is Jesus Christ.

Two things deserve emphasis here. In the first place, witness to revelation is not itself revelation. "In the Bible we meet with human words written in human speech, and in these words, and therefore by means of them, we hear of the lordship of the triune God. Therefore when we have to do with the Bible, we have to do primarily with this means, with these words, with the witness which as such is not itself revelation, but only ... the witness to it" (1/2,463). But secondly, though a "real witness is not identical with that to which it witnesses ... it sets it before us" (1/2,463). "Paul steps forth in proclamation, not as a religious personality, but as an apostle of Jesus Christ, so that Jesus Himself is present in him" (1/1,149). Accordingly, if "we want to think of the Bible as a real witness of divine revelation, then clearly we have to keep two things constantly before us and give them their due weight: the limitation and the positive element, its distinctiveness from revelation, in so far as it is only a human word about it, and its unity with it, in so far as revelation is the basis, object and content of this word" (1/2,463). "Holy Scripture is the record of a unique hearing of a unique call and a unique obedience to a unique command" (1/1,115).

The two phrases, "unique hearing" and "unique obedience," point to two sides of the existence of a witness, a passive side and an active side. "Passively, as distinct from us and all other men, [the witnesses] were those who have seen and heard the unique revelation as such, and seen and heard therefore in a unique way ... But the function of these men has also and necessarily another and active side. As distinct from us and all other men, they were those who have to proclaim to others, and therefore to us and all other men, revelation as they encounter it" (1/2,490). The prophets and apostles are not ones who speak *in the name of* God; rather, they are ones who have *witnessed* God's revelatory speech and who then, in turn, *witness to* that. Barth understands the prophets and apostles not at all as deputies; purely as witnesses. They are the ones who are compelled to speak of the revelation which they have seen and heard.[6]

Barth is fully willing to take the bit by the teeth and embrace the implication, of his concept of the witness. Witnessing is human speech, nothing more. The witness does not speak in the name of God. Furthermore, though the Spirit does superintend the witness's witnessing-of and witnessing-to revelation, so that his or her words genuinely present God's revelatory speech, it does not superintend that witnessing-of and witnessing-to in such fashion as to prevent all error and blot out all human particularity. If "we are speaking of a miracle when we say that the Bible is the Word of God, we must not compromise either directly or indirectly the humanity of its form ... [T]he prophets and apostles as such, even in their office, even in their function as witnesses, even in the act of writing down their witness, were real, historical men as we are, and therefore sinful in their action, and capable and actually guilty of error in their spoken and written word. If the miracle happened to them that they were called to be witnesses of the resurrection and that they received the Holy Spirit, it was to them it happened, leaving them the full use of their human freedom and not removing the barriers which are therefore posited for them as for all of us ... [E]very time we turn the Word of God into an infallible biblical word of man or the biblical word of man into an infallible Word of God we resist that which we ought never to resist, i.e., the truth of the miracle that here fallible men speak the Word of God in fallible human words" (1/2,529; cf.508–9). The scope of error extends even to the ethical and theological views of the biblical writers.

Thus the unity of the Bible does not consist in a unified theology or worldview. There is no "Christian view of things," "no biblical theology" (1/2,483). The unity of the Bible consists – so Barth insists – in the unity of its content, in the fact that all its parts point, in one way or another, to Jesus Christ. "The unity of revelation guarantees the unity of the biblical witness in and in spite of all its multiplicity and even contradictoriness" (1/1,117). Accordingly, "to understand the Bible from beginning to end, from verse to verse, is to understand how everything in it relates to this [*Deus dixit*] as its invisible-visible centre" (1/1,116). If we would read the Bible as it wishes to be read, we must attend centrally to the *what is said*. Barth argues that this principle "is necessarily the principle of all hermeneutics"; but "because of the unusual preponderance of what is said in [the Bible] over the words as such," it holds especially for biblical hermeneutics (1/2,468). "It cannot ... be conceded that side by side with this there is another legitimate understanding of the Bible, that, e.g., in its own way it is right and possible when we hear and understand and expound the Bible not to go beyond the humanity as such which is expressed in it" (1/2,468; *cf.* 1/2,471–2).

We have seen that it is the nature of proclamation in general to speak of the revelatory speech of God, thus to speak of Jesus Christ. But contemporary proclaimers, who are not witnesses, have no other access to that revelatory speech than through their access to the witnesses. Thus it is that within the long succession-line of proclaimers there is that fundamental internal distinction between the primary and the secondary. Contemporary proclamation must be based on, and governed by, its recollection of the witnessing-of and the witnessing-to of the witnesses. "The Church can say anything at all about the event of God and man only because something unique has taken place between God and these specific men [who were witnesses], and because in what they wrote, or what was written by them, they confront us as living documents of that unique event. To try to ignore them is to ignore that unique event. The existence of these specific men is the existence of Jesus Christ for us and for all men. It is in this function that they are distinguished from us and from all other men, whom they resemble in everything else" (1/2,486).

And just as it is only through the witnesses that you and I today have access to God's revelatory word consisting in Jesus Christ dwelling among us, so also it is only through Scripture that we have access to those witnesses. Revelation is mediated by the witnesses and the witnesses are mediated by Scripture (see 1/1,104–6). There can be no leaping over Scripture.[7] Accordingly, "it necessarily acquires in the Church, as distinct from all other words and signs, the dignity and validity of the Word of God" (1/2,459). Scripture and only Scripture "recollects the incarnation of the eternal Word ... Thus Scripture imposes itself in virtue of this its content. In distinction from all other scripture the Scripture with this content – really this! – is Holy Scripture. When the Church heard this word – and it heard it only in the prophets and apostles and nowhere else – it heard a magisterial and ultimate word which it could not ever again confuse or place on a level with any other word" (1/1,108).

"As I see it," says Barth, "this does not mean an annulling of the results of biblical scholarship in the last centuries, nor does it mean a breaking off and neglect of efforts in this direction. What it does mean is a radical re-orientation concerning the goal to be pursued, on the basis of the recognition that the biblical texts must be investigated for their own sake to the extent that the revelation which they attest does not stand or occur, and is not to be sought, behind or above them but in them" (1/2,494). The Bible is not "to be read as a collection of sources" (1/2,492). The preacher and the theologian must "leave the curious question of what is perhaps behind the texts, and ... turn with all the more attentiveness, accuracy and love to the texts as such" (1/ 2,494).

Apart from God's revelation in Jesus Christ, we have heard nothing so far about any *speech* of God. This is far from accidental on Barth's part. Though the witnesses' acts of witnessing-of and witnessing-to revelation occur under the superintendence of the Spirit, the speech of the witness remains purely human speech. So also, though contemporary proclamation concerning revelation is under the guidance of the witnesses, the speech of the preacher remains purely human speech. Barth makes the point emphatically, over and over: Scripture and contemporary proclamation as such are not the Word of God. "[W]e cannot regard the presence of God's Word in the Bible as an attribute inhering once for all in this book as such and what we see before us of books and chapters and verses. Of the book as we have it, we can only say: we recollect that we have heard in this book the Word of God" (1/2,530). The Bible is not God's book; God did not speak by way of the authoring of these books nor by way of the assembling of them into a canon. God speaks by way of a human being only if God *is* that human being – Jesus Christ. This is fundamental in Barth!

Nonetheless, Scripture and contemporary proclamation do become the instrument of God's speaking to particular persons – always to particular persons – on specific occasions. "[T]he presence of the Word of God itself, the real and present speaking and hearing of it, is not identical with the existence of the book as such. But in this presence something takes place in and with the book for which the book as such does indeed give the possibility ... A free divine decision is made. It then comes about that the Bible, the Bible *in concreto*, this or that biblical context, i.e., the Bible as it comes to us in this or that specific measure, is taken and used as an instrument in the hand of God, i.e., it speaks to and is heard by us as the authentic witness to divine revelation and is therefore present as the Word of God" (I/1,530). God's speech by way of Scripture is for Barth what I have called *presentational*, rather than *authorial*, speech.

Apart from God's speaking in Jesus Christ, there is thus in Barth's understanding of how God speaks a relentless *eventism*, as one might call it. "[F]aith in the promise of the prophetic and apostolic word, or better, the self-imposing of the Bible in virtue of its content ... is ... an event, and is to be understood only as an event. In this event the Bible is God's Word. That is to say, in this event the human prophetic and apostolic word is a representative of God's Word in the same way as the word of the modern preacher is to be in the event of real proclamation" (1/1,109). "[R]evelation is originally and directly what the Bible and Church proclamation are derivatively and indirectly, i.e., God's Word. We have said of Church proclamation that it must continually become God's Word. And we have said the same of the Bible: it must continually become God's Word" (1/1,117).

What is Barth getting at here with this emphatic eventism? Well, we talk sometimes of some text or speech "not speaking to" us. We understand it. But it "means nothing" to us; it doesn't shape our feelings and imaginings, our doings and respondings. It remains "out there." Often this is true for Scripture and preaching as well. We read it, we hear it, we understand it; and that which we read and hear and understand is, on Barth's view, the written record of a witness to revelation, or the spoken recollection of some such written record. But it doesn't "speak to" us. That is, the "matter" of it, the content, doesn't speak to us. Something more has to happen if revelation is to "speak to" us than just that it be presented to us by witness or recollector of witness. For "men acquainted with God's Word through revelation, Scripture and proclamation, God's Word can and must become true in such a way that its truth becomes their own and they become responsible witnesses to its truth" (1/1,214). They must be "determined by the Word of God in their existence, i.e., in the totality of their self-determination" (1/1,214). Their relation to revelation must become "the relation of acknowledgment" (1/1,214).

How does that happen? What is the "more" that has to happen? The "more" that has to happen is that, on the occasion of one's reading the writing of a witness or hearing a contemporary proclamation grounded on recollection of a witness, God "speaks to" one, in the sense that now one responds in faith to this presentation of Jesus Christ. One acknowledges it. "The man who so hears their word that he grasps and accepts its promise, believes. And this grasping and accepting of the promise: Immanuel with us sinners, in the word of the prophets and apostles, this is the faith of the Church" (I/I, 108; *cf.* I/I, 160, 214, 230).[8] Faith is the response of acknowledgment to God's revelation. "Only when and as the Bible grasps at us ... is this recollection [of God's past revelation] achieved. If this takes place, if the Bible speaks to us thus of the promise, if the prophets and apostles tell us what they have to tell us, if their word imposes itself on us ... all this is God's decision and not ours ... The Bible is God's Word to the extent that God causes it to be His Word, to the extent that He speaks through it ... The Bible, then, becomes God's Word in this event, and in the statement that the Bible is God's Word the little word 'is' refers to its being in this becoming" (I/I, 109–10).

## *Why there's less in Barth on God speaking than first appears*

I began my opening chapter by pointing to Augustine's citation of three episodes of God speaking. One of the three was God's speaking to Antony on the occasion of Antony's hearing a passage from the Gospel of Matthew read aloud in a Coptic church; another was God's speaking to Augustine himself on the occasion of Augustine's reading at random a passage from a letter of St. Paul. Barth would regard these two as paradigmatic examples of divine discourse, specifically, of divine discourse in the mode of proclamation. But is it in fact clear that on Barth's analysis of such episodes as these, God *speaks* on these occasions. Clearly God does something. But is it *speaking?*

There is room for doubt. I have spoken, I have written. But the content of what I have said doesn't "speak to" you. You understand it. But something else has to happen for it to "speak to" you. If I say something else, might that bring it about that what I said earlier now "speaks to" you? It might. Sometimes more speaking makes the content of one's first speaking "speak to" someone. But I think it's clear that Barth does not think of God's presentational discourse as saying anything else or anything more than what God already said in God's revelatory discourse.[9] And if that's true, then a different sort of action than speaking is called for. That which God said in Jesus Christ and is presented to me by Scripture and contemporary proclamation – that must be made "to grab me." God must so act on me that I am "grabbed" by the content of what God has already said. I see no reason to call this action "speech." It happens on the occasion of a human being witnessing, or recalling some witness. But it doesn't itself consist in God *saying* something. It consists, instead, in God working on the heart of the auditor to get him or her to acknowledge the "truth" of what the human discourser said.

It's surprising. Barth is the great theologian of the Word of God. One gets the impression upon first reading him that many are the episodes of human speech which are media of divine discourse. But close scrutiny proves that to be not true. It is of course true that Jesus was a human being, and that by way of Jesus speaking, God spoke. But Jesus was God as well; so one could also say that it was by way of God speaking that God spoke. What God does in addition is bring it about that what God said in Jesus Christ is both presented to us and, by some of us, acknowledged.[10] But that "bringing about" is something different from speaking. Barth's thought is that the very being who is the content of Scripture and proclamation, namely, Jesus Christ, the Word, the speech, of God, so acts on us that we acknowledge that content. True enough. But is that action *more speaking?*

Sometimes – so it seems – Barth himself is on the verge of recognizing the point I am making. He says in one place, "To bring it about that the *Deus dixit* is present with the Church in its various times and situations is not in the power of the Bible or proclamation. The *Deus dixit* is true ... where it *is* true, i.e., where and when God, in speaking once and for all, wills according to His eternal counsel that it be true, where and when God by His activating, ratifying and fulfilling of the word of the Bible and preaching lets it become true" (I/1,120). That is it precisely: God speaks in Jesus Christ, and only there; then on multiple occasions, God activates, ratifies, and fulfills in us what God says in Jesus Christ.[11]

Why does Barth so consistently avoid, and so determinedly resist, saying that human beings sometimes speak in the name of God, and that human speech is sometimes appropriated for divine speech? The answer appears to be twofold. For one thing, Barth repeatedly suggests that the only way of both honoring the legitimate results of biblical criticism and holding that Scripture somehow gives us God's speech is along the lines that he worked out; in the face of the results of biblical criticism, we can no longer hold that the human authors of Scripture were "inerrant." In later chapters I will develop a quite different way of both honoring those results and holding that Scripture gives us God's speech.

Secondly, Barth regarded the claim that God speaks by way of authoring Scripture as compromising the freedom of God. God and God alone speaks for God. "That the Bible is the Word of God cannot mean that with other attributes the Bible has the attribute of being the Word of God. To say that would be to violate the Word of God which is God Himself – to violate the freedom and the sovereignty of God. God is not an attribute of something else, even if this something else is the Bible. God is the Subject, God is Lord. He is Lord even over the Bible and in the Bible. The statement that the Bible is the Word of God cannot therefore say that the Word of God is tied to the Bible. On the contrary, what it must say is that the Bible is tied to the Word of God. But that means that in this statement we contemplate a free decision of God" (1/2,513). If it is indeed a limitation on God's freedom that God would commission a human being to speak "in the name of" God, then perhaps we have to take seriously the possibility that God is willing on occasion to limit God's freedom in that way – or alternatively, consider the possibility that we are working with an alien and inapplicable concept of freedom. But in the case of appropriation, it's hard to see how God's decision to appropriate certain human speech as the medium of divine speech is in any way at all a compromise of divine freedom! Probably Barth never even considered the appropriation model as a way of thinking of God as author!

"*Tolle lege, tolle lege*," chanted the child. Augustine was persuaded that by way of the child chanting, God was speaking to him. Would Barth agree? Even after Barth's expansive discussion, it's not clear; and that's interesting. Says Barth: "we have certainly to reckon with the fact that the living Lord Jesus Christ who encounters and deals with man wholly from without is not bound to preaching and the sacraments in the work of His Holy Spirit seizing and altering man within, but may very well, *extra muros ecclesiae* and independently of the ministry of His community in the world and humanity reconciled to God in Him, know and tread the very different ways of very different possibilities of most effective calling" (IV/3.2, p. 516). So it doesn't matter that the child was not a Christian; what matters is whether she was witnessing to Jesus Christ or recollecting the witness of a witness. Was she?

CHAPTER 5

# *What it is to speak*

What naturally comes to mind, when we think of performing speech actions, is the picture of someone discoursing by writing down or uttering aloud certain words. We saw in our third chapter that that is a very blinkered view. To answer the question looming before us in this segment of our discussion, viz., whether it is coherent to attribute discourse to God, it was necessary to remove the blinkers and get in view the many modes of discourse.

Now we must reflect on the very nature of speech, of discourse. That will complete the task of showing the difference between speech and revelation. More importantly, nothing short of digging down to the very nature of speech will give us a footing solid enough for addressing the question whether it is coherent to suppose that God speaks.

To say it once more, when I speak of "speaking" (and "discoursing"), I will always have in mind speech actions – that is, actions which can function as what J. L. Austin called *illocutionary* actions. No doubt ordinary English usage is such that in speaking of "speaking," one could also have in mind *locutionary* actions: actions consisting of uttering or inscribing or signing some words.[1] So my usage represents a regimentation of ordinary English.

I shall assume, without argument on this occasion, that performances of speech actions are not, in their nature, a species of exerting influence over someone, nor a species of communicating or expressing one's inner states. I fully realize that these assumptions are contested.

I grant, of course, that by uttering and inscribing words we do, typically, influence others, in fact and by intent. More specifically, I grant that there are what Austin called *perlocutionary* actions. But I dissent from the behaviorist attempt to understand speaking as consisting, in its very nature, of producing effects. In particular, I hold (as did Austin) that illocutionary actions cannot be reduced to perlocutionary ones; and that to ignore illocutionary actions is to ignore what lies at the very heart of speech. It may be added that perlocutionary actions, as Austin understood those, occur only if one's auditor apprehends or thinks he apprehends an illocutionary action that one has performed, and only if that apprehension (or purported apprehension) evokes the effect in question. One can frighten someone by talking loudly and suddenly; one can also do so by asserting something that one's auditor understands (or thinks he understands) and finds frightening. Only the latter, not the former, is a perlocutionary action on one's part. One's theory of speech must be adequate for distinguishing the two sorts of cases.

But I also dissent from the expressionist (Romanticist) view of speaking as consisting in the intentional expression of inner states by way of uttering or inscribing some bit of language. Naturally I grant that very often in and by the performance of speech actions we express our inner states – sometimes by intent, sometimes not. But the great obstacle for the expression theory is the presence of insincerity, deception and inadvertence in our speaking. I may assert what I do not believe, and profess to feeling no anger when feeling intense anger; but I cannot express beliefs and feelings which I do not have. A theory of speech must also be adequate for accounting for these facts.

Neither behaviorism nor expressionism is devastated by these few brief and quick remarks; if they were, they wouldn't have been around so long. I make the remarks not to devastate the alternatives but to highlight the perspective from which I shall be looking at speaking. Looking at language and speech from the anti-behaviorist and anti-Romanticist perspective of speech-action theory, I shall try to develop an account of what it is to speak. The account which emerges might be called a *normative theory of discourse*.

### *Attempts to account for the generation of discourse*

A few ontological clarifications and assumptions are indispensable.

I assume that there are actions – that in addition to walking animals there is walking, that in addition to barking dogs there is barking, that in addition to kicking horses there is kicking. Actions are *predicables*: entities susceptible of being predicated of something. And many are *universals*: susceptible of being predicated truly of more than one thing. In other words, many are such that they can be multiply and/or repeatedly exemplified.

A particularly useful test for the non-identity, of any actions x and y, is this: If it is possible that there be something which exemplifies x and not y, or y and not x, then x and y are not the identical action. This is a sufficient condition for the non-identity of actions; I do not assume it to be a necessary condition.

Suppose, then, that I ask you to open the door and that I do so by uttering the sentence, "Would you open the door?" I would then have performed the two distinct actions of asking you to open the door and of uttering the English sentence, "Would you open the door?" For clearly I can ask you to open the door without uttering that sentence; for example, I can do so by uttering a different sentence from some other language. And I can utter that sentence without making that request or any other; I can, for example, just enounce it. Nonetheless it's also true that, between the two distinct actions which I performed, there is in this case an intimate relationship. The two actions are two of the terms in the three-term relationship of x performing the action of y *by way of* performing the action of z.

Let's take note here of an ontological ambiguity in the English word "action." When speaking of actions, I have had in mind predicables of a certain sort – attributes. But when speaking of actions, one might also have in mind an *instance* , a *case*, of some such predicable – an entity of a sort which is nowadays sometimes called an *abstract particular* or a *trope* by ontologists, what the medievals called a *qualia*, what Aristotle called an *entity present in* something. My uttering at a certain time of the sentence, "Would you open the door?", is an example, as is my asking you to open the door at a certain time. The former of these is an instance, a case, of that predicable which is the action of uttering the sentence "Would you open the door?"; the latter is a case of that predicable which is the action of requesting you to open the door. It is fortunate for our purposes that English has the word "act" as well as the word "action." I shall regiment the language a bit and use the word "action" exclusively for predicables of a certain sort, and "act" exclusively for instances, cases, of actions.

Let us return to our original thought example. If on a certain occasion I ask you to open the door by uttering the sentence, "Would you open the door?", then there is in existence at the time in question an instance of each of the two actions of requesting and uttering. Specifically, there then exists an act consisting of my making that request and an act consisting of my uttering that sentence.[2] But obviously these acts are intimately connected. A standard way of expressing the connection is this: my uttering the sentence *counts as* my making the request. Though an act consisting of my uttering that sentence *need not* so count – though, for example, I might just be sounding out an example of a well-formed English sentence – in fact it does, on the occasion imagined, so count.

Here, then, is an example of the (sort of) question I want to pursue in this chapter: what brings it about that *by* performing the action of uttering the sentence "Would you open the door?", I perform the action of requesting you to open the door? Or in other words, what brings it about that my performing of the former action *counts as* my performing the latter? And what is it, for one's performance of one action to *count as* one's performance of another? My own conviction is that there is no more fundamental question posed by human discourse than this. How can it be that by uttering the little word "Guilty," someone condemns another to be shot at dawn?

It's obvious that there is no necessity here – that is, no *ontological* necessity. Things might well have been such that my uttering the sentence "Would you open the door?" did not count as my requesting you to open the door. But the connection is also not causal. Sometimes it is the presence of causal efficacy which brings it about that by doing one thing one does another. By flipping the switch I turn on the light; that is so because the event of my flipping the switch causes the event of the light's going on. But it's not causal efficacy that underlies the phenomenon before us; it is not by virtue of the causal texture of nature that by uttering the sentence, I make the request. Whatever it is in the ambient situation that accounts for it, that something may be missing – missing without the causal texture of nature being disrupted. When that something is present, my utterance is freighted with the significance of discourse. But what is that something?

It is regularly said or assumed that the something in question is the existence of certain conventions. For example, Alvin Goldman calls that species of doing one thing by doing another on which I am focusing attention, *conventional generation*. And then he says this: "Conventional generation is characterized by the existence of rules, conventions, or social practices in virtue of which an act A′ can be ascribed to an agent S, given his performance of another act, A″. As examples of conventional generation Goldman gives these, among others: S's signaling for a turn by S's extending his arm out the car window; and S's checkmating his opponent by S's moving his queen to king's knight 7. He then continues: "In each of these cases there is a rule, R, according to which S's performance of A justifies the further ascription of A′ to S. In the first example there is the rule, 'extending one's arm out the car window while driving counts as signaling for a turn'." He concludes, "With these examples in mind, we can state the following condition for conventional generation. Act-token A of agent S conventionally generates act-token A′ of agent S only if the performance of A in circumstances C (possibly null), together with a rule R saying that A done in C counts as A′, guarantees the performance of A′."[3]

One reason this will not do – it's a point which has been made by several writers – is that often our speaking just doesn't follow the linguistic rules. We speak, one might say, *loosely*. Yet we do really say something – do really perform a speech act. As when I request someone to pass the salt with the sentence, "Could you pass the salt?" The response of the whipper-snapper teen-ager who replies, "Yes, I suppose I could" and then does nothing, highlights the difference between what was asked and what the rules of the language would tell us was asked.

It's also worth pointing out that sometimes it is iconicity rather than conventional rules that determine what was said. A condition of picturing something is that to picture, say, a cat, one must produce a design which, by appropriate persons, can be seen as a cat. (This is a necessary condition for picturing, not sufficient.) And even beyond picturing, we all operate with a rough informal convention of saying things by producing iconic signs. Once, when driving down the highway with my family, we were overtaken by a car whose passengers gestured vigorously to us. My children quickly understood what they were saying. They were telling us that one of our rear lights was out. The gestures they were using were related to the broken light iconically.

Perhaps it's possible to expand the concept of *a rule* in such a way as to take account of these two points. Then what should be noted is that the mere *existence* of a convention or rule (I shall for the moment follow Goldman in taking these as the same) "saying that A done in C counts as A′," is surely not sufficient for A in fact to count as A′. What needs to be added is that the rule must hold, or be in effect, for the relevant parties. If there is a rule relevant to the case but that rule does not hold for the agent, the one act will not count as the other. But what brings it about that a rule holds? And what is it, for a rule to hold?

These points, important though they be for an adequate theory, nonetheless pertain to the periphery of Goldman's suggestion. The fundamental flaw in Goldman's suggestion is that it simply doesn't constitute an answer to our question – nor to his. We want to understand what it is for one act to *count as* another. Goldman observes that there are conventions among us for (correctly) ascribing one act to an agent on account of his having performed another act. Given suitable qualifications, that's true. But we couldn't have a convention whereby, say, we (correctly) ascribe to an agent *having winked* on the ground of his having *scratched his ear.* What Goldman has in mind is ascribing action B to an agent when he has performed some other action, A, which *counts as* B. It's by virtue of a convention being in effect – not any old convention, a *counting-as* convention – that one act counts as another. But what is it for the one to count as the other? Goldman notices that only if there is a convention in effect, or something convention-like, will A count as B. But that doesn't tell us *what it is* for A to count as B. That's our question!

There's a passage in John Searle's book, *Speech Acts,* which makes a suggestion worth reflecting on. Searle says that "Such facts as are recorded in my above group of statements I propose to call *institutional facts* ... [T]heir existence ... presupposes the existence of certain human institutions. It is only given the institution of marriage that certain forms of behaviour constitute Mr. Smith's marrying Miss Jones. Similarly, it is only given the institution of baseball that certain movements by certain men constitute the Dodgers beating the Giants 3 to 2 in eleven innings ... These 'institutions' are systems of constitutive rules. Every institutional fact is underlain by a (system of) rules(s) of the form 'X counts as Y in context C'."[4]

The context makes clear that Searle wishes to suggest that the phenomenon of an utterance of mine counting as a request of mine is an institutional fact of the same sort as someone's hitting a ball over a fence counting as his hitting a home run. Two things recommend this suggestion. For one thing, the rules of baseball are such that they can hold or not hold for a certain group of people at a certain time. The umpire calls, "Play ball," and the rules hold. Secondly, when the rules of baseball hold, then the mere action of hitting a ball over a fence about 400 feet away counts as the very different action of hitting a home run. Searle's suggestion is that if we look closely at how this can be, we will come to understand how it can be that by some rule's fiat, my making some noises counts as my requesting something.

Baseball is a contest game. It provides us with a way of winning. There are lots of contest games: baseball, bridge, Monopoly, Scrabble, chess, go. And each, by virtue of its rules, provides a distinct way of winning. In certain highly complex games, the rules will be formulated by way of concepts introduced to apply to certain actions which have a special significance within the game. In baseball the concept of a home run is introduced, the concept of a bunt, the concept of a balk, etc. And it does indeed seem appropriate to call something like a home run an "institutional fact." A certain action's being a home run is entirely internal to the game of baseball. By contrast, hitting a ball over a fence is a non-institutional fact. It can be given significance in many different games, and can occur outside of any game. Within that entire system of rules for baseball which provide one with ways of winning, hitting a ball over a distant fence counts as a home run if done under circumstances specified in the rules. In another game, that same action will have quite a different significance – will count as something quite different

But though on first glance it seems promising to understand asserting, commanding, and similar, as institutional facts, rather like hitting a home run and committing a balk, the promise proves illusory. For whereas the action of hitting a home run is *constituted* by a particular set of rules, surely an action like assertion is not so constituted. There are many different ways of asserting; there could be more. If, in a given situation, we are for one and another reason dissatisfied with the standard ways available to us of asserting something, we can devise a new way. We have a concept of assertion which is, in that way, rule-independent. By contrast, one cannot devise alternative actions which will count as hitting a home run. Of course the *word* "home run" can be used for happenings outside of baseball. And the rules of baseball specifying what counts as a home run can be altered somewhat. But hitting a home run is a baseball-embedded phenomenon. It cannot occur outside of baseball.

If asserting is to be compared with anything in games, it is best compared with *winning*, not with such game-embedded, rule-defined, actions as hitting a home run. For of winning we have a concept independent of any particular game; we can devise new ways of bringing it about that someone has *won*.

We say such things, sometimes, as that a certain dance *counts as* a jig, that a certain organism *counts as* an animal, and so on. What we mean, I take it, is that the concept of jig *fits* the dance, that the concept of animal *fits* the organism. It is this that is meant when we say that hitting the ball over the fence in a certain situation counts as hitting a home run. The concept of home run *fits* the action; the action *satisfies* the concept of a home run. Of course the *concept* of home run is rule-constituted in a way in which that of animal is not, with the concept of jig somewhere in between. But in all these cases, counting-as is merely concept-satisfaction.

It seems clear, by contrast, that to say that such-and-such actions count as winning, is not just to say that they satisfy the concept of winning. So too, to say that uttering a certain sound counts as asserting so-and-so, is not just to say that that act of uttering *satisfies the concept* of asserting so-and-so. Uttering so-and-so is one thing; asserting such-and-such is another. Somehow these get hooked up by the relation of counting-as. What *is* that hook-up, and how does it come about?

## Normative ascriptions of normative standings

Let me see if I can evoke a sense of the mysteriousness of the phenomenon on which I am focusing. How can an action just be ascribed to a person? I do not mean, How can an action be predicated of a person? That's easy. I mean, how can an action *belong* to a person *by ascription?* A person utters something. And if the requisite arrangement is in effect, then that other very different action of requesting something also belongs to her by – well, I don't know what other word to use than "ascription." She doesn't have to do anything else for it to be one of her actions. Sometimes she utters a sentence and that's the end of it. But in other cases she utters a sentence *and by virtue of that*, this other very different action of requesting something is something she does as well. Yet in an obvious way she hasn't done anything different in the second case; she hasn't done anything "in addition". She has done something "over and above" uttering the sentence, without that "over and above" something being a causal effect of her action of uttering. A visiting Martian would find this very mysterious. I submit that so would we, if it weren't so familiar. Searle's institutional explanation claims that something like this also happens in games. But it doesn't really. There we have nothing more than the attribution to a certain physical action of a certain significance within the game.

A satisfactory account of the counting-as relation will have to do something to dispel this mystery. And will have to do so in such a way as to illuminate the fact, on which we dwelt for some time in our third chapter, that very many speech actions can be performed by proxy, by the actions of a deputy. Given that Truman has deputized Kennan as his ambassador, Truman can now deliver a warning to Stalin by way of Kennan performing certain illocutionary actions. But so too, by way of a proxy uttering the words **I do** in a marriage ceremony, I can promise to take another person as my wedded spouse. By way of a proxy uttering **Aye** in a stockholders meeting, I can vote for a certain motion. I myself will have done so. I may be asleep, even unconscious. Yet I will have promised, I will have voted. On the basis of what my proxy has done, I can be brought to court, or bring to court.

Can the mystery be dispelled? Well, let's begin with two analogues. Consider the first-born male child of some royal parents. Though this child looks and acts like other children, there is something very different about him. He is crown prince. This is his standing in his society. On account of the standing of his parents and of his being their first-born male child, the standing of crown prince belongs to him in that society. Belongs to him, in the sense that he has the duty (once he matures) to treat others, and they the duty to treat him, as one who has that standing – which, of course, is quite another matter from the actualities of mutual treatment. His possessing that standing consists in its being *normatively ascribed* to him. This standing is itself defined in part by a unique complex of mutual (prima facie) duties: the (prima facie) rights and duties of crown prince. The standing of crown prince is thus itself a *normative standing*. A certain normative standing is normatively ascribed. Though this infant looks and acts pretty much like his infant peers, by virtue of his parentage and the monarchical structure of the society, he fits into the texture of mutual obligations in his society in a very different way from those others.

Or imagine someone in our society driving down the road and flipping on the left-side blinkers of his automobile as he approaches an intersection. *By* so doing, he signals a left turn. Without stretching the concept of *standing* very much, we can think of this too as consisting in his acquiring a certain standing among us – the standing of one who has signaled a left turn – by flipping on the left-side blinkers. His acquisition of that standing consists in his now having the duty to treat others, and they the duty to treat them, as one who has signaled a left turn. The standing is *normatively ascribed* to him. In turn, that standing which he has acquired, of being one who has signaled a left turn, is itself defined in part by a complex of mutual (prima facie) obligations; it too is a *normative standing*. What's most obvious here is that, as one who has the standing of one who has signaled a left turn, he is now (prima facie) obligated to turn left soon. Reflection on the situation when he does not turn left but instead, say, turns right and causes an accident, makes this especially clear; in that situation he obviously has culpabilities which he would not have had, other things being equal, had he not acquired the standing of one who has signaled a left turn. But it's also true that, since he now has the standing of one who has signaled a left turn, *we* now have (prima facie) duties toward *him* which we would not have had had he not acquired this standing. We now are (prima facie) obligated to drive in a manner appropriate for driving behind a car which will shortly turn left; reflection on cases in which some calamity is caused by our failure to acknowledge this duty of ours again makes clear its presence.

I suggest that the phenomenon of one's utterance of a sentence counting as one's performance of some speech action is to be understood along these same lines. So that one's uttering of a sentence may count as one's making a request, it is not necessary that one and one's fellows *actually count it* as that; they may fail or refuse to count it as that even though it is that, and may count it as that even though it is not that. Yet speaker and audience performing the action of counting it as that is indeed intimately related to *its* counting as that. The relation is that speaker and audience *ought to* count it as that – *ought to* acknowledge it as that in their relations with each other. And the standing that thus gets normatively ascribed to one is itself a normative standing – that is to say, it is itself defined in part by (prima facie) mutual duties between speaker and others. To institute an arrangement for the performance of speech actions is to institute a way of acquiring rights and responsibilities.

Imagine, for example, a field worker uttering in the hearing of his fellow worker the words, "would you hand me a drink of water," thereby requesting the other to hand him a drink of water. The standing of having issued that request is now normatively ascribed to him. And part of what thus having that standing entails is that if the addressee understands what was said, and the speaker's request is not undercut for him, then the addressee is (prima facie) obligated to hand the speaker a drink of water. (Shortly I shall explain what I mean by a speech action being undercut.) By uttering that sentence, the speaker has altered the moral relationship between himself and his fellow worker.

Or suppose I utter the sentence, "I'll write you a recommendation," thereby promising to write you a recommendation. The standing of having promised to write you a recommendation is now normatively ascribed to me. And my having that standing entails, among other things, that I am now (prima facie) obligated to write you a recommendation – assuming that my promise is not undercut for you. My uttering that sentence has altered the moral relationship between us.

This way of seeing the situation probably seems least plausible, on first glance, for assertions. But suppose I utter the words, "I saw Jim drive off with your car," and thereby acquire the normative standing of telling you that I saw Jim drive off with your car. This too alters the moral relation between us. I have not merely transmitted some information; indeed, I may not even have done that. If you understood what I said, then, unless my assertion is undercut for you, you are now (prima facie) obligated to take me at my word that I saw Jim drive off with your car. Asserting that so-and-so introduces into human relationships the (prima facie) right to be taken at one's word that so-and-so. We say, "It's your own fault; you should have accepted what I said."

It seems no great mystery that a child who looks and acts pretty much like any other child should have the special standing, in morality and law, of crown prince. Likewise it seems no great mystery that someone who turns on his left-side blinkers as he approaches an intersection should have, in morality and law, the standing of having signaled a left turn. I suggest that if we think of the performance of speech actions along these same lines, namely, as acquiring the normative ascription of some normative standing, we are well on the way to penetrating the mystery of how it can be that by way of someone's uttering some brief, breathy, innocuous-sounding words, he condemns someone to the firing squad. Though there is very much that is worth reflecting on in the phenomenon of acquiring rights and duties by virtue of causally bringing about some action to which those rights and duties are not inherently attached, there is – so it seems to me – nothing especially mysterious in it. It may be wrong, as such, to make a certain sound in a certain situation; it would hurt one's auditors ears, let us say. But in addition, normative import (and conditions) may have become *attached to* it; that, I suggest, is what lies at the bottom of discourse.

## *Why do we ascribe normative standings?*

We have thus far seen only the tip of the iceberg of the ways in which speaking is related to accountability. Let us set out to see what more there is by asking: why do we have arrangements in which the normative standing of signaling a left turn is normatively ascribed to someone who has flipped on a blinking light? Or more dramatically: why do we have arrangements in which the normative standing of pronouncing someone guilty is normatively ascribed to someone who has pronounced the little word **guilty** – given all the consequences that ensue therefrom: certain people are now entitled to drag a man out of the room in which the little word was pronounced and place him before a firing squad? Why do we human beings find it necessary or useful to invest phenomena so innocuous with import so weighty? The import attached to flipping blinkers, pronouncing words, and making marks, seems so wildly out of proportion to the phenomena themselves. What's the point?

Well for one thing, it's important for us to be able to issue requests, make promises and assertions, signal turns, and pronounce people guilty. Indeed, "important" is too weak a word. We cannot imagine a human life devoid of speech actions. But how else are we going to do such things as these except by such profoundly different actions as flipping switches and making noises? There isn't any other way for us. One can't, right off, assert or signal or request. These are not candidates for basic actions. They can be done only by doing something else. Furthermore, in most cases, the more innocuous the generating action and the simpler to perform, the better. We want asserting to be something that can be done easily. And if the generating action is *not* innocuous, then too often there will be claims and obligations attaching to it as such which will thoroughly confuse the situation.

But we can go deeper. When the requisite signaling arrangement is in effect, then the action of flipping on the blinker is not at all so innocuous as on the surface it appears to be. For then there is a *normative condition* (prima facie) attached to flipping on the blinker: one ought not flip on the left-side blinker unless one intends for oneself, and wants others, to carry out the obligations inherent in the standing of signaling a left turn – for example, one ought not turn on the left-side blinker unless one intends soon to turn left. That obligation attaches to that otherwise innocuous action because, in the first place, the subjunctive conditional holds, that if one *would* flip on the left-side blinker, then one *would* acquire the standing of signaling a left turn; and because, secondly, the action of signaling a left turn has normative conditions attached to it. In particular, it has attached to it the (prima facie) obligation not to *signal* a left turn unless one intends shortly to turn left.

Notice that intending to turn left soon is not a *logical* condition of acquiring the standing of signaling a left turn. Even if one has no such intention, even if one flips on the blinker just to see how those behind will respond, nonetheless, if the relevant signaling arrangement is in effect, one acquires in morality and law the standing of having signaled a left turn. Yet there is obviously something ill-formed about such a signaling, *normatively* ill-formed. Unless there are extenuating circumstances, one *should not* signal a left turn unless one intends soon to turn left.

Again, suppose that someone utters in the assertoric mode the sounds, a tornado has been sighted a mile to the West. If English is in effect for that person, he will thereby have acquired the standing of having asserted that a tornado has been sighted a mile to the West. And he will have acquired this standing whether or not he believes that a tornado has been sighted there. Yet he is (prima facie) obligated to not utter those sounds when that linguistic arrangement is in effect unless he believes that. For he ought not *assert* that unless he believes that. And given that English is in effect for him, it is the case that if he would utter those words, he would make that assertion. The words as such are innocuous; but the normative condition attached to pronouncing the words yields the consequence that uttering them is not at all innocuous.

Assuming that the sentences uttered are well-formed, we can organize under three headings the ways in which speech acts can be malformed. For one thing, a speech act may not bear a well-formed relation to the mental states of the speaker. The speaker may assert something without believing it, may promise something without intending it, may request something without wanting it and so on. Secondly, a speech act may not bear a well-formed relation to the facts of the world. The speaker may assert what is in fact false, ask someone to do what has in fact already been done, baptize someone who has in fact already been baptized. Thirdly, a speech act may not bear a well-formed relation to social norms. The speaker may promise to sell what he has no right to sell, ask someone to do what he has no right to ask. This last sort of case shades into those cases where only certain people have the competence – in the lawyer's sense of "competence" – to perform certain speech actions. Only an umpire can pronounce someone "Out" in baseball, only a clergyman or justice of the peace can pronounce a couple married, only the chairman of the meeting can pronounce the meeting adjourned, only a judge can pronounce someone guilty.

By no means all of the various ways in which a speech act can be malformed are signs of some defection of responsibility on the part of the speaker. It is especially malformations of the first sort which are such signs. Indeed, it appears to me to be the case that, for every speech action, there is a mental state such that if a speaker performs that speech action without being in that state, he has done what, prima facie, he ought not to have done. Thus not only does one's performance of a speech action consist in a certain normative standing being normatively ascribed to one, on the ground of one's causal bringing about of some event; there are normative conditions attached to the very bringing about of that generating event (by virtue of being attached to the speech act which it generates). Speaking is, through and through, a normative engagement.

It is because speech acts can be malformed in the ways indicated that they can be "undercut." For a speech act to be undercut, for a given person, is for that person to have good reason to think that it is malformed in such a way that the prima facie rights and responsibilities which accrue to speakers and hearers upon its performance do not, in this case, actually accrue to them. Suppose someone asks me to close the door, and suppose that I understand what he asks. Then my having good reason to think that the door is already shut, is one example of the request's being undercut for me. Having good reason to think that the speaker does not really want it shut but is merely trifling with me, is another example of its being undercut for me. And having good reason to think that he has no right to ask this of me, is yet a third example of its being undercut for me. For me to have good reason to think the door is already shut, or that the speaker does not really want it shut, or that he has no right to ask me to shut it, is to be free of the prima facie obligation which otherwise I would have, to comply with his request – provided, of course, that I understand it (and that it was addressed to me).

Why is it important that the normative conditions attached to the performance of speech actions, and derivatively, to those events which generate speech acts, be honored? Why is it important that one honor the fact that it is prima facie *wrong* to assert that a tornado has been sighted a mile to the West when one doesn't believe it – and correspondingly wrong, when English is in effect, to utter in assertoric mode the words, **a tornado has been sighted a mile to the West**? Two things, I would suppose. In the first place, on the assumption that the preservation of a system of speaking is important, it is important that the participants avoid doing what would tend to undermine the system.

And it is easy to see that asserting without believing, promising without intending, requesting without wanting, if they become at all general, undermine the system. When a single boy too often cries "wolf" in the absence of wolves, we disregard *his* speech. When it becomes a habit on the part of many to cry "wolf" in the absence of wolves, our system of speaking itself is undermined. Thomas Reid argued that our human constitution includes an inherent *disposition* toward veracity in speech and, correspondingly, toward credulity in listeners. Such dispositions are indispensable to the endurance of the system.

Of course, the undermining of the system only occurs if the discrepancy between the asserting and the believing is found out, or if it is *thought* that such a discrepancy has been found out. But whether found out or not, there is a second thing wrong: deception or attempted deception has occurred. We have no direct way of knowing whether people believe what they assert, intend what they promise, want what they request. We trust them. We trust that the normative conditions for speaking have been satisfied. To speak without satisfying those conditions is to abuse trust. If there is any place where the notion – so popular in the seventeenth and eighteenth centuries – of an *implicit compact*, is appropriate, it is here!

### Arrangements for speaking

There are in principle many other arrangements whereby one could signal a left turn than our arrangement of flipping on one's left-side blinkers; many other arrangements whereby one could pronounce someone guilty than ours of uttering the word **guilty**; many other arrangements whereby one could declare that what stands in one's IRS form is correct than ours, of signing one's name. So it always is for an act which something counts as, in the way we have been exploring. There could have been something else which counted as it – *could have been* without any alteration in either the order of ontological or causal necessity.

How shall we think of what I have here been calling *arrangements* – arrangements for signaling a left turn, arrangements for pronouncing someone guilty, arrangements for declaring that the figures in one's tax form are correct? I suggest that we think of an arrangement for signaling a left turn as an ordered pair, one member of which is the action of signaling a left turn. And what is the other member? Well, two things must be brought into the picture. One is some other action, such that by performing it, one signals a left turn. The example I have been using all along is that of flipping on one's left-side blinkers. But also a certain manner and circumstance of performing this generating action is relevant. Such a manner and circumstance, paired with the generating action, will constitute the additional member of the pair – additional, that is, to the generated action. Some abbreviations and a schematism may help to show the structure of the situation. Let

S = the action of signaling a left turn,

F = the action of flipping one's left-side blinkers, and

M/C of F = a certain manner and circumstance of performing F.

The arrangement for signaling a left turn to which I have been alluding will then have this structure:

[{F, M/C of F}, S].

If we do think of arrangements along these lines, then it becomes easy to say what it is for such an arrangement to be *in effect* for certain persons at a certain time; and secondly, what it is for it to be *used* by a certain person at a certain time. A given arrangement for acting, for example, [{F, M/C of F}, S], is *in effect* for person P at time $t$ just in case *if* P *would* perform F at time $t$ in manner and circumstance M/C, his doing so *would* count as his performing S. And that arrangement for acting is *used* by P at $t$ just in case P at $t$ performs F in manner and circumstance M/C – the act of his doing so then counting as an act of his performing S.

Of course we do not usually operate in the piece-meal fashion which this might suggest. Drivers have available to them a whole system for signaling, speakers have available to them a whole system for asserting. It would not be worth our time going into the details of how such systems can best be thought of. Here, let us just think of them as *sets* of arrangements for acting.

The most interesting question raised by this account of what it is for an arrangement for acting to be in effect at a certain time for a certain group of people is this: What *brings it about* that one arrangement for signaling turns is in effect for a given group of people at a given time rather than another – or rather than none? Or to ask the same question in another way: under what *conditions* is a certain arrangement for signaling turns in effect?

Though a detailed answer to this question would take a long time to develop, I take it that the general outlines of the correct answer are clear enough; I have already hinted at them. For one thing, a given arrangement may be in effect for a person at a time by virtue of *stipulation*. The card player may say to his partner: if I kick you, that means, bid four. It may be the speaker himself who does the stipulating; but it need not be. Someone else may make the stipulation for a prospective speaker; and if that prospective speaker knows or should know about the stipulation and does not dissent from it, that does as well.

Secondly, it seems correct to say that an arrangement for acting may be in effect for a given person at a given time by virtue of *convention*. But how are we to think of a convention here? It's natural to think of it as a social practice. And perhaps that in turn can be thought of along the lines suggested by David Lewis in his *Convention*: a convention is a coordination of actions by different actors. But I think this is not what the conventions here are. For what are the actions to be coordinated? No doubt there is a certain coordination between a driver signaling a left turn when approaching an intersection and those behind him engaging in various defensive reactions. But we wanted to know what makes the subjunctive conditional true for a person at a time, that *if* he would flip on his left-side blinkers, he *would be* signaling a left turn. How does the existence of coordinations answer that question?

I have no detailed taxonomy and theory of conventions to offer here. But perhaps it's best to think of the conventions in question on analogy to stipulations: a convention, of the sort relevant here, is a sort of social stipulation. Just as some musical works are composed whereas others merely arise in a society, so some arrangements for acting are in effect by virtue of explicit stipulation whereas others are in effect by virtue of something like a stipulation just arising in society. As it were, society stipulates and we assent.

However, it has to be more than the mere *existence* of a convention, thus understood, in a group of which a person is a member, for a certain arrangement for acting to be in effect for that person; since, as observed earlier in our remarks about Goldman, conventions themselves can exist without *holding for* a given person. So what brings it about that a convention which is *in effect* in a certain group, *holds for* a certain member of that group (on a particular occasion)? Perhaps the right way to get at the question here is from the negative side: when does a convention, a social stipulation, *not* hold for a person who is nonetheless a member of the relevant society? There is little hope of giving a complete answer to this question; the matter is too subtle for that. But some general patterns can be brought to light. We can think of conventions as holding for *qualified parties*. What makes someone a qualified, or dis-qualified, party with respect to a given convention at a certain time?

In most cases, if one doesn't know about a stipulation or convention, then it's not in effect for one. One is not a qualified party. If one doesn't know that there is a convention in our society according to which flipping on the left-side blinkers when approaching an intersection counts as signaling, then one does not signal by flipping on one's blinkers in that circumstance. So too, if a person who doesn't know German just happens when in Germany to make the sounds of some German sentence, her act of doing so does not count as an act of her asserting something. But there are cases in which a convention or stipulation holds for a person in spite of her ignorance – the reason being that her ignorance is culpable ignorance. She *should have* known; she *should have* found out. (No doubt in such cases of ignorance, however, there is only a hazy line between generating some act without actually knowing the convention when one should have, and culpably doing something that leads people to believe one has generated the act when one has not; either way, culpability for calamity may fall on one's head.) But in any case, conventions and stipulations do not hold for those who neither know them nor ought to have known them. (And knowing them involves having *some* grasp of the standing which the convention or stipulation ascribes.) Thus the signing of one's name does not constitute contracting for something if one is a small child, or severely diminished in intelligence, or *non compos mentis*.

For many conventions it's also true, as we have already seen, that the set of qualified parties is limited by a restriction built into the convention, to the effect that only a person occupying a certain institutional position can perform the generated action. Though any of us can assert that a person is guilty of some crime, only a judge can *pronounce* him guilty. Though any of us in the United States can say, "Let's go to war," only Congress can *declare* war. Though any of us can say that the runner was out at home plate, only the home plate umpire can *declare* him out. And so forth.

But even when one knows about a convention or stipulation and even when one occupies whatever institutional position is required to be a qualified participant under the convention, nonetheless one may remove oneself from the sway of the convention by dissenting from it and publishing one's dissent in such a way that others who are affected by one's dissent know about it or ought to know about it. (*Mental* reservations will not do!) Suppose we still had the convention in our society of signaling a left turn by extending one's left arm straight out the driver's side window. A driver who suffered from a partial paralysis of the left arm, making it impossible for him to raise it, could presumably remove himself from the sway of the convention by attaching a large sign to the rear of his vehicle, saying "This driver cannot signal turns." Of course, one cannot *actually* dissent from conventions and stipulations whenever one wishes. Not all attempts at dissent succeed.

## Concluding points

If the normative analysis of speaking which I have offered is approximately correct, then it follows that to understand the ways in which we human beings interact with each other, one cannot adopt as one's sole model that of exerting causal influence over someone. Speech presents us with another, profoundly different, phenomenon: that of acquiring rights and responsibilities and of doing so in accord with, or in violation of, obligations. Any attempt by sociologists, philosophers, psychologists, or whomever, to understand what transpires in human society will have to move beyond attempts at causal explanations to take account of these normative phenomena. Of course, if we could not *causally* bring about such phenomena as gesturing limbs or mouthy noises or squiggly inscriptions, we could not speak. Someone entirely paralyzed cannot speak. But speech requires that we be related to material reality and to each other in ways over and above that of causal interchange. It is because normative conditions have been attached to the pronouncing of so innocuous a word as **guilty**, and because the pronouncing of that word has been invested with normative import, that by pronouncing this word we can speak. By the acquisition of normative standings, we take up the material world into our service.

But even more important for our subsequent purposes is the fact that to speak is not, as such, to express one's inner self but to take up a normative stance in the public domain. The myth dies hard that to read a text for authorial discourse is to enter the dark world of the author's psyche. It's nothing of the sort. It is to read to discover what assertings, what promisings, what requestings, what commandings, are rightly to be ascribed to the author on the ground of her having set down the words that she did in the situation in which she set them down. Whatever be the dark demons and bright angels of the author's inner self that led her to take up this stance in public, it is that stance itself that we hope by reading to recover, not the dark demons and bright angels.

I close on a point which will serve as transition to the subsequent chapter. I have assumed, without argument, that the rights and duties which are connected with discourse in the ways described are *moral* rights and duties. But are they?

Why might one hesitate? Well, suppose that I was a Norwegian living in Norway during the time of the Quisling regime. Suppose further that I refused to accept the legitimacy of the regime. Then if some representative of the regime issued an order to me to do one thing and another, I would not regard myself as under even a prima facie *moral* obligation to obey. I might in fact obey. But not out of any recognition of moral obligation. So if speaking does involve claims and duties in roughly the way indicated, they cannot in general be *moral* claims and duties but *linguistic* ones.[5]

I do not think the objection holds. The commands in view in the example are not the ordinary commands issued by human beings in ordinary interactions with each other. No doubt those persons who are functionaries of the Quisling regime also issue such commands. But the commands in question are *official* commands, commands issued "in the name of the law," commands issued by functionaries when acting as functionaries. Now for a given person actually to issue *such* a command, the person must be what I called, a few paragraphs back, a *qualified party*. Any one of us can assert that someone is guilty of a crime. But for someone to make the *judicial pronouncement* that he is guilty of the crime, the person must be a judge. And what the Norwegian citizen who refuses to acknowledge the legitimacy of the Quisling regime actually holds, is that all or most of the functionaries of that regime are not qualified parties. They lack legitimacy. They are not capable of giving orders in the name of the law – any more than I am. They are not capable of pronouncing people legally guilty. So it's not that some functionary *did* issue that order, without putting me under even a prima facie moral obligation to obey. He did not even issue it. He used the words, alright. But his using the words simply does not *count as* his issuing legally binding orders.

And now, more generally, I see no reason to doubt that the rights and duties of which we have been speaking are moral ones. Speaking introduces the potential for a whole new range of moral culpabilities – and accomplishments. At bottom, it is our dignity as persons that requires that we be taken at our word, and take ourselves at our word. Other things being equal, of course.

## CHAPTER 6

# Could God have and acquire the rights and duties of a speaker?

It is time to ask whether God could speak. Not whether God *does* speak; we'll get to that later. But whether God *could do* such things as make assertions, issue commands, and make promises.

We'll have to presuppose certain things in our discussion or we'll never get to the issues that immediately concern us. The proposition that God speaks entails that God exists; so if it couldn't be that God exists, then it couldn't be that God speaks. Here is not the place to consider that issue. And if God were merely some abstract factor in reality – the *ground of being*, say – rather than personal, then God could not speak. But here is also not the place to consider that issue.

Let us suppose that in their use of the word "God," the Hebrew and Christian scriptures (in their English translations!) were referring to something that really exists. And let us assume that among the things those scriptures got right about that being, is their presumption that God is personal: a center of consciousness who forms and acts on intentions and has knowledge of entities other than Godself. Can that being do what's necessary for speaking? Can that being function as a participant in the community of discoursers; in particular, can that being be active in that community, as itself a discourser? The writers of these scriptures repetitively applied the language of speaking to God. So one aspect of our question is whether, understanding that language literally, they could have been right about that. Or was their application of such language to God only metaphorically true at best, and misguided at worst?

I judge that the account of speaking which I developed in the preceding chapter gives special urgency to two questions: could God fit into the texture of moral rights and duties in the way necessary for speaking? And, could God causally bring about the generating actions necessary for speaking? Let us consider the former of these questions in this chapter; and the latter, in the next.

95

The main question which I posed in the preceding chapter was this: what it is for one's causal bringing about of some action to *count as* one's performance of some speech action? The judge's uttering of some words *counts as* his pronouncing the defendant guilty. In what does this relation of *counting as* consist? The only thing the judge brings about causally is the utterance of those words; what then is it for his doing that to *count as* his also performing the very different action of pronouncing the defendant guilty?

The answer I proposed is that it consists in the fact that, on account of his having uttered that word, the *standing* of one who has performed the action of pronouncing the defendant guilty is now *normatively ascribed* to him. That is to say, we are now morally obligated to treat him, and he us, as one who has made that pronouncement. We, the hearers, may refuse to so treat him – may refuse to acknowledge his standing among us as one who has pronounced the defendant guilty, may refuse in our actions to *count him* as having made that pronouncement. But that doesn't alter the fact that he has acquired the right to be so treated and we, the obligation to so treat him. If that were not the case, his making those sounds would not *count as* his making that pronouncement. They would count as something else, or wouldn't count as anything at all.

I added that the standings which consist in having performed some speech action are themselves *normative standings*, in that intrinsic to having performed some speech action is having acquired certain (prima facie) moral rights and duties. In promising to do something, for example, one acquires the (prima facie) obligation to do what one promised. And I argued that there are also *normative conditions* for the acquisition of such standings. For example, one is (prima facie) obligated not to assert something unless one believes it.

Assuming this account is correct, the central question before us is whether God could have the obligations, and could acquire the rights and duties, requisite to speaking. The normative standing which consists in commanding something typically includes the (prima facie) right to have one's command obeyed. Could God acquire such a standing and thus acquire such a right – by causally generating some action, or by someone else doing so when acting as God's deputy? The normative standing which consists in having promised something typically includes the (prima facie) obligation to do what one promised. Could God acquire such a standing, and thus acquire such an obligation? And is it the case for God, as it is for us, that there are normative conditions on the performance of such actions? Is it, for example, a *prima facie* obligation for God as well as for us that one not promise something unless one intends to do it, and not command something unless one wants it done?

The issues hang, in good measure, on how we understand *being obligated* to do something. A theory of obligation which is extremely attractive, initially, at least, to many in the Jewish, Christian, and Muslim traditions, and which at the same time has important implications for how, if at all, God can participate in the community of discoursers, is the divine command theory. So let us enter the issues here by considering the tenability of this theory, after taking note of its precise bearing on the questions at hand.

### The divine command theory of obligation

The theory is attractive to a great many theists both when considered "from above" and when considered "from below." Its attractiveness to many when considered "from above" lies in the fact that it offers an account of obligation which saves God's unconditionedness. Deep in the traditional theological and philosophical articulation of Judaism, Christianity, and Islam, has been the conviction that God is unconditioned by anything not identical with Godself – that God in no way depends for God's existence, attributes, or actions on anything other than God. In particular, then, if God has the property of being obligated to do certain things, that must not be on account of something other than God somehow placing God under obligation.

The divine command theory offers a brisk way of honoring this conviction. It simply denies that God has any obligations. Or to be more explicit: when the theory is understood as including the thesis that God can not (or does not) issue commands which apply to Godself in such a way as to obligate God, then it *implies* that God has no obligations. Robert M. Adams, who has done as much as anyone in the contemporary world to resuscitate the divine command theory, explicitly draws out this implication (indicating thereby, though without ever explicitly calling attention to the matter, that he understands the theory as including that thesis):

If we accept a divine command theory of ethical rightness and wrongness, I think we shall have to say that *dutifulness* is a human virtue which, like sexual chastity, is logically inapplicable to God. God cannot either do or fail to do his duty, since he does not have a duty – at least not in the most important sense in which human beings have a duty.[1]

We will shortly return to this implication of the theory.

The *prima facie* attractiveness of the divine command theory to theists when approached "from below" is stated nicely by Adams in another passage. There is, he says,

> much in the phenomenology of obligation, and the related phenomena of wrongdoing and guilt, that supports an understanding of obligation in terms of social requirements. The great difficulty with such a view, to sum it up bluntly, is that human social requirements are not good enough. If we seek a better sort of social or quasi-social requirement, something transcendent, that might ground a more perfect system of ethical obligations, the most obvious candidate is divine commands.[2]

The reason divine commands seem "the most obvious candidate" to theists is, of course, that "God's commands constitute a law or standard that seems to believers to have a sanctity that is not possessed by any merely human will or institution."[3]

But though the divine command theory of moral obligation, for the reasons cited, is very attractive to a good many theists, it has been widely held, within as well as outside of the theistic traditions, that "all those theories are indefensible which attempt to explain in terms of the will or commands of God what it is for an act to be ethically right or wrong."[4] If that opinion were correct, we could set the theory aside and go on to other matters. So let us briefly consider the matter.

The objections which are widely held to be decisive against all versions of the theory are these: if God's commanding something were what made an act morally obligatory, then it would not be wrong for God to command, say, the wanton torture of children; and if God did command that, it would be morally obligatory for us to do that. But surely these implications are a *reductio ad absurdum* of the theory. It would be wrong for God to command that. And so far from its being morally obligatory for us to torture infants wantonly should God command it, it would remain morally *wrong* for us to do so; God's commanding it wouldn't change its moral status at all.

There have been many attempts on the part of divine command theorists to avoid these *reductios* of their theory. Most of them take either the form of arguing that the antecedent of the counterfactual *could not be true* – God could not command that – or the form of arguing that we can trust that the antecedent *will not be true* – God will not command that. Rather than entering the issues involved in considering whether either of these lines of response is satisfactory, let me call attention to what seems to me the much more satisfactory response of Adams to the challenge. Adams responds by introducing a modification into the traditional theory. He suggests that the property of moral wrongness is not the property of being contrary to the command of God, but the different property of being contrary to the command of *a loving* God.

To understand the import of this modification, we must be aware of the fact that the terms "ought," "ought not," and "permitted," along with their synonyms, constitute just one cluster within the totality of terms for the evaluation of action and character. Thus an action may be a good thing for someone to do without its being obligatory for that person to do it, and it may be a bad thing for that person to do without that person's being obligated not to do it. What will be the case is that an action is bad if wrong and good if obligatory. Thus the central question to which Adams addresses himself can be put like this: what has to be added to a bad action to make it a morally wrong action? His answer is that it must be contrary to the command of a loving God.

To the objection that it would be wrong *for God* to command the wanton torture of infants, Adams' reply, then, is that though it would be profoundly bad and morally repulsive, it would not be wrong; there's not something morally obligating God not to do this. And to the objection that it would remain morally wrong *for us* to torture infants wantonly even if God did command it, Adams' reply is that though it would certainly remain bad for us to do so, it would not be wrong; for though in that situation there would be *commands* of God, there would be no such thing as the commands of a *loving* God.

I judge that Adams' modification of the traditional divine command theory defuses the objections while yet retaining the core of the theory, with the consequence that the theory's initial attractiveness for theists is retained. So we cannot set it aside; we must move on to consider its implications for the issues at hand.

### *The implications of the theory for the issues at hand*

The divine command theory not only *allows* for God's participation in the community of discoursers as an agent therein; it *requires* it. More strongly yet: the theory places it on center stage. For at the *heart* of the theory is God's performing speech actions of commanding things.

Yet the theory also implies – ironically – that there is a massive restriction laid on God's participation in the community of discoursers. For the theory, when understood as including the thesis that God can not, or does not, give commands which apply to Godself in such a way as to obligate God, implies that God has no obligations. God can participate in the community of discoursers only in such ways as do not imply that God has or acquires obligations – only in such ways as imply that God has or acquires *rights*.

Perhaps the most important consequence is that certain sorts of speech actions are simply not available to God for performing – promising and covenanting, for example, since it is inherent in making a promise or covenant that one obligates oneself to do something. Of course it's only a *prima facie* obligation; when, in a given case, all things are considered, one may not have the obligation. But it's a consequence of the divine command theory that God doesn't have even *prima facie* obligations; and in any case, it would be bizarre to hold that, though God makes promises and is *prima facie* obligated to do the thing promised, God is never *in fact* obligated to do the thing promised when all things are considered.

This implication of the divine command theory has not escaped the notice of some, at least, of those who have written about it; William P. Alston is an example. Indeed, Alston not only takes note of this implication but embraces it; and does so with equanimity, so far as I can tell. He observes that "God is represented in the Bible and elsewhere as making promises, for example, to Noah and to Abraham, and as making covenants with Israel, and the very concept of a promise or of a covenant involves engendering obligations." "So how," Alston asks, "can God fail to have obligations?" His answer is this:

I think this argument does show that if God has no obligations it is not strictly true that He makes promises or covenants. Does my view then imply that all these reports are false? No. We can hold that the Biblical writers were speaking loosely, analogically, or metaphorically in so describing the transactions, just as they were in speaking of God "stretching out His arm" and doing so-and-so. They were choosing the closest human analogue to what God was doing in order to give us a vivid idea of God's action. It would be more strictly accurate to say that God *expressed the intention* to make Abraham's descendants as numerous as the dust of the earth ... Just as we can express intentions without obligating ourselves (provided we don't promise), so it is with God.[5]

That there should be some kinds of speech actions which are not available to God for performing is, of course, entirely unsurprising; it is, in fact, to be expected. But the implication that God cannot make promises or covenants should, in my judgment, be unsettling for at least all those theists who are of the view that their scriptures are a medium of divine discourse. What Jews, Christians, and Muslims must all reckon with is that, in their respective scriptures, the language of promising and covenanting is as prominent in the discourse of the writers about God as is the language of commanding. The theory of interpreting for divine discourse which I will articulate and defend in later chapters implies that, unless there is good reason to act otherwise, the writers of scripture should be interpreted as speaking literally on this matter; and implies that, unless there is good reason to do otherwise, God should be interpreted as saying what the writers said.

Furthermore, what contributes essentially to making the divine command theory of moral obligation initially attractive to the theist is that he brings to his assessment of the theory the background conviction that God does issue commands. But his background conviction that God issues commands is only one component in his much more comprehensive background conviction about the discourse of God: He brings to his assessment of the divine command theory the conviction that God performs speech actions of a wide variety – commanding, yes, but also promising, covenanting, asserting, asking, and so forth. The reason the theist comes with this comprehensive picture of the speaking God is, of course, that the writers of his sacred scriptures attributed, or appear to have attributed, exactly such a wide variety of speech actions to God. Accordingly, accepting the divine command theory requires wrenchingly altering the very framework of conviction which helped to give the theory its *prima facie* plausibility.

But not only does the divine command theory of moral obligation imply that the sorts of speech actions available to God for performance are significantly limited, compared to us human beings; it implies that God's participation in the community of discoursers is, in general, deeply idiosyncratic. Notice, first, that while it is intrinsic to the performance of some speech actions that one takes onto oneself (prima facie) obligations, it is intrinsic to others that one imposes (prima facie) obligations on others. It is typically the case, for example, that if one asks a question of someone, then one's addressee is (prima facie) obligated to answer, and that if one tells someone something, one's addressee is (prima facie) obligated to take one at one's word. But none of this will hold for our speaking to God if the divine command theory is true; nothing we can say to God will in any way obligate God. God, out of goodness, may respond to what we ask and what we say; and if God does so, that will be praiseworthy. But God will never be obligated to do so.

Furthermore, not only is God not obligated to take me at my word when I say things to God, nor obligated to answer my questions and requests; God is not even obligated to *count me*, to *acknowledge me*, as having said something. In my preceding lecture I asked what it is for a person's performance of one action to *count as* that person's performance of some speech action. And the account I offered, it will be recalled, was that it consists in that person now being obligated to treat us, and we him, as someone who has the standing of one who has performed that action. We are obligated to *count him*, and he is obligated to *count himself*, as one who has that standing. But an implication of the divine command theory is that God is not obligated to count us as having the standing of having performed any speech action – nor, of course, obligated to count himself as having any such standing. Our confidence in God's goodness will lead us to expect that God will so count Godself and us; if God does, that will be praiseworthy. But it will not mark the satisfaction of an obligation on God's part.

And lastly, the divine command theory implies that, unlike your and my speaking, there are no normative conditions attached to God's speech. We human beings live under the (prima facie) obligation not to assert something unless we believe it, not to promise something unless we intend to do it, not to command something unless we want it done. But if God neither has nor can acquire obligations, it just follows that such normative conditions do not pertain to God's speech. Our confidence in God's goodness may again lead us to expect that God will say only what God believes, command only what God wants done, and promise only what God intends to do – though the story of the binding of Isaac casts a cloud over such expectations. If God does so act, that will be praiseworthy; but it will not constitute the satisfaction of obligations. In short, if the divine command theory of moral obligation is correct, God's participation in the community of discoursers will be deeply idiosyncratic, when compared to yours and mine.

Maybe we should acknowledge that that's how it is. Maybe there are good reasons for accepting the implications of the divine command theory that though God is capable of performing speech actions of commanding, nonetheless, since God does not have and cannot acquire obligations, God's participation in the community of discoursers is idiosyncratic in the ways indicated.

One set of reasons for the theist to accept these implications is just the grounds mentioned of the theory's attractiveness – its attractiveness "from above" and "from below." But is there nothing more to be said? Is the theist limited to weighing up those grounds of the theory's attractiveness, versus whatever unattractiveness he may find in the theory's implications, and going with the stronger? No, I think not. In the same article in which Alston embraces the theory's implication that God makes no promises, he offers an independent argument for the conclusion that God has no obligations. He does so because he himself is not committed to the divine command theory of moral obligation; his aim in writing the article was simply to offer advice and assistance to those who do embrace the theory. Thus his own embrace of the thesis that God has no obligations could not rest on the theory but needed an independent argument. So let us look at Alston's argument.

### Alston's first argument against divine obligation

The argument Alston presents is an adaptation of the Kantian argument, that a holy will has no obligations. Alston assumes that God is essentially perfectly good; that is to say, that "it is metaphysically impossible that God should do anything that is less than supremely good …"[6] What he argues, then, is "that the lack of any possibility of God's doing other than the best prevents the application of terms in the 'ought' family to God" (258). For someone like Adams, who does not assume that God is essentially good, this argument begs a fundamental question. Nonetheless, it raises important issues; and in any case, probably most theists agree with Alston rather than Adams on this matter.

The "intuitive idea," says Alston,

is that it can be said that agents ought to do something, or that they have duties or obligations, only where there is the possibility of an opposition to what these duties require. Obligations *bind* us, *constrain* us to act in ways we otherwise might not act. They *govern* or *regulate* our behavior, *inhibit* some of our tendencies and *reinforce* others. We can say that a person ought to do A only where there is, or could be, some resistance on her part to doing A. (258)

But how, he asks, "to support this intuition?"

He remarks that it's tempting to support it with an argument which takes as a premise the observation that "to the extent that we think there is no possibility of S's failing to do A, we don't tell him that he ought to do A, or speak of S's duty or obligation to do A" (258). But in fact it would be fallacious, Alston insists, to move from this observation about linguistic usage, that in such-and-such circumstances we wouldn't *say* that someone has a certain duty, to the conclusion that in those circumstances he doesn't in fact have that duty. I think Alston is right about this.

But it's also worth noting that Alston's observation about linguistic usage, which is the premise in that fallacious argument, is itself mistaken. Oddly enough, Alston himself, in the same paragraph, provides a counter-example. He asks us to imagine an academic department with himself as chairman and an assistant professor as member who has "unfailingly taught his classes and, furthermore, has conscientiously performed all his academic duties, even engaging in acts of supererogation." Suppose, then, says Alston, that "I were to remark to him, when passing in the hall one day, 'You ought to meet your classes regularly.' That remark would naturally evoke intense puzzlement." No doubt it would. But note that Alston has himself described the situation as one in which the assistant professor "performed all his academic duties"; and surely there's nothing at all puzzling about that description. So it's not true that "to the extent that we think there is no possibility of S's failing to do A, we don't ... speak of S's duty or obligation to do A." We do; and Alston does.

What is true is that it would be strange to single out some of the duties that the assistant professor was unfailingly performing and then, in *imperative tone*, say *to him* that he ought to be doing those things. About this particular oddity, Alston is right in observing that it doesn't follow from the oddity of the comment that the assistant professor wasn't in fact obligated to do those things. The oddness has "to do only with the conditions of appropriateness for certain kinds of illocutionary acts, and not at all with the truth conditions of ought judgments. Even if there would be no point in my *exhorting* or *enjoining* my colleague to meet his classes, the fact remains (I am assuming) that it is his duty to do so, that he ought to do so, however little possibility there is of failure" (258).[7]

How, then, does Alston attempt to defend his "intuitive idea"? He offers two arguments. The first I find relatively clear but unpersuasive; the second, obscure but suggestive. Let's start with the first:

One thing required for my having an obligation to do A, e.g., to support my family, is that there are general principles, laws, or rules that lay down conditions under which that action is required (and that those conditions are satisfied in my case). Call them "practical rules (principles)". Practical principles are in force, in a nondegenerate way, with respect to a given population of agents only if there is at least a possibility of their playing a governing or regulative function; and this is possible only where there is a possibility of agents in that population violating them. (262)

The argument is stated elliptically. But I take it to be something like this: it is indeed possible to apply the concept of *obligation* in purely descriptive fashion – for example, by remarking about someone that supporting his family is a matter of obligation. But any particular judgment specifying what is not merely good but obligatory, whether that judgment be in the imperative or in the declarative mood, presupposes some general principle specifying the sort of conditions under which that sort of action is not only good but obligatory. For example, there is some principle stating what when a person of such-and-such a sort is in such-and-such circumstances, then it is not only good but obligatory for that person to support his family. All such presupposed general principles are *practical* principles, in that they specify something to be done; more specifically, they specify something which is *morally required* to be done. Now it is intrinsic to a principle's being a practical principle in force for a certain population that, among the various ways it can be used by the members of that population, it can be used by them to guide and regulate their actions. That is to say: that it can be used by them as a rule for acting on. But a principle can be used by the members of a population as a rule for acting on only if they don't, when they are in the circumstances specified, *necessarily* perform the action specified by the principle as not only good but morally required of persons in such circumstances. Consider, then, a population whose sole member is God. Since God *necessarily* does what's good, we get the conclusion, by *modus tollens*, that no particular ought judgments, specifying what is not merely good for God to do but morally required of God to do, are true.

Many things could be said about this argument; I shall have to restrain myself and make just two points. The argument pivots on the thesis that a principle which specifies some action as not only good but morally required in such-and-such circumstances is in force for a population only if it can be used by members of that population as a rule on which they act; and it is assumed that it cannot be thus used if the members of the population perform that action ineluctably when in such circumstances. But why suppose that this thesis is true? Suppose that there is a principle specifying the sorts of conditions under which it is not only good but obligatory for a person to try to support his family. And now imagine a population in which, *mirabile dictu*, the ties of familial affection are so strong that everybody in that situation just does ineluctably try to support his family.[8] Suppose further that this fact about their make-up prohibits anyone from taking the principle and using it as a rule on which he acts. Why is it mistaken to describe that situation as one in which everybody ineluctably does what is morally required in this regard? Alternatively, why is it mistaken to describe it thus: everybody acts *in accord with* the rule specifying what is obligatory in this situation, without anybody acting *on* that rule? Alston's argument gives no answer to these questions; the argument is conducted as if the thesis in question were self-evident.

But secondly, suppose, for the sake of argument, that Alston is right about that thesis. And imagine, this time, a population in which, though some people are ineluctably disposed to support their families when they find themselves in the sort of circumstances which, according to the family-support principle, make it obligatory to do so, others are not thus ineluctably disposed. Then, even on Alston's assumptions, this principle can function in that population as a rule on which members act. It cannot, on Alston's assumptions, function that way for everybody in the population; but it can function that way in the population at large. So why, in such a situation, wouldn't it be right to say, about those people with those strong familial ties, that they ineluctably do what they ought to do with respect to family support?

This sort of case suggests, in turn, the following question: Alston assumes that the relevant population, when we are considering the application of his thesis to God, is that population whose sole member is God. But why assume that? Why isn't the relevant population one that includes human persons along with God? Then, on Alston's principles, the moral frailty of human beings will insure that there are a great many practical principles of moral obligation which are in force for the entire population, including God; and some of those will apply to God, even though God ineluctably obeys them.

I have been assuming that by speaking of a principle's being "in force" for a certain population, Alston means this: a principle of obligation, to perform action A when in circumstance C, is in force for a certain population if and only if it is the case that, for any member of that population, that person has the obligation to perform action A when in circumstance C. That seems to me to provide the best interpretation of the various things he says, and at the same time to be something very naturally meant with those words. It would not be entirely unnatural, though, to use that phrase to mean this instead: the population for which a principle of obligation is in force consists of those persons who *are in fact* obligated to do A on account of *actually being* in circumstance C. And maybe that's what Alston meant. But this alternative understanding doesn't undercut the points I have just made; it only requires that they be formulated just a bit differently. For clarity's sake, let us use the phrase "applies to" for this alternative understanding of "is in force for"; and retain the phrase "is in force for" for the original understanding. There is some principle of obligation concerning promising such that anyone who has promised something has the obligation to do what he has promised when none of the defeating conditions $D_1 \ldots D_n$ obtains. So consider the population of persons to whom that principle applies. Suppose that some of them ineluctably do what they promise upon being in those conditions, and that some do not. The fact that some do not is sufficient for that principle of obligation to serve as a rule to be acted on in that population. And nothing that has been said implies that God is not a member of that population.

Before moving on to Alston's second argument, let us glance back at the divine command theory with this last point in mind, about God being a member of the relevant population. I have been construing the theory as including the thesis that God can not, or does not, issue commands which apply to Godself in such a way as to obligate God. And I have been doing so because the form of the theory which I have been using is the modified form developed by Robert Adams, and Adams clearly takes the theory as including this thesis; otherwise it wouldn't imply that God has no obligations. It's my clear impression that Adams is in the main line of divine command theorists on this matter. But why construe the theory in that way? A human sovereign might promulgate a law which applies to a population which includes herself – not to mention that she might promulgate a law which *is in force for* a population which includes herself. So too, a legislative body might pass a law which is not only in force for, but applies to, a population which includes within it members of that legislative body. Why can't it be like this for God? What prevents God from legislating that persons, who find themselves in a situation in which none of the promise-defeaters, $D_1 \ldots D_n$, is present, are not to promise to do something unless they intend to do that; and from God being in that sort of situation? Why suppose that God's legislation is limited in force or application to persons other than God? The effect of God's promulgating legislation which includes God in its scope of application would be that God promulgates legislation which requires certain things of Godself. But why is that impossible? A human legislature, to say it again, can pass legislation which requires certain things of the legislators themselves. In short, it's not at all clear that the divine command theory has to be construed in such a way as to imply restrictions on God's participation in the community of discoursers.

## Alston's second argument

But let us return to Alston. The questions I raised about Alston's first argument get answers, of a sort, in his second argument; for I judge that the second argument, though somewhat more obscure in its structure than the first, does, along the way, give a clue to how Alston was thinking. In his second argument, Alston tries to get the conclusion that God has no obligations *directly* from particular ought judgments, rather than from the nature of the general principles which particular judgments supposedly presuppose. Here is how he states the argument:

Under what conditions does the principle that *one ought to take account of the needs of others* apply to an agent, as well as the evaluative principle that it is a good thing for one to take account of the needs of others? For reasons of the sort we have been giving [in the first argument], it seems that such a principle has force, relative to an agent or group of agents, only where it has, or can have, a role in governing, directing, and guiding the conduct of those agents. Where it is necessary that S will do A, what sense is there in supposing that the general principle, *one ought to do A*, has any application to S? Here there is no foothold for the "ought"; there is nothing to make the ought principle true rather than or in addition to the evaluative statement plus the specification of what S will necessarily do. (263)

Rather than undertaking to exegete this passage, and trying to lay out the argument it contains, I brashly propose undertaking to say what Alston is trying to get at. That little phrase in the last sentence, "no foothold for the 'ought'," is the clue. Fundamental to Alston's thought is his conviction that what obligation adds to goodness is *requiredness* – *moral* requiredness, of course. He doesn't commit himself on what that *requiredness* consists in – perhaps it consists in being commanded by a loving God, perhaps not. Whatever it be, Alston's central point is that an action cannot have that property of *requiredness* for an agent unless it's possible for that agent not to perform that action. If there's no possibility of deviation, there is "no foothold for the 'ought'." All we would have then is goodness, not that additional property of *requiredness*.

Now it may well be that two agents and one action are such that, though for both agents the action is a good thing to do, one agent is ineluctably disposed to perform the action whereas the other agent is not. Then the action cannot be required of the former, whereas it might, so far forth, be required of the latter. *Requiredness* is thus a person-relative property. It follows that Alston's talk about populations was not really to the point. In trying to determine whether a person, and an action which is good for that person to perform, can together satisfy the Alstonian precondition for that action being *required of* that person, we must consider the capabilities and incapabilities *of that person*; the capabilities and incapabilities of other persons are irrelevant. Furthermore, if some action is not only *good* for a person to do but satisfies the Alstonian condition for being *required* of that person, then, presumably, the formulation of that requirement can have "a role in governing, directing, and guiding the conduct" of that agent. But rather than that being the fundamental fact, as Alston's first argument suggested, it's only a consequence of what is truly the fundamental fact, namely, that an action which is good for a person to do can only have the property of being *morally required of* that person if that person is not necessitated to perform it.

But why suppose it to be a fact that only the possibility of deviation gives a foothold for *requiredness*? That's obviously the crucial question. Alston explicitly deprives himself of the Kantian argument for this claim – the argument that having it in one's power to do otherwise is a condition of being obligated to perform some action A; for though he thinks that one can be obligated to perform A only if one can perform A freely, he does not think that a condition of performing A freely is that one have it in one's power to act otherwise. It "is not at all clear," he says, "that if God acts from the necessity of His own nature that prevents Him from acting freely in a way that is required for moral obligation" (257).

The truth is that Alston offers no argument for the thesis that only the possibility of deviation gives a foothold for requiredness. His second argument, at least as I have construed it, doesn't argue for that thesis but *presents* it to us, in the hope that when the thesis is put clearly before us, we will find it self-evident. That's how Alston himself understood his second argument, if "argument" it can be called. "I do not," he says, "have a knock-down argument for my thesis [that God has no obligations]. In fact I doubt that there is a more fundamental and more obvious feature of moral obligation from which the feature in question, the possibility of deviation, can be derived. All I can hope to do is to indicate the way in which this feature is crucial to obligation" (261).

### Advancing the discussion

But what are we to do if we, Alston's readers, do not find the thesis self-evident – as I do not? Is there any way of advancing the discussion past the stalemate of one party claiming that it finds it self-evident and the other party replying that it doesn't even find it true, let alone self-evident? Well, suppose there were a way of elaborating the divine command theory which allowed for God's full participation, in non-idiosyncratic manner, within the community of discoursers; suppose that it achieved this result by calling attention to a way in which an action might be required of God without any norm being imposed on God from outside; and suppose, finally, that this way of elaborating the theory remained neutral on the issue of God's essential goodness. Describing that way of elaborating the divine command theory of moral obligation would certainly advance the discussion. So let me try to do that.

At the core of the account of moral requiredness offered by the divine command theory is the phenomenon of *someone* requiring something of someone. Perhaps it was because Alston was thinking of moral requiredness along those lines, maybe without full awareness of doing so, that it seemed obviously true to him that moral requiredness requires the possibility of deviation: can my requiring some action of you get any grip on you if you are ineluctably going to perform the action anyway? At the core of the proposal I will sketch out is a quite different kind of requiredness – a kind of requiredness which doesn't consist in *someone* requiring something of someone, but just in *something* being required of someone.

Begin by noting that certain sorts of morally admirable character-formations are such that a distinction can be drawn, within the totality of the actions of a person who has that character and which are expressions thereof, between those which that particular character-formation *required*, and those which are expressions of that character without being required by it. Call these, respectively, *character-required* actions and *character-supererogatory* actions of the person. (The actions are, of course, required or supererogatory not *per se* but only with respect to some particular character-formation of a particular person.) For example, imagine someone of courageous character. If that person is to conduct himself "in the character" of a courageous person, certain actions will be required of him; not to do them would imply that he, at that point, was not conducting himself "in (courageous) character." Those are character-required actions – with respect, of course, to that particular person's courageous character. By contrast, other actions of that person will be such that, though they are expressions of the person's courageous character, the person would not be conducting himself "out of (courageous) character" if he didn't perform them. Those are character-supererogatory actions – with respect to that person's courageous character. Throwing himself on the grenade to protect the child was certainly an expression of the soldier's courage; but it went beyond what courage required. So too, if one has a loving character: some actions will be required of one if one is to conduct oneself "in (loving) character"; others, though expressive of that character, will not in that way be required. In drawing this distinction, I have said nothing about whether or not it is *possible* for one to act "out of character." Surely such silence is appropriate; the distinction doesn't at all depend on that.

Now let us suppose that God has a morally admirable character – specifically, a loving character. Adams assumes that God has that character contingently; Alston, that God has it essentially. We can remain neutral on that issue. I suggest that this same concept of character-required actions which applies to us applies to God; specifically, that it applies to God with respect to God's loving character. Some of God's actions are such that they are required of God if God is to act "in loving character." Whether there are also character-supererogatory acts in God's case, with respect to God's loving character, is less clear; possibly it is our peculiarly human frailties which make possible the performance of supererogatory actions.[9] But notice that the fact that certain actions are character-required of God, with respect to God's loving character, is not the consequence of something's being imposed on God from outside; it is simply an aspect of the internal structure of that character-formation which is *being a loving person*. To say that a certain action is character-required of the loving God is not to say that God is required to be loving in character; it is rather to say that the action is required for God's conducting Godself in loving character.

For the character-formation of being loving, and perhaps for others as well, it is possible, in turn, to go inside the set of character-required actions and distinguish two grades of requirement. Suppose that I, a person of loving character, am a lifeguard at the beach. Suppose, further, that three persons are visibly drowning in the tide; but that they are so widely separated that though there is a real chance of my saving one of them, there is no chance whatsoever of my saving more than one. In that situation, none of them has a *right* to be saved by me. Yet it is required by my loving character that I do try to save one of them. Thus the requirements of love sometimes go beyond the honoring of rights – though always they include that. The ground floor, as it were, of a loving character, is a rights-honoring character. It would be worth considering whether this same sort of thing is true for God: is it the case that, within the set of actions required of God for God to act in loving character, there is a sort of ground floor consisting of those required of God for God to act in rights-honoring character.

Now if God always acts "in character" as a loving person, then God's issuing of commands to us human beings is an expression of God's character. But given what we human beings are like, it seems eminently plausible to suppose that if God does issue commands to us, God's doing so is not just an expression of God's loving character but is *required by* that character. If so, then God's requiring of me that I do A, by commanding me to do A, is grounded in the requirements of God's character of love. What God requires of me is what God's character requires that God require of me. The phenomenon of God's requiring something of me is parasitic on the more fundamental phenomenon of the requirements of God's character. On this way of thinking of things, it might still be right to identify obligation with what is required by the commands of the loving God. But if so, there would be a form of requirement more fundamental than obligation, on which obligation depends; that form of requirement, namely, which consists of something being required by the love of God.

In summary: we have found no reason to conclude that God cannot have the rights and duties – or rights and requirednesses – necessary for participating fully in the community of discoursers. In fact, we have found two ways of so construing or elaborating that particular theory of moral obligation which is the divine command theory as to render it compatible with God's full participation in that community: the elaboration which I have just outlined, and the construal mentioned earlier, according to which the scope of application of (some of) God's legislation includes God. As to whether the divine command theory of moral obligation is true – I haven't even so much as *raised* that issue! It wasn't necessary.

## CHAPTER 7

# *Can God cause the events generative of discourse?*

Our topic, in this chapter and the preceding, is whether it's possible for God to speak – given the understanding of speaking developed in Chapter 5. Is God like what God would have to be like, and can God do what God would have to do, if God were to speak? In the preceding chapter we considered whether God could have and acquire the rights and obligations necessary for God to speak. In this chapter we will consider whether God could bring about the events generative of God's speaking.

## *Must God cause events if God is to speak?*

First, though, we'd better assure ourselves that God does indeed have to bring about certain events if God is to speak. Couldn't it be that we human beings bring about the events which count as God speaking – the events generative of divine discourse?

How could that be? Isn't it obvious that to perform a speech action one has to bring something about causally? That one can't just sit back passively? That one has to bestir oneself?

Well, we saw in Chapter 3 that, when words are the instruments of one's discourse, one needn't oneself have produced tokens of those words. One may instead take tokens produced by someone else and *authorize* them as the instruments of one's own speech – whereby they become that.

But what, then, about the authorizing? An act of authorizing is itself a speech act. So some event has to occur which generates it – which *counts as* it.

Yes; but we also saw that that generating event doesn't have to be brought about by oneself; it can be performed by one's deputy. One may deputize someone to perform "in one's name" an action which generates one's authorizing. The same is true for a vast variety of other speech actions as well; the speech action of authorizing is not peculiar in this regard. One can perform many if not most of the speech actions available to one for performing by the combination of oneself deputizing someone to perform "in one's name" an action generative of that speech action, and that deputized person then doing so. It's these facts that suggest the radical possibility: could God speak without causally bringing about any actions generative of that speech? Must God *do* something to speak? couldn't it all be done *for* God, by us?

Well, suppose one deputizes one's secretary to perform "in one's name" an action generative of one's authorization of the draft letter she has typed; typically nowadays that action consists of the secretary inscribing one's name in the appropriate place on the letter. And as to the deputizing, the customary way of accomplishing that is by oneself speaking directly to one's secretary. But one could do it instead by deputizing one's spouse to speak "in one's name" to one's secretary; if one's spouse then says the appropriate thing to one's secretary, one would have deputized one's secretary to authorize the draft of the letter in one's name. One's spouse might in turn deputize ones son to act in her name; or one might deputize one's spouse to deputize one's son; and so forth. In short, there may be a sizable number of intermediary deputies and deputizings between the person who eventually performs the generat*ing* action, and the person who performs the generat*ed* action of authorizing the letter – or whatever else the generated speech action might be. The question before us then is whether this discrepancy between agent of action generative of speech action, and agent of generated speech action could be the end of the matter?

One is initially inclined to think not. Though one can perform some speech action by deputizing someone to perform "in one's name" some action generative thereof, and deputize someone to deputize someone, and so forth, it would seem that the sequence must begin by *oneself* performing some action *generative* of one's initial action of deputizing. One must oneself *do* something which counts as deputizing. One must initiate the sequence by deputizing "in one's own name." One's speaking, so it would seem, cannot all be done in the mode of someone else performing "in one's name" an action generative thereof; one must perform some generative action "in one's own name," even if what one generates thereby is only a highly general deputation.

Further reflection shows, however, that this is not true – surprisingly. It sometimes happens, in cases where a human being is incapable of performing speech actions, even the action of deputizing, that law or custom allows another human being to function as proxy or deputy: witness a regent acting in the name of an infant king or the child of someone suffering from Alzheimers Disease acting in the name of her parent. In such cases, one human being acts as the deputy or proxy of another without having been deputized so to act by that other – and so, perforce, without that other having performed any action which *counted as* deputizing.

Could it go that way in God's case? Could God speak entirely by way of the actions of deputies and never, as it were, in God's own voice? Could it be that whatever deputizing God does is itself done by way of the actions of deputies? Could it be that at the beginning of whatever chains of deputation there are, someone acts as God's deputy without God doing anything to deputize that person?

Bizarre thought! The sorts of cases we have cited from human affairs all incorporate a legal fiction. Law (or custom) applies to some human being in such a way that it is imperative that that human being perform some action characteristic of persons. But the human being in question is incapable on his or her own behalf of performing that action; he or she does not yet possess, or does not presently possess, or does no longer possess, the requisite degree of personhood. In that extremity, law or custom allows the human being in question to perform that act by way of some human being who is a full person acting as the proxy of that immature or impaired or enfeebled human being. If God's personhood were for a time undeveloped or impaired or diminished, then, by analogy, it would make sense to think along the lines indicated. But how could that be! And in any case, then at some other time God must have the degree of personhood requisite for speaking in God's own name; then at some other time God does, or is at least capable of doing, something which generates God's speaking.

Though it is incoherent to suppose that God gains and loses personhood, the same can probably not be said about the supposition that God is not at all personal – never was and never will be. But if God were just an impersonal factor in reality, then to regard certain human beings as deputized to act in God's name would be to act out a fiction with no point. The legal fiction gets its point from the fact that human beings who are incapable of functioning as persons are *deficient* human beings: immature or temporarily diminished or permanently malformed. There would be no analogy in God's case.

In short, though it may well be the case that a great deal of God's discourse is accomplished by way of deputation and appropriation, it can't all be like that. At some point God must Godself do things which generate God's acts of discourse. And in any case, the religious traditions on which we have our eye – Judaism, Christianity, and Islam – are replete with purported cases of God discoursing in God's own voice, without resort to deputation or appropriation.

## Must God intervene if God is to speak?

So God must act if God is to speak. That is to say, God must causally bring about events *generative* of divine discourse. Now in our century there has been a veritable assault on the notion of God intervening in history. Ironically, certain theologians have been in the vanguard of this assault. Where once theologians saw it as their calling to defend not just the possibility but the actuality of divine intervention against the doubters, now a good many see it as their calling to defend the improbability if not the impossibility against the affirmers. Must we enter this debate, or can we can make an end-run around it? might it be the case that God's performance of actions generative of divine discourse does not require particular intervention on the part of God?

Perhaps we ought to allow for the possibility that sometimes an event generative of God's discourse is not part of any plan of God. This would happen, for example, if God deputized someone to speak in God's name, and then, as to content, allowed the person freely to decide the specifics of what to say – within a certain range, of course. In such a case, the event of God's saying what God did say by way of the actions of that person would not have been part of any plan of God; and that might be the case even though God foreknew what that would be. Not everything that one knows will happen, as the consequence of implementing some action-plan that one has, is part of the plan. But we can safely assume that that is not how it went with Augustine in the garden. There was something quite specific God wanted to say to Augustine then and there. And God's bringing it about that the child chanted *"tolle lege"* must have been part of God's action-plan for generating that discourse-event. Here then is the question we must reflect on: might it be that all those events generative of divine discourse, which have been part of some enacted plan of God, were part of God's plan at creation – so that no particular intervention has ever been required?

We need a bit of ontology and theology here. Let us suppose that God has causal powers; that is to say, that God is capable of bringing about events. And that God's exercise of God's causal powers is the consequence of free choice on God's part, that it is not determined. Let us furthermore suppose that among God's causal powers are the powers of immediately bringing entities into existence and of endowing them, in turn, with causal powers. Some of the causal powers with which God endows an entity may belong to its essence, so that the endowing comes along with the bringing into existence; others may not belong to its essence. If we were occasionalists, we would insist that God endows only persons with causal powers; and that these persons, in turn, are incapable of endowing anything other than persons with causal powers. For our purposes here, though, let us not think occasionalistically; let us rather suppose that non-persons such as plants, animals, minerals, atoms, and so forth, also have causal powers. Let us, in traditional fashion, call God's exercise of God's powers of immediately bringing entities into existence and of endowing them with causal powers, *creation.*

Let us suppose that among the causal powers with which God endows the entities God brings into existence are the powers of bringing new entities into existence and of endowing them with causal powers. Obviously God as creator is also ultimately behind all such bringing into existence and endowing with causal powers on the part of creatures; but let us confine the word "creation" to those cases of God *singly* and *immediately* bringing some entity into existence and/or endowing it with causal powers. The fact that God has already created entities with the causal powers of bringing entities into existence and endowing them with causal powers does not, of course, prohibit God from singly and immediately bringing new entities into existence and endowing them with causal powers, nor of singly and immediately altering the causal powers of some entity already in existence. *Original* creation does not prohibit *subsequent* creation. Nor does it prohibit God from intervening in such a way as to singly and immediately bring about some event without either bringing any new entity into existence or altering the causal powers of some extant entity.

Let us suppose, in addition to the above, that God not only has the causal power of bringing entities into existence and of endowing them with causal powers, but the power of *sustaining* them and their causal powers in existence throughout a duration. Let us call the exercise of these powers on God's part, *sustenance;* and let us suppose that only if God sustains an entity and its causal powers in existence at a certain time does that entity exist at that time and retain its causal powers.

It was part of traditional Christian doctrine to add to creation and sustenance a third, related, activity on God's part, called *general concurrence*. The idea was that if entities are to *exercise* their causal powers and not just *possess* them, God has to do something more than just create and sustain them and their causal powers; God has to *concur with* that exercise. There was much dispute as to what concurrence came to; but the orthodox consensus was that concurrence, whatever it may be, is not just God's *letting* things exercise their causal power but represents the exercise of some additional causal power on God's part. For our purposes here, we can be noncommittal on the nature of *general concurrence* while assuming its existence.

Perhaps just a word should be said here about the distinction, used above, between doing something *immediately* and doing something *nonimmediately*. I have in mind the distinction, common in action theory, between *basic* and *nonbasic* actions. Much of what we do, we do *by way of* doing something else. I ask a question by uttering some words. My uttering the words *counts as* my asking the question. It *generates* my asking the question; and it does so in the *counting-as* mode. Or I turn off the flashlight by sliding the button. My sliding the button *causes* the flashlights being turned off, and thereby it *causally generates* my turning off the flashlight. A basic action, then, is something one does without doing it by way of doing something else. There must, in the nature of the case, be such actions. Of course, not every effect of one's basic actions is to be reckoned as something that one brings about – and hence, as one of one's causally generated actions. Many of them are to be reckoned as events to whose coming about one only makes a causal contribution. Where exactly the line is to be drawn between these two sorts of cases, and why it is to be drawn there, are difficult questions which I will not pursue. What especially makes them difficult is that even when I am reckoned as the agent of some causally generated action, a vast number of other entities must exercise their causal powers if I am to do what I did.

And now, once again, our question: might all the events generative of divine discourse which are part of some plan of God be part of a plan God formed and initiated at original creation, requiring, in addition, only sustenance and general concurrence for their coming about? Not all that transpires as the result of original creation, sustenance and concurrence, need have been part of a plan God had at original creation; the effects, even the foreknown effects, might extend beyond the plan. But consider all the events generative of divine discourse which are part of some plan of God – our question is whether all of those might have been part of God's plan formed at original creation *and requiring only sustenance and concurrence for their coming about* – no particular intervention. It might have been part of God's plan at creation not just subsequently to sustain creation and concur in its workings but to intervene at certain points in history – singly and immediately to bring about some such event as creating a new entity, altering the causal powers of some extant entity, and so forth. If so, we are to exclude such parts of the plan from consideration. It might also have been part of God's plan at creation to perform some particular intervention if such-and-such should happen. This is different from planning that particular intervention; planning to water the lawn if it doesn't rain for another week is not yet planning to water the lawn. Nonetheless, such planned conditionalized interventions require particular intervention for their implementation; so they too are excluded from consideration. The event of that child chanting *tolle lege* across the wall from Augustine – might God's plan at creation have included a plan for bringing about that event then and there without particular intervention, and might the event have come about because God implemented that plan at creation?

Well, if all events in the created order were brought about by the activation of creaturely causal powers, and if the activation of those powers was always deterministic in character, then, given omniscience on God's part, presumably so. Someone might reply that if the child's chanting of *tolle lege* at that time and place was just the consequence of the unrolling of the divine plan formed before the founding of the world and implemented at its founding, then there would be no reason to suppose that that event had this quite special character of being generative of divine discourse. But why should that be? You and I form and implement action-plans for bringing about events. For many of those there comes a time when the remainder of the events comprising the plan occur without one's having to perform any additional basic actions to bring them about; one can sit back and let events take their course. The events comprising such action-plans may well include, among others, events of discourse and their generating events. Why should it be different in God's case? A significant feature of what transpired in the garden, as Augustine reported it, is that Augustine did not, before concluding that God was speaking to him, determine to his satisfaction that he was confronted with a case of *particular* divine intervention. The question was never raised. It was the uncanniness of the coincidence between his situation and the child's chanting those particular words that led him to his conviction. His conviction was reinforced by the uncanny relevance of what he read when he opened his book; one can imagine his having read something there which would have led him instead to retract his conviction that God had spoken to him through the chanting of the child.

Let it be clear that we are asking our question about our world, not about some other possible world. That event of God speaking to Augustine in the garden: for all we know, might it be the case that that event and the event generating it were effectively planned by God before the foundations of the world were laid? Might it be the case that the bulk of the discourse-events attributed to God by the scriptures and traditions of Judaism, Christianity, or Islam were similarly so planned and brought about? Might it be the case that in our universe, as it actually is, all the events generative of divine discourse were contained in God's pre-creation plan and come about as the consequence of initial creation, plus sustenance and general concurrence?

Well, it is apparently highly unlikely that in our actual universe all events are brought about by the activation of creaturely causal powers, and that the activation of those powers is always deterministic in character. Our scientists tell us that many micro-events happen purely by chance. Nothing causes particles of certain sorts to jump this way rather than that; they just do. In addition, a good many actions of human beings are freely chosen by the agents of those actions.

Now the fact that everything could come about by divine plan if the universe were deterministic is due to the fact that sufficient counter-factuals would then be available for constructing the plan. If such-and-such entities were created with such-and-such causal powers, then event E would occur down the road somewhere. If those-and-those other entities were created with those-and-those other causal powers, then event E would not occur. Knowing these counterfactuals of causal necessity, God would choose which entities to create and which powers to endow them with in the light of whether or not God wanted E to occur.

But suppose there are also counterfactuals pertaining to free agency; then planning can be done on the basis of those as well. Planners can afford to be indifferent as to the mode of the counterfactuals that they know. Suppose I know that if I would say P to Joe, then Joe would say Q to George; and that if Joe would say Q to George, then George would do X. Suppose I also know that if I would say R to Jonathan, then Jonathan would say S to George; and that if Jonathan would say S to George, then George would not do X but would instead do Y. Then I could choose what to say to whom in the light of whether I wanted George to do X or Y; and the fact that Joe, Jonathan, and George are all free agents with respect to the actions in question – that their actions were not causally necessitated – wouldn't make any difference.

As many readers will know, the area we have now entered is one of deep controversy. The issue is whether there are true counterfactuals of freedom – true propositions, concerning some free agent and some possible situation, to the effect that if that agent were in that situation, he would freely do so-and-so – not that he would *probably* do so-and-so, but that he *would* do so-and-so. Presumably if there are any such true counterfactuals of freedom, then for every free agent, for every situation in which that agent could find himself, and for every action which that agent is capable of performing freely in that situation, there is a truth of the matter as to whether that agent would perform that action were he or she in that situation. More generally yet: given an ontologically adequate construal of the notion of *possible* free agents, there are presumably such truths for all possible free agents. If there are, and if God's knowledge at creation were such as to include them all, then God could of course make comprehensive use of that knowledge in planning what to create. God would know that that freely acting child would chant *"tolle lege, tolle lege"* if he or she were in such-and-such a situation; and God would then take that into account in forming His grand plan. If it weren't for the disrupting factor of chance in the physical dimension of reality, God could then just watch the scroll unroll.

I suggested that it is a deeply controversial matter among philosophers as to whether or not there are true counterfactuals of freedom; I am myself inclined to think there are not.[1] Here is obviously not the place to enter the debate, however. We must leave the issue at the point of observing that if there aren't such true counterfactuals, then obviously God cannot just watch the scroll unroll.

It will be said that even so, we plan. And so we do; we calculate the chances and go with the probabilities. Though there may be no fact of the matter as to what Jonathan would do if I said I didn't like his speech, there may be a fact of the matter as to what he would *probably* do; so I plan in the light of that. May it be so with God as well? May it be that God plans in the light of the chances? God wanted a chanting of *tolle lege* that would seem uncanny to Augustine, and took a chance on the child stepping outdoors and starting his sing-song. But then God also had to take a chance on Augustine stumbling out into the garden; otherwise the child's chanting would have been to no avail. And a chance on Ponticianus' telling the story of Anthony, since it was that which cast Augustine into the crisis which propelled him into the garden. And a chance on Augustine and Alypius telling Ponticianus that they had never heard of Anthony, since it was that which led Ponticianus to tell the story. And so forth and so forth. A sequence of diminishing chances, approaching zero.

### The claim of theologians that God does not intervene

I asked whether, in elaborating the implications of the claim that God speaks, we could make an end-run around the opposition of contemporary theologians to the view that God intervenes in history. I think it is very likely, in the light of the preceding considerations, that the events generative of divine discourse cannot all be the consequence of God's implementation of a plan formed at creation – highly likely that many if not most of the purported episodes of divine discourse are the result of direct intervention on God's part. So we cannot make that end-run. We must ask why it is that theologians think God does not directly intervene in the course of history.

Let us allow one or two of them to speak for themselves, in representative passages. Here is a passage from a widely cited and influential essay by Langdon Gilkey:

contemporary theology does not expect, nor does it speak of, wondrous divine events on the surface of natural and historical life. The causal nexus in space and time which Enlightenment science and philosophy introduced into the Western mind ... is also assumed by modern theologians and scholars; since they participate in the modern world of science both intellectually and existentially, they can scarcely do anything else. Now this assumption of a causal order among phenomenal events, and therefore of the authority of the scientific interpretation of observable events, makes a great difference to the validity one assigns to biblical narratives and so to the way one understands their meaning. Suddenly a vast panoply of divine deeds and events recorded in Scripture are no longer regarded as having actually happened ... Whatever the Hebrews believed, *we* believe that the Biblical people lived in the same causal continuum of space and time in which we live, and so one in which no divine wonders transpired and no divine voices were heard.[2]

And here is a passage from John Macquarrie's book, *Principles of Christian Theology*. The traditional account of the distinctiveness of miracle, says Macquarrie,

makes the concept very difficult for modern minds, and might even suggest to the theologian that "miracle" is a discredited and outmoded word that ought to be banished from his vocabulary. The way of understanding miracle that appeals to breaks in the natural order and to supernatural interventions belongs to the mythological outlook and cannot commend itself in a post-mythological climate of thought ... The traditional conception of miracle is irreconcilable with our modern understanding of both science and history. Science proceeds on the assumption that whatever events occur in the world can be accounted for in terms of other events that also belong within the world; and if on some occasions we are unable to give a complete account of some happening – and presumably all our accounts fall short of completeness – the scientific conviction is that further research will bring to light further factors in the situation, but factors that will turn out to be just as immanent and this-worldly as those already known.[3]

The central claim is that modern science "proceeds on the assumption that whatever events occur in the world can be accounted for in terms of other events that also belong within the world." Engaging in any practice whatsoever requires taking certain things to be true, making certain assumptions; the suggestion is that engaging in modern science requires making this assumption. Of course, the fact – if it is a fact – that engaging in this practice requires making this assumption gives us, so far forth, no reason to think that the assumption is true. But I dare say that Gilkey and Macquarrie regard the practice of modern science as so successful in achieving its aims and so important for our lives that it would be silly and irresponsible to undermine it by surrendering the assumption. And I would guess that both of them would point to the *success* of modern science as some evidence, at least, for the truth of this assumption.

In an unpublished article in which he discusses these same passages from Gilkey and Macquarrie, along with another from Gordon Kaufman, William P. Alston makes a number of points in rebuttal. In the first place, it's just not true that engaging in the practice of modern science requires assuming a closed natural order. The "only thing a scientist is committed to assuming, by virtue of engaging in the scientific enterprise, is that there is a *good chance* that *the phenomena he is investigating* depend on natural causal conditions *to a significant degree*. These three qualifications mark three ways in which he need not be assuming strict naturalism. (1) He need only assume a significant probability. (2) He need only make his assumption for the particular area of his investigation. And (3) he need not assume even there that natural causes do the whole job in every instance."

On that last point, Alston observes that the assumption of medical research, for example, is that by discovering natural causes of pathological conditions, "we can put ourselves in a better position to forecast, prevent, and cure diseases." Believing that not every detail of every disease and of every recovery is due to natural causes, believing that some are due to particular divine intervention, scarcely precludes one from engaging in medical research. As a matter of fact, every medical researcher and every medical practitioner comes across cases that he finds inexplicable. Why would either research or practice be undercut if he believed that some of these are due to particular divine intervention? "So long as it is *generally* the case that the onset, development and cure of pneumonia follows certain natural regularities, that will give the scientist all he needs; a few exceptions don't matter."

But doesn't modern science give us reason to believe that all that happens in the natural order happens in accord with "laws of nature"; and wouldn't particular divine intervention be a violation of such laws? Alston makes three rejoinders. For one thing, many of the law-statements scientists embrace are "idealizations" "to which actual occurrences only approximate." Secondly, a good many of the laws discovered by twentieth-century science are probabilistic rather than deterministic in character; such laws "would not be 'violated' by an influence that results in the occurrence of what they imply to be improbable." But thirdly, and most interestingly: even for those deterministic natural causal laws which fit the phenomena with great precision, "if we suppose divine intervention would be a violation, it is because we are thinking of physical laws (of a deterministic form) as specifying *unqualifiedly* sufficient conditions for an outcome." In fact, though, all such laws as we have good reason to accept are *ceteris paribus* laws. "The most we are ever justified in accepting is a law that specifies what will be the outcome of certain conditions *in the absence of any relevant factors other than those specified in the law*. The strongest laws we have reason to accept lay down sufficient conditions only within a 'closed system', i.e., a system closed to influences other than those specified in the law. None of our laws takes account of all conceivable influences ... Since the laws we have reason to accept make provision for interference by outside forces unanticipated by the law, it can hardly be claimed that such a law will be violated if a divine outside force intervenes, and hence it can hardly be claimed that such laws imply that God does not intervene ... Thus even if physical laws take a deterministic *form*, the above considerations show that they by no means rule out the possibility of direct divine intervention in the affairs of the physical world."

So far, Alston's rebuttal; an impressive rebuttal indeed. To engage in modern science one does not have to assume anything which entails that particular divine intervention never occurs; surely Alston is right about that. So too he is right in his claim that the conjunction of all the law-statements which enjoy consensus or near-consensus among present-day scientists does not entail that particular divine intervention never occurs. Possibly such intervention is slightly improbable on the evidence of *just those laws*; but that, then, is the most that can be said.

### Do the theologians have more in mind?

Yet I am left with the nagging suspicion that the objectors had something more in mind than Alston has dealt with in his rebuttal. Those laws of our science which are not probabilistic in form give us no more than approximations to the patterns in the phenomena; and when not pertaining to closed idealized situations, always have *ceteris paribus* clauses attached. All true. But how are we to think of the goings-on in nature, from the scientific study of which such law-statements as these have emerged? I mean: how are we to think of those goings-on *when God is not intervening?* Is it of merely epistemological significance that our law-statements have those *ceteris paribus* clauses attached? Do the attachments merely point to the fact that we haven't yet discovered all the conditions – maybe never will, and usually wouldn't know when we had? Or is there something ontologically mistaken in the very notion of *a totality of sufficient conditions?* And does the fact that so many of our law-statements fit the data only approximately merely indicate that we have bought simplicity at the price of accuracy, or does it point to the ontological fact that often below a certain threshold of specificity there aren't any laws?

It would be entirely appropriate for Alston to reply that science as we have it is compatible with a variety of different answers to these questions. But perhaps what those theologians had in mind, whose claims about the import of modern science Alston is rebutting, was not modern science all by itself but modern science coupled with a widely held understanding of the nature of scientific explanation. We can get at the point I have in mind by asking what are those *laws of nature* to which Alston refers? Actually neither Gilkey nor Macquarrie, in the passages cited, uses the concept of *laws of nature*; but I don't think Alston was misinterpreting them when he cast their thought into this terminology.

In the course of a fine discussion about medieval Aristotelianism and its dispute with occasionalism, Alfred Freddoso remarks that "All the thinkers discussed in this essay take causation in the most basic and proper sense to be a relation between substances on the one hand and states of affairs on the other. Typically, substances (agents) act upon other substances (patients) to bring about or actualize or produce states of affairs (effects)."[4] Compare that with the following passage about modern science from Bas C. van Fraassen's recent book, *Laws and Symmetry*: "All bodies near the earth fall if released because such bodies *must* fall – and this is because of the *law* of gravity. Naïve as this may sound, it presents the paradigm pattern of explanation by law. If we take it completely seriously, it signals that a law is not itself a necessity but accounts for necessity. The law itself, it seems, is a fact about our world, some feature of what *this* world is actually like, and what must happen is due to that fact or feature."[5]

Two profoundly different mentalities are coming to expression in these two passages. The mentality coming to expression in the former passage is that of which I made use earlier in this chapter, when I was arguing that divine discourse requires particular intervention. The fundamental thought is that substances bring about states of affairs by virtue of the activation of causal powers which they possess. The activation of particular causal powers happens of necessity under certain circumstances. Causal laws are regularities of such necessitation. Historically what lay behind calling them "laws" was the conviction that their holding is to be attributed to God's creating, sustaining, and concurring wisdom and power. They are the ordinances of the Master of the Universe.

The mentality coming to expression in the latter passage does not think in terms of agents bringing about states of affairs but in terms of pairs of events, one member of which *necessitates* the other. The slipping of the glass of milk out of my hand *necessitates* the falling of that glass of milk to the floor. Obviously not every pair of events is such that one member of the pair necessitates the other. So the question arises: what accounts for the fact that the members of some pairs stand in that relationship and the members of other pairs do not? The answer is that it is *laws of nature* which account for event-necessitation. Thus laws of nature are not just spatio-temporal regularities among events. They are not even regularities of necessitation relationships among events. If that's all they were, necessitation relationships among events would be brute facts which just so happened to exhibit certain regularities. The laws *account for* the necessitation relationships; those relationships are *due to* the laws. And the laws are the truth-makers for counterfactuals; it's because of the law of gravity that this glass of milk would crash to the floor if I released it.[6]

Of course, the existence of such laws does not remove brute factuality from the picture; it moves it to a different and higher level. For though the laws of nature account for the necessitation relationships among events, they are themselves logically/ontologically contingent. It's just a brute fact about our actual world that there are such-and-such laws of nature accounting for the necessitation relationships among events. In other possible worlds, the laws of nature are different; in some, there are no laws of nature.

The business of science, then, is to discover the laws of nature. In so far as it does so, science *explains* what transpires in our world. Thus we get the common contemporary view that science explains by appealing to laws of nature, in contrast to the traditional Aristotelian view, that science explains by appealing to the causal powers of agents.

I have made no attempt, in this brief exposition, to explain what *laws of nature* are; I have only pointed to their function in this way of thinking. My own view is that the best attempts to argue for the existence of these entities and to explain their nature are seriously deficient; and that scrutiny of the actual practice of natural science does not yield the conclusion that the aim of scientists is to discover such entities. But I cannot develop these points here; let me just refer the reader to van Fraassen's book, where they are developed and argued with great force. It will be enough for us here to ask: does the case against particular divine intervention become compelling when laws of nature are thought of along these lines?

Well, in this different mode of thinking we cannot think, strictly speaking, about divine intervention – about God singly and immediately bringing about some event in the course of history. Instead of thinking in terms of agents bringing about events we are to think in terms of events necessitating other events. Thus, instead of thinking of God's immediately bringing about the event of the child's chanting *tolle lege* we must, let us say, think of the event of *God's resolving that the child would chant tolle lege* necessitating the event of *the child's chanting tolle lege*. But that done, then it becomes clear that there is nothing at all in this view which entails that that episode of event-necessitation could not have occurred, since there is nothing which entails that there couldnt be a law of nature grounding the fact that the former of those events necessitates the latter. And if it be said, in response, that though this view of law doesn't *by itself* tell us that, contemporary natural science understood as assuming and discovering such laws does tell us this, then all we have to do is first recast and then rehearse Alston's arguments.

But though the existence of laws of nature, thus understood, is entirely compatible with particular divine intervention, it is not compatible, surprisingly and ironically, with the view that laws of nature are all instituted by God. God, on this view, can act within the causal order but cannot bring the whole of it about. To see this, recall again that we are to think in terms of events necessitating events rather than in terms of agents exercising their causal powers. So take an example; say, the event of God's resolving that there should be a firmament necessitating the event of the firmament's coming into existence. Now if the latter of these events really is necessitated by the former, rather than just following upon it, that is on account of some law of nature. So might it be that God brought about that law of nature? Well, if so, that bringing-about must also be analyzed in terms of event-necessitation, perhaps like this: the event of God's resolving that there should be such-and-such a law of nature necessitated the event of the holding of that law of nature. But now we are off on an infinite regress, since this event-necessitation is also grounded in the existence of a law of nature. It's just a brute fact about actuality that there are certain laws of nature. Somewhere along the line, the fact that some event is necessitated by an event consisting of God's doing something must be grounded in the brute fact of the existence of a law of nature.

The upshot of our inquiry then is this: divine discourse of anything like the range and diversity claimed in the scriptures and traditions of Judaism, Christianity, and Islam, almost certainly requires direct intervention by God in the affairs of human history; and contemporary science provides us no good reason for thinking that such intervention does not occur.

## CHAPTER 8

# In defense of authorial-discourse interpretation: contra *Ricoeur*

We have been exploring the possibility that God speaks. It is time now to turn to issues of interpretation. When confronted with a purported case of divine discourse, how does one set about interpreting the phenomenon so as to find out what God said? Of course, Antony and Augustine didn't do anything that could be described as "setting about" interpreting. Though they interpreted, they didn't *set about* doing that. They just found themselves believing that God was then and there saying so-and-so to them – rather as we, when engaged in conversation, typically interpret what our conversational partners say without *setting about* doing so. We must not lose such cases from view; they occupy an important place in the whole picture of divine discourse. But in my discussion of interpretation, I propose focusing on cases in which we do *set about interpreting.*

I also propose focusing on the interpretation of *texts.* I have repeatedly called attention to the fact that the Judaic, the Christian, and the Islamic traditions all claim that the media of divine speech comprise much more than texts – indeed, much more than words, whether those be in the form of texts or not. God speaks by way of burning bushes, mystical experiences, national calamities – and centrally, so Christians claim, by the very presence among us of a certain person, Jesus of Nazareth. Nonetheless, the medium of the text has been seen as fundamental in all three of these religions. At the end of my discussion, when I move from hermeneutical to epistemological issues, I will once again widen my focus.

When it is appropriate to move from generalities to particularities, it will be on the text of *the Christian Bible* that I will focus my attention. I think that most of what I have to say applies straightforwardly to interpreting the Hebrew Bible for divine discourse, to interpreting the Koran for divine discourse, and so on. But since it is with the Christian Bible that I am most familiar, and with the tradition of its interpretation, it's best for me to refrain from generalizing over areas where I am relatively ignorant, and let those readers who know well one or the other of those other texts and traditions make the applications

Lastly, I shall focus my attention on that particular interpretative practice which assumes that the Christian Bible as a whole is a medium of divine discourse and then, when confronted with a particular passage, seeks to discern what God was saying by way of that passage from the whole. I know, of course, that in the modern world that particular interpretative practice is deeply contested – both *within* the Christian community and outside. Some of the alternative practices within the Christian community operate on the assumption that God does not speak. They assume, instead, that God *reveals* – in that mode which, in Chapter 2, I called the *manifestation* mode of revelation. Or they don't even assume that; they assume no more than that the Bible is one of the finest flowerings of the human religious imagination. Furthermore, not all of those who confess that God speaks would grant that the Christian Bible is a medium of God's discourse; Karl Barth would not grant that. *Paulus dixit, non deus dixit*, says Barth. So I recognize that that interpretative practice which reads and interprets the Christian Bible so as to discern what God was saying thereby is only one among many alternative, contested, practices. Though it was the dominant interpretative practice in the Christian community for about 1500 hundred years,[1] it is my impression that it has pretty much disappeared from the academic community and now puts in its appearance mainly in homiletical and devotional settings. My reason for nonetheless choosing to focus on it is this: those interpretative practices which assume that God does not speak are obviously not germane to our interests here. And from among those practices which do grant that God speaks, this one – call it the *traditional* practice – raises far and away the most interesting issues of interpretation. To this I may add that many of the objections commonly alleged against this practice seem to me to have little force; some of that will become evident in the course of our discussion. The practice is more viable than customarily supposed.

One more prefatory point: God speaks, so the Christian tradition has claimed, not only by way of *authoring* the Bible but also by way of *presenting* someone with a passage of the biblical text on a particular occasion; the Antony and Augustine cases fit that description. The assumption of my discussion has been that God might well speak both ways. But though I will make a remark or two about the interpretation of presentational discourse, my focus will be on the interpretation of authorial discourse.

We read texts for many reasons. When the participants in a liturgy together read aloud one of the Psalms, they are reading so as thereby to speak their own praise and penitence. When someone who knows well a sonnet of John Donne reads it once again, she ordinarily does so in order once again to delight in the words and the world of the poem. Without forgetting that diversity, I will focus my attention, in what follows, on a species of reading texts with the aim of finding out something.

Reading with the aim of finding out something is itself highly diverse; we read many different sorts of texts to find out many different sorts of things. But one of the things we all do, for at least some texts, is read to find out what the person who authored the text was saying thereby. We read to discover what I shall call the *authorial discourse* of the text. Suppose, for example, that I want to find out the population of China in 1980. Trusting the *Encyclopedia Britannica* on such matters, I turn to its article on China. Assuming that my trust is well placed in this case, I then find out the population of China in 1980 by finding out what the author of that article said it was – by finding out that element of the authorial discourse of that article. Reading to discover what God said by way of a sacred text is a special case of reading to discover authorial discourse.

Common though it is to read and interpret texts to discern authorial discourse, the practice has been the target of unremitting attack for more than fifty years – not just the practice of reading *sacred texts* to discern *divine* discourse, but the practice of reading *any* text to discern *any* authorial discourse. And rather than wearing itself out by more than half a century of punching, the attack has increased in fury in recent years. Evidently authorial-discourse interpretation is an extremely resilient opponent!

One recent line of attack, that of the deconstructionists, with Jacques Derrida as undisputed master, says that authorial-discourse interpretation, though it may be unavoidable for practical reasons in various situations, is nonetheless intellectually indefensible, since to think of speech or writing as an instrument of authorial discourse is to presuppose the discredited metaphysics of presence. The other, more moderate, line of attack, formulated with more profundity by Paul Ricoeur than anyone else, holds that though there is indeed the phenomenon of authorial discourse, nonetheless the goal of interpretation, when it comes to texts, must be to discover *the sense of the text.*

Ricoeur's attack on authorial-discourse interpretation of texts takes the form of arguing that it is *textual sense* interpretation that we must practice when dealing with texts – this even though the text originated as a medium of authorial discourse. Or at least, that must be our goal when confronted with texts of a certain very general sort of which the Bible is a paradigmatic example.

I propose discussing Ricoeur's argument in this chapter and Derrida's in the next. In addition to their obvious relevance to our investigation, what makes it worth discussing these attacks is that, for some time now, Ricoeur's approach to these matters has enjoyed wide influence among theologians and theologically inclined biblical scholars, and Derrida's approach is today rapidly gaining influence within those same circles.

Though my main aim in these chapters is to defend the integrity and legitimacy of authorial-discourse interpretation, I will, along the way, have occasion to make points that will prove indispensable to our own subsequent discussion. And perhaps I should say that, even though I won't here emphasize it, very many of the points made by Ricoeur and Derrida are ones that I agree with and also want to make. My response is not to be understood as unremittingly negative!

### *Ricoeur's account of discourse and sense*

Let me quote a brief passage or two from Ricoeur himself for an intimation of where he will be trying to take us. "With writing," says Ricoeur, "the verbal meaning of the text no longer coincides with the mental meaning or intention of the text. This intention is both fulfilled and abolished by the text, which is no longer the voice of someone present. The text is mute ... The text is like a musical score and the reader like the orchestra conductor who obeys the instructions of the notation."[2] The "text's career escapes the finite horizon lived by its author. What the text says now matters more than what the author meant to say, and every exegesis unfolds its procedures within the circumference of a meaning that has broken its moorings to the psychology of its author."[3]

Ricoeur's argument has two main components. First he offers an account of discourse in general. Then he draws a contrast between two sorts of situations in which discourse or its trace is the center of attention. One of those is the dialogic situation of face-to-face contact. Typical of that sort of situation is that the speaker says something which is addressed to someone, which is said about some objects in the situation, and which both expresses the speaker and incorporates references to him or her: something said, a person addressed, objects spoken about, speaker expressed and referred to. The contrasting situation is that of a person reading a text some time after its composition, in a place different from that of its composition, in the absence and unavailability of the author. The text, in this situation, is distanciated from addressee, referents, and speaker; and that, says Ricoeur, "entails a veritable upheaval in the relations between language and the world, as well as in the relation between language and the various subjectivities concerned (that of the author and that of the reader)" (HHS 147). "Hermeneutics begins where dialogue ends" (IT 32).

To get to Ricoeur's account of discourse, we must begin with a brief rehearsal of his account of language. Language (*langue*), says Ricoeur, "is the code – or the set of codes – on the basis of which a particular speaker produces *parole* [discourse] as a particular message" (IT 3). A language as such is a system which has "mere virtuality." It "does not exist. It only has a virtual existence" (IT 9). Discourse, by contrast, consists of events which, though transitory and perishing, are nonetheless real. Discourse "gives actuality to language"; "discourse grounds the very existence of language since only the discrete and each time unique acts of discourse actualize the code" (IT 9). And discourse actualizes the code by producing something which, though composed of words from the code, is not itself an element of the code, viz., a sentence. To the "unidimensional approach to language, for which signs are the only basic entities," says Ricoeur, "I want to oppose a two dimensional approach for which language relies on two irreducible entities, signs and sentences" (IT 6).

Our main concern here is with Ricoeur's account of discourse; but let me make a parenthetical remark or two about Ricoeur's ontology of language, since it differs from the ontology of language I am using in this discussion and is, to my mind, exceedingly implausible. Fundamental to my own ontology of language is the type/token distinction; Ricoeur, by distinguishing between the potentiality and the actuality of particulars, attempts to make do with only particulars in his ontology of language. His crucial move is to think of an event of uttering or inscribing a word as *actualizing* a possibility. But what exactly is that possibility? Suppose that I utter the word "sybaritic" at the end of a stretch of time during which no one was uttering or inscribing it. What then was the situation just before I uttered it? Did the word then not exist? Was there only the *possibility* that it would exist; and did my uttering it actualize that possibility? That interpretation is suggested by Ricoeur's words, it "does not exist." On this view, all the words that there are, are actual. Alternatively, did it exist all along, but in the mode of virtual or possible existence; and did my uttering it change its mode of existence, from virtual to actual? Does the realm of Being include possible words in addition to actual words? That interpretation is suggested by Ricoeur's words, it "has a virtual existence."

Either way, we confront the following question: when a word gets actualized by an event of uttering or inscribing, with which entity in that event is the word to be identified? Surely not with *the act* of uttering, nor with *the act* of inscribing;[4] rather, with the *content*, with *what is uttered* or *what is inscribed*. (Let it be noted, by the way, that though sounds are indeed transitory, characters typically endure; Ricoeur's claim that what endures in discourse is to be identified with meaning, will not do.)

Once we see clearly that words are to be identified with what is uttered or inscribed rather than with the act of uttering or inscribing, then we are confronted with the phenomenon which led Peirce to make his now-famous type/token distinction. Suppose I am asked to count the different words in the sentence preceding the present one; I can correctly answer either "43" or "37," depending on whether I count the two inscriptions of each of "we," "are," "or," and "the," and the three of "with" as, in each case, one word, or two or three. I find Peirce's account of this situation compelling: in each of these five cases we have multiple tokens of a single type; the question I was asked was ambiguous as between being asked to count word-tokens in a sentence-token, and word-types in a sentence-type. An adequate ontology of language requires acknowledging two different categories of entities, universals and particulars; we can't make do just with particulars, even if we postulate the being of merely possible particulars. And as to the conditions under which a word-type, say, "sybaritic," exists: surely it's not a condition of its existing at a certain time that there exists at that time a sounding out or an inscription of it; it is sufficient that people *remember* the word.

What happens in discourse of the most straight-forward sort is that we produce *word-tokens* of *word-types* – word-types being such that they can be repeatedly tokened, some of the tokens being perishing in character, some, enduring. We don't bring into fleeting existence what was before, and will be subsequently, only a possible particular; nor do we merely actualize a particular when before there was only the possibility of there being that particular.

But back to *discourse*. In addition to the linguistic code and sentences, there's discourse – all those perishing but real events in which, as Ricoeur sees it, the code gets actualized. Ricoeur insists, however, that within a discourse-event there's more than just what's transitory and perishing. If that were not so, "the ontological priority of discourse would be insignificant and without consequence" (IT 9). What's not merely transitory and vanishing is *what's said*. This "may be identified and reidentified as the same so that we may say it again or in other words. We may even say it in another language or translate it from one language into another. Through all these transformations it preserves an identity of its own which can be called the propositional content, the 'said as such'" (IT 9). And what is the propositional content of the discourse-event? It is, says Ricoeur, the *sense* of the sentence used in that event.

Ricoeur's appeal to *the sense* of the sentence(s) used in an event of discourse will prove to be a linch-pin in his argument. So let us take some time to get hold, as firmly as we can, of what he has in mind, beginning with the various things he says about sentential sense, and then asking what it might be, if anything, that all these things are true of. Already we have these two considerations: the sense of a sentence is something which can also be expressed by other distinct sentences; and the sense of a sentence is something which can be said. Add to these considerations that Ricoeur distinguishes, over and over, between *what is said* and *what it is said about* – between *sense* and *reference*, as he puts it. His view is that, though what is said is normally referred to something, that is not necessary: "the same sense, may or may not refer depending on the circumstances or situation of an act of discourse" (IT 20). Further, what is referred to, if something is, need not be the same from case to case. Thus a sense has its identity independently of whatever speakers may refer that sense to. Of the many passages in which Ricoeur speaks along these lines, one of the clearest is this: Another "pair of opposing features is the polarity ... between sense and reference. That is, discourse implies the possibility of distinguishing between *what* is said by the sentence as a whole and by the words which compose it on the one hand, and *that about which* something is said on the other. To speak is to say something about something ... I shall try to connect the problem of explanation to the dimension of 'sense' or the immanent pattern of discourse, and the problems of interpretation to the dimension of 'reference', understood as the power of discourse to apply itself to an extra-linguistic reality about which it says what it says" (HHS 167–68).

Another of Ricoeur's claims concerning sense is this: sentences – and let us recall that discourse requires sentences – sentences can each be analyzed into a logical subject (or subjects) and a logical predicate. Ricoeur would no doubt grant that the words uttered in some discourse-event need not constitute a complete sentence, and that that incompleteness might be such that the words do not display a logical subject/logical predicate structure; but he would contend that, in such a case, a sentence with that structure is "understood." Ricoeur thinks of subjects and predicates as the bearers of two distinct functions. The function of the subject, he says, is to "pick out" something singular; logical subjects have a singular identification function (IT 10). A predicate, by contrast, "designates" a universal (IT 11) and says something about what is picked out by the logical subject. Ricoeur speaks of the identification function and the predicative function as "intertwining" and "interplaying" so as to compose the "synthetic sense" of the sentence.

Though it follows from the above considerations that the intertwining of a certain identification function with a certain predicative function, so as to compose a sense, occurs independently of what speakers refer to in saying that sense, nonetheless "The speaker refers to something on the basis of, or through, the ideal structure of the sense. The sense, so to speak, is traversed by the referring intention of the speaker" (HHS 20). Thought "is directed through the sense towards different kinds of extralinguistic entities such as objects, states of affairs, things, facts, etc." (IT 34).

The sense of the sentence uttered, in addition to being what is said in a discourse-event, is also that toward which some illocutionary stance is taken up. The act of discourse, says Ricoeur, "is constituted by a hierarchy of subordinate acts distributed on three levels: (1) the level of the locutionary or propositional act, the act *of* saying; (2) the level of the illocutionary act (or force), what we do *in* saying; (3) the level of the perlocutionary act, what we do *by the fact that* we speak. If I tell you to close the door, I do three things. First, I relate the action predicate (to close) to two variables (you and the door): this is the act of saying. Second, I tell you this with the force of an order rather than a statement, wish or promise: this is the illocutionary act. Finally, I can provoke certain consequences . . . " (HHS 134–35).

Lastly, as to the ontological status of the sense of a sentence, it is, says Ricoeur, *ideal*. He explicitly allies himself at this point with Frege and Husserl. "For Frege and Husserl a 'meaning' ... is not an idea that somebody has in his mind. It is not a psychic content, but an ideal object which can be identified and reidentified by different individuals at different times as being one and the same. By ideality they meant that the meaning of a proposition is neither a physical nor a psychic reality" (IT 90).

These are the things Ricoeur says about the sense of a sentence, when that functions as what is uttered or inscribed in an event of discourse. But what, then, is the sense of a sentence, as Ricoeur understands that? What is he talking about? Let me make a proposal. The proposal goes beyond what Ricoeur explicitly says; but it fits with almost everything he says, and makes it intelligible. Essential to my making my proposal is that we first take note of the presence in our linguistic practice of two different criteria for *the identical thing* having been said in two distinct acts of discourse. The distinction will not only prove useful in exegeting Ricoeur, but indispensable for our discussion in subsequent lectures.

Suppose – to adapt an example from Richard Swinburne in his discussion of these same matters – that a Latin speaker of the fourteenth century assertively utters, "Regina mortua est," that a Dutch person of the late twentieth century assertively utters, "De koningin is dood," and that an English person of the late twentieth century assertively utters, "The queen is dead." Suppose further – what I think is true – that each of these sentences has just one meaning, and suppose that all three speakers spoke literally. It would then be correct to say that these speakers all said the same thing. Their thought was the same; and toward that thought they all took the same illocutionary stance, namely, assertion. We need some terminology here. Let us say that the *noematic content* of their illocutionary acts was the same.[5]

It will have been noticed that though what was said about something was the same in the three cases, what it was said about was not the same. The Dutch person was speaking of Queen Beatrix, the English, of Queen Elizabeth. That observation leads one to notice that we also operate with another and distinct criterion for identity and diversity of things said. Suppose I assertively utter at a certain time, "I have a cold." Suppose that my wife, addressing me, assertively utters at the same time, "You have a cold." And suppose that a third person with the same time in mind but speaking a day later assertively utters, "The Wilde Lecturer for 1993 had a cold." And let us suppose, here too, that each of these sentences has just one meaning; and that the speaker in each case speaks literally. Clearly the thought expressed (and asserted) is different in each of these cases; the noematic content of the illocutionary act differs from case to case. Yet it would be correct to say that all three speakers said the same thing, with the criterion for identity and diversity being whether the same property was predicated of the same thing as being possessed by it at the same time. Let me introduce some terminology here too. Let us say that the *designative content* of those three illocutionary acts was the same.[6]

Though the three expressions, "I," "you," and "the Wilde Lecturer for 1993" pick out or identify the same person in these last examples, they do so in three quite different ways; similarly, though the distinct tenses of "have" and "had" pick out the same time in the examples, they do so in different ways. The contrast with our first three examples is clear: there, though three different persons were picked out, they were identified in the same way; namely, as the present queen of the speaker's country. It is these differences that account for the fact that in the first case the noematic content was the same but the designative content different, whereas in the second case, the noematic content was different but the designative content, the same.

At times in our discussion it will be – and has already been – convenient not to distinguish between the noematic and designative content of speech actions. When that is the case, I will speak of *propositional* content.

When we interpret Ricoeur with this distinction between noematic and designative content in mind, it's clear that, in speaking of *sense*, he has his eye on *noematic* content rather than *designative* content; I shall henceforth so interpret him.

There remains one important question. My distinction between noematic and designative content is a distinction within the content of illocutionary acts, whereas Ricoeur's *senses* are also somehow "of" sentences: when a sentence is uttered or inscribed in some act of discourse, then the sense is not only identical with that toward which some illocutionary stance is taken up, but is also "of" the sentence used. So, what does that "of"-relation come to?

Let me again make a suggestion. In each of the six discourse events which I invited us to imagine, I specified that the person spoke literally. How shall we understand that? Well, let us assume that the well-formed sentences of a language *have meanings* – that they come with meanings. Then, if a person who uses the sentence speaks literally, the noematic content of what the person says is just what the sentence means – or in case the sentence has several meanings, the noematic content is one of the things the sentence means. That is to say, the thought expressed is one of the meanings of the sentence. The Dutch sentence, "De koningin is dood," means that the queen is dead; and if I speak literally when assertively uttering this sentence, then the noematic content of my discourse is the meaning of the sentence. In such a case, then, it is the meaning of the sentence in the language that is the *sense* of the sentence on this occasion of utterance.

But much of the time we don't speak literally; someone might well have spoken truth if, upon Margaret Thatcher's fall from power, he had assertively uttered the sentence, "The queen is dead." So what is the sense of the sentence on such an occasion of use? The clues as to how Ricoeur is thinking on this matter are not many; and those there are, are not very clear. My guess, though, is that Ricoeur is not only assuming that a *sentence per se* has a meaning (or meanings), but is also assuming that a *sentence in a particular linguistic context* has a meaning (or meanings) – taking *a linguistic context* to be that complex of other sentences which the speaker wants the sentence under consideration to be regarded as part of.[7] In the case of written discourse, the context will be a text. The meaning of a sentence in one such linguistic context will in general differ from its meaning in some other linguistic context, and may well differ from its meaning *per se*.

Whether this notion of *the meaning of a sentence in a particular linguistic context* is coherent, is an issue that must be postponed until a later chapter. Here let us just suppose that by the *sense* of a sentence used in some particular event of discourse, Ricoeur has in mind the meaning of that sentence in whatever be the relevant linguistic context on that occasion – the limiting case being that of a sentence constituting its own context. Fundamental to Ricoeur's thought is then the following thesis as to the connection between, on the one hand, the sense of a sentence, when that sentence occurs in some event of discourse, and, on the other hand, the noematic content of the illocutionary act which is an ingredient in that event of discourse: when someone performs some illocutionary act by uttering or inscribing some sentence, the noematic content of that illocutionary act is identical with the sense of the sentence on that occasion – this in turn being the meaning of that sentence in what is then its relevant linguistic context.[8]

## *Ricoeur's case against authorial-discourse interpretation*

With Ricoeur's account of discourse in hand, along with his concept of sentential (textual) sense, we are ready now to move on to his case against authorial-discourse interpretation, in favor of textual sense interpretation. Ricoeur conducts the argument by contrasting two sorts of situations in which interpretation takes place: situations of participating in face-to-face dialogue, and situations of reading texts produced at times and places distant from those at which we are reading them, by absent and inaccessible authors. Let me call these, respectively, the *dialogic utterance* situation and the *distanciated text* situation. Ricoeur argues that if we move from interpretation in dialogic utterance situations, to interpretation in distanciated text situations, a "veritable upheaval" takes place, an upheaval so drastic that we must be content, in distanciated text situations, with trying to discover the sense of the text.

Let me concede at once that Ricoeur does not himself describe what he is doing as contrasting those two *situations* in which we conduct interpretation. What he says, instead, is that he is contrasting inter-pretation of *utterance* with interpretation of *writing*. But as we shall see, interpretation of utterance does not in general differ from interpreta-tion of writing in the ways Ricoeur cites, whereas interpretation of utterance in the dialogue situation, and interpretation of writing in the distanciated situation, do so differ – or very nearly so. Furthermore, there are various "interlinear clues" to the effect that it is not really on the interpretation of utterance and writing as such that Ricoeur has his eye, even though he talks as if he does, but on the interpretation of utterance in dialogic situations and of writing in distanciated situations. So I propose departing from what he says he is doing and interpreting him in accord with what he appears to be "getting at."

Ricoeur will be arguing that interpretation in the distanciated text situation has to be fundamentally different in three ways from what it is, and can be, in the dialogic utterance situation; and that the upshot of those differences is that interpretation in the former situation has to be textual sense interpretation. He appears to regard the argument as a cumulative case argument; but it is the third, given my arrangement, that he quite clearly regards as the most weighty.

The first point of contrast is this: in the dialogic utterance situation, the discourser addresses someone; and the addressee has the chance to respond, in particular, to ask the discourser for assistance in interpreting what she said. By contrast, though a few of the texts we read in distanciated situations were addressed to us, most of them were not; indeed, for many of them we would be at a loss to pick out anyone at all to whom the writer addressed his text. If someone insists that he must have addressed it to someone, then often the best thing to say is that he addressed it to whoever might read it. But in any case, when reading a text in a distanciated situation, one cannot respond to the author; in particular, one cannot ask her for assistance in interpreting what she said. The author is alienated from the interpretative activity; inaccessible[9]

This difference, Ricoeur insists, is momentous in its consequences for interpretation. It is, he says, "one thing for discourse to be addressed to an interlocutor equally present to the discourse situation, and another to be addressed, as is the case in virtually every piece of writing, to whoever knows how to read. The narrowness of the dialogical relation explodes. Instead of being addressed to you, the second person, what is written is addressed to the audience that it creates itself ... The co-presence of subjects in dialogue ceases to be the model for every 'understanding'" (HHS 202–3).

> The writing-reading relation is thus not a particular case of the speaking-answering relation. It is not a relation of interlocution, not an instance of dialogue. It does not suffice to say that reading is a dialogue with the author through his work, for the relation of the reader to the book is of a completely different nature. Dialogue is an exchange of questions and answers; there is no exchange of this sort between the writer and the reader. The writer does not respond to the reader. Rather, the book divides the act of writing and the act of reading into two sides, between which there is no communication. The reader is absent from the act of writing; the writer is absent from the act of reading. The text thus produces a double eclipse of the reader and writer. It thereby replaces the relation of dialogue, which directly connects the voice of one to the hearing of the other. (HHS 146–47)

Incidentally, this passage is particularly apt for substantiating my claim that what Ricoeur "really" had in mind was not the contrast between interpretation of utterance and of writing as such, but the contrast between interpreting utterance in the dialogic situation, and interpreting writing in the distanciated situation. For here he explicitly cites interaction in a dialogic utterance situation, and reading a text in a situation where there is no communication with the author. If utterance and writing are not considered in these sorts of situations, the contrast disappears. For utterance does not only occur in the context of addressing someone who can respond by initiating a dialogue in which the discourser aids in the interpretation; witness the situation of a formal scientific address in which no one at all is really addressed, and no one is given an opportunity to respond. Conversely, witness a written correspondence between two persons, in which they address each other and ask each other what they meant.

Ricoeur regards all three points of contrast to which he will call attention as rooted in the enduringness of writing as opposed to the perishingness of utterance; he is fond of saying that discourse is "fixed" in writing. But we can already see that this too is not on target. For one thing, our technological ability to *record* utterance has the consequence that nowadays not only writing but also utterance must often be interpreted in situations temporally distanciated from the discourser; utterance can be made to endure as long as writing. And secondly, as will become particularly clear when we move on in a moment to discuss reference, it is not only the *temporal endurance* of texts but also the *spatial transportability* of texts which grounds the difficulties of interpretation to which Ricoeur calls attention. But our technological ability to broadcast utterance, as well as record it, has the consequence that we are forced to interpret even "live," non-recorded, utterance in situations spatially distanciated from the originating situation. Thus what Ricoeur attributes to writing is in fact equally true of recorded and broadcast utterance. Ricoeur conducts his discussion as if we were living in a pre-Edisonian age!

Let us move on to the second point of contrast which Ricoeur sees and emphasizes between interpreting utterance in the dialogic situation, and interpreting writing in the distanciated situation. In spoken dialogue, the speaker uses pronouns and indexicals to refer to a wide variety of spatio-temporal particulars which are present in the situation common to speaker and addressee, and discernible by both. The *here*'s and the *now*'s of the utterance refer to the times and places of the dialogue situation; the *I*'s and the *you*'s of the utterance refer to the participating members of the dialogue; and the *it*'s of the utterance, many of them, refer to objects in the situation. Furthermore, the speaker is able to supplement her verbal references by a variety of clarifying gestures.[10] But when texts are read in the absence of their authors, and at a distance of space and time from their origin, our way of finding out the referents has to be profoundly different. We the interpreters have to make do without any clarifying gestures from the author; and for all the *here*'s and *now*'s of the text, all the *there*'s and *then*'s, we have to go through complicated, albeit familiar, processes of making "allowances" if we are to determine the referents.[11] Determination of reference is profoundly altered by the distanciation.

Ricoeur has an additional point that he wants to make about texts and reference; but before moving on to that, it's worth noting that, once again, the contrasts to which he points are not grounded in the difference between utterance and writing as such, but in the difference between media of discourse which do not leave their originating situation, and media which do leave it, by temporally enduring, or spatially reaching, beyond it. If two people exchange notes in a certain situation rather than talking to each other, the *here*'s and *now*'s, *there*'s and *then*'s of their sentences function exactly as they would if they were talking; and they are as much able and entitled to supplement their writing with gestures as they are to supplement their talking. Conversely, the very same problems for determining reference which Ricoeur points to for writing, arise for utterance which is preserved for later times by recording, or utterance which is transported into distant places by recording and broadcasting.

But back to what Ricoeur has to say about texts and reference. We have heard him saying that there are large differences between how reference is accomplished and interpreted in dialogic utterance situations, and how reference is accomplished and interpreted in distanciated text situations. He goes on to argue that since the text has a sense independent of what the author referred to, it's quite possible to interpret texts without making any attempt at all to discern what the author referred to. The text "frees its reference from the limits of situational reference"(IT 36). Indeed, so Ricoeur argues, this is how "poetic" texts must be read – "poetic" is here a term of art covering religious, fictional, and poetic texts; for their authors, in composing them, were not referring to anything.

Ricoeur insists, however, that it would be a mistake to conclude from this that the sense of such a text is a self-contained entity. The sense of a "poetic" text reaches beyond itself, by way of projecting a way of being-in-the-world – or just a *world*, for short.[12] Most commentators on this part of Ricoeur's thought remark on the obscurity of the notion of *a world* to which he here appeals. What seems to me more obscure is his notion of *projection*: what is it for a sense to project a world? How must it be related to a world to project it? Does every sentential sense project a world? Does it just so happen that in dialogic situations we are typically more interested in the references that the discourser makes than in the world projected by the sense of his sentences? Or is it only the sense of a *text*, of a *writing*, that projects a world?[13] What then about a text of history? Do historical texts project worlds, and is it just a matter of interest on our part whether we will attend to the writer's references or ignore those and attend to the world that the sense of his text projects? Or is it only "poetic" texts that project worlds? In spite of the obscurities, Ricoeur clearly attaches great importance to this part of his theory; it is his way of superseding structuralism.

Let us move on to the third point of contrast Ricoeur draws between interpreting utterance in a dialogic situation, and interpreting writing in a distanciated situation. In the latter situation, as contrasted with the former, sentential sense has pulled loose from authorial intention, and authorial intention has become, if not inaccessible, then at least unimportant. This is what he says:

In discourse ... the sentence designates its speaker by diverse indicators of subjectivity and personality. In spoken discourse, this reference by discourse to the speaking subject presents a character of immediacy that we can explain in the following way. The subjective intention of the speaking subject and the meaning of the discourse overlap each other in such a way that it is the same thing to understand what the speaker means and what his discourse means. The ambiguity of the French expression *vouloir-dire*, the German *meinen*, and the English "to mean", attests to this overlapping. It is almost the same thing to ask "What do you mean?" and "What does that mean?" With written discourse, the author's intention and the meaning of the text cease to coincide. This dissociation of the verbal meaning of the text and the mental intention is what is really at stake in the inscription of discourse. Not that we can conceive of a text without an author; the tie between the speaker and the discourse is not abolished, but distended and complicated. The dissociation of the meaning and the intention is still an adventure of the reference of discourse to the speaking subject. But the text's career escapes the finite horizon lived by its author. What the text says now matters more than what the author meant to say, and every exegesis unfolds its procedures within the circumference of a meaning that has broken its moorings to the psychology of its author. (HHS 200–1; *cf.* IT 29–30)

What is Ricoeur getting at here? Is he just observing that sometimes a writer fails to achieve his intentions, in that the sense of the sentence which he writes down isn't identical with what he *intended* to say? If so, surely the same thing holds for speakers. Is he making a comparative claim, to the effect there are more slips between intent and pen than between intent and tongue? That's doubtful. But even if it were true, why would it be important?

Let me once again propose an interpretation which, though not compelled by what Ricoeur says, is consistent with it and makes sense of it. First, let's have some relevant passages before us.

> With writing, the verbal meaning of the text no longer coincides with the mental meaning or intention of the text. This intention is both fulfilled and abolished by the text, which is no longer the voice of someone present. The text is mute. (IT 75)

> [W]riting renders the text autonomous with respect to the intention of the author. What the text signifies no longer coincides with what the author meant; henceforth, textual meaning and psychological meaning have different destinies. (HHS 139)

> Inscription becomes synonymous with the semantic autonomy of the text, which results from the disconnection of the mental intention of the author from the verbal meaning of the text, of what the author meant and what the text means. The text's career escapes the finite horizon lived by its author. (IT 29–30)

> [T]he intended meaning of the text is not essentially the presumed intention of the author, the lived experience of the writer, but rather what the text means for whoever complies with its injunction. (HHS 161)

> [W]hat is "made our own" is not something mental, not the intention of another subject, nor some design supposedly hidden behind the text; rather, it is the projection of a world, the proposal of a mode of being-in-the-world which the text discloses in front of itself by means of its non-ostensive references. (HHS 192)

> What we make our own, what we appropriate for ourselves, is not an alien experience or a distant intention, but the horizon of a world towards which a work directs itself. The appropriation of the reference is no longer modelled on the fusion of consciousnesses, on empathy or sympathy. The emergence of the sense and the reference of a text in language is the coming to language of a world and not the recognition of another person. (HHS 178)

"Mental meaning," "psychological meaning," "mental intention," "lived experience," "something mental," "the intention of another subject," "some design," "alien experience," "distant intention." Ricoeur's thought begins to emerge. A discourse-event – and it makes absolutely no difference whether the sentence used be spoken or written – a discourse-event emerges from the mental life, from the "lived experience," of the discourser. At its *terminus ad quem*, that mental life includes such intentions as the intention to address someone, the intention to refer to various things, the intention to perform certain illocutionary and perlocutionary actions, and so on.

Ricoeur is strongly disinclined to say much about the lived experience, the mental life, from which discourse-events emerge; to discuss that in any detail would bring him too close to those Romantic hermeneuticists from whom he is struggling to break free (without falling entirely into the clutches of the structuralists). But there is one interesting passage in which he overcomes his disinclination and briefly develops the thought that discourse represents a dialectic of the private and the public. To each human being there is, he says, a "fundamental solitude." "[W]hat is experienced by one person cannot be transferred whole as such and such experience to someone else. My experience cannot directly become your experience. An event belonging to one stream of consciousness cannot be transferred as such into another stream of consciousness" (IT 15–16). But in addition to the "experience as experienced, as lived," which remains ineradicably private, there is "its sense, its meaning" (IT 16); this sense or meaning of an experience can go public by becoming the propositional (noematic) content of discourse, which is at the same time the sense of the sentence uttered or inscribed. This "going public" can be described from two different angles. Seen from one angle, it represents communication, or at least the *possibility* of communication. The sense or meaning of an experience transcends the experience; and the sense of a sentence, because it "is, so to speak, 'external' to the sentence ... can be transferred" from the speaker to listener or reader. Accordingly, when, in discourse, the sense of an experience coincides with the sense of a sentence, communication occurs, or at least becomes possible, and "the radical non-communicability of the lived experience as lived" is overcome (IT 16). Seen from the other angle, the "going public" of the sense of an experience represents the *expression* of that experience. "Language is the exteriorization thanks to which an impression is transcended and becomes an ex-pression, or, in other words, the transformation of the psychic into the noetic. Exteriorization and communicability are one and the same thing for they are nothing other than this elevation of a part of our life into the *logos* of discourse. There the solitude of life is for a moment, anyway, illuminated by the common light of discourse" (IT 19).

Here's the thought: it's typical of a person engaged in face-to-face dialogue with someone to want to come to know something of the lived experience, including then the intentions, from which the discourse-events emerge. Empathy is one of our goals in dialogue. The goal is a realistic one. For not only does "the speaking subject [present] a character of immediacy"; we can follow up our uncertainties with questions to the discourser. Naturally it's possible to engage in dialogue without any desire to enter the mental life of the discourser; it's possible to be concerned only with *what she said*. But typically these goals are so intertwined in dialogue that our question, "What do you mean?" can be, and should be, construed both ways.

Now consider reading a text in the absence of the author; and not only in the absence of the author, but when "the author is not available for questioning" (IT 30). Suppose, for example, that I am reading some text of Plato with philosophical interests in mind. Then I'm simply not interested in gaining acquaintance with the lived experience of Plato from which this text emerged; I'm not interested in "the psychology of the author" (IT 30). I do not have the aim of "coinciding with a foreign psyche." If I aim "to coincide with anything, it is not the inner life of another ego, but the disclosure of a possible way of looking at things, which is the genuine referential power of the text" (IT 92). I have no interest in treating the text as "the voice of someone present. The text is mute" (IT 75).[14]

### What happened to discourse in Ricoeur?

In summary: when we are interpreting texts in distanciated situations, the author is entirely absent from the interpretative process, ordinary reference, if it is present at all, must be determined in roundabout ways, and the mental life of the author from which the text emerged is unimportant if not inaccessible. The upshot, says Ricoeur, is that interpretation in such situations must aim at discerning the sense of the text. Interpretation in such situations must be textual sense interpretation.

Ricoeur began his line of argument with a clear-eyed recognition of discourse – that is, of the performance by agents of speech actions such as asserting something, promising something, commanding something, and so on. Texts, he said, are composed as media of discourse – with discourse itself the outcome of the mental life, including the intentions, of the agent. He went on to distinguish what is asserted from the asserting of it, what is promised from the promising of it, what is commanded from the commanding of it – calling what is asserted, promised, or commanded, the *propositional content* of the discourse; he propounded the thesis that the propositional (noematic) content of an act of discourse is identical with the sense of the sentence used; and that, he insists, is what interpretation at a distance must aim at.

Somewhere along the way, something strange has happened: discourse proper has disappeared, and all that remains in our luggage when we arrive at our destination is the sense of the text, on the one hand, and the mental life of the agent which gave rise to the text, on the other.[15] We are then asked to decide which of these to concern ourselves with, when interpreting texts at a distance. But why accept this disjunction? Why not practice authorial discourse interpretation? Why not interpret with the aim of discerning the authorial discourse of which the text is the medium – its illocutionary stance, its noematic content, its designative content? The event of discourse will have been motivated by the mental life of the discourser, and the sentences of the text will have meanings. But in addition to all that, the author will actually have performed certain speech actions by inscribing this text. Why not interpret to discern those? How could Ricoeur give central importance to authorial discourse in his philosophy of language, and then, in his theory of text interpretation, acknowledge only textual sense interpretation?

Possibly Ricoeur confused *the intention to perform* some speech action with *the intentional action of performing* that speech action – confused, for example, the intention to say that the cat has to be fed with the intentional action of saying that the cat has to be fed. A great many writers have confused these.[16] When they are confused, then to reject *intentions* to perform speech actions, as what interpretation attempts to discern, is perforce also to reject those *intentional actions* which are speech actions, as what interpretation attempts to discern.

Though this confusion may have played some role in Ricoeur's thought, I doubt that it was decisive. I suggest that mainly what accounts for Ricoeur's ignoring the option of authorial discourse interpretation of texts was his conviction that it's not really a distinct option. His assumption, never-quite-spoken, was that, for an interpreter of a text in a distanciated situation, everything of significance in the act of discourse, of which that text was the medium, has been lodged in, and is therefore recoverable from, the sense of the text which was composed. Though the act of discourse is indeed distinct from the sense of the text, that distinctness, to the interpreter at a distance, makes no difference.

So is that assumption on Ricoeur's part correct? One can spy

Ricoeur himself hesitating on two points. On the matter of illocutionary stance: one thing we try to discern, as we engage in authorial-discourse interpretation, is the illocutionary stance of that discourse. Is it, for example, a question that the writer was asking, or an assertion that he was making? Ricoeur doesn't really doubt that the discerning of illocutionary stance is a legitimate goal of interpretation at a distance. His hesitation is over whether one must exit the sense of the text to make that discernment. He insists that sentences carry determinants of illocutionary stance, and therefore clues thereto. But he also concedes that the determinants are by no means always all located there; typically some are found in various aspects of the non-linguistic context of the act of discourse. The mere sentences of a novel may well not reveal that it is fiction rather than biography one has in hand. But in so far as that is true, something in the act of discourse which is of significance for interpretation at a distance is not lodged in, and therefore is not recoverable from, the words of the text and their meanings.

Secondly, we saw earlier that often there is a *designative* content of discourse distinct from its noematic content, this determined in part by references which belong to the act of discourse. And often one of the goals of interpretation is discovering those references and that designative content – discovering what property the discourser predicated as belonging to what entity at what time. But reference is determined not just by the words one uses but by various features of the non-linguistic context of discourse; accordingly, to discover reference, and the designative content which reference helps to determine, we once again must exit the sense of the text and uncover the relevant non-linguistic features of the context of discourse.

Ricoeur's hesitation here is over whether the determination of reference is indeed a legitimate goal of the interpretation of texts at a distance. He argues that those acts of discourse performed by the composition of texts which are, in his terminology, "poetic" texts, do not include "ostensive" reference; the poet and the fictioneer, so he claims, do not refer, nor does the writer of a religious text. The text produced has a sense, and that sense projects a world; but the discourse of which the text is a medium is devoid of ostensive reference. And so, of course, there is no reference which interpretation at a distance could try to discern, and no designative content in the act of discourse. I have argued elsewhere that this assumption, that the discourse productive of "poetic" texts is devoid of reference, is mistaken.[17] Here let me simply remark that a great many texts are not, in Ricoeur's sense, "poetic" texts – texts of history and biography, for example. Though Ricoeur recognizes the point, strangely it does not deter him from his insistence that interpretation at a distance must be textual sense interpretation. In fact what is needed is authorial-discourse interpretation. In the case of non-"poetic" texts, there is something in the act of discourse which is of significance to the interpreter but is not lodged in, and hence is not recoverable from, the sense of the text – namely, the designative content and the references.

But what, lastly, about the noematic content of the discourse? Is Ricoeur at least right about that? Is noematic content determined by the sense of the text – that is, by the meanings of the sentences in their linguistic context – and hence recoverable from that?

No it is not. Imagine some act of discourse whose text consists entirely of a single sentence, say, "The bank is empty of people." This sentence is ambiguous; it has at least two meanings, in one of which "bank" means a financial institution of a certain sort, in the other of which it means a river's verge. But the noematic content of the act of discourse would normally be just one of those. From which it follows that the noematic content of the discourse is not recoverable from the sense of the text. The sentence, which in this case is the text, has too many meanings; information from elsewhere has to be introduced to figure out which of those is the noematic content of the discourse.

Or imagine a case in which some act of discourse is performed by using a single sentence non-literally. For example, someone saying something about the end of the Thatcher regime by assertively uttering, "The queen is dead." In such a case, the noematic content of the discourse is perforce not identical with the meaning of the sentence *per se*. But what leads us to infer that the sentence is being used non-literally is not facts about how it functions in its linguistic context, since it has none other than itself; but rather our knowledge that the speaker wouldn't have wanted to say what he would have to be reckoned as saying if he had been speaking literally.

It will be replied that what I have invited us to suppose is an impossibility; there are no sentences which lack a relevant linguistic context – alternatively described, no sentences whose relevant linguistic context is nothing but themselves. My answer is that my second argument didn't depend essentially on the sentence having no relevant linguistic context. It may, for example, have had a linguistic context which was just as hospitable to a literal interpretation as to the non-

literal interpretation which we adopted. What led us to discard the
literal interpretation was our knowledge that that was not what the
speaker wanted to say.

Obviously this places in question the whole notion of the meaning of
a sentence in a particular linguistic context. I see no good reason for
doubting that, given a certain language, the well-formed sentences *per
se* of that language have a meaning – or meanings. What is in question
is the notion of *the meaning of a sentence in a particular linguistic context*. In
other words, what is in question is the notion of *textual sense*, where that
is thought of as something other than the meanings of each of the
sentences *per se* of the text – thought of instead as the meaning of each
of the sentences in that linguistic context. But I will be discussing that
issue in a later chapter. Here it is enough to have seen that the *meaning*
of the sentence used in some act of discourse, coupled with the *linguistic
context* of the sentence on that occasion, is not enough to determine the
noematic content of that act of discourse.

Ricoeur's overarching goal in developing his theory of text interpretation was to avoid Romanticism on the one hand and structuralism
on the other: Romanticism, which says that the goal of interpretation is
to enter into the mental life of the author, structuralism, which says
that we are to treat the sense of a text as a self-contained entity. His
strategy for achieving this goal was to accept the structuralist's notion
of the sense of a text, but then to argue that it is mistaken to think of
such an entity as self-enclosed. A text's sense projects a way of being-in-
the-world. Ricoeur was right to look for a practice of interpretation
located in the space between Romanticism and structuralism. But what
occupies that space is not the practice of textual sense interpretation
but the practice of authorial-discourse interpretation – a specific
version of this being the practice of reading sacred texts to discern
divine discourse.

CHAPTER 9

# *In defense of authorial-discourse interpretation:*
# contra *Derrida*

Our scrutiny, in the last chapter, of Ricoeur's theory of interpretation, eventually revealed that his advocacy of textual sense interpretation, for interpreting texts at a distance, was not based, strictly speaking, on a rejection of authorial-discourse interpretation, but rather on the claim that to discover the sense of the text *just is* to discover the content and stance of the authorial-discourse; those have been fully incarnated in the sense. It was, strictly speaking, an argument against the *autonomy* of authorial-discourse interpretation. And my argument in response was that the content and stance of discourse cannot, in general, be inferred from the meaning of the sentences *per se* and their linguistic context. But if Ricoeur's attack was thus not truly radical, a truly radical attack on authorial-discourse interpretation is waiting in the wings; namely, that of Jacques Derrida. Derrida contends that authorial discourse interpretation is untenable because the very notion of authorial discourse is untenable. Not only is Derrida's attack thus more radical; for many readers today, it is also, more compelling. So if for no other reason than its massive appeal, we must consider what he has to say.

Let me say at the outset that it will be *authorial-discourse* interpretation that I will apply to Derrida's own text; I will try to find out *what he was saying* and then to state (some of that) in my own words. It might seem perverse to practice discourse interpretation on the texts of someone who attacks discourse interpretation. But clearly that's what Derrida himself wants us to practice on his texts, at least on those that I will be considering. Paradoxical as it may seem, he wants us to apply to his own texts that very mode of interpretation against which he launches a general attack; he wants us to interpret his texts for what he was saying and to get that right. Just one piece of evidence, from among many, is this passage: "I can be reproached for being insistent, even monotonous, but it is difficult for me to see how a concept of history as the

153

'history of meaning' can be attributed to me ... I find the expression rather comical ... Nor can I go through, line by line, all the propositions whose confusion, I must say, rather disconcerted me ..."[1] If we can arrive at the point of understanding why Derrida not only lives with, but embraces, the paradox mentioned, we will have understood a great deal of what he is up to.

### The mode of interpretation which Derrida attacks

We are confronted, says Derrida, with "two interpretations of interpretation." The one "seeks to decipher"; it holds out the "dream that by deciphering" it will discover something that "escapes play," something that escapes "the order of the sign," something that exists apart from signs and thus "lives the necessity of interpretation as an exile."[2] We can call that something "meaning." This view of interpretation assumes that "whether or not it is 'signified' or 'expressed,' whether or not it is 'interwoven' with a process of signification, 'meaning' is an intelligible or spiritual *ideality* which eventually can be united to the sensible aspect of a signifier that in itself it does not need. Its presence ... is conceivable outside this interweaving ..." Signification "would only bring meaning to light, translate it, transport it, communicate it, incarnate it, express it, etc ... The relationship between meaning and sign or between the signified and the signifier, then becomes one of *exteriority*: or better, as in Husserl, the latter becomes the exteriorization (*Äusserung*) or the expression (*Ausdruck*) of the former. Language is determined as expression – the expulsion of the intimacy of an inside ..." (P 31–32). And determined as "*communication*, which in effect implies a *transmission charged with making pass, from one subject to another, the identity of a signified* object, of a *meaning* or of a *concept* rightfully separable from the process of passage and from the signifying operation" (P 23–24).

This understanding of interpretation is the one Derrida attacks. As formulated, it fits Ricoeur's understanding of textual sense interpretation somewhat better than mine of authorial-discourse interpretation. So let me highlight what it is in authorial-discourse interpretation that Derrida will place under attack. I assumed that, for many illocutionary acts, one can distinguish between the *content* of the act and the illocutionary *action performed on* that content – asserting, wishing, commanding, and so forth. And I argued that we ought in turn to distinguish between two sorts of content: *noematic content* and *designative content.* I think it is pretty clear that what I call *noematic content* is what Derrida calls *meaning*. It will turn out that the disagreement between us pivots almost entirely on the status of meaning – or as I shall sometimes also call it, *thought* (using "thought" to refer to *what is thought* rather than to the thinking).

I have not contended that the noematic contents of illocutionary acts are entities capable of existing "on their own." For all I have said, and for all my theory requires, they may be nothing more than "respects" in which distinct acts of speech and mind are just like each other – rather as distinct color patches may be just like each other in respect to hue. What I have contended or assumed is that distinct mental and illocutionary acts of a given agent can have the same noematic content; that mental and illocutionary acts of different agents can also have the same noematic content; and that readers of texts can often find out the noematic content of the discourse of which the text is the medium – so that, in that sense, noematic content is "transferable" from one mind to another. I have assumed, furthermore, that something may be the noematic content of an agent's mental act before it is the content of an illocutionary act of that agent – one may, for example, believe something before asserting it. And I have assumed that a pair of illocutionary acts may have the same designative content but different noematic content – as when my wife, referring to me, assertively utters (speaking literally), "You are ill," and someone else, referring to me at the same time, assertively utters, "The Wilde Lecturer is ill." We can, if we wish, say that in such a case the same designative content is "conceived" differently. I have assumed, lastly, that the noematic and designative content are true or false; and that what makes them true or false is the facts of the matter – specifically, whether the facts are as the designative content represents them as being. So I assume facts – entities in relationship – in addition to illocutionary content. All these contentions and assumptions, Derrida contests.

### *Derrida's case against authorial-discourse interpretation: contra Metaphysics*

How does his attack go? Well, begin with some of what he says about his own alternative understanding of interpretation. This alternative "affirms play and tries to pass beyond man and humanism, the name of man being the name of that being who, throughout the history of metaphysics or of ontotheology ... has dreamed of full presence, the reassuring foundation, the origin and the end of play" (WD 292). The alternative assumes that meaning "must await being said or written in order to inhabit itself, and in order to become ... what it is: meaning ... [T]he notion of an Idea or 'interior design' as simply anterior to a work which would supposedly be the expression of it, is a prejudice ..." (WD 11).

Note the portentous words: "Metaphysics," "ontotheology," "presence," "foundation," "origin." The prominence in the mentality of the West of that understanding of interpretation which Derrida attacks is not, on his view, the consequence of some inadvertent error on the part of earlier theorists of interpretation which we, bright people of the late twentieth century, have spotted and can correct and be on our way. To the contrary; it goes hand in hand with metaphysics, with ontotheology, with what since Aristotle has been called "first philosophy": the science of Being as such and simultaneously of the Supreme Being. Metaphysics invites and is required by that view of writing which sees texts as devices for putting thoughts ("meanings") into words so as to communicate them from author to reader, and by that view of interpretation which takes as its goal the recovery of those thoughts from those words. The question, "How shall we interpret interpretation?" confronts us with the question of metaphysics.

Derrida is metaphysics' relentless, indefatigable, fight-to-the-death opponent; his brief against discourse interpretation is that it is metaphysical. In fact, all of Derrida's writing is the provocative, rhetorically brilliant, teasing out of the implications – or better, the "elective affinities" – of metaphysics and of the rejection of metaphysics. No matter what aspect of the traditional thought of the West one tugs at, Derrida finds metaphysics at the other end. Tug, for example, on the concept of a sign, or signifier. The concept of a *signifier* presupposes the concept of a *signified*; the concepts come paired and each can only be understood as a member of the pair. But

the maintenance of the rigorous distinction ... between the *signans* and the *signatum*, the equation of the *signatum* and the concept [i.e., that which is thought] inherently leaves open the possibility of thinking a *concept signified in and of itself*, a concept simply present for thought, independent of a relationship to language, that is of a relationship to a system of signifiers ... [It leaves open the possibility] of what I have proposed to call a "transcendental signified," which in and of itself, in its essence, would refer to no signifier, would exceed the chain of signs, and would no longer itself function as a signifier. (P 19–20)

The concept of "the sign, by its root and its implications, is in all its aspects metaphysical ..." (P 17).

So what does Derrida have in mind by "metaphysics"? The core of metaphysics, as he understands it, is the assumption of *presence*. Metaphysics represents "the determination of Being as *presence* in all senses of this word. It could be shown that all the names related to fundamentals, to principles, or to the center have always designated an invariable presence – *eidos, arche, telos, energeia, ousia* (essence, existence, substance, subject) *aletheia*, transcendentality, consciousness, God, man, and so forth" (WD 279–80). To put metaphysics into question is to put "into question the major determination of the meaning of Being as *presence*, the determination in which Heidegger recognized the destiny of philosophy" (P 7).

And what is *presence?* Let me say in advance of offering an answer that we are entering murky territory here. The main lines of Derrida's thought are clear enough; its details are far from that. I won't by any means attempt to dissipate all the murkiness; only enough for our purposes. And beyond a doubt the results of my attempt to spy what Derrida was getting at can be reasonably contested at various points. Presence, as Derrida understands is, has two dimensions: *self-presence* and *presence to consciousness*. But before I can explain what those are, we must take note of a fundamental presupposition of the affirmation of presence. Exposition will go somewhat more smoothly if we take note of it by noting its denial – that is, by noting what Derrida wants to affirm in opposition to metaphysics.

*Meaning*, claims Derrida, *is a creature of signification*. It does not exist anterior to signification. And even when brought into existence, it does not exist as something separate with a life of its own, transportable from one sentence into another, from one speaker to another, from one language to another. It does not exist except in and as meaningful signification. Meaning is not substantival but adjectival. "[T]he signified is inseparable from the signifier ... the signified and signifier are the two sides of one and the same production" (P 18). There is no possibility of "a transcendental signified ... every signified is also in the position of a signifier" (P 20). And, to cite again a passage already cited: meaning "must await being said or written in order to inhabit itself, and in order to become ... what it is: meaning ..." One of metaphysics' root errors is its denial that meaning is a creature of signification.

An assumption of my own theory, though there hasn't been any occasion to emphasize it, is that noematic content – thoughts, meanings, propositions – are to be distinguished from facts. Facts are the ways things are: entities in relationship. They are what make "meanings" true or false. Without facts, there is no world. Would Derrida accept this distinction? Is he talking only about *meanings* and not about *facts*? To the best of my knowledge, he never raises the issue in this form. But I think it's about as clear as anything in Derrida that the answer is No. There is no transcendental signified – that is, nothing transcendent to signification. There is no way things are independent of, and anterior to, signification. Which is not, perhaps, quite to say that there is *nothing* before signification. But there's nothing expressible in a 'that' clause; that's the point. "There is nothing outside the text" (OG 158).

And now for presence. Let us begin with self-presence. We can approach the point here in the same way Derrida himself sometimes does; namely, by recalling one of Ferdinand Saussure's doctrines concerning the sounds, the "phonic substance," of (natural) languages. Every language canonizes certain *differences* among sounds as linguistically significant (and others as linguistically insignificant); English, for example, canonizes as linguistically significant the ever-so-slight difference of sound between the 'e' of "merry" and the 'a' of "marry." Of course there have to be *bearers* of these differences for there to be these differences among sounds; there have to be sounds which sound different. Saussure is sometimes interpreted as if it were his doctrine that the "phonic substance" of a language is nothing else than canonized differences. But that's nonsense. There have to be "nodes" of difference.[3] Furthermore, it's equally true of the phonic substance of a language that it canonizes various *similarities* among sounds as linguistically significant (and others as linguistically insignificant). Confronted with the array of sounds that we human beings are capable of making with our vocal apparatus, and confronted with the discernible similarities and differences among those sounds, different languages carve out different units of linguistic significance.

Derrida's claim is that this is how it also is for concepts. Each concept occupies a place in the space of concepts; and that place is essential to it. A concept can't move to a different place in the conceptual space and retain its identity. It's not an accidental feature of the concept of a *signifier* that it comes paired with the concept of a *signified*. But that pairing is only the most obvious way in which occupation of that particular locus in the space of concepts which the concept of *sign* does occupy is essential to it.

Now recall the earlier dictum, that meaning (along with factuality) is a creature of signification. It follows, as Derrida sees it, that we must give up the assumption of metaphysics that things have self-presence; that they are what they are independently of how they are related to other things. At bottom, nothing is fully present *to us* because nothing is fully present *to itself* – fully self-present. Everything is a "trace" of what's absent. Essential to writing, for example, is the spacing between the letters in the sentences. "That spacing is the impossibility for an identity to be closed on itself, on the inside of its proper interiority or on its coincidence with itself. The irreducibility of spacing is the irreducibility of the other [and the impossibility of any identity without the other]" (P 94). Reality does not consist of an infinite array of Monads each exhibiting Plotinean independence. "The other is in the same . . ." (WD 296). "Being must always already be conceptualized" if we are to speak of it. This "must always already" "precisely signifies the original exile from the kingdom of Being, signifies exile as the conceptualization of Being, and signifies that Being never is, never shows *itself*, is never *present*, is never *now*, outside difference (in all the senses today required by this word). Whether he is Being or the master of beings, God himself is, and appears as what he is, within difference . . ." (WD 74).

So what exactly is it that Derrida wishes to affirm in all of this? I tender my answer with apprehension; but perhaps something like this: essential to every entity is that entity's bearing relations, within certain definite categories of relations, to entities distinct from itself. It is because of this feature of reality that to understand some entity we must always "go outside" that entity; it's never fully present. Everything is a "trace" of other things. Everything points to other things, "signifies" other things; everything is a signifier. The identity of the concept of *a signifier*, for example, incorporates various relations of that concept to the other, distinct concept of *a signified*. And the identity of one letter in the inscription of a sentence incorporates the relation of being spatially separated from the other distinct letters comprising that sentence. There's nothing which satisfies the classical medieval picture of God as bearing no true relations to anything outside Godself – not even God, if God there be.[4]

As a way of capturing this all-pervasive feature of reality (and its production) Derrida introduces the neologism *différance*, by which he means both *the different* and *the deferred*: *deferred difference*.

*Différance* is the systematic play of differences, of the traces of differences, of the *spacing* by means of which elements are related to each other . . . The activity or productivity connoted by the *a* of *différance* refers to the generative movement in the play of differences. The latter are neither fallen from the sky nor inscribed once and for all in a closed system, a static structure that a synchronic and taxonomic operation could exhaust. Differences are the effects of transformations. (P 27).

We have been discussing metaphysics' affirmation of *self-presence*, and what form Derrida's denial of self-presence takes. The other mode of presence which haunts metaphysical thought and language is *presence to consciousness*: "presence of the object, presence of meaning to consciousness, self-presence in so called living speech and in self-consciousness" (P 5). How, asks Derrida, could anything be present – fully present – to consciousness when always it is partly absent? When what is *here* is never more than a *trace* of what it is? "Experience itself and that which is most irreducible within experience: the passage and departure toward the other; the other itself as what is most irreducibly other within it: Others" (WD 83). Thus the absence of presence to consciousness is seen by Derrida as a consequence of the absence of self-presence.

One important aspect of metaphysics, as Derrida understands it, remains to be mentioned: the theology side of ontotheology. Derrida quite clearly understands it as a consequence of the preceding; but it deserves to be mentioned on its own. Before doing so, however, let me quote a passage, occurring in an interview from which I have already taken several citations, which is as good a brief statement of the points made thus far as any to be found in Derrida. The passage, as it stands, is a statement of Derrida's own *anti*-metaphysics; but from that it's clear what he takes metaphysics to be:

Nothing – no present and in-*different* being – thus precedes *différance* and spacing. There is no subject who is agent, author, and master of *différance*, who eventually and empirically would be overtaken by *différance*. Subjectivity – like objectivity – is an effect of *différance*, an effect inscribed in a system of *différance*. That is why the *a* of *différance* also recalls that spacing is temporization, the detour and postponement by means of which ... the relationship to the present, the reference to a present reality, to a *being* – are always *deferred*. Deferred by virtue of the very principle of difference which holds that an element functions and signifies, takes on or conveys meaning, only by referring to another past or future element in an economy of traces ... [T]he subject, and first of all the conscious and speaking subject, depends upon the system of differences and the movement of *différance* ... the subject is not present, nor above all present to itself before *différance* ... the subject is constituted only in being divided from itself ... in deferral ... At the point at which the concept of *différance* ... intervenes, all the conceptual oppositions of metaphysics ... – to the extent that they ultimately refer to the presence of something present (for example, in the form of the identity of the subject who is present for all his operations, present beneath every accident or event, self-present in its "living speech," in its enunciations, in the present objects and acts of its language, etc.) – become nonpertinent. They all amount, at one moment or another, to a subordination of the movement of *différance* in favor of the presence of a value or a *meaning*, supposedly antecedent to *différance*, more original than it, exceeding and governing it in the last analysis. This is still the presence of what we called ... the "transcendental signified." (P 28–29)

Suppose it to be true that meaning is a creature of language. Then the "theology" in "ontotheology" will have to go as well as the "ontology." In metaphysics we over and over come across the dream that "There is only one Book, and this same Book is distributed throughout all books"; that "there is only one book on earth, that is the law of the earth, the earth's true Bible. The difference between individual works is simply the difference between individual interpretations of one true and established text" (WD 9–10). If meaning is not anterior to signification but a creature of signification, of *our* signification, then there is no divine Book on which we are to model our books, no divine thoughts after which to think our thoughts. The God of Leibniz – indeed, the Jewish God – will have to go. "To write is to know that what has not yet been produced within literality has no other dwelling place, does not await us as prescription in some *topos ouranios*, or some divine understanding. Meaning must await being said or written in order to inhabit itself, and in order to become, by differing from itself, what it is: meaning" (WD 11). Or to look at it from the other direction: "[N]othing is more despairing, more destructive of our books than the Leibnizian Book" (WD 10).

God separated himself from himself in order to let us speak, in order to astonish and to interrogate us. He did so not by speaking but by keeping still, by letting silence interrupt his voice and his signs, by letting the Tables be broken ... Writing is, thus, originally hermetic and secondary. Our writing, certainly, but already His, which starts with the stifling of his voice and the dissimulation of his Face. This difference, this negativity in God is our freedom ..." (WD 67)

Our theology – if theology we would have – must be wrought in the struggle to think "the unpenetrated certainty that Being is a Grammar; and that the world is in all its parts a cryptogram to be constituted or reconstituted through poetic inscription or deciphering; that the book is original, that everything *belongs to the book* before being and in order to come into the world; that any thing can be born only by *approaching* the book, can die only by failing *in sight of* the book; and that always the impassible shore of the book is *first*" (WD 76–77).

This, then, is metaphysics. Derrida's case against authorial-discourse interpretation is that such interpretation presupposes metaphysics – and that metaphysics invites this interpretation.

### Metaphysics unavoidable

Yet Derrida does not draw the conclusion that we ought to put authorial-discourse interpretation behind us and conduct our interpretation exclusively in accord with his alternative understanding. As we saw earlier, he doesn't tell us to put it behind us even when interpreting his own writings! Because we can't put it behind us. And we can't put it behind us because we can't put metaphysics behind us. Several times over Julia Kristeva, in her published interview with Derrida, invited him to discuss strategies for "escaping metaphysics" and to describe the workings of language after the escape. Each time Derrida's answer was the same: "I do not believe, that someday it will be possible *simply* to escape metaphysics ..." (P 17).

This is one of the most persistent and striking themes in Derrida's writing: escape is not possible. It's not possible to conduct one's writing and one's interpreting, not much of it anyway, outside the language of ontotheology. Not possible *for us*, that is. One can speculatively imagine a human being escaping;[5] but *you and I* cannot escape. For metaphysics is not a special language, found in the books of certain philosophers, which one can write and speak for a while and then return to our customary ways of writing and speaking. Our customary ways are all metaphysical ways. Metaphysics is not "a regrettable and provisional accident of history," "a slip," "a mistake of thought occurring *within* history." Metaphysics "is the fall of thought into philosophy which gets history under way" (WD 27).

The case against metaphysics was itself conducted, and could only have been conducted, in the language of metaphysics; we have no other language in which to conduct it. "[E]verything that is exterior in relation to the book, everything that is negative as concerns the book, is produced *within the book*" (WD 76). We saw, for example, that the concept of a *sign* is implicated in metaphysics. "But we cannot do without the concept of the sign, for we cannot give up this metaphysical complicity without also giving up the critique we are directing against this complicity ... And what we are saying here about the sign can be extended to all the concepts and all the sentences of metaphysics [which are needed for the overturning of metaphysics] ... [T]hese concepts are not elements or atoms, and since they are taken from a syntax and a system, every particular borrowing brings along with it the whole of metaphysics" (WD 281).

Writing and speaking about writing and speaking as if they were devices for incarnating some "transcendentally signified" content or meaning in language so as to communicate it to others is error indeed. But fated error. The upshot of Derrida's line of thought is not that we should cease the practice of discourse interpretation but that, when we do practice it, as we sometimes should and must, we should recall that we are thereby implicated in systemic error. In that recalling, is our freedom. And let it be noted that the concepts of *truth* and *error* themselves belong to metaphysics!

Engagement in the practice of discourse interpretation is indeed fated. Derrida is right about that – though the fate is to be located in the requirements of human community and of respect rather than in the fact that we can't escape the language of metaphysics. Living together as human beings requires attending to what it is that our fellows are saying; likewise, respecting them *as persons* requires such attention. But though some interpretation must be discourse interpretation, not all need be; in particular, it's possible for a religious community to practice some other mode of interpretation on its sacred texts. That might amount to failure to accord due respect to God; but then, such failure is eminently possible. So our response to Derrida's case against discourse interpretation cannot consist just of noting his acknowledgment that we are fated to practice it, and then proceeding to the practice. We have to contest his claim that its practice is complicity in systemic error.

Complicity is conceded. Authorial-discourse interpretation is incompatible with Derrida's anti-metaphysics. That is not to say that holding the theory commits one to the entire scheme of metaphysics, as Derrida understands that. For example, we need not reject Derrida's claim that *différance* is a pervasive and necessary feature of how things are. Perhaps that claim is incompatible with the Hegelian picture of reality as pervaded by what he, Hegel, called *Aufhebung* – though I think the matter not quite so clear as Derrida often presents it as being. But even if reality cannot exhibit both *différance* and *Aufhebung*, all that follows is that *those who are Hegelians* will have to reject Derrida's claim.

The crucial issue is the thesis that nothing expressible in a "that" clause antedates or transcends the use of language signifying that so-and-so – no fact that so-and-so, no thought that so-and-so. Indeed, Derrida would not even concede the fundamental distinction with which we have been operating between *locutionary* acts and *illocutionary* acts. So how to proceed? We might consider a critical analysis of the case Derrida makes in favor of his thesis. But Derrida doesn't do anything that could be described as "making a case" in favor of his thesis. His reflections are all reflections conducted in the light of the prior conviction that meaning does not supersede language. We might, then, try the tack of noting the many points of self-referential incoherence in Derrida's line of thought. The incoherence, for example, of conceding that truth and falsehood are metaphysical concepts that have to go, while arguing that metaphysics has to go because it is false. Self-referentially incoherent arguments are bad arguments. But Derrida is there before us. He concedes the incoherences. But what he concludes from the presence of these incoherences is not that there is something wrong with the line of thought exhibiting them but that there is something fundamentally wrong with the metaphysical language which permits, even encourages, such a line of thought. We might, then, move on to try the *reductio ad absurdum* strategy. No thought that so-and-so, no fact that so-and-so, is prior, says Derrida, to someone's signifying that so-and-so. That implies, for example, that it was not the case, before we human beings signified that there were dinosaurs, *that there were dinosaurs*. But that's preposterous; we have it on eminently reputable science that dinosaurs roamed the earth for a long stretch of time before human beings appeared on the scene, not to mention, before they starting talking about dinosaurs. Only a few creation-scientists would deny that. Derrida's response would be, I take it, that if one is speaking the language of metaphysics, that is indeed the right thing to say. But there is something fundamentally amiss with the language of metaphysics. How could there possibly have been *the fact* that there were dinosaurs, prior to human beings signifying that there were dinosaurs – a *meaning* just floating around somewhere, waiting to be put into words? Unless there is God – Leibniz's God, but more fundamentally, the Jewish God.

I think we have to leave it there, at the point of a fundamental clash of intuitions. And a clash of something like emotions. Derrida speaks often of the *anguish* of the person who wants to write against metaphysics but finds that he has no other language in which to write against metaphysics than the language of metaphysics, and the even greater anguish of the person who tries, now and then, to write outside of metaphysics. The person who believes that meaning is not of signification born will contemplate such anguished thrashings about with *bemusement*. He sees in them confirmation of his own conviction that what the anti-metaphysician is struggling against is true.

### Metaphysics resisted: archi-writing

Let us return to the topic of our fatedness; for Derrida has additional things to say on that topic which will help to round out the picture of his thought and will also prove of use to us in our subsequent discussions. Metaphysics is ineluctable. Nevertheless, "we must not abandon ourselves to this language ..." "Emancipation from [it] must be attempted." Not by launching an escape attempt, "an *attempt* at emancipation from it"; for this is both "impossible unless we forget *our* history," and "would be meaningless." Worse, it would "deprive us of the light of meaning." Emancipation can only take the form of "the dream of emancipation" and of "resistance ... , as far as is possible" (wD 28).[6] *Resistance* and *the dream of emancipation*: those are the moves of Derrida, the anti-metaphysician, caught in the web of metaphysics, knowing that he cannot escape, but always struggling.

Resistance to metaphysics takes the form of "deconstructing" metaphysics: assembling whatever resources metaphysics provides for the purpose of showing to the satisfaction of metaphysics that some part of metaphysics cannot be true. This typically involves what Derrida calls a "double gesture" or "double movement": "an overturning deconstruction and a positively displacing, transgressive, deconstruction" (P 66). An overturning deconstruction starts with a "classical philosophical opposition," that of *signifier* and *signified*, for example, or that of *speaking* and *writing*. It then calls our attention to the fact that with such an opposition we are not dealing with "peaceful coexistence" but with a "violent hierarchy. One of the two terms governs the other (axiologically, logically, etc.) ..." Repression is at work.[7] For example, in the philosophical tradition, *the signified* has "the upper hand" over *the signifier*, for signifiers are said to exist for the purpose of presenting to us the signified. And *speaking* has "the upper hand" over *writing*, for in speech, so it is said, there is presence.[8] To deconstruct is "first of all," then, "to overturn the hierarchy" (P 41), to give the repressed element status. One's only resources for doing so are the resources of the language of metaphysics itself.

Derrida is of course famous for celebrating writing as opposed to speech; and probably there are some who take that to be the whole of what he wants to say on the topic. Derrida makes clear that it is not: "it has never been a question of opposing a graphocentrism to a logocentrism, nor, in general, any center to any other center ... It is not a question of returning to writing its rights, its superiority or its dignity" (P 12). After overturning the traditional hierarchy of speaking over writing, we must move on to introduce a concept which is neither the concept of speaking nor the concept of writing, nor an amalgam of those, but a new and non-metaphysical concept designed to fill the space in which that pair has been rotating. Sometimes Derrida calls this new concept by the old word, "writing." On other occasions, he uses one or another new name: *gram*, or *différance*,[9] or *archi-writing* (P 7–8). In the same way, after overturning the traditional hierarchy of signified over signifier, we introduce into that space of rotation a new and non-metaphysical concept of a sign whose relations of significance are not to some non-linguistic *signified* but to other signs: an "archi-sign." And so it is in general: after an overturning deconstruction we move on to a positively displacing deconstruction. In "the interval between inversion, which brings low what was high," there occurs "the irruptive emergence of a new 'concept,' a concept that can no longer be, and never could be, included in the previous regime" (P 42).

A new concept of writing – of archi-writing – for those who do not believe in metaphysics. To write, in this sense, "is not only to know that the Book does not exist and that forever there are books." "It is not only to have lost the theological certainty of seeing every page bind itself into the unique text of the truth ..." "It is also to be incapable of making meaning absolutely precede writing: it is thus to lower meaning while simultaneously elevating inscription. The eternal fraternity of theological optimism and of pessimism: nothing is more reassuring, but nothing is more despairing, more destructive of our books than the Leibnizian Book ... To write is to know that what has not yet been produced within literality has no other dwelling place ..." (WD 10–11).

[T]o write is to draw back. Not to retire into one's tent, in order to write, but to draw back from one's writing itself. To be grounded far from one's language, to emancipate it or lose one's hold on it, to let it make its way alone and unarmed. To leave speech. To be a poet is to know how to leave speech. To let it speak alone, which it can only do in its written form. *To leave* writing is to be there only in order to provide its passageway, to be the diaphanous element of its going forth: everything and nothing. For the work, the writer is at once everything and nothing. Like God. (WD 70)

Are there any examples or intimations of such writing? Is there somewhere a "dream of emancipation"? Or is the double gesture of the deconstruction of metaphysics all there is? The answer is that

Here or there we have discerned writing: a nonsymmetrical division designating on the one hand the closure of the book, and on the other the opening of the text. On the one hand the theological encyclopedia and, modeled upon it, the book of man. On the other a fabric of traces marking the disappearance of an exceeded God or of an erased man. The question of writing could be opened only if the book was closed. The joyous wandering of the *graphein* then became wandering without return. The opening into the text was adventure, expenditure without return. (WD 294)

Where have we discerned such writing? In certain modern literary texts. In "the poetic revolution of our century, [we see] the extraordinary reflection of man finally attempting today – and always in vain – to retake possession of his language (as if this were meaningful) by any means, through all routes, and to claim responsibility for it against a Father of Logos" (WD 73).[10] Here in this poetic revolution we get intimations of writing which "is not expression but creation"(WD 7), of writing which "runs the risk of being meaningless, and would be nothing without this risk" (WD 74), of writing which risks "meaning nothing" so as "to start to play" (P 14), of writing which "is *inaugural* . . . because of a certain absolute freedom of speech" (WD 12), of writing which "marks an irreducible and *generative* multiplicity" (WD 45), of writing in which the author finds himself "facing infinity, the white page" (WD 70), of writing which is "a book about nothing" (WD 8), of writing which "is a departure from the world toward a place which is neither a *non-place* nor an *other* world . . . , [writing which is] the creation of 'a universe to be added to the universe' " (WD 8), of writing which is "born as language" when "that which is written is *deceased* as a sign signal . . .; for then it says what is, thereby referring only to itself, a sign without signification, a game or pure functioning, since it ceased to be *utilized* as natural, biological, or technical information, or as the transition from one existent to another, from a signifier to a signified" (WD 12).[11]

No doubt what Derrida wants to call to our attention with this
flowering of different expressions is the existence, in modernist
poetry (and quasi-poetry), of texts whose writers did not compose
them *as instruments of discourse*. The writer of the text was not saying
something by composing it. Of course, that's the truth of the matter
for all texts, on Derrida's view. So what he means is that it would
be mistaken, *even in the language of metaphysics*, to describe these as
instruments of discourse. But what Derrida means by writing is more
than just that – though it is at least that. "Writing" – archi-writing –
is "the anguish of writing" of those who have rejected ontotheology
(WD 9). It is writing practiced in the face of menace; those who write
see that "language itself is menaced in its very life, helpless, adrift in
the threat of limitlessness," so that it has ceased "to be self-assured,
contained, and *guaranteed* by the infinite signified which seemed to
exceed it."[12]

One finds this same theme of "the death of the author" in other
writers of our day – most famously, in Michel Foucault and Roland
Barthes.[13] Mostly, though, the phenomenon to which they point, to
show that certain contemporary literary texts are not instruments of
discourse, is different from that which Derrida has in his sights. What
Derrida mainly has in view is highly metaphorical specimens of poetry
and quasi-poetry. What they tend to point to is texts of fiction in which
we find that structural feature whose standard analysis nowadays is that
the fiction as a whole has an implied narrator who is not to be
identified with the actual writer, this narrator being the one who speaks
the words of the text and performs illocutionary acts thereby. It should
be noted that it doesn't follow from this that the author was not
performing illocutionary acts by composing the text; at most what
follows is that he was not, in general, performing those that the implied
narrator performs. But Foucault and Barthes (along with almost all
other critics) overlook this point and conclude that such works are not
works of authorial discourse.[14]

I think it is pretty clear why Derrida is not inclined to cite such works
as illustrations of what he has in mind by writing: nothing at all about
such works requires that the author be one who is resisting metaphysics.
There isn't even any particular "elective affinity" between such works
and being opposed to ontotheology.

And now, at last, we come full circle, back to Derrida's alternative
"interpretation of interpretation." If a text was not composed as an
instrument of discourse, then of course one cannot practice discourse

interpretation on it.[15] On such texts, and especially on those among them which are examples of "writing," of archi-writing, what is called for is that other mode of interpretation which "affirms play and tries to pass beyond man and humanism, the name of man being the name of that being who, throughout the history of metaphysics or of on-totheology ... has dreamed of full presence, the reassuring foundation, the origin and the end of play" (WD 292). *Play*, because in the text to be interpreted there is "something missing ... a center which arrests and grounds the play of substitutions. One could say ... that this movement of play, permitted by the lack or absence of a center or origin, is the movement of *supplementarity*. One cannot determine the center and exhaust totalization because the sign which replaces the center, which supplements it, taking the center's place in its absence – this sign is added, occurs as a surplus, as a *supplement*. The movement of significa-tion adds something, which results in the fact that there is always more, but this addition is a floating one because it comes to perform a vicarious function, to supplement a lack on the part of the signified" (WD 289). "The birth of the reader must be at the cost of the death of the Author," says Barthes.[16]

Two interpretations of interpretation. I have not argued against the practice of Derrida's alternative. I have only rejected the imperialism of Derrida's rejection of authorial-discourse interpretation – rejected the repression and suppression indigenous to his line of thought, rejected his violence against authors. There are a few texts, and passages in a fair number of texts, which call for exactly Derrida's style of interpretation. One doesn't have to repudiate ontotheology to say that – though I will, in the next chapter, domesticate Derrida's alternative by arguing that it is only a special case of a much more general mode of interpretation which I will call *performance* interpreta-tion. The presuppositions of performance interpretation are coherent and tenable; no need to embrace Derridean ontology and episte-mology. And it constitutes a genuine alternative to discourse interpreta-tion, in that every text on which discourse interpretation can be practiced is also one on which performance interpretation can be practiced. So at the end we'll have to face up to this question: Why shouldn't a religious community – Jewish, Christian, or Muslim, for example – be content to practice performance interpretation on its sacred texts? What does it lose if it doesn't interpret for what the author was saying?

[T]he poet does not simply receive his speech and his law from God. Judaic heteronomy has no need of a poet's intercession. Poetry is to prophecy what the idol is to truth.

Between the fragments of the broken Tables the poem grows and the right to speech takes root ... The necessity of commentary, like poetic necessity, is the very form of exiled speech. In the beginning is hermeneutics. But the *shared* necessity of exegesis, the interpretive imperative, is interpreted differently by the rabbi and the poet. The difference between the horizon of the original text and exegetic writing makes the difference between the rabbi and the poet irreducible. Forever unable to reunite with each other, yet so close to each other, how could they ever regain the *realm*? The original opening of interpretation essentially signifies that there will always be rabbis and poets. And two interpretations of interpretation. (WD 67)

True indeed. But we know now that there aren't many poets – "poets," archi-poets. Aeschylus, Virgil, Chaucer, Dante, Milton, Shakespeare, Donne, Goethe, Dickinson, Eliot, Joyce, Rilke, none of them is a poet. Kafka? Probably not.

## CHAPTER 10

# Performance interpretation

Let us review where we are in our discussion of interpretation. I have defended the *legitimacy* of discourse interpretation against Derrida's attack, or more precisely, against Derrida's *rejection*, by observing that whereas Derrida argues that discourse interpretation rests on assumptions characteristic of what he calls "metaphysics," when it comes to metaphysics itself he doesn't argue but simply declares his rejection. And I have defended the *autonomy* of authorial-discourse interpretation against Ricoeur's attempt to assimilate it to textual sense interpretation.

## *Why there's no such thing as the sense of a text*

I want now to take this last point farther, and argue that there is no such thing as *the sense of a text*, as Ricoeur and those in the general tradition of New Criticism understand that. It follows that textual sense interpretation is not a viable mode of interpretation. That does not leave authorial-discourse interpretation to occupy the field of interpretation all by itself. There is another coherent and viable mode of interpretation – *performance interpretation*, I will call it. After showing the non-viability of textual sense interpretation, I will go on to explain this alternative mode; and then conclude by pointing out why it is not relevant to our purposes here.[1]

The sense of a text is understood to be a function of the meanings of the sentences comprising the text; so that, for a given text, if one knows the sentences comprising the text and the meanings of those sentences, one knows everything necessary to determining the sense of that text. Ricoeur speaks regularly of the "semantic autonomy" of the text. Secondly, the sense of a text is understood to be the sort of thing that can function as the *noematic* content of discourse, though not as the *designative* content, since the sense of a text is to be independent of what, if anything, singular terms in the text were used to refer to. And thirdly, the sense of a text is not to be identified with the totality of the meanings of the sentences comprising the text. The textual sense interpreter distinguishes between the meaning of a sentence *per se*, and the meaning of a sentence in some particular linguistic context. The *sense* of a text is that totality of meanings which the sentences comprising the text have in that linguistic context which is the text. Though the meanings of some of the sentences in context will be the meanings that those sentences have *per se* – those will be literal meanings – the meanings of many others will be metaphorical meanings, ironic meanings, and so on. Furthermore, many of the sentences comprising the text have multiple meanings *per se*, and some of those, in the context of the text, have only one of those (literal) meanings. The idea is that linguistic context both eliminates many ambiguities of literal meaning and forces and determines non-literal meaning.

I contend that it does nothing of the sort; and that, accordingly, this concept of *the sense of a text* is an incoherent concept. Or to put it differently: there is no such thing as the sense of a text.

The phenomenon of tropes makes this especially clear. Let's take an example. In the course of reading along in the text of John Locke we come across the sentence, "Reason is the candle of the Lord." By "the Lord," Locke had in mind *the Lord God*; so let us take the sentence as elliptical for this one: "Reason is the candle of the Lord God." It appears to me that this sentence *per se* is not ambiguous, and that its meaning is clear. It means that there is exactly one thing which is the candle of the Lord God and that thing is Reason.

Now whether we understand metaphor as a matter of meaning or of usage – I will discuss the issue in the next chapter – we all agree, I take it, that Locke must at this point be interpreted metaphorically. The textual sense theorist would put the point by saying that the meaning of this sentence in the context of the Lockean text is metaphorical.

But why so? Why not interpret the sentence literally? Because, so it will be said, the context prohibits a literal interpretation, forces a metaphorical interpretation. How so? Because, so it will be said, we cannot arrive at a consistent interpretation of the Lockean text as a whole if we interpret this sentence literally.

To this, these are two responses. Why *must* we come up with a consistent interpretation? Why can't texts have inconsistent senses? Why can't they have breaks and ruptures in their senses? But secondly, and more interestingly, what is it that makes it impossible to interpret this sentence literally and still arrive at a consistent sense for the totality of the text? Doing so would require the acknowledgement of tropes at quite unexpected places; sentences that one was first inclined to interpret literally would have to be given quite astonishing tropical interpretations. But why not? Why not interpret the whole in a consistent but wildly imaginative way?

Because, it will be said, it's patently false – perhaps *necesssarily* false – that there is exactly one thing which is the candle of the Lord God and that one thing is Reason. So what? we may ask in turn. Well, the sense of the text as a whole must be capable of functioning as the noematic content of someone's discourse. But why isn't the wild sense we have arrived at capable of functioning thus? Because one would have to be mad to say seriously that there is exactly one thing which is the candle of the Lord and that one thing is Reason, and insanely mad to affirm the totality of a sense which includes the literal meaning of this sentence. But some people *are* insane!

The point is now clear enough. If the only requirement for arriving at a sense of a text is that, given the meanings of the sentences *per se* and their position in the text, one arrives at a consistent meaning which can in principle function as the noematic content of someone's discourse, then no text has one sense, but all have a huge number of senses. There is no such thing as *the* sense of a text; textual sense interpretation, accordingly, is not a viable mode of interpretation. Textual sense interpretation assumes that every text has one sense – or, in recognition of ambiguities, a rather limited number of senses. That assumption is false.

The actual reason we don't interpret that sentence in the Lockean text literally is surely that Locke would have had to be mad to say that seriously, whereas we all know he wasn't mad. So that can't have been what he intended to say. In short, though we may profess to be engaged in textual sense interpretation, we all of us, surreptitiously or openly, engage in authorial-discourse interpretation.

## Performance interpretation

Let me begin my explanation of what I have in mind by *performance* interpretation with an example. It's the famous opening paragraph of Section One of Book Two of Kant's *Religion within the Limits of Reason Alone*. Kant is offering his interpretation of the Prologue to St. John's Gospel. The paragraph goes like this:

*Mankind* (rational earthly existence in general) *in its complete moral perfection* is that which alone can render a world the object of a divine decree and the end of creation. With such perfection as the prime condition, happiness is the direct consequence, according to the will of the Supreme Being. Man so conceived, alone pleasing to God, "is in Him through eternity"; the idea of him proceeds from God's very being; hence he is no created thing but His only-begotten Son, "the *Word* (the *Fiat!*) through which all other things are, and without which nothing is in existence that is made" (since for him, that is, for rational existence in the world, so far as he may be regarded in the light of his moral destiny, all things were made). "He is the brightness of His glory." "In him God loved the world," and only in him and through the adoption of his disposition can we hope "to become the sons of God"; etc.

It would be singularly implausible to construe Kant as here engaged in discourse interpretation. One would not get him to withdraw his interpretation by convincing him that his paragraph is not a statement of what the author of the Prologue was saying. In fact, not only was it not Kant's goal to find out, and then to state, what the author of the Prologue was saying; it's doubtful that it was his goal to find out anything at all. Not authorial discourse, not textual sense; nothing. That doesn't mean that Kant's interpretation is impervious to criticism; but it does force us to acknowledge that not all interpretation is a species of trying to find out something. But neither was Kant's interpretation just one move in a play of interpretations. Interpretation was for him not just an exercise of the imagination; he wanted, in some sense, to "get it right." In making these points I am assuming, of course, that in the paragraph quoted, Kant was in fact offering *an interpretation.*

It is sometimes said that what one does in such cases is "make sense" – or try to "make sense" of the text. And that way of speaking, as far as it goes, is quite acceptable. But it doesn't go very far. What is it to "make sense" of a text? What is one doing when one does that? In Kant's case there was already a way of making sense of the text available to him – that of the Christian tradition. Why did Kant want to "make sense" of it in a different way?

The strategy which I will use for illuminating what Kant was doing, and more generally, for explaining that form of interpretation which I am calling "performance interpretation," is this: I will take a certain activity which is familiar to us outside the field of text interpretation, I will highlight certain features of that activity, and then I will use that as a model for thinking about interpretation. Some readers will recognize that, on Mary Hesse's view, this sort of strategy is fundamental to the construction of natural science.[2]

A useful way to get at the activity I have in mind is to quote a passage from Ricoeur in which he alludes to the activity that I will be taking as model. The passage is couched almost entirely in the language of *finding out* – of finding out *the sense of the text*, for that is how Ricoeur understands interpretation. But in the middle of it another note is struck, a note from a different key, if you will. This is how the passage goes:

> The necessity of guessing the meaning of a text may be related to the kind of semantic autonomy that I ascribed to the textual meaning ... With writing, the verbal meaning of the text no longer coincides with the mental meaning or intention of the text ... there is a problem of interpretation not so much because of the incommunicability of the psychic experience of the author, but because of the very nature of the verbal intention of the text. The surpassing of the intention by the meaning signifies precisely that understanding takes place in a nonpsychologial and properly semantical space. The text is like a musical score and the reader like the orchestra conductor who obeys the instructions of the notation. If the objective meaning is something other than the subjective intention of the author, it may be construed in various ways. Misunderstanding is possible and even unavoidable. The problem of the correct understanding can no longer be solved by a simple return to the alleged situation of the author. The concept of guess has no other origin. To construe the meaning as the verbal meaning of the text is to make a guess. But as we shall see below, if there are no rules for making good guesses, there are methods for validating those guesses. (IT 75–76)

In the middle of all his talk about guessing the right answer, Ricoeur speaks of interpreting a text as like an orchestra conductor being guided by a musical score. He uses the same image in another essay: "Reading is like the execution of a musical score; it marks the realisation, the enactment, of the semantic possibilities of the text" (HHS 159). In neither essay does Ricoeur *develop* the suggestion that we ought to think of interpretation on the model of being guided in musical performance by a score; he simply inserts the suggestion into passages which speak pervasively of interpretation as a species of trying to find out something, as if the allusion somehow elucidated that understanding of interpretation. But the two ways of thinking are in conflict: being guided in musical performance by a score is not a case of trying to find out something – though it presupposes having done that.

A score is, among other things, a set of guidelines for producing a musical performance. And when the score is a score of a *musical work*

– as most scores produced in Western society over the past five or more centuries have been – then it is at the same time a specification of what constitutes a *correct* performance of the work.[3] Scores differ in how detailed are the instructions they give. Scores for classical music produced in the twentieth century tend to be much more detailed than those produced in earlier centuries; J. S. Bach did not even specify the instrumentation for his *Musical Offering*. But there are exceptions to the generalization; the instructions in some of John Cage's scores are very nearly as far from being "highly detailed" as instructions for musical performance can be. No matter how detailed, however, scores always come far short of specifying the resolution of all the issues that must be faced if the score is to be "realized." When the score is for a musical work, that fact has this consequence: performances which sound significantly different and are executed in significantly different ways may nonetheless all be correct performances of the same work. Of course, a musical performance need not be a *correct* performance of a work to be a performance of it; and when we compare *all* the performances of a work, incorrect along with correct, then the differences in sound and execution are even more striking.

The fact that a score's specifications are never sufficient for fully determining its realizations is what makes interpretation not only possible, but necessary. Interpretation occurs in the space between a score's specifications and its realizations; there is no other way to traverse that space than by interpretation.

Performers are not thrown entirely onto their own devices for interpretation. They are inducted into interpretative traditions, and sometimes affiliate themselves with traditions into which they were not themselves inducted. For if a score has been repeatedly realized over several centuries, it will almost always be the case that there are for it distinct performance traditions of interpretation. That is what made possible the fascinating dispute, over the last couple of decades, between those who advocated recovering the interpretation tradition of the Baroque era and performing Baroque music in accord with that, and those who defended continuing to perform it in accord with the late-Romantic tradition. On the other hand, imaginative performers sometimes emerge who depart significantly from all traditions in their realizations of certain scores; think of Glenn Gould performing Bach. And if one knows how some composer realized certain of his own scores – how Stravinsky conducted Stravinsky, how Messiaen performed Messiaen, etc. – then it's possible to model one's own realization of the score on the composer's.

Let us now use this activity, of interpreting a musical score so as to achieve a realization thereof, as a model for thinking about the sort of interpretation in which Kant was engaged. And notice that in normal usage we do regularly speak of both activities as "interpretation." What's given to the musician is a score; what's given to the reader is a text. The musician performs by producing sounds in accordance with the score's guidelines, filling in what is not specified with her interpretation, thus arriving at a realization of the score. What analogue might there be in interpretation to producing sounds in accordance with the score's guidelines? What analogue might there be to resolving by interpretation the issues not specified? What analogue might there be to a realization of the score? What analogue might there be to the boundaries outside of which performances of the work, no matter how good, are incorrect, and inside of which, no matter how bad, are correct?

We often speak of texts as *saying* things. It's easy to dismiss this as wrong-headed: "How can a text say something; only persons can say things." True enough. But on this occasion, rather than dismissing this as stupidly false, let us take this personification of the text – for if only persons can say things, then that's what this is – let us take this personification of the text as a clue. "The text of the Prologue says that *Mankind in its complete moral perfection is that which alone can render a world the object of a divine decree and the end of creation.*" Thus, Kant. I suggest that what Kant was doing was imagining what someone might say by inscribing the words of the Prologue, and then presenting to us some of the results of his imagining. The person Kant imagined was, of course, a person of Kantian conviction. The question he posed to himself which generated his interpretation was this: "What might someone who shared my convictions have said by inscribing the words of the Prologue?"

We sometimes respond to what we regard as far-fetched interpretations with the exclamation, "I can't imagine how anyone could possibly have meant that with those words!" Thereby we give voice to our recognition of the outer boundaries. If we can't imagine someone saying that with those words, then we won't accept that as an interpretation of them. Not, anyway, on our own authority; we may be so intimidated by Kant's brilliance and integrity that we accept that he has succeeded in this feat of imagination though we ourselves have

failed to duplicate it. It would help, though, if Kant gave us some hints
to get us started on imagining someone saying that with those words. In
realizing a score, our interpretations have to fall within the boundaries
of the pitches, rhythms, and so forth specified by the score. In
"realizing" a text, our interpretations have to fall within the boundaries
of the meanings of the sentences in the text, plus established tropic (and
indirect) usages of those,[4] in this way: we have to be able to imagine
someone saying that with those words. Of course, we may misread the
text at certain points, just as we may misread a score; or the copy of
text or score we have may be corrupted, or we may deliberately alter
text or score at certain points. Then one's realization is, strictly
speaking, of something other than the text or score.

The act of interpreting within the guidelines of the score finds its
fulfilment in a musical performance – understanding "performance"
here in both its senses, as the act of performing and as the sequence
of sounds produced by the act. Scores are "realized" in performances. What is a realization of a text? In what does the act of
interpreting within the guidelines of a text find its fulfilment? I think
it would be a mistake to think of that paragraph I quoted from
*Religion within the Limits of Reason Alone* as presenting to us Kant's
realization of the text of the Prologue – a counterpart, let us say, to
a musical performance by Alfred Brendel being one of his realizations of the score of the *Hammerklavier Sonata*. What Kant gives us
here is more like Brendel's giving one of his pupils some suggestions
for interpreting the *Hammerklavier*, it then remains for the student to
play the sonata, to realize the score.

A realization of a text comes about when we actually read the text
and imagine someone saying certain things with the words. Kant, in
the paragraph I quoted, makes suggestions for a realization of the
Prologue of John's Gospel. It's up to him and to us then actually to
realize the text by reading through it in such fashion as to imagine
sayings that accord with his suggestions. The counterparts of performers of scores are readers of texts, not critics offering us their
interpretations; the counterpart of actually performing the score is
reading through it and imagining things said with the words one reads.

I remarked earlier that we should not picture the situation in the
field of music as solitary musician sitting before isolated score trying to
decide how to realize it. Unless the score is not only new but strikingly
original, the musician, by virtue of her training, will have been
inducted into a way of realizing scores such as this, the way in question

usually not being idiosyncratic to the teacher but a way which is a tradition of a community. The musician may eventually react against certain aspects of the way into which she has been inducted. That reaction may take the form of realizing the work in a truly original way, or the form of imitating the composer's realizations, or the form of inducting herself into some tradition which is an alternative to the one into which she was inducted by her instructors. All of this makes possible a wide variety of distinct ways of evaluating realizations. "A very original interpretation of the *Goldberg Variations*; nonetheless, aesthetically inferior to the best of those that follow Baroque performance practices." "As good an example of the Romantic way of performing the *Messiah* as one will ever get; but lacking the urgency and pungency of some of the recent ones that recover the practices of Handel's own day." And so forth, on and on.

## *Why engage in performance interpretation?*

There are close analogues in the field of text interpretation. The late Yale theologian, Hans Frei, in one of his last essays, titled "The 'Literal Reading' of Biblical Narrative in the Christian Tradition: Does It Stretch or Will It Break?"[5] remarks at one point that "Established or 'plain' readings [of sacred texts] are warranted by their agreement with a religious community's rules for reading its sacred text" (McConnell 68). And he then points his reader to something that he said at the beginning of the essay: "I believe that the tradition of the *sensus literalis* is the closest one can come to a consensus reading of the Bible as the sacred text in the Christian church ... " (McConnell 37). What Frei is saying here is that there is a way of interpreting the Gospels which is traditional in the Christian church. In other passages in the essay he describes that way in some detail; here he simply alludes to it as "the tradition of the *sensus literalis*." If one's aim is to interpret the text of the gospels in accord with that tradition, it will not be sufficient, as a defense of some proposed interpretation, to say that one can imagine someone saying that with these words. That is minimally necessary, indeed. But one has to do more: one has to show that one's proposed interpretation is in accord with the community's rules for interpreting this text. Kant, of course, did not share the aim of which Frei speaks.

Frei goes on to describe what he sees as the appropriate way of defending the practice of interpreting these texts in accord with that tradition. The issue is whether the practice shows "continued viability.

That viability, if any, will follow excellently from the actual, fruitful use religious people continue to make of it in ways that enhance their own and other people's lives, without the obscurantist features so often and unhappily associated with it. And even if, as may be expected, there is a continuing decline of the felt pertinence of this way of reading among those who do not make a direct religious use of it, this in no way alters the case for its viability in principle to Christian people, no matter how distressing it is bound to be to them as an actual cultural fact" (37). These words seem to me wise and perceptive – and that in several ways. Naturally a particular interpretation of a text, and a whole way of interpreting a text, may operate on false and otherwise untenable assumptions; we should, accordingly, not play down the relevance of the work of critics to our decision as to whether ourselves to interpret a text in a certain way. Assuming, however, that the interpretation is not susceptible to that sort of objection, the decision has to be made by reference to the value of reading the text, of realizing it, in that way, in one's own life and the lives of others. The decision is to be made not by reference to arguments of theorists about such realizations, but by reference to the actual value of the actual realizations. The proof of the pudding which is the poem is the reading thereof.

Furthermore, given that we human beings live, and are committed to living, different kinds of lives, with different sensibilities, different convictions, different commitments, different tasks, a given realization of a given text will be of value to one person and not to another. If one doesn't share Kant's convictions about the moral life, then there won't be much value in reading the Prologue of St. John's Gospel in accord with Kant's suggestions. But if one does share those convictions, one might find it not only interesting but illuminating; one might find oneself seeing the same things in a new light. If one shares Frei's conviction that the Chalcedonian formula fits Jesus of Nazareth, then it's very likely that one will find it worthwhile to interpret the gospels in accord with the interpretive tradition which Frei calls "the tradition of the *sensus literalis*"; after all, the tradition developed among those who shared that conviction. But if one doesn't share that conviction – as Kant, for example, did not – then, depending on the details of one's alternative convictions, one might well find an interpretation which does not focus on the *sensus literalis* more valuable. Or one might conclude that none has any value for oneself.

These remarks pertain to how one defends one's realization of a text when it is performance interpretation in which one is engaged; if it counts as a realization of this text, then one defends it by reference to its value for this or that sort of person. I must emphasize that when it is discourse interpretation in which one is engaged, then one has to defend one's interpretations in a very different way. The issue then is whether one's conclusions are correct, whether they are true – whether the discourser did in fact, by authoring or presenting this text, say what one claims that he said.

As to the issue of whether, confronted with a text, to engage in discourse interpretation or in performance interpretation, that is not an issue of correctness and incorrectness but of value and disvalue. But once one has opted for discourse interpretation, then the issue is not whether one's interpretation is valuable in one way or another – exciting, original, imaginative, provocative, beneficial – but whether it is true.

I mentioned in the last chapter that that style of interpretation which Derrida regards as faithful to anti-metaphysics, the "play of interpretations" style of interpretation, is really a special case of performance interpretation. It's that special case in which the interpreter doesn't have any special sort of person in mind when imagining what someone might have said with these words but rather finds it fascinating to run through a number of different possibilities. The great desideratum is originality and creativity in interpretative imagination.

Why not content ourselves with performance interpretation, of Scripture and everything else? Well, what performance interpretation ignores, by its very nature, is the actual acts of discourse: my promising to do the grocery shopping, your inquiring after the cause of Beverly's death, St. John's testifying to what he had seen. Rather than trying to discern what the author was promising or asking or testifying to, by inscribing these sentences, we just imagine what someone might say with these sentences. Of course we might, if we wished, imagine someone very much like the author; we might even imagine someone *just like* the author – in which case the outcome of the two styles of interpretation is the same, with this big difference: The performance interpreter doesn't claim to have *found out* what the author said.

Now when it comes to fiction and mathematics, often not a great deal of value is lost by ignoring the discourse events. I read the novel and rather effortlessly arrive at a realization which I find fascinating. Perhaps if I worked hard in literature courses I could get at the details of what the writer was actually inviting me to imagine; and that might prove more fascinating than the realization at which I effortlessly arrived. But I run the risk that the extra fascination would not be sufficient to pay for the extra labor.[6] And as for mathematics: no doubt the mathematician who wrote this text has all sorts of insights which I don't have and which I would like to have; but if I follow the proofs he sets out, that's it.

Promising is different. Confronted with the words you wrote, it may be interesting for me to imagine what someone might promise with those words you wrote. But even more often, it's important for me to know *what you actually did promise me.* So too for asking. You may find it fascinating to imagine what a person of a certain sort might say with the words I penned. But often what matters to me is that you realize that by writing them, I was asking you something. So too for testifying. It may be fun to imagine what someone of a certain sort might say with these words of a witness. But often it's extremely important to us that we know what the writer was actually claiming that he saw happen. So I think we can see why we are so often content to practice performance interpretation on fiction, and why we don't often practice it on contracts, requests, and testimony.

The bearing of this point on my topic of inquiry in these lectures is obvious. If God said or is saying something by way of this text, it is presumably important for some or all of us to find out what that was or is; it's hard to imagine God engaging in small-talk. But if we confine ourselves to performance interpretation, we will miss that.

We must be careful, though, not to exclude the possibility that God would speak to us not only by way of authoring the text of Scripture but by way of our interpreting it, be our interpretation within a tradition, or original to the point of bizarre. Antony made no attempt to arrive at an accurate interpretation of what God had said by way of the text of Matthew; no consultation of commentaries. An interpretation just came into his head. If God spoke to him on that occasion, it was by way of that.

## CHAPTER II

# Interpreting the mediating human discourse: the first hermeneutic

Interpretation, on the expressionist view of discourse characteristic of the Romantics, traverses the process of discourse in reverse. Whereas speakers start from inner life and then form and implement a plan for producing externalizations expressive of that inner life, interpreters start from the externalizations and proceed by inference to the inner life of which those were, by intent, expressive.

It's an elegant picture; but misleading. The essence of discourse lies not in the relation of *expression* holding between inner life and outer signs, but in the relation of *counting as* holding between a generating act performed in a certain situation, and the speech act generated *by* that act performed in that situation. The goal of interpretation, correspondingly, is to discover what counts as what. The discourser takes up a normative stance in the public domain by way of performing some publicly perceptible action.

Nonetheless, the Romantics had their eye on something real. Typically there's something that the discourser wants to say, some speech action he wants to perform; his desire to do that may or may not be motivated by the desire to express some inner state. To perform that speech action, he has to causally bring about (or a deputy of his has to causally bring about) some action which will count-generate that speech action. In the case in which he speaks in his own name, he performs and then implements an action-plan; he causally brings about some action which he believes will count-generate the speech action on which he has his eye. If all goes well on both sides, the interpreter, in discerning what counts as what, will perforce discern the content of that implemented action plan; and typically the sequence of her discernment will reverse the sequence of its formation: the discourser started with a speech action he wanted to perform and then settled on an action he thought might count-generate it; the interpreter starts with that latter action and tries to discern what speech action might be

count-generated thereby. But everything may not go well, even on the
discourser's side. What he causally brings about may not count as what
he thought it would count as – not count as the speech action that he
intended to perform. Or it may count as quite a bit more than he had
in mind; and with that more, he may be less than happy.

We have established that authorial-discourse interpretation is, in
general, a legitimate mode of interpretation. So the question now
before us is this: how, on what I have called the *traditional* practice, do
we go about interpreting the Christian Bible for divine discourse?
Before we set out, though, let me call attention to a striking feature of
how the Bible is used in the Christian community: the Bible has not
been filed away. Christians keep on reading it, and doing other things
with it. Not just the novices in each generation, but those who have
read it from childhood up. The same is true for the Hebrew Bible in
Judaism and for the Koran in Islam.

Why is that? If it's an instrument of divine discourse, or alternatively,
a medium of divine revelation, why don't those who have discerned
what is thereby said or revealed move on to other things? Not move on
to things other than the *content* of the discourse or revelation; that's
eminently worth keeping in mind. But move on to other things than
the medium. Normally when something of importance is said or
revealed to us, we don't keep coming back to the instrument of
discourse or the medium of revelation; the instrument or medium has
done its work and we move on. Why this endless returning to the
Bible?

If one saw no way of improving on this way of saying what God said,
or on this way of communicating what God revealed, then of course it
would be important to keep on introducing new members of the
community to the Bible. But why do the old ones keep coming back?
And as to unimprovability: don't our pastors and Bible interpreters and
theologians in fact tacitly assume that the medium can be improved
on? Don't they assume that, all in all, the Bible's way of accomplishing
the discourse or communicating the revelation is rather difficult and
obscure, that, nonetheless, if one works at it one can see what is said
and can state it more clearly, and that they have in fact done this? But
if so, why not make do with the clarification wrested from the text?
Why endlessly return to the text from which the clarification was
wrested?

What seems to me the right answer to this question has two parts;
and it's especially the second part of the answer that we must keep in

mind, lest we inflate the significance of our inquiry. The first part is that the community assumes, by its practice, that no matter how successful prior interpretations, additional discernment is always possible; the activity of discerning the divine discourse is forever *incomplete*. It is that in two ways. For one thing, I cannot in general just assume that what God said to me in my situation, or to my group in our situation, by way of this text is exactly the same as what God said to other earlier readers and interpreters in their situations. But if there is indeed a rich diversity in the particularity of what God said to different people by way of authoring this text, then those different people have to try to discern that. Secondly, the fact that interpretation is forever incomplete is grounded in the subtlety of the text as well as in the diversity of what was said to whom. Sometimes we're stymied in our attempts at interpretation; often our interpretations get it wrong. The Bible is a rich and subtle letter from a friend of ours to a group of us. Over and over when we come back to it, whether as individuals or as a group, with the question in mind of what the friend was saying, we are rewarded with new insight. In part that is because each of us at a particular stage in our lives is cognitively privileged with respect to certain facets of reality and cognitively underprivileged with respect to others. If one has lived in luxury all one's life, certain aspects of the biblical text will almost certainly escape one's attention; if one has lived under oppression, certain aspects will jump out.

The other part of the answer is that the community assumes, by its practice, that the significance of the Bible goes beyond its being a instrument of divine discourse. The community assumes a surplus of significance for the Bible. For one thing, the words and the worlds projected prove worth contemplating in their own right; there is an art of biblical narrative, an art of biblical poetics, and fascinating resonances among the parts of the text and the worlds. Furthermore, the church down through the ages has found itself drawn to using the words of Scripture for its own discourse: it speaks its own praise and lament in the words of the psalms, it speaks its own blessings in the words of Paul, it speaks its own hopes in the words of Revelation. But thirdly, and perhaps most importantly, the church has wanted to be so formed by the very phrases and images of scripture, the narratives and songs, the preachments and visions, that it sees reality and imagines possibilities through those phrases and images, through those narratives and songs, through those preachments and visions. A poem is a piece of discourse; and a good poem is rich and subtle in the discourse of which it is the instrument. But a good poem is more than that, much more than that, more than a subtle instrument of rich discourse; it is discourse with a surplus of significance. It provides stuff for our meditation, offers words for our voice, gives form to our consciousness, shapes our interpretation of life and reality. After Shakespeare, many are those for whom the world's a stage and all the men and women, merely players.

### Opening assumptions

To get our inquiry going, we have to make some assumptions. First, that the books of the Bible did not come about by God directly producing inscriptions on parchment but by human beings doing so. Second, that by way of doing so, those human beings were themselves performing acts of discourse; they were not just writing words down. And third, that God's discourse is a function not just of those human acts of inscription but of *those human acts of discourse generated by those human acts of inscription.* To know what God was saying, we have to know more than just the Hebrew and Greek text; we have to know what was being said with those texts – what was being said with them by whatever human beings authorized them in their present form to count as *their* discourse.

And one more assumption: in our earlier discussion on the many modes of discourse, I distinguished two ways in which it may come about that one person's discourse counts as another person's discourse. One of those I called *deputation.* If one person is deputized to speak in the name of another, then the deputy's discourse counts as the other person's discourse. The other I called *appropriation.* If one person appropriates another's discourse by such words as "I agree with that" or "that speaks for me too" or "I second that," then the appropriated discourse counts as the appropriator's discourse. That particular practice of biblical interpretation on which I am focusing my attention, in these discussions on interpretation, is that practice which takes the Christian Bible as a whole to be an instrument of divine discourse; for the sake of convenience, I have called it, the *traditional* practice. In my discussion I am going to assume that, given the extraordinary diversity of the biblical text, the best model for those who engage in the traditional practice to use as they think about the way in which God is the author of scripture is the *appropriation model.*

There can be no doubt, of course, that within the totality of the appropriated discourse which constitutes the Bible, some of it is prophetic, and hence deputation, discourse – as is some of the discourse *reported by* the biblical writers. But it's not at all plausible to think of all of it as that – to think of the Psalms, for example, as prophetic discourse, or the book of Esther, or the Song of Songs. Of course it would be bizarre to think of God as just finding these books lying about and deciding to appropriate them; the appropriation model calls for supplementation with some doctrine of inspiration. But what's worth noting is that, on this way of thinking of the matter, a doctrine of inspiration really is a supplement. However these books came about, the crucial fact is that God appropriates that discourse in such a way that those speakings now mediate God's speaking.

Given these assumptions, how do we go about interpreting the text so as to discern God's discourse? Let me say, before I set out, that I have found Richard Swinburne's recent book, *Revelation*, extremely helpful in thinking about these matters – far and away the most helpful book around. The structure of my proposal will be different at many points from the structure Swinburne proposes – some of those differences, though by no means all of them, the consequence of the fact that Swinburne is discussing divine revelation whereas I am discussing divine discourse. But whatever the differences, Swinburne's discussion marks a signal contribution to our understanding of these issues.

### Beginning with the appropriated human discourse

If the goal of our interpretation is to discern the divine discourse mediated by the appropriated human discourse, we begin our interpretation by trying to discern that appropriated human discourse. We begin by trying to discern the noematic and designative content of the illocutionary act, and the illocutionary stance taken toward that content. If I appropriate someone else's discourse by saying some such words as, "Those are my sentiments as well," then the attempt to figure out what I was saying thereby must begin by figuring out the illocutionary stance and content of that discourse which I appropriated. When one person speaks by appropriating another person's discourse, then that appropriated discourse anchors everything. Possibly it was on this fact that Karl Barth had his eye when he argued that the freedom of God would be compromised if scripture were an instrument of divine discourse.

What follows is that the work of scholars who open up to us a better grasp of what the human authors of Scripture were saying is of indispensable importance for the discernment of divine discourse. This declaration will cause alarm in some quarters. It appears to place between the devout, unsophisticated reader of Scripture and the divine discourse of which that Scripture is the medium a mass of intimidating scholarship; he can't get from here to there without going through all that.

The alarm can be alleviated somewhat. A good deal of the scholarship I have in mind is not some looming intimidating barrier confronting the ordinary reader. It is almost invisible to him or her; it finds its manifestation in the flow of new and better modern language translations. Secondly, given the new translations, the ordinary reader can get the drift of many passages of Scripture without much in the way of additional help from scholars. And thirdly, I have spoken only about discerning the human discourse of Scripture; I have not spoken about discerning the divine discourse in the human discourse. Nonetheless, whether or not the principle evokes alarm, the "logic" of the situation makes it inescapable. And the practice of the church down through the ages makes clear that it has recognized this.

What should be added is that we are not talking here about all cases of God saying something by way of some part of the biblical text, but only about God saying something by way of *authoring* the biblical text as a whole, understanding that authoring as consisting in the appropriation of prior human discourse. To use terminology which I employed earlier: we are talking about the discernment of *authorial* discourse, rather than the discernment of *presentational* discourse. It may help to recall the example I used earlier of presentational discourse, viz., that which brought about the conversion of St. Antony. Antony, you will recall, happened to be present in church when the passage from St. Matthew about the rich young man was read. Upon hearing the words of Jesus as reported by Matthew, "If you wish to be perfect, go, sell your possessions, and give the money to the poor, and you will have treasure in heaven; then come, follow me," Antony found himself convinced that God had spoken to him then and there, telling him to give away his possessions.

Now suppose that on some later occasion Antony had undertaken to study with care this passage from St. Matthew and had concluded that Jesus was speaking metaphorically when he said "sell your possessions." Suppose further that Antony had been right in that conclusion. It seems to me about as clear as anything can be that he would not have been right, that Jesus was speaking literally. But let us suppose, for the sake of our example, that Jesus had been speaking metaphorically. Would it follow that God did not on that occasion say to Antony what Antony took God as saying to him? Alternatively, would it follow that Antony now had a reason for seriously reconsidering whether God had said that?

I think not. For Antony was presented with a case of divine presentational discourse, rather than divine authorial discourse. It doesn't really matter what Jesus meant by those words, nor what Matthew took Jesus as meaning. It was by way of that lector's *locutionary act* of uttering those words that God performed the *illocutionary act* of speaking to Antony. It was not divine discourse mediated by human *discourse*, but divine discourse mediated by human locution.

What is before us for consideration here, though, is not cases such as these of God *presenting* someone with some passage from Scripture, but the case of God *authoring* the Bible as a whole by appropriating all that human discourse which the human authors of the various parts of the text used their texts to perform. For this, interpreting the text for divine discourse must begin by interpreting the text for human discourse, trying to discern the illocutionary stance and content thereof.

How does someone do that? Since this is not a text on hermeneutics, I shall have to content myself with describing the main features of what seems to me the appropriate procedure – though even here, there will be plenty of points which are controversial.

### Discerning the noematic content of the appropriated discourse

A central part of the totality of what we want to discern is the *noematic* content of the discourse. To do that, we begin with the meanings of the sentences in whatever be the language in use. The anchor of the appropriating divine discourse is the human appropriated discourse; and one of the main anchors of the human discourse is the meanings of the sentences used.

I assume that the well-formed sentences of a language do have meanings. We, who are taught to use an extant language, don't have to do something to *give* a well-formed sentence a meaning; it *comes* with that. And if we don't already know that meaning, there are ways of finding out – though naturally our use of those ways doesn't always yield success. Let it be added that many sentences in any natural language have more than one meaning.

What about sentences containing proper names; do they have meanings? One sometimes hears philosophers arguing that sentences containing proper names don't have meanings because the proper names don't have meanings; and arguing for that, in turn, by claiming that one can't find the meaning of a proper name by looking it up in a dictionary. Now there might be other reasons for dictionaries not giving the meanings of proper names than that proper names don't have meanings; for this argument to be compelling, that possibility would have to be eliminated. But in fact the claim is mistaken. I open at random the dictionary I have at hand and find at the top of the right-hand column on the right-hand page this entry: "Narbonne: A town in southern France; pop. 32,000. Ancient Narbo Martius."

But "Narbonne," it may be said, is a very uncommon proper name; what about, say, the name "John"? Well, for this my dictionary has several entries, thirteen as a matter of fact – though for some of the thirteen, "John" is treated as part of a longer name, such as "John III" and "John Barleycorn." Pretty clearly the makers of this dictionary were thinking of the character-sequence J-o-h-n as the character sequence of many different words, each of those words having its own meaning; and the reason they don't give all those words with their meanings is that it would be impossible to do so. They content themselves with giving the meanings of those proper names whose bearers they judge to be most significant for their readers.

Possibly there was some naiveté in the thinking of those who composed the dictionary I have at hand; perhaps they had never read Mill, Frege, and Kripke on proper names. But then again, maybe they had; it may be that a good deal of informed and sophisticated thought had gone into their decision to handle proper names in this way. The proper analysis of the workings of proper names remains a highly controverted matter among philosophers; and one can imagine an intelligent line of thought eventuating in the practice adopted by those who composed the dictionary I have at hand. In any case, it will speed things up, and do no harm, if we do think of proper names as having meanings; and it won't much matter whether we think, as my dictionary makers were thinking, of a huge number of different names "John," each with its own meaning but all sharing the same character-sequence J-o-h-n, or if we think of there being just one proper name, "John," highly ambiguous as to meaning. Purely for the sake of convenience, I will think and speak in the latter way.

We want to get to the noematic content of the discourse. And we start, I said, with the meaning, or the meanings, of the sentences used. What do we do then? Suppose that each of the sentences used has just one meaning. Then we take the noematic content of the discourse to be the meaning of the sentence, unless we have good reason for doing otherwise. There are those – John Searle is an example – who would describe our practice in the following way: we take the *speaker's utterance meaning* to be the *sentence meaning*. I strongly prefer not talking about speaker's meaning, confining the word "meaning" to something that sentences have; and then talking about the noematic (and designative) content of the speaker's illocutionary act.

So once again: the base line from which we operate is that of reckoning people as having said what their sentences mean – in other words, reckoning them as having spoken literally, strictly and directly so. In the most fundamental sense of the words, that's what it is to speak in strict and direct literal fashion: to say what one's sentence means. We reckon people as speaking in strict and direct literal fashion unless we have good reason for not doing so. If someone performs an act of discourse by uttering the sentence "The bell is on the cat," then, since his sentence means that the bell is on the cat, we conclude that that's what he said, that that's the noematic content of his illocutionary act – unless we have good reason for not doing so.

What do we do if the sentence has several meanings? We consider the possibilities: the possibility that the noematic content of his discourse is meaning A of the sentence, the possibility that it is meaning B of the sentence, the possibility that it is meaning C of the sentence, and so on. And then, in the light of all we believe, we settle on that one which is the noematic content of the speech act that we judge to have the greatest likelihood of being the one that he intended to perform with this sentence. Unless, in the light of all we believe, we judge it unlikely that he intended to perform any speech act of which one of those sentential meanings is the noematic content. In the most straightforward case, the speaker *tells us* which meaning of the sentence is the relevant one, and does so with an unambiguous sentence.

The theme, of the interpreter forming judgments as to the speech actions that the discourser is likely and unlikely to have *intended* and *not intended* to perform, is going to turn up repeatedly in my discussion of how interpretation proceeds; let me postpone, until later, commenting on this theme as such.

Suppose we conclude that the discourser is not speaking literally in strict and direct fashion – that the noematic content of his discourse is not to be identified with any of the meanings of his sentence. What do we do then? We consider the possibility that he is speaking literally but not strictly – that he is speaking loosely. Especially we who are philosophers constantly make the judgment, as we interpret texts, that the writer was speaking loosely at a certain point; we do so on the basis of our judgment that the discourser didn't intend to say quite what his sentence means. Often it's clear to us what he wanted to say instead; so sometimes we count his inscription of the sentence as a loose way of saying that. Sometimes writers themselves tell us that they will be speaking loosely; to speak strictly would be too cumbersome, too infelicitous, or whatever.

Or we consider the possibility that the discourser is speaking literally but not directly – speaking with indirection. "Could you pass the salt" says someone at table. We know that he didn't want to say what that sentence means – that that was not his intention. In fact it's as clear as anything could be what speech action it is that he did want to perform. So we count his utterance of that sentence as a performance of that speech action. He has performed it indirectly, by indirection. Typically it's the wish to avoid bluntness, the desire to be circumspect, polite, coy, or sensitive to the addressee's feelings, that leads us to speak with indirection.

Or we consider the possibility that he was speaking non-literally – *tropically*, as I shall call it. It seems unlikely to us that he intended to say any of the things he would have to be reckoned as saying if he were speaking literally – be it strict or loose, be it direct or indirect. So we consider the possibility that he is using one or more words in the sentence as a trope – as metaphor, as hyperbole, as irony, as metonymy, as synecdoche, as personification, or whatever. With the various possible tropic uses in mind, and recalling our beliefs about his intentions, we run through such possibilities as occur to us, settling finally on that noematic content which the linguistic practice allows to be said in this tropic fashion, and which, of all the possibilities, he is most likely to have wanted to say – and wanted to say in this fashion.

It is no part of my aim here to develop an account of the workings of the various literary tropes. My aim is rather to describe the main lines of how interpretation proceeds, and then to single out for special attention one recurrent theme, that of what the discourser intended to say. But I should highlight one facet of how I am thinking of tropes. It will be easier if I formulate my point in terms of metaphors, though I mean the point to apply to all the tropes.[1]

I hold that literality and metaphoricity are a matter of *use* rather than of *meaning*. Thus I side with Searle and Davidson in my understanding of tropes, against the majority.[2] A well-formed sentence of a language has a meaning, or perhaps several. Not a literal meaning, not a metaphorical meaning, not an ironic meaning; just a meaning. Nor does a sentence have one meaning relative to one context and another meaning relative to another context – with perhaps one of those literal and the other, metaphorical. It always has just the meaning that it has *per se*. What differs from occasion to occasion is not the meaning of the sentence but the noematic content of what is said by using the sentence. We can *use* it literally, strictly and directly; we do so when, by uttering it in a certain circumstance, we perform an illocutionary act whose noematic content is the meaning (or one of the meanings) of the sentence. But we can also use it metaphorically. For me to use it metaphorically, it must have a meaning and I must know that meaning; the metaphoricity of my use inheres in a certain relationship between the meaning of the sentence and the noematic content of what I say. To explain that relationship is the central challenge which a theory of metaphor tries to meet and overcome. Such a theory, on my view, would take as its underlying framework, that sentences do not acquire metaphorical meanings but are put to metaphorical uses.

Some of those writers who see literality and metaphoricity as a matter of meanings rather than as a matter of uses, work out this view by attributing literal and metaphorical meanings to the *tokens* of sentences rather than to the sentences themselves. They hold that well-formed sentences – that is, sentence-types – have a meaning in the language; that, in addition, sentence-tokens have meanings; and that it is at the level of sentence-tokens that we can distinguish literal meaning, metaphorical meaning, ironic meaning, and so on. Richard Swinburne is an example. This is what he says in one place:

> a token sentence "I shut the sheep in the pen" could have a meaning other than the normal meaning of the type sentence: for example, in a fairy story about sheep being shut in a giant fountain-pen. Context (of paragraph, speaker, hearer, and environment) selects among the normal meanings of type sentences and may give to a token sentence a meaning other than a normal meaning. A token sentence must be presumed to have among its possible

meanings the one which makes it a natural thing to say in the context, if with all other meanings it is not. This may be because only so would it be relevant to the subject of the conversation; or because otherwise it would be obviously (to the speaker and hearer) false. If with two or more meanings the sentence is a natural thing to say in the context, whereas with all other meanings it is not, then it is ambiguous between interpretations with the former senses.[3]

The main question to be faced by someone who wishes to follow the strategy Swinburne adopts here, of attributing meanings of diverse types to sentence-tokens, is the question: what *is* a meaning of a sentence-token. We *come to* hermeneutical reflections with a concept of sentence meaning. The concept of sentence-token meaning, by contrast, is a philosopher's artifact. It would be easy to explain Swinburne's notion of the metaphorical meaning of sentence-tokens in terms of the conceptuality with which I am working. It would go thus: consider a case of someone performing some illocutionary act by inscribing some sentence which is such that the person used the sentence metaphorically; then the metaphorical meaning of the sentence-token produced by that action of inscribing is the noematic content of the illocutionary act. But Swinburne wouldn't accept this as *his* explanation of the concept of the metaphorical meaning of sentence-tokens, since he wants to make the notion of sentences and sentence-tokens expressing propositional (noematic) content basic, rather than parasitic on the notion of the noematic content of illocutionary acts.

What do we do if none of the above strategies works out? We conclude that some sort of malformation has taken place. That the speaker mis-spoke himself, absent-mindedly saying "Locke" when all the while he meant to say "Hume." Or that he was operating under some mis-apprehension: he thought he knew the meaning of "serendipity" when clearly he didn't; he kept on referring to the man in the corner as the man drinking the martini when in fact the man was drinking Perrier. Or that he really didn't succeed in saying anything – didn't succeed in performing any illocutionary act.

In the outline I have offered of the strategy we follow for interpreting human discourse, I have several times claimed the decisive relevance of the interpreter's beliefs concerning the illocutionary actions that the discourser was likely and not likely to have wanted and not wanted to perform with that locutionary act in that situation. Appeals to authorial intention have received such a bad press in our century that most readers will probably boggle at this point. So let me take a moment to reflect on the matter further.

John Searle, in his discussion of metaphor, suggests that to arrive at a metaphorical interpretation of some remark, one must apply in succession three strategies. The first is the one of concern to me here. Searle describes it thus: the interpreter "must have some strategy for determining whether or not he has to seek a metaphorical interpretation of the utterance in the first place" (114). Searle's description of this strategy is then as follows:

Suppose [the interpreter] hears the utterance, "Sam is a pig." He knows that that cannot be literally true, that the utterance, if he tries to take it literally, is radically defective. And, indeed, such defectiveness is a feature of nearly all of the examples that we have considered so far. The defects which cue the hearer may be obvious falsehood, semantic nonsense, violations of the rules of speech acts, or violations of conversational principles of communication. This suggests a strategy that underlies the first step: *Where the utterance is defective if taken literally, look for an utterance meaning that differs from sentence meaning.* (114)

Searle adds that "This is not the only strategy on which a hearer can tell that an utterance probably has a metaphorical meaning, but it is by far the most common ... But it is certainly not a necessary condition of a metaphorical utterance that it be in any way defective if construed literally. Disraeli might have said metaphorically, 'I have climbed to the top of the greasy pole,' though he had in fact climbed to the top of a greasy pole."[4]

But surely this cannot be right, as it stands. People all the time do actually say things that hearers or readers judge to be defective, seriously defective: patent falsehoods, irrelevant comments, points that scarcely need to be made, and so forth. Surely the reason that the patent falsehood, the irrelevant comment, the point that scarcely needs to be made, prods us into looking for some interpretation other than the strict and direct literal, is that we believe that the strict and direct literal interpretation gives us something that he would not have wanted to say – would not have *intended* to say – on this occasion in this way. Our basis for that judgment may be very direct; the speaker may announce that he is not speaking literally. But usually we have to make inferences from whatever knowledge is available to us. Searle's last example, about Disraeli, makes the point especially clearly. The reason we would take Disraeli's remark to be a metaphorical comment about his rise to the Prime Ministership is our conviction that he wouldn't have intended on this occasion to say that there was a greasy pole to whose top he had managed to climb – even if there was such a pole.

Or consider part of the passage already quoted from Swinburne:

"A token sentence must be presumed to have among its possible meanings the one which makes it a natural thing to say in the context, if with all other meanings it is not. This may be because only so would it be relevant to the subject of the conversation; or because otherwise it would be obviously (to the speaker and hearer) false." We look, says Swinburne, for an interpretation of the person's remark which makes it "a natural thing to say in the context"; and the irrelevance or obvious falsehood of the remark as interpreted literally prods us into looking for some other than literal interpretation. As Swinburne recognizes, the issue is not what would be natural for *me* to say in the context, but what would be natural *for the person speaking* to say in the context. But "what would be natural to say" has to be parsed as meaning: what that person would be likely to have intended and not intended to say, in this way on this occasion. Whether or not his remark is natural or unnatural in some other sense, or whether he thinks it is, is not relevant. In some sense of "natural," *asserting that P* may be a very unnatural thing for him to say and he may realize that it is. Yet we may recognize that that is exactly what he intended to say with those words; and that if we construe them metaphorically, that's exactly what we interpret him as saying. That, then, is the relevant consideration.

It follows that interpreters cannot operate without beliefs about the discourser; specifically, beliefs as to the relative probability of the discourser intending and not intending to say one thing and another. If I have no beliefs as to what you're likely and unlikely be intending to say, then I must refrain from interpreting your utterances. But no matter who you are, I will have such beliefs; for you are a human being. Sometimes beliefs of such generality won't get me very far, however. Then I may have to concede that, even though I understand the language you are using, I can't figure out what you said.

Where do we get our beliefs as to what some speaker is likely and unlikely to have intended and not intended to say? Some of them we bring with us to the particular episode of discourse which we are interpreting. "Given what I have long known about Victor, it's most implausible to suppose that he intended to say, with those words, that his father was a liar." Others are beliefs concerning what is true of the speaker in the context of his discourse; they are, then, acquired from our knowledge of that. Partly the linguistic context consisting of other things the person has recently said: "Given that Victor had already said that the car was out of gas, it's not very plausible to suppose that, in saying what he did, he intended to ask her to start up the motor." In the case of texts, the *genre* of the text is often an important clue. But also, features of the non-linguistic context: "Given that she was standing right in front of him, it's implausible to suppose that in saying what he did, it was his intention to ask where she was."

## The role of authorial intention

These reflections, about the role of judgments concerning the discourser's intentions in the process of interpretation, induce the following perplexity: if it is our aim to discern the illocutionary actions which the discourser *did* perform, why bother with what he *intended* to perform? Haven't we inadvertently slid back into the confusion between *intending to perform* some action, on the one hand, and, on the other, *intentionally performing* some action, or performing some *intentional action*? If I want to know, say, whether Amy set on the tea water, I don't ask whether she *intended* to set on the tea water, but whether she did in fact perform the intentional action of setting on the tea water. Why isn't the same true here, when we are dealing with speech actions? If discoursing is, as I have argued, the acquisition of a normative standing in the public domain by the performance of an action which is itself publicly perceptible, how could the discourser's *intention* to acquire such-and-such a normative standing be relevant to our determination of what normative standing, if any, he *did* acquire? Is there not, perhaps, something deeply askew in the whole conceptuality we have developed?

I think the resolution of this perplexity goes along the following lines: the person who is discoursing by using a certain natural language is operating a certain *system* for saying things. If that system were such that every well-formed sentence of the language had just one meaning, were such that no discrepancy was allowed between the noematic content of one's illocutionary act and the meaning of the sentence one used, and were such that the only relevant feature of the generating act was the inscribing or uttering of a sentence, then appeals to what the author intended to say would have no place in the process of interpreting what he did say; if he intended to say *that p*, whereas the meaning of the sentence he used is *that r*, then if he said anything, he said *that r*, and that's the end of the matter.[5]

But that's exactly how our natural languages *do not* work. Many well-formed sentences have multiple meanings; and in addition, to learn to use the language is to learn to use sentences in other ways than literally.

It's as if the user of a natural language had before him a vast board on which the well-formed sentences of the language are all arrayed. From each sentence, various paths go out: from sentence S, the path which consists of using S (directly and strictly) literally with meaning M, the path which consists of using S (directly and strictly) literally with meaning N, the path which consists of using S indirectly literally with meaning M, the path which consists of using S with meaning M metaphorically, and so forth. Whenever a person wishes to use the language to say something (and doesn't want to speak ambiguously), he must not only select a sentence but must also select a path leading from that sentence. Sometimes he has options: a variety of different combinations of sentences and paths will give him the noematic content that he wants.

Each of the paths going out from a sentence has a gate at the entrance. Once the person utters a sentence and selects a meaning thereof, one gate will automatically open – viz., the gate leading to the (strict and direct) literal usage of that sentence with that meaning. The exception is that some genres are such that if he is discoursing in that genre, then one of the non-literal gates is the one that automatically opens up. So if that's not the path he wants, he must close that automatically opened gate and open another.

Now you and I, to discern what he said, must not only know what sentence he used, along with various features of the context of utterance, but must also know what gate he opened (or left opened) to a path leading from the sentence he uttered or inscribed. Sometimes he will tell us. He will explain in which sense he is using the word "bear," he will state that now he is speaking literally. But he can't make such explanations for everything; in particular, he can't *keep on* making them for his explanations. So we operate with two general presumptions, and the speaker knows that we do: we presume that he is speaking literally – and then directly so, with more or less strictness. Or for certain distinct genres of discourse, we presume that he is discoursing in accord with the conventions of that genre. We continue in these presumptions until something turns up to disturb the presumption – something which makes us suspect, for a certain sentence, that the speaker closed the gate which was automatically open and opened up another. Then we do our best to infer which gate he opened up instead. And a prominent role in these inferences is played by beliefs we have as to which illocutionary action he probably would have wanted to perform with that sentence in that situation, and which ones he probably would not have wanted to perform.

Starting from the sentence he used, we reflect that the path of strict and direct literal use of that sentence with meaning M would lead to such-and-such speech action. But we judge it most unlikely that when he chose to use that sentence, it was *that* speech action that he wanted to perform; so we conclude that he must have closed the gate that opens to the path of strict and direct literal use with meaning M, and opened up another. Or we judge that it was probably so-and-so that he wanted to say, and that he probably wanted to say it with indirection; so he must have closed the gate which leads to strict and direct literal usage, and opened the one that leads to indirect literal usage.

So our interest as authorial-discourse interpreters is indeed in what the speaker said – not in what he intended to say, but in what he did say, if anything. But saying is an intentional action. And more importantly, we have to know how he was operating, or trying to operate, the system. Given all those distinct meaning- and usage-paths going out from each sentence, we have to know which path he was using, or trying to use. And in coming to know that, a crucial role is played by our beliefs as to which plan of action for saying something he probably implemented, and which ones he probably did not implement. He, in turn, if he wants to communicate, must take account of which interpretations we are likely to put on his words; he must, in that way and for that reason, take expected audience reaction into account.[6]

### *Discerning illocutionary stance and designative content*

We have now spent a good deal of time on the topic of how we go about discerning noematic content; our remarks on illocutionary stance and designative content will, accordingly, have to be very brief. The main clues to illocutionary stance are carried by the moods of our sentences: declarative, interrogative, optative, and so forth. But literary genre also carries clues; in our culture, to be told that a piece of prose is a novel is to be told that the illocutionary stance of most of the discourse therein is fictive. Here too, though, linguistic clues are neither sufficient nor decisive; the determination of stance requires the use of considerations about what it is likely that the discourser intended, in ways similar to those outlined in our discussion of the determination of noematic content.

I have assumed that for the determination of noematic content, the only considerations relevant are considerations about the meanings of sentences, considerations about tropic uses established in the linguistic culture, and considerations of probability and improbability as to what the discourser had and didn't have as his intention to say. The determination of designative content is very different. To discover what the discourser referred to, and what he predicated of the entities referred to, one must, with noematic content in mind, exit the meanings and tropes of language and the action-plans of discoursers and enter the real world so as to discover which entity if any the definite descriptions designate, which time the tenses designate, which persons the personal pronouns designate. Here, non-linguistic features of the context of utterance are decisively important. Two people utter the sentence "My queen is dead." Both speak literally; so that – given the assumption that this sentence has only one meaning – the noematic content of the two illocutionary acts is the same. But the one predicates of the Dutch queen that she is dead; the other predicates of the English queen that she is dead. The designative content of the illocutionary acts is different. It is that because one speaker is Dutch and the other is English.

Let me close with a disavowal. What I have said may well have given the impression that, when discourse is well-formed, then the discourser has a clear and distinct apprehension of the noematic content of her discourse; and that, as a consequence, there is a definite answer to the question as to whether something does or doesn't belong to that content. We the interpreters may not know that answer; but it's there for the finding out. For I said that in the well-formed case, discoursing-by-inscribing and discoursing-by-uttering are the implementation of an action-plan on the part of the discourser: the speaker intended to say that, and intended to utter that, and intended to say that *by* uttering that. And I said that, in trying to find out the noematic content of what someone said, we operate on the principle that she said what her sentence means, unless, in the light of whatever evidence is available to us, it is implausible to suppose that that is what she wanted to say. Then we run through the other things that the linguistic practice in question allows one to say with this sentence; and pick that one, from all those, that she is most likely to have wanted to say in this situation, with some usage other than the strict and direct literal. Unless, in the light of the evidence available to us, it is implausible to suppose that she wanted to say any of those either. Then we go for a fall-back option and attribute some defect to her attempt at discourse.

But what it is that a speaker wants to say, and what it is that a speaker does say, will sometimes be relatively indeterminate. Or may have a richness of content which she herself only dimly apprehends. This dimness of apprehension may itself come in degrees: some parts she sees yet more dimly than others. As she probes deeper and deeper into the depths of that, she will come across things she wasn't even aware of having said – and things she's not sure whether or not she did say. Especially is this true when we speak metaphorically. When reflecting on one's own metaphorical speech, one sometimes has the sense of learning what one said – be it with delight or dismay.

CHAPTER 12

# Interpreting for the mediated divine discourse: the second hermeneutic

Suppose one has discerned the human authorial discourse of the biblical writings. How does one then move on, as the traditional practice assumes one must, to discern the mediated divine discourse? And let me say, once more, that to understand how the Bible as a whole, with its extraordinary diversity of texts, could be an instrument of God's discourse, I am working with the *appropriation* model; different models would yield a somewhat different answer to our question.

It would, in my judgment, be a mistake to move on too quickly. Perhaps even those who read while running can get something out of Plato's *Republic,* and Dante's *Divine Comedy.* But the experience down through the ages of those who participate in Western culture is that these works repay repeated and close reading; subtleties and profundities never noticed when we read as we run come to light when we meditate on these works. Surely we must suppose the same for God's book; we must suppose that God's book requires and rewards close attention to what its human authors wrote. For it is by way of that, that God discourses. The truly dazzling contributions which critics have made in recent years to our understanding of biblical narrative and poetry have mainly come from those who disavowed any explicit theological concerns. Their contributions are nonetheless of inestimable worth for those who do read for theological concerns – more specifically, for those who read to discern the speech of God. God is in the details. It's the details of texts that resist imposed interpretations. Only by attending to the details does it become likely that one is oneself interpreted by the text – or by that One who is the author of the text.[1]

Here is also the place to remark that, even when considering the Bible as God's one book, one might well have other "interpretative" interests than discerning the divine discourse. One might be interested in applying to our contemporary situation what God said by way of

202

authoring scripture; traditionally, that was called *tropological* interpretation. Or one might be interested in what might be called *simile* interpretation: using one part of the world projected by the biblical writers as an image for describing another part: "As Moses raised the serpent in the wilderness, so God raised Christ ..." In his book, *Discerning the Mystery*, Andrew Louth includes a chapter on biblical interpretation which he calls "Return to Allegory." Unfortunately, a sizeable number of rather different phenomena are lumped together by Louth under the rubric of "allegory," with next to no attempt at differentiation. But when one scrutinizes the examples of so-called "allegorical interpretation" that he culls from traditional exegesis, one sees that most of them are of this "*as X, so also Y*" pattern. "A good example," he says, of allegorical interpretation

can be found in interpretations of the narrative of our Lady's Visitation of Elizabeth. When Elizabeth hears Mary's greeting, the baby John the Baptist, still in her womb, leaps for joy. Max Thurian comments: "John the Baptist is like David who danced and leapt with joy before the Ark of the covenant at the entering-in of Jerusalem ... the Son of God in Mary produces in her a kind of messianic exaltation, even as the sacred presence in the Ark calls King David to dance and tumble with joy."[2]

Thirdly, one might be interested in *typological* interpretation – which, as I indicated earlier, is a species of *extrapolation*. Extrapolation consists of determining what else would be the case, if what some writer projects by way of his or her text were the case. You and I tend to confine ourselves to the use of logical and causal principles in answering this question. But suppose one believed that there are not only causal relations among entities in the world, but also relations of natural signification: that things have been so created as to signify other things. Then in fleshing out the projected world of a work, beyond what is specified and suggested, one would find it natural to point out some of the signification relations that hold among the entities in the world. And that was what typology, traditionally understood, was concerned with.[3]

### *How to interpret for appropriating divine discourse*

My concern here, however, is how we discern the divine discourse. Suppose we have figured out the meanings of the sentences of the biblical text and what the authors of the various parts of that text said by authoring those parts; how do we get from there to the appropriating divine discourse? Let us once again start by reflecting on the human case. Suppose that I appropriate your discourse-by-inscription for my own discourse. How does an interpreter go about figuring out what I have said – figuring out the stance and content of my appropriating discourse?

The most fundamental principle, I submit, is this: the interpreter takes the stance and content of my appropriating discourse to be that of your appropriated discourse, unless there is good reason to do otherwise – such "good reason to do otherwise" consisting, at bottom, of its being improbable, on the evidence available, that by my appropriation in this situation, I would have wanted to say that and only that. At those points where the interpreter does have good reason to do otherwise, he proceeds by selecting the illocutionary stance and content which have the highest probability of being what I intended to say in this way. If the most probable of those is nonetheless improbable, then he adopts some such fall-back option as that I didn't really appropriate that discourse but only appeared to do so, that in appropriating it I said something I never intended to say, that I misunderstood the discourse I appropriated – or that *he* has misunderstood the appropriated discourse.

This, I say, is how interpretation proceeds when one human being appropriates the discourse-by-inscription of another human. I see no reason to think that it proceeds differently when it is God who appropriates the discourse-by-inscription of some human being – except that some of the fall-back options are excluded. God does not unwittingly say things God never intended to say, nor does God misunderstand the discourse God appropriates!

It follows that we do our interpreting for divine discourse with convictions in two hands: in one hand, our convictions as to the stance and content of the appropriated discourse and the meanings of the sentences used;[4] In the other, our convictions concerning the probabilities and improbabilities of what God would have been intending to say by appropriating this particular discourse-by-inscription.

One of the most important contributions of Swinburne's discussion in *Revelation* is his emphatic reminder that it was part of the traditional practice of Christians to regard the Bible as *one book* – not as approximately sixty-six books published together in one binding but as *one* book with approximately sixty-six clearly distinguished parts.[5] An implication of this, given the framework within which Swinburne conducts his discussion, is that the literary unit relevant for determining the meaning of a token sentence from, say, the Gospel of Matthew, is not just the text of Matthew, and certainly not some small pericope from Matthew, but the text of the whole Bible. I have my doubts, expressed in the preceding chapter, about the wisdom of ascribing meaning to token sentences, as I have my doubts, expressed yet earlier, about the wisdom of introducing the notion of context-relative meanings of sentences and of then ascribing meanings to sentences-in-context. Nonetheless, Swinburne's point has its close analogue in the conceptuality which I have been using and developing for understanding the traditional practice of interpreting for divine discourse.

Suppose someone remarks, "You'll get what I want to say if you take what Ruth said just now along with what she said yesterday," or alternatively, "You'll get what I want to say if you take what Ruth said just now along with what Michelle said." Then, to discern the appropriating discourse, we have to consider those two pieces of appropriated discourse *together*, as a unit. So too, to discern what God is saying by way of the Bible, we have to take these sixty-six or so biblical books *together*. For some purposes it's relevant to take the book of Isaiah as one complete text; perhaps there are also purposes for which it's relevant to take so-called First Isaiah as a complete text, so-called Second Isaiah as another, and so forth. But to discern God's discourse, we have to treat the text of Isaiah as no more than part of a much larger book, the Bible.

The situation is not that for a sentence occurring in so-called Second Isaiah, there is one thing which is its meaning all by itself, perhaps another thing which is its meaning in the text of Second Isaiah, perhaps another which is its meaning in the text of Isaiah, perhaps another which is its meaning in the text of the Old Testament, and perhaps yet one more thing which is its meaning in the text of the Bible. The situation is rather this: when the instrument of someone's discourse is an extended text, the evidence to be considered by an interpreter in trying to determine what that person said with one sentence of his text has to include the fact that his saying something with this sentence is only part of an extended discourse of which the text as a whole is the medium. We the interpreters have to juggle tentative interpretations of the parts of the text until we arrive at the best interpretation of the total text – at that interpretation which has the highest probability of being the totality of what he intended to say with this total text. (Unless that interpretation is such that it's improbable that he would have intended to say that; then we adopt some fall-back option.) And in particular: when someone appropriates for his own the discourse-by-inscription of others, we as interpreters have to interpret parts of what he appropriated in the light of the totality of what he appropriated, whether that be just one sentence and what was said thereby, or a whole text, or several texts by a single person, or several texts by several different persons.

There's a strand of radical Protestantism which would protest vigorously what I said above, that we do our interpreting for divine discourse with convictions in two hands – in one, convictions as to the human discourse and meanings of the sentences used, in the other, convictions as to what God would and wouldn't have intended to say by appropriating this totality of discourse and locution. That strand would insist that interpretation for divine discourse must be interpretation with one hand: no convictions about God are to be employed in the practice of interpretation which do not themselves emerge from interpreting the human locution and discourse of the Bible. Perhaps the simplest and most decisive way of seeing that this cannot be correct is the following: in our interpretations, we make use of the conviction that God speaks consistently. If we didn't, then even the fact that one's tentative interpretation of two parts of the biblical text has the implication that God's discourse was contradictory would be no reason for not adopting that interpretation. Indeed, so fundamental and pervasive is our use of this conviction in our practice of interpretation that we rarely notice we are using it. But if we didn't bring this conviction *to* the practice of interpretation, rather than waiting until it emerged *from* the practice, we couldn't take even the first steps in the practice of interpreting for divine discourse. For suppose we approached the text with a truly open mind as to whether God's discourse is contradictory, and then read in the text the sentence, "I, God, do not contradict myself." How are we to interpret that very sentence? If we already believed that God does not contradict Godself, then we would interpret it literally, and rightly so – unless something in the context indicated that the sentence was being used in an unusual fashion. But if we had no view on the matter of God's consistency, we would be without good reason to adopt either a literal or non-literal interpretation, say, an ironic interpretation. We couldn't adopt any interpretation; we would be stymied.

That God does not speak in contradictions is both the most fundamental and the least controversial of the prior convictions about

God's nature and purposes that the church, down through the ages, has used for interpreting for divine discourse.[6] To get a better notion of the role of such prior convictions, let me cite two or three others which, while not entirely non-controversial, have none the less been prominent in the tradition. One is formulated by Augustine in a famous passage from his *de doctrina Christiana*:

we must show the way to find out whether a phrase is literal or figurative. And the way is certainly as follows: Whatever there is in the word of God that cannot, when taken literally, be referred either to purity of life or soundness of doctrine, you may set down as figurative. Purity of life has reference to the love of God and one's neighbor; soundness of doctrine to the knowledge of God and one's neighbor. (III,10,14)

The idea is this: we are considering whether so-and-so is something that God said by way of a certain part of the appropriated discourse-by-inscription. If God's saying that would not conduce to our love of God and neighbor, or if its content is incompatible with Christian doctrine, then it follows that God did not say that. Accordingly, if we the interpreters *believe*, on careful reflection, that it would not so conduce or is thus incompatible, we are to conclude that God did not say that. It was pretty much accepted Christian doctrine in Augustine's day that God does not have emotions; accordingly, in his own interpretations of Scripture Augustine concluded, using the principle of interpretation enunciated, that the use in Scripture of the language of emotions about God must be interpreted metaphorically – as must, for the same reason, all language which implies change in God.

Almost certainly Augustine, when speaking of "doctrine" in the passage quoted, had *Christian* doctrine in mind – official church teaching. God does not assert anything inconsistent with that, the unspoken reason being that Christian doctrine is true. But most if not all Christian interpreters, including Augustine, have operated with a much broader principle concerning the truth and falsehood of divine discourse than this. They have said or assumed that we are not to interpret God as asserting falsehood of any sort, on the ground that God, unlike human beings, does not and would not assert a falsehood. In the words of John Locke, "Whatever God hath revealed, is certainly true; no doubt can be made of it" (*Essay* IV,xviii,10).[7]

Thirdly, convictions as to God's *purpose* in speaking to us by way of Scripture have also been used in conducting interpretation A common formulation of one such conviction is that God speaks to us only on matters of faith and morals. If our tentative interpretation of some passage has the consequence that God would have spoken on some matter other than faith and morals, we are, on this principle, to conclude that God did not say that.

Whether or not these particular principles concerning God's nature and purposes are entirely correct is, of course, a legitimate topic for debate; but appeal to some such principles, so I have argued, is indispensable if one is to interpret for divine discourse. At the same time, it's no doubt natural for Christians to feel wary of making use of such principles as these in the practice of interpreting for divine discourse – and for Jews and Muslims to feel so as well. Divine discourse threatens to become a wax nose molded in the image of our own beliefs. I will discuss this worry in the next chapter.

### *Structure of the relation between appropriated discourse and appropriating divine discourse*

In the meanwhile, let us imagine that we have been engaged in the practice of interpreting the human discourse of the Bible for the mediated divine discourse, that we are well along in the process, and that we now take a moment to catch our breath and survey the path we have been led to take from the mediating human discourse to the mediated divine discourse. The following question comes to mind: at those points where we have found ourselves forced to depart from the baseline of construing the stance and content of God's discourse to be that of the human discourse, how is God's discourse related to the locutions and discourse of the human authors which mediated it? We should shy away from the expectation of ever formulating a set of informative generalizations which catch all the cases; the relationships are much too subtle for that. But some persistent patterns there will be.

For one thing, it will often be the case that to arrive at the correct *rhetorico-conceptual structure* of the divine discourse, we had to alter systematically that of the mediating human discourse. What I have in mind can best be explained with an example. In the 9th verse of his letter to the Romans, Paul says that "God, whom I serve with my spirit by announcing the gospel of his Son, is my witness . . ." By inscribing these words, Paul said that *God, whom he serves with his spirit by announcing the gospel of God's Son, is his witness.* But we cannot suppose that God, by way of appropriating this passage, says that *God, whom he, God, serves with his spirit by announcing the gospel of his Son, is his, that is, God's, witness.* Why not? Well, the rhetorico-conceptual structure is all wrong. It's incoherent, it makes no sense, to suppose that God said this; it can't be true. It makes eminently good sense for Paul to say that *he* serves God; but it makes no sense for *God* to say that *God* serves God. So whatever we take God to be saying by way of this passage, its noematic content will have a different rhetorical structure from the noematic content of what Paul said. The point holds for a great deal of the Bible, and is obvious and non-controversial. Much of the Bible is structured as human *speech about* God and as human *address to* God. As we move from the appropriated human discourse to the appropriating divine discourse, we must change the rhetorico-conceptual structure. Whatever God says by way of the psalmist's writing, "Have mercy on me, O God," it's not a plea to Godself to have mercy on Godself.

Secondly – and now things get more complicated and controversial – we will have found ourselves forced at various points to dig inside the human discourse, so as to bring to light its particular exemplification of a structure which inhabits all human discourse of any length – viz., the distinction between *the point*, or *the main point*, that the author wishes to make, and the author's particular *way of making or developing* that point. Having discerned this structure in the biblical discourse, we will at various points have been led to leave behind, as of purely human significance, the author's particular way of making his point, while attributing the point itself to God.[8]

Consider, for example, the opening verses of Psalm 93:

> The Lord is king, he is robed in majesty;
>     the Lord is robed, he is girded with strength.
> He has established the world; it shall never be moved;
>     your throne is established from of old;
>     you are from everlasting.

The psalmist is hymning God's majesty, strength, and steadfastness; that's his main point in this psalm. He does so by citing what he regards as manifestations of these attributes. In particular, he remarks that God has "established" the world in such a way that it will never be moved; he sees this as an example of God's steadfastness. What is coming to the surface here, of course, is the geocentric cosmology widely shared among the peoples of antiquity. The author expresses this cosmology in his discourse; it's part of what he actually says – part of the content of his discourse. But as a matter of fact the earth is moved, and we all believe that it is; it rotates on its axis, revolves around the sun, and moves with the solar system as a whole through space. So God can't be saying here that the earth is immobile. But the main point of the discourse of this Psalm, once we make the appropriate alteration of rhetorical structure, is that God is worthy of being hymned for majesty, strength, and steadfastness. So we attribute that main point to God, and discard the psalmist's particular way of making the point as of purely human significance.

Let me construct a somewhat different example of the same general point – that sometimes it will be the main point of the human author that we attribute to God (perhaps after suitable alteration of rhetorical structure), while leaving behind the human author's way of making that point. The psalmist actually *says* that the Lord "has established the world; it shall never be moved," though only as part of his way of hymning God. Suppose that he had instead written this: "The Lord, who has established the earth so that it shall never be moved, is from everlasting." Then the psalmist's belief, that the Lord has established the earth so that it shall never be moved, functions somewhat differently in his discourse. Rather than the content of the belief being something that he asserts as part of his way of hymning God, it's incorporated into his way of purportedly referring to God. God is purportedly referred to as the Lord who has established the earth so that it shall never be moved; and the logical predicate, "is from everlasting," is then predicated of him. But as a matter of fact, nothing satisfies the description, "The Lord who has established the earth so that it shall never be moved."

What is to be done with such a case? Well, the crucial question to raise when a person uses a referring expression, with the aim of referring to something, is whether in context he thereby expresses a cognitive grip on some entity which is firm enough for him to have beliefs about that entity, to make assertions about that entity, and so forth. And often it will be the case that a referring expression, even though it incorporates a certain amount of error, does express such a cognitive grip. "That large elm tree there must be diseased, since it's losing its leaves," I say, pointing to a large tree up the street. But it's not an elm; it's a sycamore. In spite of my error, my cognitive grip on that large sycamore up the street was firm enough for me to have referred to it, and to have predicated of it the property of being such that it must be diseased, since it's losing its leaves. Furthermore, the main point of my discourse was to predicate that property of that tree; my main point was to affirm the designative content of my discourse. Though the noematic content of my discourse incorporated an error, my performing an illocutionary act with that noematic content was only my way of accomplishing my principle aim of performing an illocutionary act with that *designative* content.

So too, then, for our devised example, "The Lord, who has established the earth so that it shall never be moved, is from ever-lasting." Though the noematic content of this assertion would incorporate an error, nonetheless the psalmist would surely have predicated of God the property of being everlasting; that would have been the designative content of his discourse. And it would have been the affirmation of that designative content that was the main point of his discourse. The affirmation of that is what we attribute to God; some (not all) of the noematic content is left behind.

Thirdly, sometimes the relation between the divine discourse, and the discourse-by-inscription of the human author, is that though the human writer has spoken *literally*, God, as it were, has spoken *tropically*. That is to say, the noematic content of what the human author says is identical with the meaning of his sentence, whereas the noematic content of what God says is not identical with the meaning of the sentence. To get from the sentence used to the noematic content of God's discourse, we have to construe some of the words in the sentence as being used as tropes.

This happens less often than one would initially suppose; for in our interpretation of the human discourse-by-inscription, we will already have concluded that a good deal of the human discourse was not literal. In such cases, the phenomenon in question, of God speaking tropically where the human writer spoke literally, does not arise. For example, I take it as beyond doubt that the human writers were speaking metaphorically when they spoke of the eyes and ears and limbs of God.

But what about their application of the language of emotions to God? Were they speaking literally then? I rather think they were. If so, then if we follow the tradition of the church in insisting that such language about God must be construed metaphorically, we do have a case of the human author using the sentence literally whereas God uses it metaphorically. But let us consider a more obvious and dramatic example, one familiar to everyone: Psalm 137. The psalm opens with the moving lament:

> By the rivers of Babylon –
>    there we sat down and there we wept
>    when we remembered Zion.
> On the willows there
>    we hung up our harps.
> For there our captors
>    asked us for songs,
> and our tormentors asked for mirth, saying,
>    "Sing us one of the songs of Zion!"

But then it closes with these words:

> O daughter Babylon, you devastator!
>    Happy shall they be who pay you back
>    what you have done to us!
> Happy shall they be who take your little ones
>    and dash them against the rock!

I find it difficult to believe that the human author of these last two sentences was not using them literally, not saying just what those words mean: out of angry grief speaking a blessing on those who would take Babylonian infants and smash them against rocks. But the church has rarely if ever concluded that, with these words, *God* was speaking that blessing. It has taken God to be expressing opposition to whatever opposes God's reign; and to get to that, it has always construed these words tropically, as a metaphor cluster.

We are supposing ourselves to have discerned a good deal of the divine discourse of scripture; and we are now looking back over the course we have taken so as to spy some general patterns in the relation between, on the one hand, the human locutions and discourse from which we began, and, on the other hand, the content and stance of the divine discourse which we have arrived at. Let me now call attention to a fourth such pattern.

The fundamental phenomenon, when we human beings speak for ourselves instead of either deputizing another to speak in our name or appropriating the discourse of another, is that by performing some locutionary act we perform some illocutionary act – our producing or presenting tokens of words counts as our performing some act of discourse, some speech act. More precisely, this is the fundamental phenomenon when words are the medium; words need not of course be the medium. But it also happens rather often that by performing one illocutionary action we perform another illocutionary action – that by saying one thing, we say another thing, that one of our acts of discourse counts as another of our acts of discourse. The prophet Nathan, by telling King David a story about a rich man taking the lamb of a poor man, accused David of stealing the wife of a poor man. Aesop, by telling a story about asses and grasshoppers, propounded the moral that one man's meat is another man's poison. Jesus, by telling a parable about a sower, instructed his hearers about various kinds of receptivity to the word of God. Bunyan, by telling a story about a man's mundane travels, propounded an allegory about the soul's progress. And so forth; the examples are legion.

Let us have a name for this phenomenon of one act of discourse on the part of a person counting as another act of discourse on the part of that person. Let us call it *transitive discourse*. And if we need to pick out one or the other of the two acts of discourse, we can speak of *discourse-generating* discourse and of *discourse-generated* discourse. Parables and allegories are common forms of transitive discourse; but so too is telling a story to propound a moral or make a point, if that is not already captured under the concept of *parable*.

The concept of *transitive discourse*, as I have introduced it, is such that the concept is exemplified only if two acts of discourse, related in such a way that one generates the other, are both performed by the same person. But consider the various genres of transitive discourse, parables and allegories being the most commonly recognized. It's obvious that when one person deputizes or appropriates the discourse of another, the stance and noematic content of the deputized or appropriated discourse may be related to that of the deputizing or appropriating discourse in exactly the way characteristic of a parable or allegory. So let us revise our concept of *transitive discourse* by decreeing that it also applies to such double-author cases as these. In such cases, the two discourses making up a parable or allegory are divided between two different persons.

The application to the matter at hand is obvious: rather often when we pair off the illocutionary stance and noematic content of some piece of appropriated biblical discourse, with those of the appropriating divine discourse, we have an example of *transitive discourse*: parable, allegory, or whatever. If both of the two discourses comprising the parable or allegory are present in the human discourse, then, if God appropriates that discourse as a whole, they will also both be present within the divine discourse. But if so, then it will also automatically be the case that one half of the human transitive discourse (the discourse-generating half) and one half of the divine transitive discourse (the discourse-generated half) will together constitute a transitive discourse. Perhaps the Old Testament book of Jonah gives us an example; it does so if the human author told the story of Jonah as a parable and if God does so as well.

The more interesting cases of transitive discourse divided between human and divine discoursers occur, however, when the appropriated human discourse is not itself transitive discourse. Perhaps the Old Testament Song of Songs will serve as an example. Read on its own it sounds, to my ear anyway, like a love song "pure and simple" – if one can speak of a song so rich and evocative as "simple"! The characteristics of paradigmatic parable and allegory seem missing.[9] Possibly it was nonetheless written to make a point or propound a moral – some of our contemporary novels seem to function like that even though they lack the characteristics of paradigmatic parable. But if so, the clues seem to me entirely lacking. Nonetheless, Judaism and Christianity have both traditionally interpreted the text allegorically. Suppose that we go along with this tradition when interpreting the Song of Songs as part of the discourse which God has appropriated. Then only when we pair off the appropriated human discourse with the appropriating divine discourse do we get the allegory; the *allegorizing* discourse belongs to the divine author, the *allegorized* discourse, to the human author. We don't take the human author to have been speaking of the love of God for the Church; and we don't take God to be speaking that sensuous love song which is the Song of Songs all by itself. We don't take God to be saying,

> Sustain me with raisins,
>     refresh me with apples;
>     for I am faint with love.                    (2:5)

I think almost everyone would concede that biblical *narrative* as a whole fits under this category of transitive discourse. Possibly there are some "fundamentalists," so-called, who hold that the biblical author was doing nothing else than narrating the story in declarative mood, claiming that this is how things went; and that, in appropriating it, God also was doing nothing else. But most readers have felt that these stories were being told to make a point; and certainly most of those who have interpreted these stories as part of divinely appropriated discourse have believed that God appropriated them to make a point – whether or not the human authors were making a point in telling them, and if so, whether or not God's point is the same as that of the human authors. The intensely controverted question has rather been how much of these narratives the human authors were presenting as true, and how much (if any) God was presenting as true. In a later chapter I propose discussing in some detail this matter of the illocutionary stance of the biblical narratives. Here let it simply be noted that the fact that a narrative is told to make a point – that it is one half of a piece of transitive discourse, the discourse-generating half – does not imply that it is not also presented as true, not also *asserted*. Once upon a time it was customary for historians to use their historical narrations to teach lessons. Perhaps it's still customary; perhaps the clues to didactic intent in our contemporary historians are just more subtle.

Lastly, rather often there is a relation of *specificity/generality* between the noematic content of the appropriated human discourse and that of the appropriating divine discourse. The point can again best be explained by considering an example. Let me take a passage which happens to be one whose interpretation has been the source of much controversy in recent years. In the second chapter of the first letter to Timothy we find the sentence, "I permit no woman to teach or to have authority over a man; she is to keep silent." One question to consider is how we are to interpret the human discourse here. Was the writer saying, in effect, that *in situations of the sort he is addressing*, women are to keep silent in the assemblies of the church; or was he saying, in effect, that *at all times and places* women are to keep silent? The more important question, though, is what God was saying with this passage. Suppose we come to the view that though the writer of this letter was speaking in the name of God, and though, by his writing what he did, God was saying to the people addressed that women should be silent in their assemblies, nonetheless God, by appropriating this passage along with the whole of the biblical text and discourse for God's own discourse, was not saying that women in all church assemblies everywhere should be silent. It does not follow that we then discard this passage as being of purely limited significance. Instead one considers first whether perhaps by way of this passage God is issuing to all of us a deeper and more general point, whose application in that particular kind of situation yielded the injunction that women be silent, but whose application in our situation yields a rather different injunction.

Up to this point I have been speaking as if whatever God says by way of appropriating the discourse-by-inscription of the biblical writers is said by God to one and all. But there is no reason at all to suppose that that is true. Even without transitive discourse entering the picture, we human beings sometimes say several distinct things by uttering or inscribing one sentence; and those several distinct things sometimes – though not always – are said to distinct persons. There is every reason to suppose the same for divine discourse, every reason to suppose that God's discourse is in this way rich in its diversity.

Of course, since God, unlike human beings, remains alive and active, the question What *was* God saying to us today by way of authoring this passage of Scripture? is easily confused with the question, What *is* God saying to us today by way of confronting us with this passage of Scripture? In homiletical and devotional situations the Church and its members typically ask, What does God say to us by way of this passage? That formulation is ambiguous as between the two questions; the Church doesn't distinguish, and it usually doesn't make any difference that it doesn't distinguish. The distinction is more important for theory than for practice.

These, then, are some of the patterns to be spied in the relation between the mediating locutions and discourse of the human authors of the Bible, and the mediated divine discourse. I do not claim that they are *all* of the patterns; I claim only that they are among the most prominent.

### How to decide which pattern to use

A question which comes naturally to mind when one sees the five patterns arrayed before one – supplemented by whichever others one discerns and finds worth singling out for attention – is how to decide when to follow which pattern. I introduced my discussion of these patterns by inviting us to imagine ourselves well along in the activity of interpreting for divine discourse, and then looking back to see which patterns had emerged in the results. But the fact that these patterns had emerged implies that we had at various points along the way decided to interpret in accord with one of these patterns rather than another. How did we make those decisions?

I judge that the question arises most acutely when we have to decide whether to interpret a certain passage tropically so as to arrive at God's discourse, or to apply the main point/ancillary point distinction and then assign the main point to God and leave behind the ancillary point as of purely human significance. For example, why not give a metaphorical interpretation to that line from Psalm 93,

He has established the world; it shall never be moved?

And why not apply the main point/ancillary point pattern to those lines from Psalm 137:

> Happy shall they be who take your little ones
> and dash them against the rock?

Well, as to the former case, it just doesn't work as a metaphor – not for us, anyway, with our knowledge of cosmology. If the point of the psalmist had been to emphasize the transience of human life by contrasting it with the relative fixity of the earth, we could, with no difficulty, take "established" and "never be moved" as metaphors. The earth does seem very fixed when contrasted with the human affairs that take place upon it. But that's not the psalmist's point. His eye is on God, not on human life. He wants to evoke a sense of God's ever-lastingness; he does so by saying that it's like the fixity of the earth. But for us, the place of the earth in the cosmos just won't work as a metaphor for God's everlastingness; in our mind's eye is the picture of the earth as whirling about in space at enormous speed – about as unfixed as anything could be. The point is that not every case of literal falsehood can be successfully interpreted by anybody whatsoever as a case of metaphorical truth – in part because, as we have just seen, whether an expression works for one as a metaphor depends, among other things, on one's knowledge. If there were a plausible metaphorical interpretation of the passage, I would prefer that – on the ground that a plausible metaphorical interpretation of an appropriated passage is more honoring of the passage and its appropriation than an interpretation which just leaves that passage behind as making an ancillary point. But in this case, there is none such. And as to the latter case: it appears to me that the human author's main point in the whole passage is his call to God to wreak vengeance on the Babylonians. The author's blessing of those who smash the heads of Babylonian infants against rocks is not his negotiable way of making his main point; it is very much part of what he wants to happen. For this case, however, a plausible metaphorical interpretation lies ready at hand.

In short, it often turns out, when one looks into the details of the passage to be interpreted, that the choice between these two patterns of interpretation is easy. One can't even think of how one of the two patterns might go; it doesn't prove viable. There will be other cases in which, though both are viable, one of the two proves very implausible as a construal of what God is likely to have intended to say by appropriating this particular passage. That probably leaves us with a few cases where close scrutiny of the passage, coupled with reflection on what God might have intended to say by appropriating the passage, leaves us with equally viable and plausible alternatives. I judge that then one should prefer the tropic interpretation over the main point/ancillary point interpretation, for the reason cited above.

### Frei and Swinburne on the second hermeneutic

Near the beginning of this discussion of interpreting the mediating human locution and discourse for the mediated divine discourse – the "second hermeneutic," one might call it – I suggested that such interpretation has to be conducted with two sets of convictions in hand: in one hand, convictions as to the sentential meanings of the text and the illocutionary stance and content of the human authorial discourse, and in the other hand, convictions as to what God would and wouldn't have intended to say by appropriating these particular locutions and discourse. In conclusion, I want to consider whether the traditional practice doesn't have to appeal to certain other considerations which don't fall very comfortably into either of those categories.

Let me explain what I have in mind by again introducing a bit of the thought of the (recently deceased) Yale theologian, Hans Frei. Frei remarks in several places that, among all the different interpretations which Christians traditionally gave to the biblical text, there were a few fundamental points of near-consensus. There was near-consensus around the conviction that the Bible must be interpreted as one book. There was near-consensus around the conviction that, in interpreting the Bible as one book, the gospels must be given priority. And there was near-consensus around the conviction that when it comes to interpreting the Gospels as a whole, priority must be given to what Frei called the "*sensus literalis*" of the text. Parts of the Gospels, perhaps all of the Gospels, may be given other interpretations as well; some parts of the Gospels, such as the parables, *call for* other interpretations. But as he says in one passage, "there has in effect been something close to consensus in the major Christian theological traditions of the West – from their early history to their most recent liberal and conservative expressions." And a central part of that is "a consensus that in the interpretation of Scripture, especially the New Testament, the literal sense has priority over other legitimate readings, be they allegorical, moral, or critical . . ."[10]

At several junctures Frei's thought is, admittedly, not very clear. For example, Frei never succeeded, and I think he regarded himself as never having succeeded, in explaining what he had in mind by *sensus literalis*. But the unclarities don't affect the point I wish to extract from Frei; that point is clear enough. Frei was firmly committed early on to textual sense interpretation, later to performance interpretation; throughout his career he was resolutely opposed to authorial-discourse interpretation, be the discourse in question human or divine; he had been persuaded by his New Critical colleagues at Yale that authorial-discourse interpretation makes untenable assumptions about the accessibility of authorial intentions and their relevance to interpretation. And as to theology: the core of Frei's theological vision was the Barthian conviction that Jesus of Nazareth became Christ by enacting his Messiahship, and that this enactment of identity is presented to us narratively by the Gospels. Frei made a point of saying that to construe the significance of the Gospels in the way presupposed by that theological vision is to go beyond the boundaries of interpretation, as he understood those, and to enter the quite different terrain of relating the sense of the text to the world outside the text and its sense. But he also insisted that it presupposes a certain way of interpreting the textual sense of the gospels – the *sensus literalis* interpretation.

So how to argue for the priority, in the case of the Gospels, of the *sensus literalis* interpretation? In principle Frei could have argued for it by starting from his theological convictions and arguing that those convictions presuppose this style of interpretation. But that is not what he did – not most of the time, anyway. Instead he spent the early part of his career arguing that the Gospels have a quality of "realistic narrative," as he called it; and that only a *sensus literalis* interpretation honors that quality. To interpret the gospels allegorically, for example, is unavoidably to neglect that quality of realistic narrativity. The assumption, never quite spoken, seems to have been that the sheer "thereness" of this quality of realistic narrativity is sufficient grounding for the call to honor it with our styles of interpretation.

As Frei's career progressed, however, he began to see, and reluctantly to concede, that as a pure textual-sense interpreter, his preference for the *sensus literalis* interpretation of the Gospels was highly vulnerable. Even if the Gospels do have a quality of realistic narrativity, and even if the *sensus literalis* style of interpretation is the only one that fully honors this quality, why *must* it be honored? Why not, with full self-awareness, neglect that quality, adopt an allegorical style of interpretation for the Gospels, and work out from there to the rest of the Bible?

The answer Frei began to give had two main points. The choice among large-scale interpretive strategies has to be made in terms of more and less beneficial, not in terms of true and false. And secondly, when a text begins to play a canonical or quasi-canonical role in a community, that community will typically establish a certain sense of the text as the preferred sense; it will be the slowly emergent "sense" of the community that interpreting for that sense is the most beneficial.

Specifically, then, Frei began to claim that early on in the life of the Church the "sense" emerged – as a *sensus fidelium* – that the *sensus literalis* interpretation of the Gospels is the most beneficial. What exactly that benefit might be, remains open to discussion; Frei's own conviction – here we return to his Barthian theology – was that the great benefit of thus interpreting the Gospels is that Jesus' enactment of his identity as Messiah and Son of God is then presented to us. But whatever be the benefit, to be faithful to the traditional *sensus fidelium* is to give priority to the Gospels in one's interpretation of the Bible, and to give priority to the *sensus literalis* in one's interpretation of the Gospels. This is what Frei says in one passage:

> Interpretive traditions of religious communities tend to reach a consensus on certain central texts. We have noted that the literal reading of the gospel stories was the crucial instance of this consensus in the early church. What is striking about this is that the "literal" reading in this fashion became the normative or "plain" reading of the texts. There is no apriori reason why the "plain" reading could not have been "spiritual" in contrast to "literal," and certainly the temptation was strong. The identification of the plain with the literal sense was not a logically necessary development, but it did begin with the early Christian community and was perhaps unique to Christianity. The creed, "rule of faith" or "rule of truth" which governed the Gospels' use in the church asserted the primacy of their literal sense.[11]

The differences of thought between Hans Frei and Richard Swinburne are, in general, enormous. But on this particular point, that biblical interpretation should be conducted in accord with the traditional *sensus fidelium*, there is agreement. Frei doesn't say much about what he regards as the relevant part of that *sensus fidelium* ; perhaps it's just those three principles of biblical interpretation which he claims to have been points of near-consensus in the main Christian tradition.

And as to why we must or should interpret in accord with the *sensus fidelium*, his answer is that only thus will we realize the benefits which the Church has traditionally regarded as flowing from interpretation thus practiced. By contrast, the *sensus fidelium* for Swinburne is the content of the official teaching of the Church, in, for example, its ecumenical creeds; the Bible is to be read as if it had those creeds as a preface guiding us in the overall shape of our interpretation and in the resolution of certain ambiguous cases. As to why we must or should interpret in accord with the *sensus fidelium*, Swinburne's answer is that if we don't, we are likely to miss out on what God intended to reveal to us by way of the Bible. The biblical text, without this prefatory guide to interpretation, is too open to alternative interpretations. "The idea that the Bible could be interpreted naked," says Swinburne,

without a tradition of interpretation which clarified its meaning, is not intrinsically plausible and would not have appealed to many before the fifteenth century. Theology from without always dictated which sentences of the Bible were benchmarks by which other sentences were interpreted ... A crucial consequence of this rule was, in view of what Christian teaching said about the superiority of the manifestation of God in Christ to all that had gone before, that in any apparent clash between Old and New Testaments, the New took priority. Passages in the Old Testament in apparent conflict with the New were either to be interpreted as God's temporary and limited revelation, or to be interpreted metaphorically.[12]

The similarity to Frei is obvious!

Neither Frei nor Swinburne, in their discussions of interpretation, have their eye on authorial-discourse interpretation, be it human authorial discourse or divine; in that way, their discussions are significantly different from mine. Nonetheless, their discussions certainly pose the question whether my description, of how to interpret the mediating human locutions and discourse of the biblical writings for the divine mediated discourse, was complete. Does such interpretation require, in addition, an appeal to the *sensus fidelium* of the Church, or to some functional equivalent thereof?

I have insisted repeatedly that interpretation of a biblical passage for the divine mediating discourse cannot proceed without the interpreter appealing to convictions she has as to what God would and would not be likely to have intended to say by appropriating this passage within the whole text of the Bible. And such convictions, I said, will depend crucially on what the interpreter believes about the nature and purposes of God. Naturally interpretation does not require that the interpreter be traditionally Christian in these latter beliefs. But if she is, then she will in fact, in the course of her interpretation, appeal tacitly or explicitly to what Frei calls the *sensus fidelium*, and to what Swinburne calls 'the teaching of the Church." So the point made by Frei and Swinburne is an important one; but it doesn't require from us the introduction of a consideration *in addition to* the ones already cited.

## CHAPTER 13

# *Has Scripture become a wax nose?*

I have argued that authorial-discourse interpretation requires the use by the interpreter of convictions as to what the discourser is likely and unlikely to have wanted, and not wanted, to say. When the relevant convictions of this sort are lacking, interpretation is stymied or goes astray. Let me give an example.

In Mircea Eliade's fascinating book, *The Myth of the Eternal Return*, we find this paragraph:

> During the course of the *akîtu* ceremony, which lasted twelve days, the so-called epic of the Creation, *Enûma eliš*, was solemnly recited several times in the temple of Marduk. Thus the combat between Marduk and the sea monster Tiamat was reactualized – the combat that had taken place *in illo tempore* and had put an end to chaos by the final victory of the god. Marduk creates the cosmos from the fragments of Tiamat's torn body and creates man from the blood of the demon Kingu, to whom Tiamat had entrusted the Tablets of Destiny ... That this commemoration of the Creation was in effect a reactualization of the cosmogonic act is proved both by the rituals and by the formulas recited during the course of the ceremony. The combat between Tiamat and Marduk was mimed by a struggle between two groups of actors, a ceremonial that is also found among the Hittites (again in the frame of the dramatic scenario of the New Year), among the Egyptians, and at Ras Shamra. The struggle between two groups of actors not only commemorated the primordial conflict between Marduk and Tiamat; it repeated, it actualized, the cosmogony, the passage from chaos to cosmos. The mythical event was present: "May he continue to conquer Tiamat and shorten her days!" the celebrant exclaimed. The combat, the victory, and the Creation took place *at that very moment*.[1]

"May he continue to conquer Tiamat and shorten her days," exclaims the celebrant at the New Year ritual. Eliade interprets him as saying or implying thereby that the Creation of the cosmos is taking place right then and there. No doubt the thoughts and deeds of so-called primitive peoples were very different from ours. But was the celebrant *really* saying or implying that the Creation was taking place then and there? Often in reading Eliade one gets the impression that he won't allow the primitives whom he studies any figures of speech. Christians mime the events of Christ's birth at their Christmas celebrations, and sing that the child is born – not *has been* born but *is* born, just as they sing on Easter, "Jesus Christ is risen today." But none that I have ever come across believes that Jesus is born anew each Christmas and rises anew each Easter; nor would any of them want to say or suggest this. It is because we know that about contemporary Christians that we interpret their present-tense speech on those days as tropic, or figurative. Possibly the primitive peoples were different on this score; possibly they really did think that by going through their ritual, Creation was once again accomplished. But doubt seems appropriate: would a normal adult human being really believe that?

Be that as it may, however; the point to which I wish to call attention is that the issue cannot be settled simply by turning to grammars and dictionaries of ancient languages and then, in the light of what one has learned, studying the texts. We have to exit the domain of language and come to know enough about *the mentality* of those ancient peoples to be able to determine what they would have wanted to say on this matter; only then can we decide between literal and tropic interpretations. And maybe it's no longer possible to find out enough about their mentality to make that determination with any reliability.

Primitive peoples, alien though their ways of thinking may have been from ours, were nonetheless human beings living on the same planet that we live on; for that reason, we can surmise a good deal of what they would have wanted to say, and thus interpret a good deal of their speech. Perhaps the full import of their ritual language will forever remain obscure to us; nonetheless, we are able to interpret much of their ordinary practical language with considerable reliability. But should a strange non-human creature from outer space turn up and start producing sequences of sounds, we could do very little interpreting, if any.

What, then, emboldens us to undertake interpreting God's discourse? The conviction, apparently, that we can and do know something of God and of God's intentions. The example of the aliens from outer space suggests that what in turn underlay that conviction on the part of the writers of the Bible was their conviction that we human beings are made in the image of God, so that God is not totally alien to us. Though the differences between us are immense, there are nonetheless important affinities. We are able to surmise certain things about God. The conviction that God speaks and that we can interpret that speech presupposes that God is not *ganz anders*.

## How the wax nose anxiety arises

Now we all know very well that our fellow human beings do not always say what is true nor always what conduces to love. So the fact that one's tentative interpretation of some remark of one of one's fellows has the implication that the person would have spoken falsely or mean-spiritedly if that is what he said, is, so far forth, no argument against that interpretation. Of course we would hesitate in attributing a mean-spirited remark to Mother Theresa. And as to truth, the following remark of Leibniz is to the point: "we are certain that Constantinople is in the world, and that Constantine, Alexander the Great and Julius Caesar have lived. Of course, some peasant from the Ardennes could justifiably doubt this, for lack of information; but a man of letters or of the world could not do so unless his mind was unhinged."[2] Thus considerations of truth and of what conduces to love are by no means irrelevant to our interpretations of the remarks of our fellows. If a remark by Mother Theresa taken literally would be unloving, or a remark by an educated person taken literally would imply that there was never a Roman named Julius Caesar, we are inclined to try interpreting their remarks tropically. But such considerations must, as it were, all go through the limited mind and sinful heart of the discourser. In the last resort it's not whether the remark is in fact loving or mean-spirited that counts but what Mother Theresa wanted to say; and she may be mistaken, or on a certain occasion want to say what she knows is mean-spirited. And in the last resort it's not whether there was a Roman named Julius Caesar that counts but whether the speaker wants to say or deny that there was; and even well educated persons sometimes surprise one with what they don't know, and sometimes assert what they don't believe.

The situation is strikingly different when it comes to interpreting divine discourse. As we saw in an earlier chapter, two traditional principles guiding biblical interpretation in the Christian tradition are that God never speaks falsehood and that God never says things which conduce to what is incompatible with love. So if a tentative interpretation of divine discourse has the implication, so far as one can tell, that God would have said or suggested something false or something conducing to what is incompatible with love, that alone is sufficient ground for rejecting the proposed interpretation. One doesn't have to introduce additional considerations concerning the moral character or epistemic situation of the speaker. Of course, instead of concluding that God didn't say that, one can, in principle try the opposite tack of altering one's belief about the world or about morality, so that the tentative interpretation no longer seems false or unloving. But as Leibniz's crisp comment makes clear, that strategy bumps up against limits. "A man of letters or of the world" could not come to believe that Julius Caesar never lived "unless his mind was unhinged."

As a consequence, interpreting for divine discourse is directly at the mercy of the vagaries of human belief. Here there is no looseness of connection between truth and love, on the one hand, and what was said, on the other; for there are no moral or epistemic limitations on the divine speaker, nor any absentmindedness. If the proposed interpretation is false or does not conduce to love, then God didn't say it. Accordingly, if I *believe* it is false or *believe* it does not conduce to love, I must not attribute it to God. As Augustine remarks, "it frequently happens that a man will think nothing blamable except what the men of his own country and time are accustomed to condemn, and nothing worthy of praise or approval except what is sanctioned by the custom of his companions; and thus it comes to pass, that if Scripture either enjoins what is opposed to the customs of the hearers, or condemns what is not so opposed, and if at the same time the authority of the word has a hold upon their minds, they think that the expression is figurative."[3] Or as John Locke put it, the outcome of biblical interpretation threatens to be "that the scripture serves but, like a nose of wax, to be turned and bent, just as may fit the contrary orthodoxies of different societies. For it is these several systems, that to each party are the just standards of truth, and the meaning of the scripture is to be measured only by them."[4]

Locke describes the menace vividly, but not very precisely. The menace is actually two-fold. One of the menacing possibilities is that we will miss what God has said: miss the commands, the promises, the assertions. Because we firmly believe that to say such-and-such would be to speak falsely or unlovingly, we conclude that God didn't say that. But God did. Our false beliefs prevented us from discerning that God said it; they screened out the divine discourse. The other menacing possibility is that we come to believe that God said what God in fact did not say. A bit more reflection or inquiry, or reflection and inquiry shaped less by self-interest, would have made clear that if someone were to say that, he would be speaking falsely or unlovingly; and since God doesn't do that, God didn't say that. The outcome, either way, is that instead of conforming our beliefs and actions to what God says, we so interpret God's speech as to make it conform to our beliefs. We continue to acknowledge, formally, the authority of God's speech; but what emerges from our practice of interpretation is divine speech made in our own image.

## Does inerrantism alleviate the anxiety?

Is there any way of averting this menace? Well, *inerrantists*, as I shall call them, often speak as if their strategy of biblical interpretation averts the menace. So let us see whether they are right about that. The crucial assumption, or conviction, underlying the interpretative strategy of those I have in mind by "inerrantists" is that God so moved or guided the human authors of the Bible that what they said is entirely without error. Accordingly, as we move from our interpretation of the human discourse to our interpretation of the divine discourse mediated by that human discourse, we needn't appeal to the hermeneutical principle that no speech which is either false or unloving must be attributed to God. Since the human writers said nothing false, that principle is irrelevant. It's true that the inerrantist doesn't hold, or would be well advised not to hold, that God says exactly what the human writers said. As I observed in the preceding chapter, the rhetorical structure of much biblical discourse, such as that of the Psalms, is the structure of a human being addressing God rather than that of God addressing human beings. Then too, the possibility should be kept open that God says *more than* the human writers said; perhaps by the very act of *appropriating* some narrative God is saying something that the human author of the narrative was not saying. The inerrantist can readily admit both of these points. What he insists on is just that any divergence between the mediating human discourse and the mediated divine discourse will not be due to the falsity of what the human writers said. God saw to it that the human discourse was infallible; hence, all that we interpreters need do, so as to wind up with results which satisfy the principle that God does not speak falsehood, is interpret the biblical text in accord with the ordinary practices of interpretation for getting at what some human being said. By contrast, the "errantist" holds open the possibility that those human authors may have affirmed falsehoods, and may have said what does not conduce to love. But since God does not speak falsely or unlovingly, one of the principles guiding the interpretative move from the mediating human discourse to the divine mediated discourse must be that God is not to be interpreted as saying what is false or unloving.

The intensely polemical relations in the modern world between the adherents of these two strategies obscures the fact that the differences between them are considerably less than first meets the eye. For one thing, if all goes well in the process of interpreting, both strategies yield *the outcome* that false and unloving speech is never attributed to God. However, for our purposes what is more important to observe is that neither party simply uses ordinary principles of interpretation for discerning discourse. Both parties use *the exceptional* principle, that in trying to discern what the author said, we are to keep in mind that nothing false or unloving is to be attributed to the author. The fundamental difference between the two parties lies in the fact that they use that exceptional principle at different points in the whole process: the inerrantist uses it when interpreting the human discourse, and thus has no need of it thereafter; the errantist uses it only when moving from the human discourse to discernment of the divine discourse.

Most if not all inerrantists would bridle at what I have just said. On their self-description, they use ordinary principles of interpretation to discern what the human authors said; and that just *proves to be inerrant* because of God's guidance and inspiration. Nowhere, so they say, is their interpretation guided by the principle that nothing false or unloving is to be attributed to the author in question – be that author God or some human biblical writer. But consider the example I cited earlier, from Psalm 93, where the psalmist writes that God "has established the world; it shall never be moved." It's clear that if the psalmist was speaking literally at this point, he was affirming geocentricism. But contemporary inerrantists are not geocentricists; they believe that geocentricism is false. Accordingly, they look for some non-literal interpretation of the psalmist's words which won't saddle him with a false geocentric cosmology. Yet they also go along with the standard historical view that most ancient persons were geocentricists; when ancient peoples used sentences synonymous with this one of the psalmist, they were affirming geocentricism. Nonetheless, the biblical writer, so the inerrantists say, was not speaking literally.

What makes them think not? Well, they don't base their conclusion on extensive research into the thought-patterns of ancient Hebrews.

They haven't discovered a pocket of avant-garde solar-centricists among the ancient Hebrews, of which the psalmist was a member, on the basis of which knowledge they conclude that he must have been speaking metaphorically when he said that the earth shall never be moved. Nor have they discovered some particularity about the psalmist which leads them to conclude that though he believed, along with everyone else around him, that the earth is fixed, nonetheless he was using those words about the earth's fixity metaphorically in this case. Instead, their rejection of a literal interpretation is motivated by their conviction that if the author had been speaking literally, he would have said what is false. Since, on their view, biblical writers don't speak falsehoods, it just follows that the literal interpretation must be discarded.

It follows that inerrantism does not immunize the interpretation of scripture against the vagaries of human beliefs about reality and morality. Both the errantist and the inerrantist, each in his own way, allows the conviction that geocentrism is false to shape his interpretation of what God was saying by way of that passage from Psalm 93. The strategy of the inerrantist, rather than circumventing what gives rise to the wax-nose anxiety, evokes that anxiety.

## *Does Frei's strategy alleviate the anxiety?*

But might it be that the fateful defect in the strategy of the inerrantist is that it is not radical enough? The inerrantist can keep his own beliefs about reality and morality out of the picture when he moves from interpreting the human discourse of the Bible to interpreting for the divine mediated discourse because he has already given those beliefs a decisive role in his interpretation of the human discourse. But why not go one step further and keep them out of our interpretation of the mediating discourse? Why not, in that way, make our interpretation of the biblical text truly immune to the vagaries of our convictions as to how things are outside the text?

How could we do that? Well, an important component in my argument over the past several chapters has been that if the goal of our interpretation of a text is to find out what the author was saying with that text, then we cannot just concern ourselves with the meanings of words and their place in the text but must bring into play considerations of what the author would and would not have wanted to say. We move from a literal to a figurative interpretation in a given case because we are convinced that the author would not have wanted to say what the literal interpretation would have him saying. In the context of assuming that Michael would not have wanted to say what he didn't believe, we reason, "Michael can't have meant it literally, because he knows that's not true." Of course we do learn new things about persons by interpreting their discourse; but such interpretation can only be conducted by eliminating and adopting proposed interpretations in the light of things we already know or believe about the person. Those beliefs may well be false, however. When they are, rather than enabling correct interpretation, they all too often cause false interpretation.

How could this be avoided? How could interpretation remain internal to the text and the language used in the text? Only by setting aside the practice of authorial-discourse interpretation and practicing performance interpretation. And as we saw at the end of the preceding chapter, that is exactly what Hans Frei did, once he saw that textual-sense interpretation, which he tried to practice in the early part of his career, rested on the untenable assumption that there is such a thing as *the sense* of a text. Furthermore, Frei's interpretative strategies throughout his career were chosen with the aim of alleviating a near-relative of the wax-nose anxiety which we are considering. So let us now take a closer look than we have heretofore at Frei's proposal.

Frei's best known book is *The Eclipse of Biblical Narrative*. About the book, he says in one place that

When I wrote *The Eclipse of Biblical Narrative*, ... what I had in mind was the fact that if something didn't seem to fit the world view of the day, then liberals quickly reinterpreted it, or as we say today, "revised" it. And my sense of the matter, though I'm not antiliberal, was that you can revise the text to suit yourself only just so far. There really is an analogy between the Bible and a novel writer who says something like this: I mean what I say whether or not anything took place. I mean what I say. It's as simple as that: the text means what it says.[5]

It's fairly clear from this passage alone, and it would be even more clear if this passage were read in the light of others I could cite, that Frei himself saw his work as motivated by an anxiety very like that which I have called "the wax nose anxiety." Not quite identical: Frei, in his account of biblical interpretation, was not concerned with interpreting the Bible to find out what God was saying thereby. But obviously a near relative.

Some preliminary points must be made before Frei's strategy can be presented. First, Frei's focus was entirely on the interpretation of the narratives of the Bible, and more specifically, on the narratives of the Gospels; he never, in his writings, ventured beyond that. Second, though Frei's assumption throughout *The Eclipse* was that there is such a thing as *the sense* of a text, it becomes clear from some of his late essays that he had second thoughts about that. In place of his earlier assumption that a text has a single sense, he began to claim that though there is a multiplicity of senses which the biblical text can rightly be thought of as *having*, there is one which has the status of being the *established* sense in the tradition of Church interpretation.[6] Lastly, as I mentioned above, Frei makes no use of the notion of *God speaking* by way of the text. In fact, he also makes no use of the notion of some human being speaking by way of the text. His concern is entirely with senses of the text.

When Frei surveyed the pattern of gospel interpretation in the modern and contemporary church, what struck him was the "eclipse", as he called it, of biblical narrative; that is, the obscuring of the narratives of the gospels from the view of interpreters. Something there was that made the interpreters scarcely capable of seeing the narrative. This eclipse from view seemed to Frei calamitous. In *Eclipse* it's not clear why; the impression conveyed is that the sheer *thereness* of the narrative is sufficient to ground the call for interpreters to attend to it. But Frei's other book, *The Identity of Jesus Christ*, published at the same time, makes clear that that was not his thought. The gospel narratives present to us the enactment by Jesus of Nazareth of his identity as Messiah. They are far and away our best access to that enactment; and for religious purposes, an entirely adequate access. It is the importance of reliable access to Jesus' enactment of his identity that makes attention to the gospel narratives important.

The questions to which Frei devoted most of his thought were then these: Why has biblical narrative been eclipsed from view in the modern world, especially in the Church, of all places; and what can be done to undo this eclipse? Frei claimed to have identified three assumptions which together, as he saw it, accounted for the eclipse. One was the assumption, made by almost all interpreters, that, to use Frei's words, the *meaning* of the gospel narratives is some *reference* or other. Now when those of us who have been trained in the modern philosophical tradition hear the words "meaning" and "reference" in combination, we immediately think of Frege. I submit, however, that to have Frege's distinction in mind when reading Frei is to sink into total bewilderment. By the *meaning* of a passage Frei means *its point*: what the passage is trying to set before us, what the passage is trying to call to our attention. Frei thinks that one of the fateful assumptions of modern interpreters has been the assumption that the point of the gospel narratives lies outside those narratives, in something that is supposedly *the reference* of those narratives. A second assumption has been that the purported reference of the gospel narratives – what they mean to set before us – is certain happenings in first-century Palestine. And a third assumption, arising more slowly, and interacting with those first two, has been that the events which the gospel narratives purport to present to us are very different from any events that actually transpired back there in first-century Palestine; in good measure, what they purportedly referred to was not there to be referred to.

Now most interpreters of the gospels were faithful members of the Church. Being such, they were not willing to relieve the tension among these three assumptions by concluding that these narratives lack meaning, lack point. Instead, those who were members of the liberal party surrendered the assumption that the reference was to events in first-century Palestine, and began to say that the reference must be instead to some dimension of the inner life, or to some such abstract entity such as the Kingdom of God, or Reconciliation, or Authentic Existence. But on that way of thinking, the role of the narrative is to introduce us to that other, truly important, thing, the reference; and shortly, so Frei argued, one must expect that the narrative itself will be virtually eclipsed from view, especially when that to which it supposedly refers is itself not at all narrative in character.

Members of the conservative party, so Frei claimed, also accepted the near-universal assumption that the meaning of these narratives is their reference; but since they chose to hang on to the traditional assumption that their reference is to happenings in first-century Palestine, they were forced into combating the liberals on the issue of historical skepticism so as to relieve the tension. The gospel narratives, they insisted, are fully accurate presentations of events in first-century Palestine. But it's also true on this way of thinking that the role of the narrative is to introduce us to those other, truly important, things outside the narrative. Accordingly, the narrative of the gospels themselves was as much eclipsed from their view as it was from the view of the liberals.

Frei's own proposal for relieving the tension was that we reject the assumption that the meaning of the gospel narratives is their reference – the assumption that their point is something outside themselves that they present to us. The meaning of the narrative is the narrative. What the narrative aims to set before us is itself: those events in that sequence. It means what it says, says Frei; by which he was not claiming that the narrative means what it *says* rather than what it *intends* to say, but that the point of the narrative is the narrative itself.

And as to interpreting the narrative: we are to set off to the side all convictions we may have as to how well the narrative fits anything outside itself, and just interpret the words. After all, none of us, in our interpretations of fiction, allows our interpretation to be shaped by our judgments as to how well the story fits the facts. Interpretation of the gospels by Christians is to consist entirely of working out the details of that one sense, from among the variety of possible senses of the text, which has been "established" by the church. That done, interpretation is finished. Then, but only then, is it appropriate to raise the question of truth; specifically, to raise the question of how well the established sense fits the events surrounding the historical person, Jesus of Nazareth. Some people find themselves believing that that sense does fit that historical person; they have faith. Others find themselves not believing that.

Frei's intervention in the interpretative practice of the modern Church was extraordinarily influential; it was one of the dynamics behind the recent surge of interest in biblical narrative, and it has proved provocative for a great many theologians. Interpretation first, then faith – or disbelief. In a lecture which he delivered at Harvard in 1967, titled "Remarks in Connection with a Theological Proposal," Frei remarked that "My plea here is – the more formal, the less loaded we can make the notion of understanding, the better. And that, in turn, involves a search, in deliberate opposition to most of what I find in contemporary theology, for categories of understanding detached from the perspectives we bring to our understanding, including our commitments of faith."[7]

The first thing to notice about Frei's proposal, however, is that the argument within which it is embedded is seriously out of focus. Over and over in *The Eclipse of Biblical Narrative* Frei declares that the meaning, the point, of the gospel narratives is the narratives themselves, not some supposed reference of the narratives to something outside themselves. Yet an implication of *The Identity of Jesus Christ* is that, on Frei's view, the meaning of the narratives for the believer is not the narratives themselves but those historical events back in first-century Palestine which the narratives present to us.

Imagine someone with Frei's theology practicing Frei's style of interpretation on one of the gospels. Such a person would indeed pay close attention to the narrative of the gospel; the narrative would not be eclipsed from view. But the reason she would attend to the narrative is not that she had abandoned the supposedly traditional conviction that the meaning of the narrative is its reference, embracing in its place the conviction that the whole point of the narrative is the narrative itself. She would do so out of her conviction that the narrative presents ("refers to") Jesus of Nazareth enacting his identity as Messiah. The only sort of text that can adequately render that sort of thing is a text in narrative form.

A narrative doesn't come bearing its point just *qua* narrative – come bearing its "meaning," in Frei's terminology. What else could the point of a narrative be but the point of someone's offering us the narrative – or the point of our putting the narrative to one and another use. Frei's argument, when seen in its totality, proves not to be an argument to the effect that the meaning of the gospels is the narrative thereof but to the effect that the meaning of the gospels, for Christians, is their reference to Jesus' enactment of his identity.

The question immediately comes to mind how Frei's mode of interpretation differs from that of the conservatives, as he describes that. Frei is not entirely clear on the point. But the answer, I think, is that though he regards the Gospel narratives as a whole as presenting to us Jesus' enactment of his identity as Messiah, he did not regard all parts of the narrative as presenting that enactment in the same way. The following rough and ready generalization holds: as we move from the infancy narratives to the passion and resurrection narratives, we move from the narratives functioning "symbolically" to the narratives functioning "historically." That former mode of functioning is not a deficiency in the narrative, Frei insisted; there is no better way of presenting to us the astounding reality of Jesus' enactment of what might be called his "Chalcedonian identity." The conservative, by contrast, regards the narrative in its entirety as functioning "historically."

For our purposes here we can afford to pay no further attention to the out-of-focus character of Frei's overall argument, and can concentrate just on his proposal for dealing with his near-relative of the wax-nose anxiety: those who are members of the Christian community, says Frei, should interpret for that illocutionary stance, and that overall meaning of the sentences in the context of the text, which the Church has established. All considerations as to the truth or falsity of that sense are to be kept at bay until interpretation is finished.

The proposal does not achieve the goal desired, certainly not for anyone whose concern is to interpret for divine discourse. That can best be seen by posing a dilemma. Suppose that when the biblical text is interpreted as Frei proposes, the sense assigned to some of its declarative sentences prove false – the opening of Psalm 93, for example. Then to conclude that what God said, by appropriating that sentence for His own discourse, is identical with the meaning which the established sense assigns to that sentence, would be to ascribe falsehood to God; and that won't do. So we look around for some other interpretation; and we do so *because* we are convinced that the assigned sense is false cosmology and that God doesn't speak falsehood. The wax-nose anxiety is as relevant at this point as ever.

Suppose, on the other hand, that when the biblical text is interpreted as Frei proposes, none of the senses assigned to its sentences proves false in our judgment. For example, suppose that that sentence from Psalm 93, about the earth being fixed, is assigned a figurative rather than a literal interpretation in the established sense of the Church; and suppose that that assigned tropic sense is, in our judgment, true. So far forth, then, there is no obstacle to concluding that God says, by way of a certain sentence in the text, what the established sense assigns to that sentence as its meaning. As with inerrantism, nothing in the move to the mediated divine discourse evokes the wax-nose anxiety.

But what would make things turn out so serendipitously? We know what makes them turn out thus when the inerrantist strategy is followed: the inerrantist interprets in accord with the principle that the text is never to be interpreted in such a way that the human author says something false. What would bring about this same fortuitous development on the Frei strategy?

Obviously what brings it about is the considerations that the church used in choosing a certain sense for its established sense. As we saw earlier, Frei, by the time he wrote his late essays, realized that the Church had, in principle, a wide variety of senses from which to choose. He realized that the Church has traditionally read the Bible as *one book*; and he recognized that the various books of the Bible are so diverse that the totality is susceptible to a variety of different interpretations. Accordingly, the question to ask is why the Church established the sense that it did establish.

To the best of my knowledge, Frei never addressed this question head on; the focus of his attention was always on how contemporary members of the Church should proceed, *given that a sense has been established*. But surely a large part of the answer is that the Church wanted the content of its interpretation to be true, and chose from among its options in the light of that desire. In the traditionally established sense, the language of suffering and unhappiness which is applied to God in the biblical text is all treated as metaphorical. Why is that? Because the Church believed that God is perfect and that a perfect being does not suffer.[8] In the more or less established sense of the modern liberal church, the language of miracles in the biblical text is all interpreted non-literally. Why is that? Because the liberal wing of the modern Church believes that God does not suspend natural law by miraculous intervention in the course of nature. In short, if it should serendipitously turn out that, in our judgment, all the sentences in the traditionally established sense are true, thereby making it possible to say that God speaks that sense, that is because, in deciding to establish a certain sense, the Church made use of its convictions as to what is true and what is false. But once we notice that, the wax-nose anxiety again wells up.

### Coping with the anxiety

I conclude that there is no way to avoid employing our convictions as to what is true and loving in the process of interpreting for divine discourse – no way to circumvent doing that which evokes the wax-nose anxiety, the anxiety, namely, that the convictions with which we approach the process of interpretation may lead us to miss discerning what God said and to conclude that God said what God did not say. The anxiety is appropriate, eminently appropriate, and will always be appropriate. Only with awe and apprehension, sometimes even fear and trembling, and only after prayer and fasting, is it appropriate to interpret a text so as to discern what God said and is saying thereby. The risks cannot be evaded.

But they can be diminished; and it is on that, then, that we should concentrate our attention. So let me close with some remarks on diminishing the risks. In the first place, we should remind ourselves of two presumptions in the logic for the interpretation of appropriating discourse, as I have outlined that. One, is the presumption that the appropriator says what the person whose discourse is appropriated said. The appropriated discourse anchors the appropriating discourse.

There may well be good reason for departing at certain points from the results of applying that principle; but that, then, is what we must be attentive for, good reason for departing. Absent such good reason, we interpret the appropriator or deputizer as saying what the person whose discourse is appropriated or deputized said. Appropriation is not license for unbridled play of imagination on the part of interpreters. The human authors of the Bible clearly claimed that God intervenes directly in the course of nature and human affairs; if we choose to depart from that in the course of interpreting for divine discourse, we need good reason for doing so. Likewise, they clearly ascribed unhappiness and even suffering to God; if we choose to depart from that, we need good reason for doing so. And let it be added that having good reason to depart is also not license for unbridled play of the imagination. Roughly speaking, we are to stay as close as possible to the mediating discourse, given our convictions as to what the appropriator would have wanted and not wanted to say by appropriating this discourse thus expressed. Interpretation of the mediating discourse anchors interpretation of the mediated discourse.

And just as the appropriated discourse anchors the appropriating discourse, so the meanings and accepted tropic usages of the sentences anchor the human discourse. For a presumption of authorial-discourse interpretation is that the speaker says what his sentence means. There may be good reason in a given case for departing from the results of that presumption; but that then is what we are attentive for, good reason for departing. And when we do find good reason to depart from literal interpretation, the presumption is that the speaker is using the sentence in some linguistically accepted tropic manner. In a given case there may also be good reason for departing from the results of that presumption, and concluding that he is using it idiosyncratically; but good reason for departing from the presumption is what we are attentive for. Leibniz states the point well:

But it seems to me that a question remains which the authors I have just mentioned did not investigate thoroughly enough, namely: suppose that on the one hand we have the literal sense of a text from Holy Scripture and that on the other we have a strong appearance of a logical impossibility or at least a recognized physical impossibility; then is it more reasonable to give up the literal sense or to give up the philosophical principle? There are certainly passages where there is no objection to abandoning the literal sense – for instance, where Scripture gives God hands, or attributes to him anger, repentance and other human affects. Otherwise we would have to side with the Anthropomorphites, or with certain English fanatics who believed that when Jesus called Herod a fox he was actually turned into one. This is where the rules of interpretation come into play; but if they provide nothing which goes against the literal sense in deference to the philosophical maxim, and if furthermore the literal sense contains nothing imputing some imperfection to God or involving a threat to pious observances, it is safer and indeed more reasonable to keep to the letter.[9]

Secondly, one minimizes the risk by doing one's best to remain genuinely open to the possibility that the beliefs with which one approached the enterprise of interpreting for divine discourse are mistaken. Interpreting Scripture is not an isolated enterprise but is to be seen and practiced as a component in one's attempt to arrive at that totality of beliefs which seems to one, on reflection, to have the greatest likelihood of being true. Sometimes that requires concluding that God was not saying what, on first reading, God appeared to be saying. But often it requires concluding that the beliefs one had about the world, about human beings, about history, about God, or whatever, were mistaken.

Genuine openness to the possibility that the beliefs one had were mistaken, and creative imagining of different options for achieving reflective equilibrium, are typically nurtured by breaking out of one's solitude and comparing one's own interpretations with those of others, especially with those of others whose epistemic condition and situation is significantly different from one's own: persons of different gender, persons from different positions in the social hierarchy, persons of different nationality, persons of different race, persons from different historical eras, persons with different educational backgrounds, persons of different temperament, persons of different theological orientation or ecclesiastical location. Of course, awareness of this diversity of interpretations remains relatively useless unless one also struggles to become self-critical – self-suspicious in the modern sense of "suspicion" – so as to be able to listen to those alternative interpretations, genuinely listen. Parochialism, especially arrogant parochialism, makes it inevitable that scripture becomes a wax nose in our hands.

Thirdly, one minimizes the risk of missing or misinterpreting the divine discourse by cultivating knowledge of ourselves and of the world: psychological, social, physical. Perhaps this point is the least important; nevertheless, it is to be noted that it is our science which has put us in the position of being better able to discern what God was saying by way of Psalm 93. Where once readers might reasonably have supposed that God was propounding geocentricism, we know now that that is not the case. And when we assemble the sizable number of revisions induced by what we have learned from modern science, we begin to see, or think we begin to see, a pattern: God is not interested in speaking to us, by way of scripture, about very many of the sorts of things that modern science deals with. But we must step cautiously here. There is a great deal of salesmanship in contemporary writing about science. Much of what is announced as "something science has discovered" is nothing of the sort but merely something held by certain scientists. Nevertheless, the point remains: modern science enables us to discern God's discourse with greater accuracy.

The most important point remains: one minimizes the risk that Scripture is becoming a wax nose in one's hands by coming to know God better. I have several times made the point that though our knowledge of human beings comes in good measure from interpreting their discourse, it is also a fundamental prerequisite of interpreting a human being's discourse that one already know a good deal about that person. Interpretation of a person's discourse occurs, and can only occur, in the context of knowledge of that person. When one fears that in spite of having heard all the words a human being uttered and knowing all their meanings, one is nevertheless missing or misinterpreting that person's discourse, the thing to do is get to know that person better so as to be able better to determine what they would and would not have wanted to say. So too for God: to interpret God's discourse more reliably, we must come to know God better. A hermeneutics of divine discourse requires supplementation with discussions of other ways of knowing God, and of ways of knowing God better. And engaging in the practice of interpreting texts so as to discern God's discourse requires engaging simultaneously in whatever practices might yield a better knowledge of God. Those practices will be practices of the heart as well as the head, of devotion as well as reflection.

A leisurely approach to the text, the cultivation of a quiet receptiveness which allows the Holy Spirit to speak in a man's heart as it will, patient reflection upon every detail of expression; these had long been the features of the "holy reading" (*lectio divina*) of monastic life. At its best it led to a sharp and lively perception of the text and its meaning. (G. R. Evans, *The Language and Logic of the Bible: the Earlier Middle Ages*, p. 13)

## CHAPTER 14

# The illocutionary stance of biblical narrative

How can human discourse mediate divine discourse when the human discourse in question propounds error or expresses morally offensive attitudes? That question has sounded like a ground bass throughout a good deal of our discussion; and often, when it wasn't actually sounding, it was implied. Already in Chapter 3 I observed that when double agency discourse takes the form either of deputation or appropriation, it will typically be the case that not everything said by the agent of the mediating discourse is also said by the agent of the mediated discourse. And in Chapter 12 I took note of some of the general patterns of difference which emerge when we interpret the human discourse of the Bible for the divine discourse which it mediates, given the assumption that God speaks only what is true and conducive to love.

I want now to discuss one more aspect of this general theme. Since it concerns the genre of the Bible's mediating discourse, it would have been appropriate to discuss it earlier. But if one accepts the suggestion I will be making, one will find that some of the wax-nose anxiety which I discussed in the preceding chapter is thereby alleviated; that makes it appropriate to discuss it here. Up to this point in my discussion, my concern with interpretation has been entirely hermeneutical, that is to say, methodological and second-order in character. I will now leave that realm of abstraction and take the considerable risk of discussing an issue of actual interpretation in an area where it's not philosophers but biblical scholars who are specialists.

## The issue of illocutionary stance

The Bible, as I have mentioned several times, is extraordinarily diverse with respect to the genres of its component parts. Among its diverse genres are some which are completely unfamiliar to us; and some which are not only unfamiliar to us, but strike us as exceedingly strange. Not of course the letters; we are familiar with that genre, and understand it. But prophecy is certainly unfamiliar. And apocalyptic is not just unfamiliar but strange – weird, even. Narrative, again, is familiar. And a great deal of the Bible is narrative; if the Bible is a medium of divine discourse, then God is very much a story teller. But narrative comes in many forms. The genre of biblical narrative – are we familiar with that? Do we understand it?

Many of our disputes take for granted that we do. Many of us straightforwardly interpret Matthew as asserting – literally, now – that when Jesus breathed his last breath, "the curtain of the temple was torn in two, from top to bottom. The earth shook, and the rocks were split" (27: 51); and we then dispute whether this actually happened. The "conservatives" among us insist it did, the "liberals," that it did not. Many of us straightforwardly interpret Matthew and Luke as claiming that Jesus' cleansing of the temple occurred after his final triumphal entry into Jerusalem, and John as claiming that Jesus cleansed the temple much earlier in his ministry; and we then dispute the fact of the matter. The "liberals" among us insist that at least one of these narrations is mistaken, while "conservatives" of an inerrantist stripe retort that there could well have been two cleansings – why not?

Others of us, though, notice certain features of the gospel narratives which make us wonder whether such straightforward interpretations are the correct interpretations. Comparing Matthew with Luke, we notice not only that Luke's genealogy of Jesus is very different from Matthew's; but that Matthew has stylized his genealogy into three groups of fourteen, a stylization achieved, incidentally, at the cost of placing Jechoniah within the second of these groups as its terminus and within the third group as its beginning. This, once noticed, ineluctably leads one to wonder whether, perhaps, genealogies function symbolically for the gospel writers.[1] And if we read Matthew's narration of the rending of the temple veil after immersing ourselves for some time in apocalyptic literature of the day, it strikes us immediately that Matthew is here using familiar apocalyptic imagery. These, combined with many other examples of the same sort, lead one to wonder whether perhaps the straightforward interpretation often fails to give us what the gospel writers were saying – that is, fails to give us the *noematic content* of their speech actions. Perhaps it interprets as literal, language which was in fact used figuratively.

And maybe the straightforward interpretation doesn't get the illocu-

tionary stance right. I have pointed to two discrepancies among the
gospels: the discrepancy between John, on the one hand, and Luke and
Matthew, on the other, as to the temporal location of the temple
cleansing within Jesus' ministry; and the discrepancy between Matthew
and Luke on Jesus' genealogy. But these are just two of many
discrepancies among the gospel narratives. In recent years, "redaction
critics" have been emphasizing discrepancies in theological perspective
among the gospels; that is relatively new. By contrast, the church has
long known about discrepancies among the implied chronicles of these
narratives. Indeed, the *early* church already knew about such discrepancies, since within it there were sporadic attempts at harmonizing the
chronicles. But even though it knew about the discrepancies in
chronicle, it wasn't much troubled by them. It decreed that all four
gospels were to be read in the churches; it didn't discard the four in
favor of a harmonization.

That is surprising. For these are narratives of the crucified and
resurrected Lord of the church; for the church, there were, and there
are, no more important narratives than these. Why then would the
church sit so lightly on the discrepancies? Why wouldn't it do all in its
power to get things right – or at least, to get them consistent?[2]

Well, possibly it thought they were already consistent. Possibly it
took for granted that the discrepant chronicles of the four gospels could
be harmonized – that the discrepancies were only skin-deep. But if so,
then the puzzle is that it seems to have made no serious attempt to
assure itself on this score; harmonizing, though not unknown, was
never a big concern. The ancient church seems just to have lived pretty
much at ease with its knowledge of discrepancies.

I want to explore the possibility that the clue to this puzzling
situation lies in the fact that John, for example, was not asserting, in
contrast to Matthew and Luke, that the temple cleansing took place
early in Jesus' ministry, nor did the ancient church take him as asserting
that. He was doing something else than asserting this – taking up some
other illocutionary stance toward that proposition than the straightforwardly assertive stance. And more generally, I want to explore the
possibility that often where many see error in the gospel narratives,
they and we ought instead to spy the workings of an unfamiliar
illocutionary stance.[3]

I will not, however, make things easy by arguing that these
narratives, as a whole or in large part, are fictional; for it seems to me
clear, as clear as anything in this area, that they are not fictional. A

brief word about the nature of fiction is in order, since there's a great deal of confusion on this score. Whether some discourse, or the text produced thereby, counts as fiction, is not determined by the truth or falsehood of the designative content of that discourse. The designative content of a specimen of history or biography may be massively false while yet being history or biography; conversely, the designative content of a specimen of fiction may be massively true while yet being fiction. Truman Capote's "realistic fiction", *In Cold Blood*, is an example of this latter point. Neither does the "presence" of fictional entities in a piece of discourse make it fiction; a piece of discourse may be fiction without the "presence" of any fictional entities whatsoever. Again, *In Cold Blood* is an example. What makes fiction fiction is not anything about the designative (or noematic) content of the discourse, nor anything about the relation of that content to reality. What makes fiction fiction is simply the illocutionary stance taken toward whatever be the content. Rather than asserting, the teller of fiction *invites us to imagine*. The designative content of a piece of fiction might be exactly the same as the designative content of a piece of history; what makes one fiction and the other history is simply, to say it again, the illocutionary stance taken toward that content.[4]

Though biblical narrative obviously incorporates some fiction – the parables of Jesus, for example – the overarching stance of almost all biblical narrative is not fictive. The only plausible exceptions seem to me to be the book of Job and the book of Jonah. It makes no sense to think of the overarching stance as fictive. For the underlying theological conviction is that God did actually work in history for the salvation first of Israel, and then of all humanity; the stories all presuppose that worldview.[5]

But rather than arguing this case myself, it will be sufficient for my purposes here to appeal to authority. (Though as with everything in biblical studies, the view of the authorities I will cite is contested.) First, concerning the narrative sections of the Hebrew Bible, this is what Meir Sternberg says on the matter in his brilliant, though arrogant and polemically bristling, book, *The Poetics of Biblical Narrative*:

So does the Bible belong to the historical or the fictional genre? The mist enveloping the question once dissipated to reveal its communicative bearing, the answer becomes obvious. Of course the narrative is historiographic, inevitably so considering its teleology and incredibly so considering its time and environment. Everything points in this direction. (30)

And concerning the gospels, this is what N. T. Wright says on the matter in his recent book, *The New Testament and the People of God*. He is speaking specifically about Luke; but he says the same thing, *mutatis mutandis*, about the other Gospels:

Anyone who wrote [like Luke in the opening of his Gospel] was intending to describe historical events ... Luke was precisely a *historian*, not too unlike Josephus. (378)

From this perspective, we can see that a complete account of the nature of Luke's story must include two elements which are normally thought of as quite distinct. On the one hand, we have the Davidic story as just outlined, and with it the sense that Luke is conscious of telling, in a manner similar to Josephus, how it was that Israel's long story reached its paradoxical fulfillment. On the other hand, we must take full account of the recent arguments that the gospels, and perhaps Luke in particular, belong within the broad genre of Hellenistic biography. Luke blended together two apparently incompatible genres with consummate skill. He told the story of Jesus *as* a Jewish story, indeed as *the* Jewish story, much as Josephus told the story of the fall of Jerusalem as the climax of Israel's long and tragic history. (381)

The most full and cogent of the "recent arguments" to which Wright refers is that of Richard A. Burridge in his book, *What are the Gospels?*[6] Indeed, Burridge's multi-faceted argument is such that I find his conclusion incontrovertible: "a wide range of similarities have been discovered between the gospels and Graeco-Roman *bioi*; the differences are not sufficiently marked or significant to prevent the gospels belonging to the genre of *bios* literature. The increasing tendency among New Testament scholars to refer to the gospels as 'biographical' is vindicated; indeed, the time has come to go on from the use of the adjective 'biographical', for *the gospels are bioi!*" (243; cf. 256–9).

Among the similarities which Burridge notes between Graeco-Roman biographies and the gospels, is their way of using sources. The gospel writer, displaying as he does "the freedom to select and edit sources to produce the desired picture of the subject" (205), resembles the *bios* writer, who likewise displays "a certain freedom and licence, greater than that of the historiographer, to select and edit his oral and written sources, to deal with episodes in greater or lesser detail, or even to include or omit them when composing his portrait of the subject" (143). So far, no problem: the ancient biographers select and edit their sources, somewhat more freely than do ancient historians. But then, in the course of discussing Plutarch's *Lives*, Burridge lets fall a comment which arrests our attention:

Plutarch would have read widely first, with some note-taking, and then followed one main source when writing, supplemented by notes and memory. Such a method allows for great selectivity of material, and an account of an incident in one *Life* is sometimes contradicted by another. Although this can be explained by poor memory, more often it is because he wants to tell the story this way this time to illustrate this particular person's character. (174)

In ancient biography, an author's account of an incident "is sometimes contradicted" by another account of that same incident by that same author, because the author "wants it" thus. There is here an obvious similarity to that feature of the gospels to which I pointed above. But if Burridge is right on this, what were ancient authors *doing* in writing biographies? What illocutionary stance were they taking toward the incidents they mention? Burridge himself, oddly, doesn't note this similarity of ancient biography to biblical gospel with respect to apparent illocutionary stance; his emphasis is entirely on the similarity of selecting and editing. But if we can understand the workings of this "element of imaginative 'creative reconstruction' of the truth" in at least some ancient biography – *not fiction, but biography* – perhaps we will also understand the illocutionary stance of biblical narrative.

### Sternberg on the "omniscience" of biblical narrators

What principally motivates the suggestion I will make as to the illocutionary stance of biblical narrative is, as I have indicated, the fact that even though the gospels were surely understood by the ancient church as belonging to the genre of biography rather than fiction, nonetheless, discrepancies among the narratives were by and large untroubling to it – even though it made next to no attempt to satisfy itself that these discrepancies could be harmonized. However, I propose approaching my suggestion by calling attention to a quite different feature of biblical narrative which has been elaborately discussed by Meir Sternberg. It will for some time appear that I am circumambulating whatever might be my suggestion, rather than approaching it. At the end, however, it will be clear that that was not so, since any satisfactory theory of biblical narrative will have to take account of this other feature as well.

A narrative is not a mere chronicle; nonetheless, a narrative implies a chronicle, and, conversely, everybody who composes a narrative in the assertive mood makes use of a chronicle. The narrative always goes beyond the chronicle used in that it orders and interprets the events of the chronicle in such a way that the totality is meaningful to the author and, so he or she assumes, to the intended audience. Upon reading the narrative we feel that we understand what was going on; it makes sense. It must be added at once that sequences of events can make sense in different ways; thus two rather different narratives can use exactly the same chronicle. And naturally it is the case, given the diversity of ideologies and worldviews among us human beings, that what makes sense to one audience may strike another as nonsense at crucial points. Committed Freudians are probably convinced that Erikson has made sense of Luther's life as a whole; non-Freudians will have their doubts.

Though Sternberg doesn't himself employ this distinction between chronicle and narrative to describe the pervasive feature of biblical narrative to which he insistently calls attention and for which he proposes an account, it helps to do so. The feature is this: the chronicles implied by the biblical narratives typically include (purported) designations of events and states such that the use of normal human capacities would not yield to any author a knowledge of those. This is true especially in that the chronicles include (purported) designations of the doings of God, and (purported) designations of episodes in the inner lives of human beings other than whoever might have been the author.

Having taken note of this feature of biblical narrative, Sternberg goes on to offer an account of it – an account which simultaneously deals with what he takes to be the other salient features of biblical narrative. At the center of his account is his use of the contemporary literary-critical notion of an *implied narrator*, distinct from the author. Given that feature of the implied chronicle to which I just called attention, he holds that the narrator must be understood as *omniscient*. And he notes the additional fact that, with the exception of Nehemiah and part of Ezra, this implied narrator is never *self-referencing*. Classic biblical narrative has the point-of-view of an omniscient, non self-referencing, implied narrator: that is Sternberg's central contention. He explores the ideological significance of this (purported) fact; and, with extraordinary acuity and imagination, he analyzes specific narratives in its light.

We must say a bit about what he takes to be the ideological significance. You and I are thoroughly familiar with fiction of that structure which literary critics describe as having the point of view of an omniscient, non self-referencing, implied narrator. Whether or not that description is apt, there is fiction of the structure so described and we are familiar with it. Furthermore, though most writers of fiction don't any longer structure their fiction like that, we don't find anything theoretically problematic in fiction so structured. To the question: how could anybody know about the inner life of all the characters in the projected world of the fiction, we readily and happily give the answer: fictional characters aren't persons waiting around to be known by authors; they are "created" by authors. And authors can "create" them with whatever inner life they wish.

But what, asks Sternberg, are we to make of *a work of history* which is so structured? For let us recall that Sternberg regards biblical narrative as historiographic. If we're just invited to *imagine* a projected world of this sort – no problem. But what are we to make of someone projecting a world of this sort *in the assertive mood*? It makes no sense to us.

No doubt, says Sternberg. But if it is interpretation of these ancient texts that is our concern, then the relevant consideration is not whether these texts and the discourse of which they were the medium make sense to us; the relevant consideration is whether they made sense to the ancient Hebrews. And to answer that question, we have to know something of their ideological framework.

They did make sense to them, says Sternberg, in the following way. In the first place, we must be aware that central in the theology of ancient Israel was the conviction that there is a deep epistemological divide between God and human beings: God is all-knowing, whereas every human being is radically limited in his or her knowledge. Given the omniscience of the implied narrator, it was thus an implication of the theology of ancient Israel that it is *God* who is the implied narrator of classic biblical narrative. Every such narrative is to be interpreted as if it carried the preface: "And God said:".

Secondly, the ancient Hebrews believed that we human beings are not all confined, in our cognitive access to facts, to the use of our normal cognitive capacities. Some of us are granted, by divine inspiration, cognitive access to facts beyond the reach of our normal capacities. So how did the biblical author gain cognitive access to all those facts which he implicitly says God says? Partly by normal procedures; but in addition, by special divine inspiration. The authors of biblical narrative were understood as like the prophets, in that they communicate truths revealed to them by divine inspiration.[7] Sternberg makes this last point vividly by quoting a passage from the Babylonian Talmud in which the rabbis are discussing whether the book of Esther is inspired, and hence belongs in the canon:

Rabbi Eleazar says: Esther was composed under the inspiration of the Holy Spirit, as it says, "And Haman said in his heart." Rabbi Akiba says: Esther was composed under the inspiration of the Holy Spirit, as it says, "And Esther found favour in the eyes of all that looked upon her." Rabbi Meir says, Esther was composed under the inspiration of the Holy Spirit, as it says, "And the thing became known to Mordecai." Rabbi Yose ben Durmaskith said: Esther was composed under the inspiration of the Holy Spirit, as it says, "But on the spoil they laid not their hands." (Sternberg, pp. 58–59)

That is the essence of Sternberg's hypothesis concerning the structure of biblical narrative. It must be granted that it is an imaginative hypothesis, and that Sternberg's interpretations of biblical passages, always formulated within the framework of the hypothesis, are often wonderfully perceptive. Nonetheless, the hypothesis is fatally flawed. The fundamental flaw is that the conceptual framework of the implied narrator simply doesn't fit the structure of biblical narrative.

In caustic charged language Sternberg regularly accuses his fellow biblical scholars of using modern conceptualities entirely alien to the biblical text. It is ironic that, with no discernible hesitation whatsoever, he construes the structure of biblical narrative in terms of one of the main orthodoxies of contemporary literary criticism. Deep confusion results, he says, if we fail to distinguish "the real writer ... as a historical figure" from "the author or narrator as an artistic persona" (64). "Whoever the biblical writer was, he did not speak in his own voice and by his natural privileges. Hence the imperative need to distinguish the person from the persona: the writer as the historical man ... behind the writing from the writer as the authorial figure reflected in the writing" (69).[8] I shall brave this blustering confidence and argue that, on the contrary, confusion results *from trying to apply* the distinction. The concept of implied narrator has no application here.

To see this, we must become more ontologically serious than is the wont of literary critics and ask: what is an *implied narrator* supposed to be? Sometimes Sternberg speaks of it as a *persona* which the author adopts when narrating; he speaks of "the storyteller's persona" (75). He doesn't go on to say what such a *persona* is; but I assume that to adopt the *persona* of a narrator of a certain sort is to play the role of such a narrator. In playing some such role, the author will pretend to believe, know, feel, and say things which he in fact does not believe, know, feel, or say.

I have no doubt that there are such roles, and that all of us sometimes play them; we adopt such *personae*. But I submit that our mainline historians, when writing serious history, do not do so; nor do we their readers suppose they do. The historian speaks in his own voice. He doesn't *pretend* to assert that such and such happened; he *asserts* that it happened. And we his readers wouldn't find it acceptable if he *pretended* to know what he asserts; we want him *to know* what he asserts. Sternberg claims that in the ideological background of biblical narrative is the assumption that the writer is divinely inspired, and thereby knows things beyond his normal ken. But if he is thus inspired, then he *knows* those; he doesn't play the role of knowing them. And if he is a historiographer, he *asserts* them; he doesn't play the role of asserting them.

Knowing things by inspiration doesn't make one omniscient, however. And surely the biblical writers don't pretend to be omniscient – don't pretend to be God-like.[9] They don't pretend at all. Instead what they do – or appear to do – is assert, and thereby tacitly claim to know, various things which go beyond our normal human ken. And let it be noted that to know by inspiration what Haman said in his heart, one doesn't have to be omniscient; one only has to know by inspiration what Haman said in his heart. And to assert that and thereby tacitly claim to know it, one doesn't have to play the role of an omniscient narrator; all one has to do is assert it and thereby tacitly claim to know it. In one's own voice. Sternberg says that "given the biblical narrator's access to privileged knowledge – the distant past, private scenes, the thoughts of the dramatis personae, from God down – he must speak from an omniscient position" (12). As to why Sternberg would draw that extreme inference, I can only guess that he was letting the literary critical term of art, "omniscient narrator," run away with him.[10]

I know of only one other ontologically serious way of understanding the notion of an implied narrator, and that is along the following lines. Think of both the fictioneer and the historian as *projecting worlds*, with the fictioneer (dominantly) doing so in the fictive mood and the mainline historian (dominantly) doing so in the assertive mood. The world projected, be it by the fictioneer or the historian, will have a certain structure; for various purposes it is worthwhile to single out certain types of those. One such type of structure is that of a person uttering or inscribing (in some mood or other) the words of the text, thereby performing a monologic narration. Given a projected world so structured, the fictioneer *invites us to imagine* such a narrator and narration (such a "world"), the historian *asserts the actuality* of such a narrator and narration (such a "world").[11]

When the concept of *implied narrator* is understood along these lines, then Sternberg's thesis concerning the structure of biblical narrative goes as follows: the "world" which the biblical author assertively projects has the overall structure of someone narrating by way of uttering or inscribing the words that stand in the text. That is the situation assertorically set before us. Since the narrator is, so Sternberg claims, omniscient, and since the background ideology holds that the only omniscient being is God, the narrator is understood to be God: "the biblical narrator and God are not only analogues, nor does God's informational privilege only look far more impressive than the narrator's derivative or second-order authority. The very choice to devise an omniscient narrator serves the purpose of staging and glorifying an omniscient God" (89).[12] If the biblical author were a fictioneer, he would be inviting us to imagine that God had propounded a narrative with the words that stand in the text. But he's not a fictioneer, he's a historiographer, says Sternberg; so he is *asserting* that God propounded a narrative with the words that stand in the text. It goes without saying that the claim is that God propounded the narrative assertorically; the claim of the author is certainly not that God told fiction by way of the words of the text. And how does inspiration fit into this understanding? The answer is, awkwardly, as we will see in a moment.

Let us concede at once that this way of understanding the structure of biblical narrative is at least coherent, as that earlier *persona* way of understanding was not. So the question is whether the claim, that biblical narrative has this structure, is plausible. This whole way of understanding is, of course, complex; but the central issue is this: what is the evidence for the thesis that the implicit preface of all classical biblical narrative is: "Thus spoke the Lord"?

If the writers were tacitly claiming that God said all those things, presumably they also had a view as to *when* and *where* God said them, and *to whom*. A salient feature of the explicit reports of God's speech in the Bible is that God's speaking is almost always *located*. The answer to this question would presumably be that God addressed his narration *to the author*, at a time and place unmentioned. But if so, why is nothing of this sort ever said? The ancient Hebrews to whom God spoke seem not to have been shy of reporting that. Why were the writers of narrative so inhibited?

There was a convention in effect, says Sternberg. It was conventionally understood, by author and readers alike, that if one composed and published a narrative of this classic sort, one was tacitly claiming that God had spoken all of this to one. No need to say it.

But what reason is there to suppose that there was any such convention? Let's be sure that we have the "hard data" in hand. First, the narratives of the Hebrew Bible, with the exception perhaps of Jonah and Job, are, and were understood to be, historiographic narratives. Second, the implied chronicles of the historiographic narratives include items which are beyond the normal ken of anyone who might have been the human author. (I myself think that we have rather more access by normal means to facts about the inner lives of our fellow human beings than Sternberg and the ancient rabbis suppose; nonetheless, the point remains.) Third, with the exception of Nehemiah and part of Ezra, the narratives of the Hebrew Bible are so structured as to include no first-person singular pronominal references. And fourth, the Hebrew rabbis – who first began to flourish, it should be added, many centuries after the writings in the Hebrew Bible were completed – were of the view that by virtue of divine inspiration the authors of the biblical narratives had access to facts beyond their normal ken.

Now let it be seen clearly and said firmly that it doesn't follow from these facts that it was conventionally understood among the ancient Hebrews that the writers of those narratives which are included in the Hebrew Bible all tacitly claimed that God had narrated to them the narrative of their text. Not only does it not follow; those four facts don't even constitute *evidence* for this additional claim. Indeed, there's apriori reason to think that there wouldn't have been such a convention. The implied chronicles of the biblical narratives includes items beyond the normal ken of their authors; at some stage in Israel's history, divine inspiration is brought in to account for this "beyond". But the implied chronicles also include many items which fall within the normal ken of the authors. Now the theory under consideration says that everything in the chronicles – things known by normal means along with things known by inspiration – that everything in the chronicles was spoken by God to the authors. The hypothesis is that the totality was understood as prefaced with: "Thus spoke the Lord (to me)." Divine speaking went beyond divine inspiration: that's the idea.[13] But why would God bother to say to the author all sorts of things that the author knew anyway? It seems most implausible that there was any such conventional under-standing as Sternberg postulates – so much taken for granted that it was never mentioned. We'll need strong evidence to overcome this prior improbability.

Sternberg has an inkling of the kind of evidence needed. It has to be evidence that the authors of biblical narrative were regarded, by themselves and others, as prophets, or at least as prophet-like, not necessarily in that they, like prophets, spoke in the name of God, but at least in that they were recipients and transmitters of divine discourse. And then, not just of *some* divine discourse, but of the totality of what stands in their books.

Do we have strong evidence that the writers were so regarded?[14] If so, Sternberg doesn't offer it. He concedes the truth of Momigliano's remark, "The Hebrew historian never claimed to be a prophet" (p. 32). But then he goes on to say this: "Anonymity in ancient narrative validates supernatural powers of narration; and in Israelite culture, which not only institutionalized prophecy but invested its writings with canonical authority, the narrator's claim to omniscience dovetails rather than conflicts with his claim to historicity. It is no accident that the narrative books from Joshua to Kings fall under the rubric of Former Prophets" (33). As to the former of these sentences, I am at a loss to know what evidence is being cited that might support the claim in question. As to the latter: the mere existence of this rubric, absent information about the significance of its emergence and use, constitutes at best extremely thin evidence for the existence of a convention among the ancient Hebrews to the effect that narratives structured like those of the Hebrew Bible are to be understood as bearing the tacit preface: "Thus spoke the Lord (to me)."[15]

I submit that the most plausible hypothesis about the convention in question is that it is a product of the imagination of someone looking at the phenomena of biblical narrative through the lens of one of the orthodoxies of twentieth-century literary criticism. I suggest that we reject that orthodoxy, embrace literary-critical heterodoxy, and put behind us the assumption that all narrative has an implicit narrator structure. Biblical narrative does not, nor does assertoric narrative in general. (Nor, as I have argued elsewhere,[16] does most fictional narrative; but that's another matter!)

## *Contemporary examples of the illocutionary stance of biblical narrative*

We have explored two ways of construing Sternberg's hypothesis concerning the structure of biblical narrative; neither construal works. And since (to the best of my knowledge) there is no other ontologically serious way of construing that fundamental concept of an *implied narrator* than the two we have considered, Sternberg's hypothesis must be rejected. What I earlier called the "hard data" are still in search of a satisfactory account – in particular, the "hard datum" with which I began this discussion of Sternberg, viz., the chronicles implied by biblical narratives include items which go beyond the normal ken of human beings. Any satisfactory account of biblical narrative, and more particularly, of its illocutionary stance, will have to take account of that feature of the narratives. Though the feature is probably more prominent in the Hebrew Bible, on which Sternberg focuses exclusively, than in the gospels, it's not absent there. Let me give just one commonly cited example. Luke opens his gospel by saying that his narrative is based on the collection he has made of eyewitness accounts of the events concerning Jesus; nonetheless, in chapter 22 we read the following:

Jesus came out and went, as was his custom, to the Mount of Olives; and the disciples followed him. When he reached the place, he said to them, "Pray that you may not come into the time of trial." Then he withdrew from them about a stone's throw, knelt down, and prayed, "Father, if you are willing, remove this cup from me; yet, not my will but yours be done." Then an angel from heaven appeared to him and gave him strength. In his anguish he prayed more earnestly, and his sweat became like great drops of blood falling down on the ground. When he got up from prayer, he came to the disciples and found them sleeping because of grief.

How did Luke know what transpired with Jesus when the disciples were sleeping? (The counterpart passage in Matthew, chapter 26, raises the same issue.)

But any satisfactory account of the illocutionary stance of biblical narrative will also have to take account of that combination of phenomena with which I began this chapter: there are discrepancies among the chronicles implied by the gospel narratives which are of such a sort that the chronicles can't all accord entirely with the facts; the early church knew about these, but was by and large untroubled.[17]

Our attempt to understand the illocutionary stance of biblical narrative would presumably be assisted greatly if we could find some contemporary narrative with the same combination of traits that we find so perplexing in biblical narrative. It would have to be biography of a sort, maybe even history. The implied chronicle would have to include items which the author's exercise of his natural capacities would not – perhaps even *could not* – have given him good reason to think were factual. A few items might even be such that the author believed they were non-factual. Thus the implied chronicle would have to go beyond and maybe even diverge from the research chronicle of well-evidenced facts available to the author. Lastly, the author would have to regard his composition of biography or history with an implied chronicle of this sort as a reputable enterprise, and hope or even expect that we, the readers, would do so as well.

Are there any contemporary examples of such narratives? I think there are. Gore Vidal's "novels" of Lincoln and Burr appear to me to be of this sort.[18] But an example which is more provocative and challenging, coming as it does from an esteemed (though controversial!) member of the guild of historians, is Simon Schama's recent book, *Dead Certainties*.[19]

The book has two main parts. The first, called "The Many Deaths of General Wolfe," presents various perspectives on the death of General James Wolfe in the battle on the Plains of Abraham outside Quebec; in particular, we learn about the fascination of Francis Parkman Jr. with Wolfe, and of Parkman's struggles to write a history of Wolfe's career. The second main part, called "Death of a Harvard Man," deals with the murder of Francis Parkman's uncle, George. The connecting link is, of course, the Parkman family. About that link, Schama says this in his "Afterword":

Both stories are, of course, Parkman stories, and although I arrived with happy inadvertence at the George Parkman calamity by pondering the career of his more famous nephew, there seem, in retrospect, to be compulsions and obsessions that run through the entire tragic dynasty. The Parkman inheritance – lying at the core of Boston's own ambiguous *historical* relationship with old England and New England – deeply colours both stories. In flight from the expectations of that inheritance – Unitarian, moneyed, reasonable, Harvardian – Francis Parkman seeks the prairies and the forests ... George Parkman journeys equally far, to the asylums of the insane in Paris, but fails to break free of the obligations of his property, and becomes instead its rigorous steward and, ultimately, its victim.

This is history with a point – or with a couple of points. One point is to *show* something about the British in America. The writer of the jacket blurb for the book says well what that is: "In 'The Many Deaths of General Wolfe,' witnesses, artists, eulogists and historians all compete to celebrate an act that seems to confer authority and legitimacy on the imperial destiny of the Anglo-Saxons. But the 'Death of a Harvard Man' comes as a squalid, dismaying reproach to the moral self-esteem of a cultural elite just as its credentials for governance are being tested by cholera, massive immigration and urban crime."

The other point is a self-referential point about the craft of history. The "habitually insoluble quandary of the historian," says Schama, again in his "Afterword," is "how to live in two worlds at once; how to take the broken, mutilated remains of something or someone from the 'enemy lines' of the documented past and restore it to life or give it a decent interment in our own time and place" – and how to do this in full recognition of the uncertainties in that documentation, "however thorough or revealing" that documentation be. Historians "are left forever chasing shadows, painfully aware of their inability ever to reconstruct a dead world in its completeness …" Accordingly, "Both stories … play with the teasing gap separating a lived event and its subsequent narration. Although both follow the documented record with some closeness, they are works of the imagination, not scholarship. Both dissolve the certainties of events into the multiple possibilities of alternative narrations. Thus, General Wolfe dies many deaths …"

There seems to be a non-sequitur in those last sentences. Schama remarks, about a scholarly anthology containing "exhaustive documentation" of Wolfe's career, that it "makes abundantly clear the discrepancies between the many accounts of Wolfe's final moments" ("A Note on Sources"). But if that is so, it's scholarship, not imagination, that points up the uncertainties. Schama composes different narrations of Wolfe's death in accord with the different accounts. But we all catch at once what he's doing, and it poses no threat whatsoever to our traditional picture of the responsible historian as a scholar: instead of affirming that this is how Wolfe died, Schama is affirming that this is how he died according to one account, and that is how he died according to another account.

Schama has more up his sleeve, however; and to this more, the point about imagination is indubitably relevant. Indeed, twice again he makes the point. He knows, of course, that all writing of history involves some imagination; so that's not his point. "Even in the most austere scholarly report from the archives, the inventive faculty – selecting, pruning, editing, commenting, interpreting, delivering judgements – is in full play" ("Afterword"). But about the stories in hand, more has to be said. "This book is a work of the imagination that chronicles historical events," he says in his "Note on Sources." And in his "Afterword," "Though these stories may at times appear to observe the discursive conventions of history, they are in fact historical novellas, since some passages (the soldier with Wolfe's army, for example) are pure inventions, based, however, on what documents suggest."

Part One opens and closes with the example Schama refers to in this last comment. The Part opens with a foot soldier from Wolfe's army describing what the climb up the cliff and the opening of the battle was like; it closes with the same foot soldier describing the goings-on in the battle at about the time of Wolfe's death. It sounds like a letter home from a survivor. In fact it was not discovered in an archive somewhere but composed by Schama: pure invention, "based, however, on what documents suggest." "Purely imagined fiction," "constructed [however] from a number of contemporary documents" ("A Note on Sources"). About a "fictitious" dialogue in Part Two, Schama doesn't claim documents as its source but his own "understanding of the sources as to how such a scene might have taken place" ("A Note on Sources").

But not only does Schama allow imagination to go beyond what scholarship (fully) justifies when he puts words in the mouth of persons, and when he creates characters. He also allows his imagination to go beyond what scholarship (fully) justifies when he speaks in his own voice. For example, Schama's narrative in the second section of Part One, where he is speaking in his own voice about the life of General Wolfe, is peppered with claims about Wolfe's inner life. I cite just a few: "the humiliation of his position had galled him," "he was not eased by the embarrassing recollection," "he had realized how daunting his mission was, how idle the hope," "his proclamation, written, he thought, in the most sententious French," "in vexation he had begun," "the endless sense of impotence and rage that swelled inside him," "Wolfe was agonized," "he dreaded the jeering," "painfully aware that he was losing the authority," "brooded sourly"; and so forth, on and on.

Of course it's true that it takes imagination to be a historian. Nonetheless, we in the modern world have understood our historians as *asserting* everything in the projected worlds of their works – in particular, as asserting everything in the chronicles implied by their works. And then in turn we have expected of them that they would, at a minimum, obey the standard normative condition for assertion: to assert something only if one believes it and doesn't believe one is not entitled to believe it. (I will offer an account of *entitlement* in the next chapter.)

It's pretty obvious that Schama has broken with this understanding.

But where? And what is he doing instead? Well, it's abstractly possible that he's saying things he doesn't believe; or saying things he believes but doesn't believe he's entitled to believe. But that's most unlikely. Much more likely is that he isn't asserting everything in the world he projects – isn't asserting everything in the chronicle implied by his narrative. Schama projects for us a world in which a foot soldier of General Wolfe writes the words that we find in the opening section of *Dead Certainties*; but he isn't asserting that there actually was a foot soldier of General Wolfe who said those things. On this point, Schama is explicit. The implied chronicle of Schama's narrative includes the proposition that there was an endless sense of impotence and rage swelling inside Wolfe; but Schama isn't asserting that there actually was that sense.

So was it fiction he was writing; fiction which happened in good measure to be about historical figures, but still, just fiction? Was he merely inviting us to imagine the world he projects? I doubt it. Some of his language suggests that. But whenever he suggests that it is fiction he is writing, he immediately undercuts that suggestion. Furthermore, if it were fiction he was writing, he wouldn't be showing "the compulsions and obsessions that run through the entire tragic dynasty" of those actual persons who were the Bostonian Parkmans.

So what then is he doing? It's not entirely clear; perhaps the elusiveness of Schama's self-descriptions indicates that it's not entirely clear to him either. But perhaps something like this: in offering that chronicle of Wolfe's inner life, Schama is claiming that Wolfe was such, and the situation in which he found himself was such, that he might well have thought and felt those things. And in composing that foot soldier's letter, Schama is claiming that the situation was such that a foot soldier of Wolfe's army might well have written such a letter. Recall Schama's comment: "The more purely fictitious dialogues ... are worked up from my own understanding of the sources as to how such a scene might have taken place."

Schama is making assertions, not inviting us to imagine. But at several points, what he is asserting is not *actuality* but *plausibility*. Not that things *did go* thus and so but that, whether or not they did, they *might well have gone* thus and so – given such-and-such. The relevant kind of criticism to be brought at those points is not the kind brought against standard history, namely, that we lack good reason to think it did happen; but rather, that we lack good reason to think it might well have happened, given what the author is there taking as given.

Of course we have to understand Schama, at many points, as claiming or presupposing actuality, not just claiming plausibility. There actually was a General Wolfe, whose foot soldiers actually did scale that steep escarpment, to actually fight a battle on the Plains of Abraham, in which Wolfe actually died. It's about real happenings that Schama is talking, partly asserting that so and so happened, partly filling in the gaps by asserting that so and so might well have happened. For some purposes, it would be important to sort out exactly where Schama is claiming actuality and where, only plausibility; for other purposes, that's not at all important. There's also a matter of logic involved in Schama's claiming and presupposing actuality at various points: only with respect to certain givens can one consider what might well have happened. *Given* Wolfe's character, experience and situation, one can consider whether he *might well have* felt thus and so. Otherwise, not.

But what's the point? The point, presumably, is "to take the broken, mutilated remains of something or someone from the 'enemy lines' of the documented past and restore it to life or give it a decent interment in our own time and place." If we are reluctant to describe what Schama composes as "history" or "biography," then perhaps "portrait" will do: he has composed a portrait of historical events and historical figures. And with Rembrandt in mind, can there be any doubt that sometimes there is more truth, of the sort we care about, in a portrait of a living person than in a photograph?

It's my impression that Schama only allows himself to imagine, and then assert, plausibilities at those points where the documentary record is silent; he doesn't allow himself to go against the record. In that regard, the conscience of the modern historian, traditionally understood, remains alive in him. But is that absolutely necessary, given his purposes? Isn't Rembrandt allowed to alter the appearance of his subject in certain respects, so as better to reveal that person's character? People sometimes act in flukey, uncharacteristic ways. In constructing one's portrait, it might be best either not to mention those things or to alter them a bit.

## The illocutionary stance of the gospel narratives

Perhaps the chronicle of the events surrounding Jesus that was available to one gospel writer differed a bit from that available to another gospel writer; that seems not unlikely. If so, that would account for some of the divergences among the implied chronicles. But to move from chronicle to narrative: perhaps the gospel narratives are best understood as *portraits* of Jesus, designed to reveal who he really was and what was really happening in his life, death and resurrection; and perhaps they achieve that goal by, at certain points, going beyond and even against the available chronicle, not claiming at those points that things did go thus and so, but rather that, given the identity and significance of Jesus, they might well have gone thus and so. And as to the divergences among the implied chronicles of the gospels: though some of those may reflect somewhat different understandings of the identity and significance of Jesus, it's likely that others do not. Agreeing with each other on the identity and significance of Jesus, one author claims that Jesus' cleansing of the temple occurred late in his ministry, the other claims that it might well have occurred earlier, given the identity and significance of Jesus. No conflict there.[20] And one last point: both portraits may have been inspired.

For the purposes of the modern historian of the traditional sort, it is of indispensable importance, when confronted with these portraits, to sort out where the writers were claiming actuality and where they are claiming no more than illuminating plausibility; and that done, to determine which of the former claims are true. But there are other purposes that these portraits of Jesus serve, and other purposes – so I suggest – that they were meant to serve, than the purposes of the modern historian of the traditional sort. Surely it was those other purposes that the early church embraced – which would explain why they sat so lightly on the discrepancies.[21] Earlier I quoted a passage from the recent book by Richard A. Burridge, *What are the Gospels?* in which he is discussing Plutarch's lives. I broke off my quotation before the last clause of the passage. Let me now quote the passage whole:

Plutarch would have read widely first, with some note-taking, and then followed one main source when writing, supplemented by notes and memory. Such a method allows for great selectivity of material, and an account of an incident in one *Life* is sometimes contradicted by another. Although this can be explained by poor memory, more often it is because he wants to tell the story this way this time to illustrate this particular person's character. While Plutarch did not allow himself wholesale fabrication (as happened in encomium or invective), he does have an element of imaginative "creative reconstruction" of the truth as he saw it, in order to illustrate the way "it must have been." (174)

By "the way it must have been" Burridge means, I think: "the way it might well have been." That was ancient biography, he says; and the gospels were specimens of the genre. I am in no position to advance scholarship on that point. What I have sought to do in these last pages is deepen our understanding of the illocutionary stance which Burridge attributes to the writers of ancient biography by pointing to examples which show that the genre, after being moribund for a considerable time, is now again showing signs of life. Perhaps after Vidal and Schama we can once again understand Matthew and Mark, Luke and John!

CHAPTER 15

# *Are we entitled?*

The turn of the kaleidoscope confronts us at last with questions of epistemology. After distinguishing various modes of speaking, and offering an account of its nature, I went on to argue that, from a theistic perspective, God *could* speak; there is nothing impossible in that. From those issues of discourse theory and of philosophical theology, we moved on to issues of interpretation. Here I singled out for near-exclusive attention that long-enduring, though now intensely controverted, practice within the Christian community of reading the Bible so as to discern what God said by way of authoring it. I defended the legitimacy in general of authorial-discourse interpretation; and I considered how one ought to go about interpreting scripture if it is the single divine voice that one is looking for. Now at last we are face to face with the question: *does* God speak?

Our situation is not that we and a few others have recently begun to entertain the proposition that God speaks, and are now wondering whether to accept or reject that proposition. Countless human beings, down through the ages, and on into our own time and place, have in fact believed that God speaks. Let us, then, pose our question in full recognition of that fact; let us ask how such beliefs are to be appraised.

## *Locke on entitlement to religious belief*

I began the opening chapter by recalling a conversation which took place in a villa in Milan in the year 386. I propose setting the stage for this issue of appraisal by recalling an equally fateful conversation which took place 1285 years later, in the spring of 1671 in an apartment in Exeter House in London. The participants were John Locke and some five or six of his friends; the topic was various matters of morality and revealed religion – we don't know which. The participants, Locke tells us, were scarcely into their conversation before they felt themselves stymied "by the difficulties that arose on every side." They plowed ahead and kept on talking, but they were getting nowhere. After they had thrashed about in this fashion for some hours, the thought occurred to Locke that perhaps their whole procedure was misguided. Perhaps to advance one had first to retreat: instead of continuing to worry the issues at hand in the hope that answers would turn up if they just kept at it, perhaps they ought to turn inward for a while to examine the cognitive abilities of human beings, with the aim of determining which objects the human understanding is fit to deal with, and how; and then, with illumination on those matters in hand, return to the topic. It was this thought, says Locke, that led eventually to his *Essay concerning Human Understanding.*

The general epistemology which Locke developed there has been profoundly influential in the modern West; even more influential has been Locke's application of that general epistemology to the regional epistemology of religious belief. An indispensable preparation for thinking through for ourselves how we ought to appraise beliefs that God speaks is bringing to the level of conscious self-awareness this part of our cultural inheritance.

There are things deeply amiss, Locke concluded, in the practices that his fellow countrymen – and humanity in general – typically use for arriving at beliefs, especially beliefs on matters of religion and morality. One of the worst features of those practices is their use of tradition as a basis of belief. People believe without question what others tell them; they take them at their word. Since most of what people believe on say-so is false, there is scarcely a worse basis for belief than this. Admittedly believing on say-so cannot be eliminated from our lives; no one could possibly look into everything for herself. Nonetheless, for everyone there are certain questions whose answers one is *obligated to try one's best* to discover – matters of maximal "concernment", Locke calls them.

What constitutes doing one's best? Locke assumed, without question, that for every person and for every topic, the structure of doing one's best is the same. For every person, there are certain facts of which that person is directly aware. Typically such awareness produces a corresponding belief; when it does, that belief has maximal certitude. One can't do better in one's believings than this. The scope of such directly perceptible facts is extremely limited, however: each of us can be directly aware only of those facts consisting of relationships among the ideas and acts of one's own mind, and the relationship of those to one's mind itself. So what about all the other facts; what constitutes doing one's best to get in touch with those? Well, it may be that one can construct a demonstrative argument for some of them, starting from propositions one knows because one is directly aware of the corresponding mental fact. But if that doesn't work, then, for any proposition concerning some such fact, doing one's best consists of doing the following: first, from among the facts of which one is directly aware, assembling a satisfactory body of evidence concerning the truth or falsehood of that proposition. Second, calculating the probability of that proposition on that body of evidence. And third, believing or disbelieving the proposition with a firmness proportioned to its probability on that evidence.

Once he had this general epistemology in hand, Locke returned to the issues of morality and revealed religion which initiated his line of thought. For though he believed that what is of maximal "concernment" differs in good measure from person to person, Locke was also convinced that issues of morality and religion are of maximal "concernment" to everyone; our eternal destiny depends, or may well depend, on getting the answers to such questions right. It was doxastically irresponsible for Antony and Augustine to rest content with just finding themselves believing that God had spoken to them by way of those perceived events.

The first issue which faces us is whether God exists. Now the very concept of God yields the conclusion that God is identical neither with one's mind nor with one's mental acts or ideas. It follows that God is not something of which one can be directly aware. But neither is God something of which one can be *indirectly* aware, by way of God's appearing to one; the traditional notion of the presence of God and, correspondingly, of our awareness of God, has disappeared entirely from Locke's thought. If God turns up at all in the belief systems of those who try their best, God will appear there as an inferred entity. (And so will everything else which turns up there of which one is not directly aware – everything else which is not identical with one's mind or its modifications.) It was Locke's firm conviction that as a matter of fact there is a demonstration available to each of us that God exists, starting from propositions corresponding to mental facts of which one is directly aware; and that likewise there are available to each of us demonstrations of various attributes of God. What Locke regarded as the yield of such demonstrations was a knowledge of God very much like that which the high medievals believed was the yield of natural theology.

And what about propositions to the effect that God says so-and-so? Will doing our best ever yield belief in such propositions? Locke himself never addresses this precise question; the traditional notion of God speaking has all but disappeared from his thought, its place taken up by the notion of God revealing. But we can get a good indication of what he *would* say on the topic by looking at what he says about believing that God has *revealed* so-and-so, and then extrapolating from that.[1]

Locke draws the customary distinction between original and traditional revelation in the following way: original revelation is "that first impression, which is made immediately by God, on the mind of any man, to which we cannot set any bounds"; traditional revelation is "those impressions delivered over to others in words, and the ordinary ways of conveying our conceptions one to another" (*Essay* IV, xviii, 3). The word "impression" here is vague. When Locke speaks of "an impression made immediately by God on the mind," he means, as I understand him, a *belief*; revelation occurs when God directly brings about a belief in someone's mind.[2]

It will already be clear from the foregoing that, on Locke's view, the mere fact that God has planted a belief in one's mind does not entitle one to believe it. His language is vivid and emphatic:

He ... that will not give himself up to all the extravagancies of delusion and error must bring this guide of his light within to the trial. God when he makes the prophet does not unmake the man. He leaves all his faculties in their natural state, to enable him to judge of his inspirations, whether they be of divine original or not. When he illuminates the mind with supernatural light, he does not extinguish that which is natural. If he would have us assent to the truth of any proposition, he either evidences that truth by the usual methods of natural reason, or else makes it known to be a truth, which he would have us assent to, by his authority, and convinces us that it is from him, by some marks which reason cannot be mistaken in. Reason must be our last judge and guide in every thing (*Essay* IV, xix, 14).

So suppose God has originally revealed something to someone. How is that person to proceed? Well, somehow the thought comes to mind that God revealed this. What brings that about, Locke does not say; perhaps when God directly plants a belief in someone's mind, God also directly plants the second-level thought (though not necessarily the belief) that that first-level belief is a case of revelation. Be that as it may, the thought does come to mind; and the recipient of original revelation is obligated to set about doing his best concerning the proposition *that*

*God has revealed so-and-so to him.* Doing his best requires looking around for a miracle which will confirm that it was a case of revelation. "The holy men of old," says Locke, "who had revelations from God, had something else besides that internal light of assurance in their own minds, to testify to them, that it was from God . . . [They] had outward signs to convince them of the author of those revelations . . . Moses saw the bush burn without being consumed, and heard a voice out of it. This was something besides finding an impulse upon his mind to go to Pharaoh," and also something beyond the impulse to believe that that first impulse was planted in his mind by God (*ibid.*, IV, xix, 15).[3]

Locke conceded that original revelation might still be occurring; nonetheless, he was profoundly skeptical of anyone's claim to have experienced a contemporary episode thereof. The only episodes of original revelation he was himself willing to acknowledge were those ancient episodes recorded and reported in the Christian scriptures. His own attention was focused entirely on the books of the New Testament, which he regarded as divinely inspired, infallible records of original revelation by God to the writers – these infallible records in turn including a good many reports of original revelation received by someone other than the writer, in particular, by Jesus. Thus the Bible was for him an instrument of traditional revelation, not of original revelation. Our task in reading scripture is to do our best to figure out what God revealed back in antiquity, to the writers of the biblical books and to those other ancient persons that the writers report as having been recipients of revelation.

And what does doing our best look like in this case? If one wanted to do one's best to find out whether, say, God revealed so-and-so to the apostle Peter, how would one proceed? Well, one starts with the narration by a gospel writer, Luke, perhaps, of a claim of Peter's that God revealed so-and-so to him, and of Peter's claim that he experienced such-and-such miraculous event confirming that it really was a revelation he had received. One first determines the probability on satisfactory evidence that Luke has accurately narrated what Peter reported on these two matters. If that probability proves high, one believes with an appropriate firmness that Luke accurately narrated what Peter reported. Now one is ready to deal with the accuracy of Peter's reports. First one assesses the probability on satisfactory evidence that Peter really did have the experience which he claimed to have identified as receiving a revelation from God, and the probability on satisfactory evidence that he really did experience the event which he claimed to have identified as a miracle. If the probability of both of these turns out rather high, then one believes with an appropriate firmness that Peter really did have those two experiences which he thus identified. Now one is ready to consider the likelihood that Peter's claimed identification of those experiences was correct. First one determines the probability on satisfactory evidence that that event, which Peter identified as a miracle, really was a miracle. If that probability proves rather high, one believes with an appropriate firmness that if it occurred, it was a miracle. Then one moves on to consider the probability on satisfactory evidence that that miracle, if it was that, really does confirm that Peter's experience was an experience of receiving a revelation from God. If the probability of that proves rather high, one believes with an appropriate firmness that if that was a miracle, then Peter did receive a revelation from God. Lastly, one considers the probability on satisfactory evidence that if God did indeed reveal something to Peter, then it was so-and-so that God revealed, not something else. If the probability of that proves rather high, then one believes, quite infirmly by now, that so-and-so. One needn't, before believing the content of the purported revelation, take the additional step of assessing the probability on satisfactory evidence that the revealer is veracious and reliable; for it is a necessary truth, self-evident to us, that if God reveals something, it's true.

## *Practice and entitlement*

The topic before us is how we are to appraise that enormous number of humanity's believings which consist of believing that God said so-and-so. What must first be noted is that there is a wide variety of distinct merits (and corresponding defects) which believings are capable of possessing; and that for each of these merits one can attempt to determine, for a given believing, whether that believing has it or lacks it – or to what extent it has it or lacks it. We have all been schooled to consider which believings possess the merit of being cases of *knowing*, and which possess the merit of having *true* propositional *content*. But those merits represent only a small selection from the totality. In his recent book *Warrant*, Alvin Plantinga has introduced the concept of *warrant* – by which he means, that which must be added to a belief whose propositional content is true to make it a case of knowledge. One might consider whether a given believing has that merit. William Alston, in his recent book *Perceiving God*, carves out a concept of justified belief according to which, to quote him, "being justified in believing that p is for that belief to be based on an objectively adequate ground, one that is (fairly) strongly indicative of the truth of the belief" (99). One might consider whether a given believing has that merit. Closely related, and much discussed in recent years, is the concept of being formed by a reliable belief-forming process. One might consider whether a given belief has that merit. And prominent in the philosophical tradition for many centuries have been disputes over which beliefs have the merit of *belonging to good science*.

The merit which occupied the center of Locke's attention is different from any of those I have mentioned. It is that of a belief being such that the person is *entitled* to that belief. The assumption is that *deontic* concepts, concepts of *obligation*, apply to believings. Some believings of a person are ones that he ought not to have, some, are ones that he ought to have, and some – the ones for which it is *not* the case that he *ought not* to have them – are ones that he is permitted to have, *entitled* to have. Perhaps there are also some he doesn't have that he ought to have.

Epistemology is that branch of philosophy in which we attempt to develop accounts of truth-relevant merits in believings. What makes the field so extraordinarily difficult and confusing is the combination of, on the one hand, this plethora of distinct merits, with, on the other hand, competing theories, for each such merit, as to the conditions under which a believing has it or lacks it. Despair is a natural response. But this whole array of believings, that God said or is saying so-and-so, cries out for appraisal. Some are so bizarre as to lack whatever merit one can think of. Many have proved utterly appalling in their consequences: human blood has been shed, oppression imposed, suffering experienced, as the consequence of one and another person believing that God had spoken to him. We can't let despair get the better of us and just walk away. So which, from this dizzying array, shall we focus on? We can't deal with them all.

I propose focusing on that one which was at the center of Locke's attention and which, from the seventeenth century until recently, was probably at the center of most discussions of these matters – the merit of *entitlement*. All of us would dearly love to know which, if any of these believings are true. But one can see why Locke focused on entitlement. The facts which make the propositions we are considering, and those we believe, true or false, are mainly not even in principle available to us for our awareness, certainly not for our direct awareness; by

contrast, whether or not one has fulfilled one's (subjective) obligations is
something that one can discern, at least in principle, by reflection. So
we aim at fulfilling our duties in our believings; and hope and trust that
in believing as we ought and may, we are getting truth in hand.
Furthermore, fulfilling one's duties in one's believings takes precedence
over aiming at their exhibiting one and another merely admirable
feature. Locke puts the point nicely in a well-known passage from the
*Essay*. Ignore, on this occasion, the allusions to his own views concerning the grounds of obligations and the criterion for entitlement in
belief:

> He that believes, without having any reason for believing, may be in love with
> his own fancies; but neither seeks truth as he ought, nor pays the obedience
> due his maker, who would have him use those discerning faculties he has
> given him, to keep him out of mistake and errour ... He that does not this to
> the best of his power however he sometimes lights on truth, is in the right but
> by chance; and I now not whether the luckiness of the accident will excuse the
> irregularity of his proceeding. This at least is certain, that he must be
> accountable for whatever mistakes he runs into: whereas he that makes use of
> the light and faculties God has given him, and seeks sincerely to discover
> truth, by those helps and abilities he has, may have this satisfaction in doing
> his duty as a rational creature, that though he should miss truth, he will not
> miss the reward of it. (*Essay* IV, xvii, 24)

I said that from the seventeenth century onwards the merit of
entitlement has been at the center of these discussions – *until recently*.
Recently many epistemologists have concluded that there is no such
merit in believings as *entitlement*. Members of the family of deontic
concepts – ought, ought not, duty, may, permitted, entitled, – simply
do not apply to believings. The main reason offered is that our
believings and non-believings are not the outcome of acts of will on our
part, but of dispositions.[4] One can't bring about one's believing or not
believing some proposition by *deciding* to believe or not believe it; one's
disposition to believe so-and-so is activated by some event, and the
belief just emerges, like it or not. Possibly it's true that, with the aim in
mind of believing so-and-so, one can form and act on a *long range* action
plan which has some chance of success; Pascal remarked that if one
wants to become a Catholic believer, one might try attending Catholic
mass. Evidence about belief-formation from contemporary experimental psychology gives some credence to Pascal's claim. But it seems
clear that the phenomenon doesn't come to much – not enough to
build a whole theory around.

I judge these points about belief-formation to be both true and of fundamental importance for the epistemologist. But they do not establish that deontic concepts have, at most, marginal application to our believings. A glance back at Locke can help us see why. For though it may have been characteristic of those later "Lockeans" who embraced a so-called "ethics of belief" to make naive assumptions about the power of the will over belief, Locke himself was not at all naive on the matter. He held that only rarely if ever can one come to believe something by deciding to believe it; there's little in the current near-consensus among epistemologists about belief and the will that Locke would disagree with. Yet, for all that, Locke's discussion is resonant with the language of duty. I have interpreted Locke as outlining a certain *practice* which, in his judgment, ought to be used by each of us in all cases of maximal "concernment." The clue to the applicability of deontic concepts to our believings lies in the notion of a *doxastic practice*, as I shall call it, of which the practice Locke recommends is one example.

To explain what I have in mind by such a practice, we must start at ground level. All of us, as we go about our ways of being and doing, find beliefs emerging in ourselves; and all of us find that some of these get stored in memory for retrieval. Often though not always we can identify the event which activated the disposition that produced the belief – though it must at once be added that one must be in a certain state for the event to activate the disposition: must possess such-and-such concepts, have or lack such-and-such beliefs, attend with a certain intensity, and so forth.

Among the believings that emerge, are believings about our believings – beliefs about our beliefs. The second-order beliefs that we have about our first-order beliefs often make us unhappy with the flow of our first-order beliefs, and lead us to anticipate unhappiness. That unhappiness is grounded in part in the emotional impact on us of various of our beliefs. But it's also grounded in two other features of our flow of beliefs. We find our flow of belief lacking beliefs on certain matters that we want it to include beliefs on. And we find our flow of beliefs throwing up false beliefs here and there; we want both to get rid of, and forestall, such.

How do we come to believe that our flow of beliefs throws up false beliefs? In a variety of ways – prominent among them, in my view, being that of finding oneself directly acquainted with a fact which contradicts some proposition that one believes. On this occasion, however, I don't propose exploring all the issues and controversies surrounding that claim. Suffice it to note that all of us do, rather often, find ourselves in the situation of believing, about a certain pair of our beliefs, that they aren't both true – maybe even believing that they couldn't both be true. That is to say, we find ourselves with belief-triples of this sort: the belief that $p$, the belief that $q$, and the belief that $p$ and $q$ aren't both true (or the belief that necessarily $p$ and $q$ aren't both true). But then, typically, another feature of our believings enters the picture to which I haven't yet called attention: it is with varying degrees of firmness that we believe propositions. Thus it regularly happens, after taking note of one of those troubling triples, that right away, or after a while, one no longer believes the propositional content of one member of the triple – perhaps even one believes that it's false. Perhaps the firm belief that $p$, and the firm belief that $p$ and $q$ are not both true, together oust the somewhat infirm belief that $q$ from one's belief repertoire. The fittest survive.

So once again: we come to believe that the flow of beliefs that spills into us as we go about our being and doing has these two grand deficiencies: it's not producing certain beliefs and sorts of beliefs that we would like it to be producing; and it's producing more false beliefs on certain matters than we would like it to produce. So we take steps. The flow of beliefs itself becomes a matter of concern on our part. We don't just let it occur as we go about our other concerns.

What do we do? We implement ways of using our belief-dispositional constitution so as to diminish these deficiencies, in so far as in us lies. We implement what I shall call *doxastic practices*. We implement ways of finding out about new things. We implement ways of ousting false beliefs. And we implement ways of forestalling the emergence of false beliefs, or rather, of diminishing the frequency of their emergence, so that various components of the flow become more reliable. Some of these ways we learn on our own, from experience. But massively it's the case that we learn them from others. For many are established in our society; they are *social practices*, in Alisdair MacIntyre's sense;[5] and we are inducted into them, by modeling and by explicit instruction. We learn from our parents how to determine more reliably the colors of things, from our art teachers how to look at paintings, and so forth.

But if beliefs are formed in us by the activation of our belief-dispositions rather than by acts of will, what can such "ways of using" our belief-dispositional nature possibly come to? Fundamentally they consist of doing things which we have learned will activate, or will probably or possibly activate, our dispositions. We listen attentively for certain formal features in musical compositions; that's something we can decide to do. There emerges the belief that the movement we are listening to is a rondo. We rehearse all the places we stopped during the last hour; that's something we can decide to do. There emerges the belief that we left our umbrella on the counter in the butcher shop. A doxastic practice is a way of steering one's doxastic constitution. The constitution itself also changes across the course of one's lifetime. As Hume emphasized in his account of induction, new dispositions of belief-formation emerge in the form of habits. But mostly we do and must accept our constitution, as we slowly come to know it, and then steer it – just as most of us pretty much accept how the cars we purchase are built, and content ourselves with steering them. Locke outlined for us a certain doxastic practice, a way of steering one's doxastic constitution. His claim for this practice was that, for any proposition, if you want to do your best to bring it about that you believe it if and only if it is true, then this is the practice to use. There is, so he claims, no practice more reliable than this one.

Though nothing has yet been said about entitlement, the phenomenon is now right at hand. These doxastic practices, these ways of using our belief-dispositional nature, these ways of steering our doxastic constitution, *recommend* themselves to us; otherwise we wouldn't participate in them. They recommend themselves to us as ways of finding out about this and that sort of thing, as ways of ousting false beliefs about certain sorts of things from the body of beliefs we already have, and as ways of forming beliefs about certain sorts of things *more reliably*. We come to believe, about the doxastic practices of which we know, that they hold out one or the other of those three kinds of promise. This is part and parcel of our induction into them, in case they are social practices, or of our decision to adopt them, in case they emerge from our own experience. And now for the final link in the chain: given such beliefs about the various doxastic practices of which one knows, it is often the case that one is *obligated* to try to use one of them to find out about so-and-so, or *obligated* to try to use one of them so as to sort through one's present beliefs with the aim of detecting and ousting false ones, or *obligated* to try to use one of them so as to form beliefs on a more reliable basis.

Thus it is that our conversations about belief are filled with the language of "You should have known" and "You know you shouldn't have believed that without doing so-and-so." We say, "You should have

known that Germany is not a member of the UN Security Council";
thereby we express our judgment that the addressee has failed to carry
out the obligation to take steps to find out, or recall, the proposition in
question. And we say, "You know you shouldn't have believed what he
told you about his divorce without first checking it out with people who
know him," thereby expressing our judgment that the addressee has
failed, and knows that he has failed, to carry out his obligation to acquire
a particular basis for his belief. The idea in this latter sort of case is not
that he knows he shouldn't *have decided to believe p* without doing X;
because he didn't, and couldn't, *decide* to believe *p*. The idea is rather
that he knows that he had the obligation to do X, given that he believed
*p*. Had he done X, he might now not believe *p*. Then again, he still
might; but if so, he would believe it on a different and more reliable
basis, or in the light of more of the relevant evidence.[6]

A great deal more begs to be said on all these matters; I hope, on
another occasion, to say some of that more. But I judge that, for our
purposes here, enough has been said for me to be able to explain *being
entitled* to a belief thus: a person S is *entitled* to his belief that *p* just in
case S believes *p*, and there's no doxastic practice D pertaining to *p*
such that S ought to have implemented D and S did not, or S ought to
have implemented D better than S did. (Notice that a person may be
entitled at one time to believe *p* without having implemented D, and at
a later time no longer be entitled to believe *p* without having
implemented D.)

What sort of obligations are these? Are they, in the last resort, all
moral obligations? Or is there perhaps a distinct set of *doxastic*
obligations within the totality of one's obligations? In addition to our
duties to each other, do we perhaps have a "duty to the truth"? A well-
argued answer to this question would require detailed analysis of a
rather wide range of cases; and nothing at all in what I say subsequently
hangs on what the right answer proves to be. Enough for my purposes
here that it be acknowledged that, whatever be their type, we do have
such obligations as I have been pointing to.

Whatever be their nature, it's important to realize that the obligations
in questions are *situated* obligations, in that which obligations of this sort
actually apply to a given person is a function of various aspects of the
particular situation of the person in question. To pose the abstract
question, for some proposition P, "Is *one* entitled to believe that P?" is to
pose a question void for vagueness. Which obligations of this sort apply
to a given person depend, for one thing, on the doxastic practices

available to that person, and what he entitledly believes and doesn't believe about them. We have ways now of finding out about the distance of the moon from the earth which simply were not available to persons of antiquity. Secondly, it depends on the abilities of the person. There may be some excellent doxastic practices available in a society which certain members of the society lack the ability to utilize, as there may be excellent doxastic practices available in one society which members of another society lack the ability to utilize. That cluster of extremely subtle practices which native Americans utilized for finding their way and tracking game in the forests of North America is beyond the abilities of most of us to utilize. Some of us might be able to acquire the requisite abilities; none of us has them now. Thirdly, which obligations of this sort apply to a given person depends on the totality of that person's other obligations. One may know about a more reliable way of forming beliefs on some matter; but using that way might take time away from other, more pressing, obligations. It might be irresponsible to take the time to utilize that more reliable practice.

### Was Virginia entitled?

The application, to the main issue at hand, of this last point about the situatedness of entitlement, is obvious. That main issue is which, if any, of humanity's beliefs that God said something is an entitled belief. The question can only be answered in the concrete, not in the abstract.

On which concrete examples, then, shall we focus? On those we most care about. Whether Antony and Augustine were entitled to believe that God had spoken to them is, for us, little more than a matter of curiosity. What we really want to know is whether we – intelligent, educated, citizens of the modern West – are ever entitled to believe that God speaks. Let's pick an example in which extraneous considerations are minimized – in particular, considerations pertaining to the epistemology of testimony. That leads us to look for a recent case, and one close to home.

Let me present part of the narration of some experiences which recently befell an acquaintance of mine who is a well-established member of the faculty of one of the old, Eastern seaboard universities of the United States. I shall call her "Virginia"; that's not her real name; I'll also change the name of the pastor named in the narration and call him "Byron." Perhaps I should add that though Virginia is, and was at the time, a Christian, she neither is nor was what anyone would classify as an *Evangelical.* It's worth saying that because Evangelicals have the reputation of believing that God speaks to them rather more often, and rather more trivially, than most of us think God would bother with; hence we quite easily dismiss their claims that God is on speaking terms with them.

It's probably important to know that there was a great deal of conflict in the parish of which Virginia speaks; that comes out in parts of the narration which I won't quote. Here's Virginia's narration, or part of it. I think all of us will have the sense of entering a strange and unsettling world:

On February 12, 1987, while folding laundry I suddenly knew with certain knowledge that Byron was supposed to leave St. Paul's Church. There was no external voice, but there was a brightening in the room at the moment of revelation. The experience was so overwhelming that I called my husband and invited him to come home for lunch. I did not discuss what had happened, but I needed to reassure myself of reality. Later that afternoon . . . I found myself sobbing. I knew the knowledge that I had been given was not me, and I knew that it was correct. As the day progressed, it became clear to me that there were seven, insistent statements that I needed to tell Byron. Nothing like this had ever happened to me before or to anyone I knew. I was awe-struck and terrified. Passing on the message accurately and with a preface that would allow him to hear it clearly became my goal . . .

The next morning, when I went to see Byron, I was very agitated. Byron told me to take a deep breath or I would hyperventilate. We discussed God, and belief in God, and then I prayed out loud that I would be rendered speechless if what I was about to say was not indeed God's will. I told him the seven statements: "Your work is done here. You have accomplished what you were sent to do. You are still young. There are great things in store for you. Do not be afraid. God will take care of you. I will help with the transition." This message was not a surprise to Byron. He had already come to that conclusion prior to our conversation. There had been a call committee at the church that past Sunday, about which I had known nothing . . .

Byron did not get that call . . . I began to doubt my message. As I drove home from staff meeting one day in March, I said to God that if He wanted me to believe that the message had been divine, God would either have to give Byron a call or give me a message for someone else. Both came true . . .

[A few weeks later, on a] Saturday night, there was a fierce thunderstorm which shook the screen next to our bedroom window. From 12:30 to 4 a.m. I struggled with God. There was another message. God was patient and kept repeating each sentence until I could not possibly forget it. It was only about a paragraph long. I knew it was for the Tuesday night meeting. But I did not know when to say it or how to preface it. I kept seeing the hall clock at church pointing to 8:45 . . .

The narration continues with her telling about delivering the message from God at 8:45 on Tuesday evening, and the response from the other participants in the meeting. "I was surprised," she says, "at how perfectly everybody seemed to think what I had said fit in. There was a feeling of jubilation." Still she had her doubts. She went to see a priest who was recommended to her as a spiritual director. Let me continue with her own words:

He was extremely helpful in his affirmation of my experiences. I began to see how I could use my renewed spirituality in all aspects of what I was already doing. I felt stronger but still wanted to go to see a psychologist to be sure that I was mentally fit.

I met with a psychologist at Harvard Community Health Plan and told her everything that had happened. After listening to my story, she said that these kinds of things happen all the time, and why was I surprised. She suggested a book that I might read, and thanked me profusely for sharing my experience with her. She did not feel that I required any further sessions . . .

Before we set out, a small bit of taxonomy may be helpful. Reading and interpreting sacred Scripture for the divine voice consists of taking an enduring object, a text, and reading *to find out* what God said. Virginia's case was very different. She wasn't trying to *find out* what God said – she wasn't on the lookout for divine discourse. A non-sensory, quasi-mystical, experience befell her, totally unexpected, which seems to have had the phenomenological character of God appearing to her as talking to her; and this immediately evoked in her the conviction that God was saying something to her – discoursing with her. The Augustine case was somewhat different. The phenomenology was not that of a non-sensory, quasi-mystical experience of God, appearing to him as talking to him. Its core was the sensory experience of a child's sounding out certain words – though one gets the impression that that did not exhaust the phenomenology, that there was in addition some strange sort of aura; and rather than this entire phenomenology immediately evoking in Augustine the conviction that by way of the child talking, God was discoursing with him, it seems to have triggered a rapid "best explanation" inference. Augustine rapidly inferred that the best explanation of his being confronted with the sounding out loud of exactly those words at exactly that time in his life was that God was bringing about that confrontation so as thereby to speak to him, to discourse with him. There have been other cases like Augustine's except that the person only very slowly came to the conclusion that the best explanation of the events he had experienced is that God brought about those events so as thereby to speak. Various writers testify to the fact that sometimes when reading and interpreting Scripture to find out what God said thereby, they have had an experience rather like Augustine's, which they explain as God speaking to them by way of the passage before them. In that case we have a coincidence of the two phenomena between which I have drawn my major divide. When reading to *find out*, they had an *experience* which *befell them*.

Let's assume that Virginia was entitled to her framework of basic Christian belief. I know, of course, that some will contest that assumption. But in considering issues of entitlement, one always has to take for granted that a great many – indeed, most – of the person's beliefs are entitled beliefs; otherwise one can't even get going on determinations of entitlement. It appears to me that Virginia, without having thought much (if at all) about the matter, believed that it was possible for God to speak. I doubt that she had worked through the arguments of any of the philosophers and theologians who have cast doubt on the very possibility of God speaking. I doubt that she had even heard of them. She probably just took for granted the biblical picture of God as speaking. Should she have known about the skeptical discussions of philosophers and theologians? I don't myself see why. But if you think I'm wrong about this, imagine that Virginia had once looked into these discussions and concluded that the skepticism was not well-grounded.

I'm composing this chapter in a flat on The High Street in Oxford. There's always noise coming into the flat – the rumble of traffic going past. Now and then I happen to take note of the rumble; I often take note when a vehicle goes by with siren blaring. But mostly, I pay no attention. So if my wife wants to say something to me, and wants me to take note *that* she is doing so, she can't just make noises which blend into the noise of the traffic going by – even though it is in principle possible to say things by making exactly such noises.

So it is for God as well. If God is going to say things to us, say them in such a way that there's a chance of our taking note, God has to do something which stands out from the rumble of ordinary existence. Must it be a miraculous intervention in the workings of a law of nature? That depends, in part, on what one takes *laws of nature* to be, and how much of what transpires in the world and human experience one takes to fall under their sway; and those are complicated questions. But even if we conclude that it must be a miraculous intervention, that by itself isn't enough. There may be all sorts of miraculous interventions in the workings of laws of nature of which we know nothing. If God is to speak to us, the discourse-generating event must somehow stand out from what I called "the rumble of ordinary existence." Something *uncanny* – I don't know of a better word – something uncanny must take place in one's experience. That uncanniness may take many forms: the uncanniness of Virginia's quasi-mystical experience, the uncanniness of the coincidence of Augustine's just happening to hear words so appropriate to his spiritual condition, and so forth.

But we in the modern world know that the experiences of people in a state of mental disorder also sometimes have an uncanny quality; in particular, it's not at all uncommon for people in such states to "hear voices." So Virginia did exactly what I, at least, think she ought to have done: she seriously entertained the possibility that her experience was a symptom of mental disorder rather than a case of God inwardly appearing to her as speaking, and took steps to check it out. She immediately called her husband and urged him to come home for lunch; "I needed to reassure myself of reality," she says. She is reassured. But the possibility, that the uncanny experience was a symptom of mental disorder, continued to prey on her mind for a long time, until she tells all to a professional psychologist, who in response says "You're OK." In short, Virginia explored the possibility that there is another and better explanation of her uncanny experience than the one which just overwhelmed her at the time, viz., that God was speaking to her; but she doesn't come up with a better one.

No doubt Virginia's background understanding of God was such that one can imagine a whole range of purported experiences, of God speaking to her in this quasi-mystical fashion, which she would and should have dismissed at once on the ground that the *content* wasn't something that God would say to her. If, for example, the voice had told her to call her husband to come home for lunch and then to stab him as he was drinking his coffee. (Though it's likely that if she had in fact "heard" a voice saying that, she would have been so disordered that she wouldn't have drawn the conclusion that it wasn't God speaking.) However, this test, call it the *acceptability of content* test, was not a test she applied – unless she just neglected to narrate it. Apparently nothing about the content triggered any suspicion on her part.

Instead, the narration focuses on whether or not the experiences, and her accepting that the experiences are veridical, have the consequences that one would expect if the experiences were indeed of God speaking. After some initial hesitations about the first message, she concludes that they do have those consequences. Her hesitation was induced by the fact that what God told her to tell Byron didn't come true when she had assumed it would. Eventually, though, it did. As to the message that she delivered to the whole group, that produced jubilation; people remarked about how well her remarks fitted in. Sometime later she noticed that her experiences had produced in her a "renewed spirituality."

I have been assuming that the narration is an honest one; I have no reason at all to think otherwise. So my own conclusion is that, at least by the time she wrote this narration, Virginia was entitled to believe that God had spoken to her. So far as I can see, everything she should have done to make her entitled to this belief, she had done.

It will be noted that she didn't try to implement the Lockean practice. Should she have tried to do so? Should she have tried to establish that, on evidence consisting of mental and conceptual facts of which she was directly aware, it was more probable than not that God had spoken to her?

Well, one thing Locke says does, I think, point to an important truth. Often, when we know of a more reliable practice for the formation of some belief of ours than the one we actually used, we remain more or less content with not applying that purportedly more reliable practice; we judge the practice we did use reliable enough for our purposes, and we have more pressing things to do than worry the matter further. But if there's something about some experience of mine which makes me think there's a live possibility that God was speaking to me by way of that experience, then I think it would seldom if ever be appropriate to rush on to other things on the ground that they are more important. Even if the experience produced in me the *conviction* that God was speaking to me by way of that experience, I would seldom want to rush on to other things, since I would know that lots of times when people believed that God was speaking to them, they were mistaken, often with calamitous consequences. One will want to do one's reasonable best, and probably should do one's reasonable best, to determine whether God was or was not speaking to one.

The question, though, is whether doing one's best always consists of implementing the Lockean practice. It seems to me clear that, for a vast array of facts, the Lockean practice is not in fact the best. Modern philosophy has witnessed a long and elaborate series of attempts to prove, along Lockean lines, the existence of the external world. It's the consensus of most philosophers – myself included – that all those attempts have failed. Faithful application of the Lockean practice will not yield the belief that this and that external object exists; one can't get to there starting solely from mental and conceptual facts. Nonetheless, we do have available to us very good ways of getting in touch with a great deal of the external world. Those ways are the various perceptual practices that have emerged among us and which we all use: for many facts of the external world, the best way of bringing it about that one believes the corresponding propositions if and only if they are true is to apply not the Lockean practice but one and another of our common perceptual practices.

So far forth, this leaves open the possibility that the Lockean practice is the best for finding out the truth of the matter when it comes to God speaking. But once we see that it is not in general the best practice available to us human beings, we would need some special argument for the thesis that it is the most reliable for such facts. And I, at least, fail to see what such a reason might look like.

I dare say that some of my readers remain convinced that, be all this as it may, Virginia was suffering from delusions and that she herself should have realized that. But here we must once again remind ourselves of how beliefs get formed in us, and of the role of doxastic practices in our lives. We don't *decide* to believe or not believe things; it was not in Virginia's power to *decide* to believe that it was a delusion. Beliefs are formed in us by the activation of our belief-dispositions. What we can do is *steer* our belief-dispositional nature: go out and acquire additional experiences, attend more carefully and in different ways to the experiences we are having, reflect more carefully on the things we already know and believe and how they fit together, and so forth. Beyond that, there's nothing we can do, nothing at all. Virginia did everything, so far as I can see, that one could ask of her; applied all the doxastic practices that she ought to have applied.

Some there are who will remain convinced that she didn't get it right; God didn't speak to her, she was suffering from delusions. But it's just a fundamental feature of our human existence that often two of us look at the same evidence and consider the same arguments and come out with different conclusions. We can't get past that. When that happens, the outcome is symmetrical: each party believes the other is mistaken. The skeptic believes that Virginia was suffering from delusions and mistaken in her belief that God had spoken to her; but Virginia, having done everything one could ask of her, believes that the person who thinks she was suffering from delusions is mistaken. Though the situation, as between Virginia and her skeptical critics, isn't quite symmetrical: Virginia had the experience, the skeptic didn't. And that counts for something.

So, yes; it is possible for an intelligent adult of the modern Western world to be entitled to believe that God has spoken to him or her. I draw that conclusion because the possibility seems to me to have been actualized in the case of Virginia.

CHAPTER 16

# *Historical and theological afterword*

When it came time, in the course of our kaleidoscopic look at the notion of God speaking, to consider issues of interpretation, I greatly narrowed the focus of my attention. Suppose, I said, that one considered the human discourse of the Christian Bible to be an instrument of divine discourse; how would one go about interpreting it so as to discern that divine discourse? To forestall the objection that this was a purely fanciful supposition, with no tie to reality, I observed that for centuries the Christian Bible was thought of in exactly this way; God speaks by way of these writings.

### *Is there good reason to believe that the Bible is a medium of divine discourse?*

But is there good reason for supposing that the Christian Bible is in fact a medium of divine discourse – and thus for preferring, over all its competitors, the interpretative practice which operates on that assumption? That question will have been on the mind of all my readers; I have said nothing at all by way of answering it. When it came time to reflect on epistemological issues, I concentrated on *entitlement* rather than *justification*, posing the question whether normal, well-educated human beings of the twentieth century are ever entitled to believe that God speaks; and I answered the question by focusing on a case in which extraneous issues – such as that of entitlement to believe human testimony – were reduced to a minimum. Let me now, in this "Afterword," say something about that unanswered question; what I have to say will not be an answer to the question but reflections on how to go about answering it.

Begin by noting that the position which I have been exploring, that the Bible is an instrument of divine discourse, is only one of several traditional positions – indeed, only one of several which have been expressed with some such words as that God is the author of the Bible, or that the Bible is the Word of God. Calvin, in a passage contrasting Scripture with God's revelation in creation, says that this "is a special gift, where God, to instruct the church, not merely uses mute teachers but also opens his own most hallowed lips" (*Institutes* I, vi, 1). Though the language is of course metaphorical, clearly Calvin is expressing the view we have been exploring, viz., that Scripture is a medium of divine discourse. Many other passages from Calvin could be cited in which the same point is made. But Calvin by no means speaks for everyone. Barth said such things as that God is the author of Scripture, and that Scripture conveys (or *is*) the word of God. But as we saw, it would be a mistake to interpret him as saying thereby that Scripture is a medium of divine discourse. In the case of yet other writers, it would not so much be a mistake to interpret them thus, as to put too fine a point on what they said.

Sometimes the thought expressed by saying that Scripture conveys (or is) the Word of God is not that Scripture is an instrument of divine discourse, but that God spoke to the human author of Scripture, and that the author communicates to his readers what God said – perhaps putting the "substance" of what God said in his own words, perhaps, in case God used human words, repeating God's very words. God may have spoken to the author by way of publicly discernible events; alternatively, God may have spoken privately. About a case such as this, of a human being communicating a message from God, it would not be inappropriate to say that the writer's words convey what God said – that they convey "the word" of God. But as I observed already in Chapter 3, to communicate a message from someone is not to speak in the name of that person – is not to speak on behalf of that person. The first person does not speak *by way of* the speaking of the second person, by way of the second person acting as his deputy; rather, the speech of the second person conveys or communicates *what the first person has already said*. The second person's inscription of words is not the medium of the first person's discourse; that discourse must already have had something else as its medium. The second person merely *communicates the content* of the first person's discourse.

This is Barth's view of Scripture. God speaks, in the strict sense, only in the life and words, the doings and undergoings, of Jesus; the writers of Scripture communicate what God said there, putting it in their own words. In that way, they communicate the "Word" of God. On this point of structure, Barth's view is like John Locke's. Admittedly Locke does not think of God as *speaking*; he thinks of God only as revealing.

Nowhere is there any "Word" of God. But he regards the writers of Scripture as communicating what God revealed to them and others.

Sometimes yet another, third, pattern of thought lies behind saying of Scripture that God is its "author"; the thought, namely, that God *inspired* the human authors to write (or edit) as they did. The claim that God inspired the writer is an answer to a question about *causality*: how is the author's writing what he did to be accounted for? The answer offered is that we can only account for it if we include reference to the workings of the Holy Spirit. That answer is compatible with God *never* speaking – that is, never performing acts of discourse.

Christian theologians have staked out a wide variety of positions concerning the "scope" of inspiration. Some have been of the view that God "inspired" the authors to set down the very words they wrote; the writer "took dictation." Others have been of the view that inspiration works in such a way as to allow the writer to find his own words. And whichever be the way, those who dwell on the "organic" character of inspiration have called to our attention that the resultant text reveals (manifests) various things about the writer, not just about God.

The result of inspiration is of course that God is pleased with whatever be the aspect of the text that is inspired; the text in that respect is as God wants it to be, "infallible." Seeing this, it occurs to one that it would also be possible to hold the view that God super-intends the human authors so that their writing turns out as God wants it to turn out, but that God accomplishes this result by giving the human authors free rein until such time as they are about to go astray, only then intervening with inspiration.

Now if the scope of inspiration is relatively wide, it is not, perhaps, inappropriate to say that God is the *author* of scripture. Nonetheless, as I have observed several times in the course of our discussion, the phenomenon of X inspiring Y to say such-and-such is not the same as X saying such-and-such – nor, indeed, the same as Y saying such-and-such. Divine inspiration and divine discourse are distinct, albeit inter-related, phenomena. I may dictate words to you; but of whose discourse those words are then the medium depends on which of us *authorizes* them. If, after you have finished taking dictation from me, I sign the resultant document, then they are the medium of my discourse. But if *you* sign the resultant document, then they are the medium of your discourse, and I have dictated to you what you will say. Again, a young student's paper remains the medium of his discourse even though he composes it very much under the inspiration of his professor;

while the letter which a secretary composes under the inspiration of her executive becomes a medium of the executive's discourse upon the secretary handing it to her for signing. The fact that X inspires Y to write as Y does, even to the extent of the very words Y uses, is compatible both with the resultant words being the medium of X's discourse and with the resultant words being the medium of Y's discourse. Inspiration accounts for the existence of the discourse-generating events; inspiration does not determine the agent of the discourse generated.

In short, sometimes the pattern of thought expressed by speaking of God as "author" of Scripture, and of Scripture as conveying the "word" of God, is that by way of the human discourse of Scripture, God discourses. But sometimes it is, instead, that the writers of Scripture *communicate* what God said to them, or that the writers were *inspired* by God to write what they did. And sometimes these patterns of thought will not have been distinguished in the writer's mind. Nonetheless, it does remain the case that the pattern of thought on which I focused attention was not invented for the purposes of our discussion.

### A-historical attempts to answer the question

So once again: Is there good reason for preferring, over competing views of the significance of Scripture, the view that the discourse of the biblical writers is an instrument of divine discourse – and for engaging in the interpretative practice which goes along with that? Well, suppose that someone who had been puzzling about these matters, without coming to any settled view one way or the other as to whether Scripture is a medium of divine discourse, decided to engage in the practice of reading the Bible as a medium of divine discourse; and suppose that she, upon concluding that so-and-so is what God would be saying with the passage before her if it were a medium of divine discourse, found the conviction welling up immediately within her that God did say that – not that God is saying that to her now by way of this passage, but that God did say that by way of "authoring" the passage. Would the fact that such experiences occur be good reason for us – or even for her – to prefer, over its competitors, the view that Scripture is a medium of divine discourse?

I fail to see that it would. An obvious problem is that it is a huge step from *God authored this particular passage* to *God authored the whole of Scripture*. But this does not appear to be a decisive difficulty. For there are probably people who, continuing in the "experimental" use of this interpretative practice, have the same experience each time, and thus arrive at a point when it is probable, on evidence consisting of all the propositions thus believed, that God authored all of Scripture.

A much more decisive difficulty seems to me to be this: probably the sort of thing I invited us to imagine does now and then actually happen. But I would guess it happens just as often that those who engage "experimentally" in the two alternative practices of interpretation have the counterpart experience: that those who engage in the practice of interpreting Scripture to discern the "Word of God" *spoken to and communicated by* the writer, find the conviction welling up immediately within themselves, concerning some interpretative result, that this is something *God said to the writer*, and that those who engage "experimentally" in the practice of interpreting Scripture for what God *inspired the writers to say*, find the conviction welling up immediately within themselves, that God *inspired the writer* to say this. Now I do not doubt that immediately formed beliefs of each of these sorts may, in principle, possess one or another doxastic merit: the persons in question may be entitled to them, one or the other of them may be reliably formed, one or the other of the propositions believed may be true. But you and I want to know whether the view that Scripture is a medium of divine discourse is to be preferred over its competitors. And how could the fact that a person somewhere has the experience I described be for us a good reason for preferring this view of Scripture, if other people have the counterpart experiences for their construals of Scripture's significance? And this is not even to mention the fact that others never have any of such experiences in such circumstances, and that yet others have these experiences when interpreting some passages of Scripture but not when interpreting others.

There's a famous passage in Calvin, the *testimonium Spiritus Sancti* passage in *Institutes* I, vii, in which Calvin, having claimed that the Holy Spirit produces in certain people exactly the experiences I have hypothesized (though under what circumstances, is not made clear), goes on to argue that those immediately formed convictions are preferable, in religiously significant ways, to those same convictions produced by argumentation. Or so, at least, I interpret the following, much contested, passage. "Credibility of doctrine," Calvin remarks, "is not established until we are persuaded beyond doubt that God is its Author," adding that "the highest proof of Scripture derives in general from the fact that God in person speaks in it" (*Inst.* I, vii, 4). Now if we wanted we could, says Calvin, offer cogent arguments for the conclusion that "the law, the prophets, and the gospel" come from God. Much better, though, to let ourselves be convinced by "the secret testimony of the Spirit"; this "is more excellent than all reason. For as God alone is a fit witness of himself in his Word, so also the Word will not find acceptance in men's hearts before it is sealed by the inward testimony of the Spirit" (*ibid.*).

What is that testimony, and what does it effect? This: "the same Spirit, therefore, who has spoken through the mouths of the prophets must penetrate into our hearts to persuade us that they faithfully proclaimed what had been divinely commanded." The "certainty [Scripture] deserves with us, it attains by the testimony of the Spirit. For even if it wins reverence for itself by its own majesty, it seriously affects us only when it is sealed upon our hearts through the Spirit. Therefore, illumined by his power, we believe neither by our own nor by anyone else's judgment that Scripture is from God; but above human judgment we affirm with utter certainty (just as if we were gazing upon the majesty of God himself) that it has flowed to us from the very mouth of God by the ministry of men." In such conviction thus produced "the mind truly reposes more securely and constantly than in any reasons ... " Such conviction "can be born only of heavenly revelation. I speak of nothing other than what each believer experiences within himself – though my words fall far beneath a just explanation of the matter."

Now suppose that as a matter of fact it is the Holy Spirit which produces in believers, once they have arrived at an interpretation of some Scriptural passage, the immediate conviction that it is God who said that by way of the human discourse; that doesn't turn those experiences into good reason for us to prefer, over its competitors, the divine discourse construal of Scripture's significance. We would need good reason to believe that the Holy Spirit is causing those experiences. And even if the "we" in question is John Calvin himself, I doubt that we have such good reason – given that some believers, instead of having the immediate conviction that the passage before them is a medium of divine discourse, have the immediate conviction that the passage communicates what God said to the author, and yet others, the immediate conviction that God inspired the passage. The theological considerations which persuaded Calvin that experiences of the first sort are to be attributed to the Holy Spirit also yield the conclusion, so far as I can see, that those of the latter two sorts are to be attributed to the

Holy Spirit. But then, of course we are without any reason for preferring the divine discourse construal of Scripture's significance over these competitors.[1]

Possibly there are some people who have had an "uncanny" mystical experience of God *telling them* that He is the author of the Christian scriptures, this experience immediately evoking in them the conviction that God is telling them that. Or alternatively, an experience of some "uncanny" external event whose best explanation, they became convinced, immediately or otherwise, is that God was telling them, by way of that event, that He was the author of the Christian scriptures. If there have in fact been such experiences, we would have to make a judgment about their veridicality before we could do anything with them. But since I have yet to hear of an *actual* case of either of these sorts, let us move on.

Sometimes it is said that Scripture authenticates itself as the Word of God – that it is "self-authenticating." What is meant by this might be one or the other of the options already considered; Calvin, in the passage already discussed, at one point expresses his view by saying that Scripture is self-authenticated. But if not one of those, then perhaps what is meant is that it is *self-evident* that the Christian scriptures are God's book. To this, the response can be brief: surely that proposition is not self-evident; very many people grasp it without believing it.

Or maybe what is meant is that when the Christian scriptures are interpreted for the divine discourse mediated by the human discourse, one of the things we discover that God said by way of authoring this book is that God is its author. Now if that interpretative practice applied to the Christian scriptures is in fact a reliable mode of access to divine discourse, and if that practice does yield the conclusion that God said, by way of this text, that He was the author thereof, and if the totality of one's justified beliefs contains no defeater of that conclusion, then one would, as a matter of objective fact, be *justified* in holding that belief on that basis. Nonetheless, it would, to say the least, be unhelpful to plead this kind of self-authentication in the polemic among alternative ways of construing Scripture's significance.

Lastly, a good many of those who engage in the practice of interpreting Scripture for the divine discourse testify that they find the results thereof spiritually satisfying. This requires to be seen as a significant part of the whole picture; a participant in the practice who didn't experience this result would rightly find that disturbing. But the fact that reading and interpreting the text – its narratives, its poetry, its proclamations, its prescriptions – in this fashion gives a shape to the lives of many people that they find spiritually satisfying, is at best a very weak reason for us to prefer the central assumption of this interpretative practice, that this book is God's book, over its competitors. Many of those who engage in one or another alternative practice also experience the results thereof as spiritually satisfying.

### A sketch of an historical answer

The lines of argumentation which I have just canvassed are all similar in one important respect: they are all a-historical. They say nothing about the historical origins of this text; they base their case entirely on contemporary experiences of contemporary believers or practitioners. In fact I think there is no way of making the case a-historically. We are confronted with a large number of competing construals of the significance of the Christian scriptures; the choice among these can only properly be made in terms of which constitutes the best way of fitting together a large number of different considerations: textual, historical, theological, and so forth. We look for the construal which comes closest to achieving "wide reflective equilibrium." And among our data will have to be the evidence we have concerning various developments in the early church.

Let me speak for a while only of the New Testament. There is a story about happenings in the early church which, if true, constitutes a powerful reason for preferring the divine discourse construal of the New Testament over its competitors. Part of that story was told *within* the early church; it was a component in the early church's self-narrative.[2] The story seems to me plausible. Whether it is more than plausible, whether you and I have good reason to accept it, is an issue that lies outside my purview here. The likelihood that it is true depends very much on the trustworthiness of the relevant documents. But to explore adequately the epistemology of testimony – the epistemology of *believing what a person says on his or her say-so* – would require a book all by itself. That book begs to be written; it would amount to exploring the foundations of historical inquiry.

Let me present the main outlines of the story I have in mind. The best evidence for my claim that part of the story belongs to the self-narrative of the early church is to be culled from passages of the New Testament. But before I turn to that, let me cite two extra-biblical passages which present the bare-bone outline of the self-narrative. One comes from I Clement xlii, and goes like this:

The apostles received the gospel for us from the Lord Jesus Christ, Jesus the Christ was sent from God. The Christ therefore is from God and the apostles from the Christ. In both ways, then, they were in accordance with the appointed order of God's will. Having therefore received their commands, and being fully assured by the resurrection of our Lord Jesus Christ, and with faith confirmed by the word of God, they went forth in the assurance of the Holy Spirit preaching the good news that the Kingdom of God is coming.

The other comes from Book iii of Irenaeus' discourse *Against Heresies*:

the only true and life-giving faith, which the Church has received from the apostles and imparted to her sons. For the Lord of all gave to His apostles the power of the Gospel, through whom also we have known the truth, that is, the doctrine of the Son of God; to whom also did the Lord declare: "He that heareth you, heareth Me; and he that despiseth you, despiseth Me, and Him that sent me ... For after our Lord rose from the dead, [the apostles] were invested with power from on high when the Holy Spirit came down [upon them], were filled from all [His gifts], and had perfect knowledge: they departed to the ends of the earth, preaching the glad tidings of the good things [sent] from God to us, and proclaiming the peace of heaven to men. (Preface, and Chap. I)[3]

Suppose that around 45 c.e. we had been living in the province of Galatia in Asia Minor when, one day, a Jew named Paul came around preaching what he called "the gospel of Jesus Christ." Suppose that we came to believe what he said; we accepted this gospel of Jesus Christ and formed a church there in Galatia. Now suppose, further, that after Paul moved on to other places, other itinerant evangelists turned up preaching what they also advertised as "the gospel of Jesus Christ," but with a content significantly different from that of Paul's preachment. We would then be in crisis: whom should we believe? So suppose we wrote to Paul and asked him why we should accept his version of "the gospel of Jesus Christ."

We know what Paul would have said; for we know what he did say to exactly this query from a congregation in that city at that time. I am, he said, "an apostle – not from men nor through men, but through Jesus Christ and God the Father, who raised him from the dead" (Gal. 1: 1).

What status was Paul claiming for himself in claiming that he was an apostle? We can be brief, since we discussed the matter already in Chapter 3: Paul was claiming that he had the status of having been *called or commissioned by God* to be an apostle – more specifically, that he was called or commissioned by God *through Jesus Christ.* So far as I can tell, no New Testament writer diverges from Paul in this understanding of the status of an apostle.

What made Paul think he had the status of apostle? Well, as he and everyone else acknowledged, the manner of his commissioning was unusual. It happened by way of the famous mystical experience that he had on the way to Damascus. No doubt subsequent events served to confirm him in his conviction that he had been called by God through Jesus Christ to be an apostle; but that was how it happened. He was on his way to Damascus to persecute the Christians there when he had a blinding vision and heard a voice saying, "Saul, Saul, why do you persecute me?" To the question, "Who are you, Lord?" he received the answer, "I am Jesus, whom you are persecuting. But rise and stand upon your feet; for I have appeared to you for this purpose, to appoint you to serve and bear witness to the things in which you have seen me and to those in which I will appear to you" (Acts 26; *cf.* Acts 9 and 22).

This mode of commissioning to the office of apostle was, as I mentioned, out of the ordinary; and for quite some time there were people in the church who questioned whether Paul really had been commissioned. The commissioning of all but one of the other apostles was performed by the resurrected Jesus when he was still on earth. The Gospel of Matthew reports the commissioning in these words:

Now the eleven disciples went to Galilee, to the mountain to which Jesus had directed them. And when they saw him they worshipped him; but some doubted. And Jesus came and said to them, "All authority in heaven and on earth has been given to me. Go therefore and make disciples of all nations, baptizing them in the name of the Father and of the Son and of the Holy Spirit, teaching them to observe all that I have commanded you; and lo, I am with you always, to the close of the age."

And the Gospel of Luke, in these words:

Then he opened their minds to understand the scriptures, and said to them, "Thus it is written, that the Christ should suffer and on the third day rise from the dead, and that repentance and forgiveness of sins should be preached in his name to all nations, beginning from Jerusalem. You are witnesses of these things. And behold, I send the promise of my Father upon you; but stay in the city, until you are clothed with power from on high.

Why was it thought that this commissioning by Jesus of "the eleven" to be apostles was a commissioning *by God* through Jesus? Because those who believed that Jesus was resurrected – there were doubters – believed, on that ground, that by way of Jesus acting, God was acting. Eventually the church would come to the view that Jesus' actions *just were* God's actions.

There was one other abnormal commissioning, in addition to Paul's. The persons whom the risen Jesus commissioned before his departure were his eleven remaining disciples; Judas was of course missing. The sense of someone missing, of eleven being an unsatisfactory number, seems to have been felt acutely by the apostles. Luke, in the opening chapter of Acts, tells us what happened: Peter stood up before a group of about a hundred and twenty followers and, after some preliminary argumentation, concluded thus:

So one of the men who have accompanied us during all the time that the Lord Jesus went in and out among us, beginning from the baptism of John until the day when he was taken up from us – one of these men must become with us a witness to his resurrection.

So the group

put forward two, Joseph called Barsabas, who was surnamed Justus, and Matthias. And they prayed and said, "Lord, who knowest the hearts of all men, show which one of these two thou hast chosen to take the place in this ministry and apostleship from which Judas turned aside, to go to his own place." And they cast lots for them, and the lot fell on Matthias; and he was enrolled with the eleven apostles.

We can say this, in summary: the church was only willing to acknowledge as apostles those who had been commissioned to that office by God through Jesus Christ.

What was an apostle commissioned to do? Let me begin with what is clear, and then move to what is unclear. One finds various formulations. Probably the formulation which best catches everything is that they were commissioned to be *witnesses to* – that is, *witnesses concerning* – Jesus Christ. For that, they had to have known Jesus, recall the major outlines of his life and words, be able to say who he was. Thus it is that the risen Jesus before his departure commissioned as his apostles those who had been his intimates. The thought is clear in our sources that an apostle is not left to his own devices for interpreting this exceedingly strange human being. Jesus interpreted himself. Their witnessing to Jesus was to take the form of communicating that self-interpretation – in the context, of course, of their memory of the sayings and deeds of Jesus. Not everything that they said about Jesus, in the course of

witnessing to him, consisted of repeating what he told them; much of it
came from their memories of the goings-on surrounding him.

It's clear that Paul was sensitive not only to the irregularity of his
commissioning but also to the irregularity of his way of knowing Jesus.
Obviously he had not been an intimate of Jesus during his life. But if
his knowledge of Jesus had been acquired entirely from the say-so of
those who had been intimates of Jesus, his claimed status of apostle
would clearly have had a large question mark around it. What
happened is that after his conversion, Paul went down to Arabia for a
time; and there again had some sort of mystical experience: "The
gospel which was preached by me is not man's gospel. For I did not
receive it from man, nor was I taught it, but it came through a
revelation of Jesus Christ ... I did not confer with flesh and blood, nor
did I go up to Jerusalem to those who were apostles before me, but I
went away into Arabia" (Gal. 1: 11–17).[4] Later, of course, Paul did
confer with those who had earlier been appointed as apostles, especially
with Peter.

The picture which emerges is that the early church regarded some
thirteen of its members as having a special status within the church.[5]
They had been commissioned by God through Jesus to be witnesses to
Jesus – through whom, they believed, God himself spoke; and their
knowledge and interpretation of Jesus was grounded in their special
intimacy with him.[6] Thus there emerged an apostolic teaching about
Jesus and his significance which had the status in the church of being
normative. On many issues, there was consensus among the apostles
from the very beginning. On others, consensus slowly emerged – under
the pressure of controversy, in the light of new experiences; gradually
the apostles came to see more clearly the pattern and significance of
what Jesus had said and done. On yet other matters, such as details in
the life of Jesus, there never was consensus, or at least not unanimity;
and for many such matters, there's no evidence that the lack of
unanimity was of any concern to them. Nonetheless, the "official" view
of the young church about this apostolic tradition as a whole was that it
communicated what God had said by way of the teachings and doings
and self-interpretation of Jesus. The church, says Paul in Ephesians, is
"built upon the foundation of the apostles and prophets, Jesus Christ
being the cornerstone" (Eph. 2: 20).[7]

So the apostles were commissioned to communicate what God said
and did in Jesus Christ. Were they also commissioned to represent him,
to stand in for him, to speak for him, to speak in his name, to deputize

for him, to be his proxy? Quite clearly Irenaeus regarded them as so commissioned; for he applies to them the words which Jesus, in Luke (10: 16), is recorded as applying to "the seventy" whom he sends out: "Whoever listens to you listens to me, and whoever rejects you rejects me, and whoever rejects me rejects the one who sent me." And indeed, as I myself remarked in Chapter 3, it's hard to see why the apostles would not have been so commissioned if "the seventy" were.

Perhaps more decisive, though, is the tenth chapter of Matthew, and various passages in the Gospel of John, from chapter 12 onwards. In Matthew 10 we get a narration of Jesus summoning his twelve disciples and giving them a commissioning talk. They are sent forth, with various mandates and various forms of authority. The time at which they are to *go forth* remains obscure; one gets the impression that they are to go forth and do some of these things as part of Jesus' ministry at the time. And perhaps Jesus' disciples made nothing more of his words at the time than just exactly that. But with hindsight, it is impossible to refrain from interpreting Matthew's Jesus as also having his eye on the post-resurrection apostolic commissioning; "you will be dragged before governors and kings because of me," says Jesus. In that light, it is significant then that Jesus' commissioning talk concludes with these words: "Whoever welcomes you welcomes me, and whoever welcomes me welcomes the one who sent me. Whoever welcomes a prophet in the name of a prophet will receive a prophet's reward . . . "

In John, from chapter 13 through chapter 17, we get Jesus' final address to his disciples. It too is a commissioning address; and the undertone, clear though mainly unspoken, is that the disciples are to become Jesus' *representatives*. The words that the Father gave to Jesus, Jesus gave to his disciples. They have received them, and know in truth that Jesus came from the Father. They are now to give those words, and that knowledge, to others. They are able to do so because they have been with Jesus from the beginning, and because they will receive the Advocate, the Spirit of truth, who will guide them into all truth; the Advocate will remind them of all that Jesus said to them. "Very truly, I tell you," says Jesus, "whoever receives one whom I send receives me; and whoever receives me receives him who sent me" (13: 20).

So what are we to make of these flickering indications, coupled with the overall silence of the New Testament on the issue of whether the apostles were not only commissioned to witness to Jesus but were also commissioned to speak in the name of Jesus, and thereby, of God? Much the most plausible hypothesis seems to me to be that the writers simply took for granted this understanding of apostolic commissioning; for them, it "went without saying."

What we have so far is commissioned apostolic teaching; we do not yet have a New Testament. But everyone will know, or if not know, be able to surmise, how the transition was made. It turned out that by around 200 A.D. the Church had adopted for itself a new canon of sacred writings, which eventually it called *The New Testament*. For almost 200 more years, controversies swirled around a few books as to whether they should or should not be included in the canon. But by around 200, the *practice* of treating certain books as belonging to a new sacred canon was everywhere accepted, as was, with just a few exceptions, the actual list. For most of our century, it has been the scholarly consensus that the clue to the emergence of a new canon is to be found in the fact that gradually the church came to a shared view on which books are appropriate and desirable for use in the liturgy. More recently it has been argued by Hans von Campenhausen[8] – compellingly, in my view – that the clue to the emergence of the canon is to be found rather in the need of the church to confront Marcionism on the one side and Montanism on the other. These controversies forced the church to go beyond appealing to the tradition of the apostles' teaching and to adopt certain books as normative.

The move was freighted with significance. With respect to the antecedent tradition, putting just these books together in this arrangement into a canon perforce meant seeing the tradition from a certain perspective, when in principle somewhat different perspectives – different "orthodox" perspectives – would have been possible.[9] With respect to subsequent generations, a canon of normative writings functions very differently from a normative tradition[10] – which is, of course, why the church made the move.

But though the move was, in these ways, freighted with significance, it was, nonetheless, in one way a very small move indeed. From its very beginnings, the church operated with a normative tradition – viz., the tradition of apostolic teaching. And for its canon, the church didn't just pick some books that proved edifying for reading in church or good for answering Marcionists and Montanists. It picked books which it judged to be examples of an apostle's teaching, as in the case of Paul's writings, or to be faithful representations of the apostolic teaching, as in the case of the Gospels. Indeed, concerning the latter, it wanted the faithful representations to come from the time of the apostles, even to come, if not from an apostle, then from an intimate of an apostle – someone capable of being, as it were, a mouthpiece of one of the apostles.[11] To be accepted into the canon, the book had to possess *apostolicity*. And further, as Brevard Childs observes, the status of being a normative writing is claimed by some New Testament books about themselves, and by others, about other New Testament books. There's a canonical impulse within the New Testament books; canonicity is not some fate which befalls them from outside.[12] The situation is not that a canon of normative books displaces a normative tradition; for the normative tradition itself included books claiming normative status. Perhaps sometimes the move of a religious community from a normative tradition to a textual canon is a very large move. For the reasons cited, the move of the early church from *its* normative tradition to *its* textual canon was about as small as such a move could be. Though not inevitable, it was certainly natural, and to be expected.

Let us gather the strands together. Suppose the apostles were commissioned by God through Jesus Christ to be witnesses and representatives (deputies) of Jesus. Suppose that what emerged from their carrying out this commission was a body of apostolic teaching which incorporated what Jesus taught them and what they remembered of the goings-on surrounding Jesus, shaped under the guidance of the Spirit. And suppose that the New Testament books are all either apostolic writings, or formulations of apostolic teaching composed by close associates of one or another apostle. Then it would be correct to construe each book as a medium of divine discourse. And an eminently plausible construal of the process whereby these books found their way into a single canonical text, would be that by way of that process of canonization, God was authorizing these books as together constituting a single volume of divine discourse.

Good reasons for regarding the Christian scriptures as a medium of divine discourse must obviously bring the Old Testament along with the New into the picture. But I must beg off at this point – with the observation that the widespread conviction in first-century Judaism that their sacred scriptures were a medium of divine discourse undoubtedly aided the emergence of the same conviction, among Christians, concerning the Christian scriptures.

A final point. It will be said in some quarters that to regard the Christian scriptures as an instrument of divine discourse, and to interpret them in accord with that conviction, would be to turn Christianity into a "religion of the book," when in fact it is Jesus Christ who is at the center of the Christian religion, not the Bible. The

Christian church is the Jesus party in history (more precisely, the *surviving* Jesus party).

But why would that be? The focus of the Christian scriptures is of course on Jesus Christ. Why is it that if we interpret God as telling us, by way of the scriptures, about God's entrance into our history centrally and decisively in Jesus Christ, we have turned the Christian religion into a "religion of the book" – worse yet, into *bibliolatry*?

What's true is this: I have not, in this book, focused attention on that mode of divine discourse which Christians regard as central; I have not focused on God's speaking in Jesus Christ. It would, on another occasion, be eminently appropriate to do that. As it would be appropriate to discuss the conviction, shared alike by rabbinic Judaism and classic Lutheranism and Calvinism, that by way of authorized interpretation of the sacred text, God speaks anew: the line between divine discourse and interpretation is breached.

# Notes

### I LOCATING OUR TOPIC

1 *Cf. Confessions* VIII, 4: "It would be unthinkable that men of wealth and power should be more welcome in your Church than those who are poor and unknown. For *you have chosen what the world holds weak, so as to abash the strong; you have chosen what the world holds base and contemptible, nay you have chosen what is nothing, so as to bring to nothing what is now in being.* It was through the apostle Paul that you spoke these words . . ."

2 "Revelation in the Jewish Tradition" in Seán Hand (ed.), *The Levinas Reader* (Oxford, Basil Blackwell; 1989), p. 191.

3 *Ibid.*, pp. 192–93.

4 Levinas, in the essay to which I have referred, breaks with the traditional assumption in a different and less explicit way. He sees himself as talking about revelation; yet, when he actually begins to describe the Jewish way of interpreting the Hebrew Bible, he argues that the Jew regards *prescription* as fundamental to all of it, no matter what the genre. Quite clearly he means, *divine prescription.* I will argue in my next chapter that prescription is not a species of revelation. But what is interesting about Levinas's article is that the concept of *revelation* actually plays little role in his thought; it is instead the concept of (that speech-action which is) *prescription* that proves determinative for him.

5 Moses Maimonides, *The Guide of the Perplexed*, tr. by Shlomo Pines (Chicago, University of Chicago Press: 1963), I, 46 [pp. 99–100]. A full discussion of Maimonides' account of the import of attributions of speech to God would have to take account also of the rather different point made in *Guide* I, 65, where Maimonides has the Genesis account of creation in view: "the term 'command' is figuratively used of God with reference to the coming to be of that which He has willed. Thus it is said that He commanded that this should come to be. The words are used accordingly by way of likening His actions to ours, in addition to their being used, as we have made clear, to indicate the meaning: he wished. In all cases in which *He said,* occurs in the *Account of the Beginning*, it means that He willed or wanted" (p. 159).

6 Sandra M. Schneider, *The Revelatory Text* (San Francisco, Harper: 1991),

pp. 27–29. By contrast to Maimonides and Schneider, consider Karl Barth: "Church proclamation is talk, speech. So is Holy Scripture. So is even revelation in itself and as such. If we stay with God's Word in the three forms in which it is actually heard in the Church ... we have no reason not to take the concept of God's Word primarily in its literal sense. God's Word means that God speaks. Speaking is not a 'symbol'" (*Church Dogmatics* I/I, p. 132).

7 Robert Alter, *The World of Biblical Literature* (Basic Books, n.p.: 1992), pp. 34, 40.

## 2 SPEAKING IS NOT REVEALING

1 *Cf.* John Baillie, *The Idea of Revelation in Recent Thought* (New York, Columbia University Press; 1956), p. 19: "Revelation literally means an unveiling, the lifting of an obscuring veil, so as to disclose something that was former hidden."

2 Charles Taylor, *Sources of the Self* (Cambridge, Harvard University Press; 1989), p. 131.

3 Richard Swinburne, *Revelation* (Oxford, Clarendon Press; 1992).

4 *Cf.* John Locke, *Essay concerning Human Understanding*, IV, xviii, 2: "Faith ... is the assent to any proposition, not thus made out by the deductions of reason; but upon the credit of the proposer, as coming from God, in some extraordinary way of communication. This way of discovering truths to men we call *Revelation*."

5 *Cf.* Baillie, *The Idea of Revelation*, Chapter IV, especially the opening section on "Event and Interpretation."

6 On manifestation-revelation requiring, in this way, interpretation, see Chapter 4 of Avery Dulles' well-known book, *Models of Revelation* (Garden City, N.Y., Doubleday; 1985). For example, discussing the views of William Temple, Dulles says that "Temple avoided any crude reduction of revelation to objective history. For the events to be revelation, he held, they must be understood as disclosures of God. Secondarily, then, revelation consists in the illumination of the minds of the prophets to discern what has been manifested. In Temple's words, 'The essential condition of effectual revelation is the coincidence of divinely controlled event and minds divinely illuminated to read it aright'" (54).

7 I am indebted to my colleague, Christopher Seitz, for calling this article to my attention.

8 *Cf.* Baillie, *The Idea of Revelation*, p. 62: "No affirmation runs more broadly throughout recent writing on our subject [of revelation] than ... that all revelation is given, not in the form of directly communicated knowledge, but through events occurring in the historical experience of mankind, events which are apprehended by faith as the 'mighty acts' of God, and which therefore engender in the mind of man such reflective knowledge of God as it is given him to possess. It is clear that this represents a very

radical departure from the traditional ecclesiastical formulation which identified revelation with the written word of Scripture and gave to the action of God in history the revelational status only of being among the things concerning which Scripture informed us." In addition to making this claim about the contemporary theological discussion, Baillie claims that the Bible too speaks only of the manifestational sort of revelation: "According to the Bible, what is revealed to us is not a body of information concerning various things of which we might otherwise be ignorant. If it is information at all, it is information concerning the nature and mind and purpose of God – that and nothing else. Yet in the last resort it is not information about God that is revealed, but very God Himself incarnate in Jesus Christ our Lord" (p. 28). On this claim, one should consider, in addition to the point made by Barr in the text above, what Downing has to say in his, *Has Christianity a Revelation?*

9   In his *Models of Revelation*, Avery Dulles distinguishes five theological models of revelation. These map onto the distinctions I have been making in the following way: what Dulles calls *Revelation as Doctrine* is knowledge-transmitting revelation of the assertoric form. What he calls *Revelation as History* and *Revelation as Inner Experience* are two versions of manifesting revelation, the difference between the two hinging on whether the phenomena which do the manifesting are located in external history or in the "inward self" of human beings. The fourth model, *Revelation as Dialectical Presence* is apparently that special form of (intended) manifesting revelation in which what is manifested is just the agent's presence. The last model, *Revelation as New Awareness*, is what I have called *agentless* revelation.

    George Mavrodes, in his recent book *Revelation in Religious Belief* (Philadelphia, Temple University Press; 1988), discusses three models of divine revelation. What he calls The Causation Model is a form of non-assertoric knowledge-transmitting revelation. What he calls The Manifestation Model is just manifestation revelation. And what he calls The Communication Model is assertoric knowledge-transmitting revelation.

10  Mavrodes, in *Revelation*, p. 99, says that "if something has been revealed it seems natural to suppose that there is someone to whom it has been revealed." But consider this sentence: "The old man revealed the location of the jewels in a document he wrote just before his death; but by then his hand was so unsteady that none of us has yet been able to decipher what he wrote." The use of "reveal" in this sentence seems to me not at all "unnatural."

11  This function of revelation as prolegomenal to theology is seen as problematic, but is nonetheless unwaveringly embraced, by Avery Dulles in his *Models of Revelation*: "The theology of revelation offers peculiar methodological problems. It is not a part of doctrinal theology (or dogmatics) as ordinarily understood, for doctrinal theology, as we have already seen, customarily tests its assertions by their conformity with what is already recognized as revelation. Without falling into a vicious circle,

one could not test a theory of revelation by its conformity to revelation ...
What is being attempted in this book may be described as a fundamental
theology of revelation ... Fundamental theology ... is predogmatic
because ... it does not rest on a finished theory regarding revelation and
its mediation through tradition and ecclesiastical pronouncements.
Rather, by fashioning such a theory, it contributes to the foundations for
dogmatic theology" (14–15).

### 3 MANY MODES OF DISCOURSE

1 Of course, the recipients of letters not composed by their senders will
sometimes be distinctly displeased to learn that they were composed by
someone else; the businessman who signs and sends off love letters composed
by his secretary is courting disaster. (The example was offered me by
Eleonore Stump.) And I, at least, would be upset if I learned that Lincoln's
Gettysburg Address was composed by a secretary. There's a fascinating field
here beckoning for exploration which I will refrain from entering!

2 Though it appears to me acceptable to describe any case of *acting as the
deputy of* with the words, "acting on behalf" of, not all cases of acting on
behalf of are cases of acting as the deputy of. Suppose that you have
promised the town officials to spend tomorrow afternoon filling sand bags
to strengthen the levee, but that, while playing baseball in the evening,
you break your arm. You then ask me to take your place. I show up, and
announce that I'll spend the afternoon filling sandbags and that I'm doing
it on your behalf (in your place, in your stead). The town officials then
mark your obligation as fulfilled. But *you* haven't filled the sandbags; it's
not the case that by way of what I do, *you* fill the sandbags. So *you* haven't
done what you promised. Though the content of what you promised that
you would do, fill sandbags, has been done.

3 The most elaborate indication of the continuation of the concept is this
passage, from Acts 3: 18: "But what God foretold by the mouth of all the
prophets, that his Christ should suffer, he thus fulfilled. Repent therefore,
and turn again, that your sins may be blotted out, that times of refreshing
may come from the presence of the Lord, and that he may send the
Christ appointed for you, Jesus, whom heaven must receive until the time
for establishing all that God spoke by the mouth of his holy prophets
from of old. Moses said, 'The Lord God will raise up for you a prophet
from your brethren as he raised me up. You shall listen to him in
whatever he tells you. And it shall be that every soul that does not listen
to that prophet shall be destroyed from the people'."

4 Some of the New Testament writers obviously did regard the line of the
prophets as continuing, albeit in a rather unusual way, within the
assemblies of the Church; see the descriptions by Luke in Acts, and by
Paul in his letters to the Corinthians.

5 At the beginning of his first letter to the Christians at Corinth he says that

he was "called by the will of God to be an apostle of Jesus Christ" (I Cor.
1: 1; *cf.* II Cor.1: 1, Eph.1: 1, Col.1: 1, II Tim.1: 1); in I Tim.1: 1 he says that
he was called "by command of God our Savior and of Jesus Christ our
hope"; and in Romans 1: 5 he says that his is an apostleship received from
Jesus Christ our Lord. See further discussion in Chapter 16.

6 Though my conclusion will be that they probably were understood as
deputies, I think that Rengstorff, in his article on *apostolos* in *Kittel's
Theological Word-Book of the New Testament*, is rather more decisive than the
evidence entitles him to be in his treatment of the apostles as just prophets
of a special type: "The parallel between the apostles and the prophets
which we see in Paul rests on the fact that both are exclusively bearers of
revelation, the prophets of revelation still in progress and the apostles of
completed revelation. Perhaps the different temporal relationship to the
same thing explains why the NT preaching office could not use the
ancient title for God's *messengers* (*prophetes*), to describe the messengers of
Jesus. It needed a new term corresponding to the new and altered
situation and yet still referring to the commission which Jesus gave to His
disciples." What is worth noting about this passage is that Rengstorff is
trying to explicate the notions of prophet and apostle with the concept of
*revelation*, rather than with the concept of *speaking*. Then, indeed, the
structural distinction between prophet and apostle which I am suggesting
in the text above is completely concealed from view!

7 It should be acknowledged that much of what we have in the prophetic
books may not be "a record of prophetic utterance." The connection
between what the prophets of Israel said orally to their people, and what
stands in the prophetic books, is no doubt complicated and full of
variations.

8 Naturally there may be other reasons for holding to a general doctrine of
inspiration; all I wish to emphasize is that *inspiration* and *appropriation* are
distinct, and in principle separate, phenomena; and that what is decisive
for something's belonging to God's book is appropriation, not inspiration.
A person may superintend the locution (and illocution) of someone
without authorizing that as the medium of his own discourse; conversely,
a person may authorize some words as the medium of his discourse
without having in any way superintended their production. A doctrine of
divine inspiration is thus not a doctrine of divine discourse.

9 I owe the example to Eleonore Stump.

### 4 IN THE HANDS OF THEOLOGIANS

1 Ricoeur's essay is to be found in his book, *Essays on Biblical Interpretation*
(Philadelphia, Fortress Press; 1980). I will incorporate page references into
the text above.

2 A somewhat confusing feature of Barth's presentation of his thought is
that he sometimes uses "proclamation" to cover prophetic and apostolic

witnessing along with church proclamation, and sometimes uses it (as I just did) to pick out church proclamation in distinction from prophetic and apostolic witnessing. I shall adopt the practice of always calling the former, "contemporary proclamation," reserving "proclamation" as such for the genus which covers both species, viz., witnessing, and church proclamation.

3  Thus Barth says, "When we say 'Word of God revealed,' then in distinction from the 'written' and 'preached' of the two other forms of the Word of God, 'revealed' does not belong to the predicate. It is simply a paraphrase, a second designation of the subject" (1/1, 118).

4  *Cf.* 1/1, 142: "the Word of God as the Word of reconciliation directed to us is the Word by which God announces Himself to man, i.e., by which He promises Himself as the content of man's future, as the One who meets him on his way through time as the end of all time, as the hidden Lord of all times. His presence by the Word is His presence as the coming One, coming for the fulfilment and consummation of the relation established between Him and us in creation and renewed and confirmed in reconciliation."

5  In *C.D.* IV/3.2, §71.4, Barth speaks at length of Christians in general as being called to be witnesses – as having the vocation of witness. This appears to me to be a significant change in his thought from the opening volumes of the *Church Dogmatics*, where contemporary witnessing is consistently assigned to official church proclamation, rather than to Christians in general.

6  I judge this interpretation to be decisively confirmed by Barth's discussions about "The Vocation of Man" and "The Holy Spirit and the Sending of the Christian Community" in *C.D.* IV/3.2. Never does Barth speak about the witness as commissioned to speak "in the name of" God. See especially pp. 515, 592–93, 606–10, 737–38, 835–36, 843 ff., 868 ff. From all these passages, let me quote a bit from p. 737: God "puts His word on the lips of the men of this people. That is, He gives to their lips, to their human knowledge and confession, to their human voice, the power to attest His Word and by His Word His work, and by His work Himself ... He actually does what He as the Almighty can do, namely, that He puts His Word on their lips, that He sanctifies their profane language, that He gives them the power and freedom to speak of Him in their humanly secular words and expressions and sentences, and therefore to become and to be His witnesses to other men." Barth does say in one place that "It is part of the concept of evangelist and apostle, as it is also of that of prophet, that they do not have to speak in their own name but only in the name, i.e., in fulfilment of the revelation of Jesus: to speak of Him, to speak by His commission, to speak according to His ordering, to speak of the ability which is to be expected from Him." The wording is too vague to be the basis of an interpretation.

7  "As the witness of divine revelation the Bible also attests the institution

and function of prophets and apostles. And in so doing it attests itself as Holy Scripture, as the indispensable form of that content. But because this is the case, in this question of divine revelation the Church, and in and with it theology, has to hold fast to this unity of content and form. The distinction of form and content must not involve any separation. Even on the basis of the biblical witness we cannot have revelation except through this witness. We cannot have revelation "in itself". The purpose of the biblical witness is not to help us achieve this, so that its usefulness is outlived when it is achieved. Revelation is, of course, the theme of the biblical witness. And we have already seen that the perception of it is absolutely decisive for the reading and understanding and expounding of this biblical witness. But it always is the theme of this, the biblical witness. We have no witness to it but this. There are, therefore, no points of comparison to make it possible for us even in part to free ourselves from this witness, to put ourselves into direct relationship to the theme of it ... In this question of revelation we cannot, therefore, free ourselves from the texts in which its expectation and recollection is attested to us. We are tied to these texts" (1/2, 492).

8  "We insist that faith is experience, a concretely ascertainable temporal act of a specific man, the act of acknowledgment. But experience is not self-evidently ... experience of God's Word ... It is the Word, Christ, to whom faith refers because He presents Himself to it as its object, that makes faith faith, real experience. Let it be clearly understood: because He presents Himself to it as its object. For faith is not faith by the mere fact that it has or is a reference – it might well be in reality a pointless reference to an imagined object. It is faith by the fact that the Word of God is given to us as the object of this reference, as the object of acknowledgment, and therefore as the basis of real faith" (I/1, 230; see also 1/1, 160).

9  For example, "If now it is true in time, as it is true in eternity, that the Bible is the Word of God, then according to what we have just said, God Himself now says what the text says" (1/2, 532).

10  Barth says that "God always has something specific to say to each man, something that applies to him and to him alone. The real content of God's speech or the real will of the speaking person of God is not in any sense, then, to be construed and reproduced by us as a general truth" (1/1, 140). Barth doesn't develop this thought farther in this passage; so it's not entirely clear what he has in mind. But I think his thought is not that in Jesus Christ God says something specific to each of us (though he might also hold that), but that God applies to each of us what God says in Jesus Christ. Thus my guess is that the passage should be interpreted in the light of this later passage: "Because the Word of God, unlike created realities, is not universally present and ascertainable, and cannot possibly be universally present and ascertainable, therefore, as decision, it always implies choice in relation to man. The Word of God is an act of God

which takes place *specialissime*, in this way and not another, to this or that particular man" (1/1, 159). The same point is made in 1/1, 160.

11  I should report one other line of thought on this matter in Barth. It's much less prominent than the line of thought I have presented in the text above; in fact, I know of only one passage in which it comes through at all clearly. And I don't profess to understand it. In this passage, after emphasizing that the time of revelation, the time of the witnessing, and the time of church proclamation, are three different times, Barth says that God's speaking in Jesus Christ *then and there* is contemporaneous with God's speaking *here and now*. I doubt that this is just a figurative way of expressing the line of thought in the text above, that the Spirit moves us here and now to acknowledge what God said in Christ *then and there*. See 1/i, 148–49.

## 5  WHAT IT IS TO SPEAK

1  I should say here that the concept of a *locutionary* act with which I am working differs a bit from J. L. Austin's. For him, a locutionary act consists of using words with a certain sense and reference; for me, a locutionary act consists just of uttering or inscribing (or signing) words.

2  If one's ontology leads one to hold that the former act is identical with the latter – that this act which is a case of one of these distinct action-predicables is also an instance of the other – then what follows would have to be conceptualized rather differently.

3  Alvin Goldman, *A Theory of Human Action* (Englewood Cliffs, N.J., Prentice-Hall; 1970), pp. 25–26.

4  John Searle, *Speech Acts* (Cambridge, Cambridge University Press; 1970), pp. 51–2.

5  The argument and example were posed to me by Robert M. Adams.

## 6  COULD GOD HAVE RIGHTS AND DUTIES OF SPEAKER?

1  "A Modified Divine Command Theory" in R. M. Adams, *The Virtue of Faith* (New York, Oxford University Press; 1987), p. 115.

2  From an unpublished paper by Robert M. Adams, "The Concept of a Divine Command."

3  "Divine Command Metaethics Modified Again" in *The Virtue of Faith*, p. 139.

4  Adams, "A Modified Divine Command Theory of Ethical Wrongness," in *The Virtue of Faith*, p. 97.

5  William P. Alston, "Some Suggestions for Divine Command Theorists," in Alston, *Divine Nature and Human Language* (Ithaca, Cornell University Press; 1989), p. 265. Of course, it is odd for Alston to say that in speaking of God as promising, the biblical writers were giving the closest human analogue to what God was doing, when he, Alston, gives what he regards

as a closer analogue, viz., that God was expressing an intention. Or does his point trade on "vivid idea"? Were the biblical writers sacrificing the accuracy of speaking of God as expressing intentions for the vividness of speaking of God as promising?

6 Alston, *Divine Nature*, p. 257.

7 Note that Alston again speaks of the hyper-conscientious assistant professor as having *duties*!

8 At one point, Alston says that the sort of possibility he has in mind when he speaks of the possibility of deviation is "metaphysical possibility." But nothing in his argument turns on the difference between causal and metaphysical possibility.

9 A point made by Eleonore Stump in her paper "God's Obligations," in *Philosophical Perspectives, 6: Ethics, 1992*, ed. by J. E. Tomberlin (Atascadero, CA, Ridgeview Publ. Co.; 1992). The paper should be consulted for a somewhat different line of argument against Alston's contentions from that which I have presented – though along the way, some of the same points are made.

## 7 CAN GOD CAUSE EVENTS OF DISCOURSE?

1 For a very helpful survey of the issues, see William Hasker, *God, Time, and Knowledge* (Ithaca, Cornell University Press; 1989), Chap. 2.

2 Langdon Gilkey, "Cosmology, Ontology, and the Travail of Biblical Language," reprinted in Owen C. Thomas, ed., *God's Activity in the World: The Contemporary Problem* (Chico, Cal., Scholars Press; 1983), p. 31.

3 John Macquarrie, *Principles of Christian Theology*, 2nd ed. (New York, Scribner's; 1977), pp. 247–48.

4 Alfred J. Freddoso, "Medieval Aristotelianism and the Case against Secondary Causation in Nature" in Thomas V. Morris (ed), *Divine and Human Action* (Ithaca, Cornell University Press), p. 79.

5 Bas C. van Fraassen, *Laws and Symmetry* (Oxford, Clarendon Press; 1989), p. 94.

6 *Cf.* David Armstrong, *What Is a Law of Nature?* (Cambridge, Cambridge University Press; 1983).

## 8 CONTRA RICOEUR

1 I take this claim to be amply confirmed by G. R. Evans' two books, *The Language of the Bible: The Earlier Middle Ages*, and *The Language of the Bible: The Road to Reformation* (Cambridge, Cambridge University Press; 1984 and 1985).

2 Paul Ricoeur, *Interpretation Theory* (Fort Worth, Texas Christian University Press; 1976); p. 75. Henceforth I will abbreviate references to this text as "IT," and will incorporate them into my text.

3 Paul Ricoeur, *Hermeneutics and the Human Sciences*, ed. and tr. by J. B.

Thompson (Cambridge, Cambridge University Press; 1981), p. 201. Henceforth I will abbreviate references to this text as "HHS" and will incorporate them into my text. *Cf.* "What happens in writing is the full manifestation of something that is in a virtual state ... in living speech, namely the detachment of meaning from the event" (IT 25).

4   Though Ricoeur does say, "the sentence is actual as the very event of speaking" (IT 7).

5   This is what Swinburne calls a *proposition*, in chapter 1 of his *Revelation*.

6   This is what Swinburne calls a *statement*.

7   This assumption is a standard part of the anti-intentionalist armory. For one of the best statements of it, see Monroe C. Beardsley, "The Authority of the Text," in G. Iseminger, ed., *Intention and Interpretation* (Philadelphia, Temple University Press; 1992). Beardsley summarizes his view like this: "My position is ... that texts acquire determinate meaning through the interactions of their words without the intervention of an authorial will. When possible meanings are transformed into an actual meaning, this transformation is generated by the possibilities ... themselves" (31–32).

8   The possibility should be noted that a sense of a sentence, as Ricoeur understands it, is not just a meaning but is a speech-action universal of which that meaning is not the whole but only the content. Consider the following passages: "The locutionary act is exteriorised in the sentence *qua* proposition. For it is as such and such proposition that the sentence can be identified and reidentified as the same" (HHS 135). "But the illocutionary act can also be exteriorised through grammatical paradigms (indicative, imperative, and subjunctive modes, and other procedures expressive of the illocutionary force) which permit its identification and reidentification ... Without a doubt we must concede that the perlocutionary act is the least inscribable aspect of discourse and that by preference it characterises spoken language. But the perlocutionary action is precisely what is the least discourse in discourse. It is the discourse as stimulus ... Therefore it is necessary to understand by the meaning of the speech-act, or by the noema of the saying, not only the sentence, in the narrow sense of the propositional act, but also the illocutionary force and even the perlocutionary action in the measure that these three aspects of the speech-act are codified, gathered into paradigms, and where, consequently, they can be identified and reidentified as having the same meaning. Therefore I am giving the word 'meaning' a very large acceptation which covers all the aspects and levels of the intentional exteriorisation that makes the inscription of discourse possible" (HHS 199–200). Speaking of illocutionary acts, Ricoeur also says, however, that "This 'doing' of the saying may be assimilated to the event pole on the dialectic of event and meaning" (IT 14). What might he mean? Well, suppose we keep in mind our distinction between those universals which are action-types and those particulars which are act-tokens; and suppose further that, true to Ricoeur's obvious hesitations, we

set perlocutionary acts off to the side. Then perhaps what Ricoeur is saying is this: a good many sentences express not only a certain meaning but also a certain speech action, in the sense that if one uttered them when the language is in effect, one would be counted as having performed that speech action with that meaning as its content. When that is the case, then that speech action with that meaning as its content constitutes the sense of the sentence. Take our example of someone, call the person *S*, assertively uttering "The queen is dead." If one regards the indicative mood of this sentence as an indicator that, when someone utters it, she is to be counted as making an assertion, then the sense of this sentence is the following action-type: *asserting that the queen is dead*. (Of course the indicative mood is not by itself an indicator of assertion; the sentence might occur in a piece of fiction!) Notice, however, that in the example imagined there is the following act-token particular, *S's asserting that the queen is dead*, this being a case or instance of the action-type universal. What Ricoeur is denying is that this particular is part of the sense.

9   Verbal discourse is "addressed to an interlocutor equally present to the discourse situation with the speaker" (HHS 202). In verbal discourse we witness "the temporal phenomenon of exchange, the establishment of a dialogue which can be started, continued, or interrupted" (HHS 133–34). Written discourse, by contrast, "creates an audience which extends in principle to anyone who can read. The freeing of the written material with respect to the dialogical situation of discourse is the most significant effect of writing" (HHS 139). "Whereas spoken discourse is addressed to someone who is determined in advance by the dialogical situation – it is addressed to you, the second person – a written text is addressed to an unknown reader and potentially to whoever knows how to read" (IT 31).

10  In spoken discourse, "the ultimate criterion for the referential scope of what we say is the possibility of showing the thing referred to as a member of the situation common to both speaker and hearer. This situation surrounds the dialogue, and its landmarks can all be shown by a gesture or by pointing a finger. Or it can be designated in an ostensive manner by the discourse itself through the oblique reference of those indicators which include the demonstratives, the adverbs of time and place, and the tenses of the verb. Finally, they can be described in such a way that one, and only one, thing may be identified within the common framework of reference" (IT 34). *Cf.* HHS 141 and 148.

11  "Letters, travel reports, geographical descriptions, diaries, historical monographs, and in general all descriptive accounts of reality may provide the reader with an equivalent of ostensive reference in the mode of 'as if' ('as if you were there'), thanks to the ordinary procedures of singular identification. The heres and theres of the text may be tacitly referred to the absolute here and there of the reader, thanks to the unique spatio-temporal network to which both writer and reader ultimately belong and which they both acknowledge" (IT 35).

12  "A second extension of the scope of reference is much more difficult to
    interpret. It proceeds less from writing as such as from the open or covert
    strategy of certain modes of discourse. Therefore it concerns literature
    more than writing, or writing as the channel of literature. In the
    construction of his schema of communication, Roman Jakobson relates
    the poetic function – which is to be understood in a broader sense than
    just poetry – to the emphasis of the message for its own sake at the
    expense of the reference. We have already anticipated this eclipsing of the
    reference by comparing poetic discourse to a self-contained sculptural
    work. The gap between situational and non-situational reference, implied
    in the "as if" reference of descriptive accounts, is now unbridgeable. This
    can be seen in fictional narratives, i.e., in narratives that are not
    descriptive reports where a narrative time, expressed by specific tenses of
    the verbs, is displayed by and within the narrative without any connection
    to the unique space-time network common to ostensive and non-ostensive
    description.
       "Does this mean that this eclipse of reference, in either the ostensive or
    descriptive sense, amounts to a sheer abolition of all reference? No ... In
    one manner or another, poetic texts speak about the world. But not in a
    descriptive way ... the reference here is not abolished, but divided or
    split. The effacement of the ostensive and descriptive reference liberates a
    power of reference to aspects of our being in the world that cannot be
    said in a direct descriptive way, but only alluded to, thanks to the
    referential values of metaphoric and, in general, symbolic expressions" (IT
    36–37).
       If "the suspension of ordinary discourse and its didactic intention
    assumes an urgent character for the poet, this is just because the reduction
    of the referential values of ordinary discourse is the negative condition
    that allows new configurations expressing the meaning of reality to be
    brought to language. Through those new configurations new ways of
    being in the world, of living there, and of projecting our innermost
    possibilities onto it are also brought to language" (IT 60).

13  Ricoeur remarks that texts extend "the scope of reference beyond the
    narrow boundaries of the dialogical situation ..." (IT 36). On first
    reading, this is very strange; one is not, in utterance, confined to referring
    to entities in the discourse situation. In principle, anything that one can
    refer to in writing, one can refer to in utterance. But probably what he
    means is that texts make possible that mode of reference which is world-
    projection. It is in that way that they extend reference; they extend it
    beyond ordinary reference. He says in the same passage, "Thanks to
    writing, man and only man has a world and not just a situation ... For us,
    the world is the ensemble of references opened up by the texts, or, at least
    for the moment, by descriptive texts" (IT 36). Which implies that
    utterance in dialogic situations lacks the world-projective mode of
    reference. But I know of no place in which Ricoeur works this out. In

general, his comments about reference are among the most confusing aspects of his exposition.

14  If the response be forthcoming that discerning the intentions of the author is relevant not only to the aim of entering the lived experience from which the text emerged, but also to the aim of discerning the sense and reference of the text, the answer is that it is a mistake to suppose that we can or should conduct our interpretation under "the tutelage of the mental intention" (HHS 201). "The fact is that the author can no longer 'rescue' his work ... His intention is often unknown to us, sometimes redundant, sometimes useless, and sometimes even harmful as regards the interpretation of the verbal meaning of his work. In even the better cases it has to be taken into account in light of the text itself" (IT 75–76).

15  Though the possibility discussed earlier should be kept in mind, that the sense is a speech action whose content is a meaning.

16  Even Monroe Beardsley, one of the most lucid writers on these matters, confused them, in, for example, the article already cited, "The Authority of the Text." He distinguishes there between what he calls "textual meaning" and "authorial meaning"; but he makes no distinction, within the latter, between what the author actually meant (i.e., said) and what the author meant to mean (i.e., to say).

17  In my *Works and Worlds of Art* (Oxford, Clarendon Press; 1980), Part Three.

## 9  *CONTRA DERRIDA*

1  Jacques Derrida, *Positions*, tr. and ed. by Alan Bass (Chicago, University of Chicago Press; 1981), pp. 50–51. Henceforth I will abbreviate references to this text as "P", and incorporate them into my text.

2  Jacques Derrida, *Writing and Difference*, tr. by Alan Bass (Chicago, University of Chicago Press; 1978), p. 292. Henceforth I will abbreviate references to this text as "WD" and incorporate them into my text.

3  Derrida would not disagree: "It is evident that the concept of spacing, by itself, cannot account for anything, any more than any other concept. It cannot account for the differences – the different things – between which is opened the spacing which nevertheless delimits them" (P 81).

4  On this theological application, see especially Derrida's essay, "Edmond Jabès and the Question of the Book" in WD.

5  Though perhaps one is then imagining a logical rather than a causal possibility: "the debate is interminable. The divergence, the *difference* between Dionysius and Apollo, between ardor and structure, cannot be erased in history; for it is not *in* history. It too, in an unexpected sense, is an original structure; the opening of history, historicity itself. *Difference* does not simply belong either to history or to structure" (WD 28).

6  Perhaps I should quote as a unit the passage which I am here interpreting: "Emancipation from this language must be attempted. But

not as an *attempt* at emancipation from it, for this is impossible unless we forget *our* history. Rather, as the dream of emancipation. Nor as emancipation from it, which would be meaningless and would deprive us of the light of meaning. Rather, as resistance to it, as far as possible. In any event, we must not abandon ourselves to this language ..."

7 "To 'deconstruct' philosophy, thus, would be to think – in the most faithful, interior way – the structured genealogy of philosophy's concepts, but at the same time to determine – from a certain exterior that is unqualifiable or unnameable by philosophy – what this history has been able to dissimulate or forbid, making itself into a history by means of this somewhere motivated repression."

8 "*Phone*, in effect, is the signifying substance *given to consciousness* as that which is most intimately tied to the thought of the signified concept. From this point of view, the voice is consciousness itself. When I speak, not only am I conscious of being present for what I think, but I am conscious also of keeping as close as possible to my thought, or to the 'concept,' a signifier that does not fall into the world, a signifier that I hear as soon as I emit it, that seems to depend upon my pure and free spontaneity, requiring the use of no instrument, no accessory, no force taken from the world. Not only do the signifier and the signified seem to unite, but also, in this confusion, the signifier seems to erase itself or to become transparent, in order to allow the concept to present itself as what it is, referring to nothing other than its presence. The exteriority of the signifier seems reduced. Naturally this experience is a lure ..." (*Positions* 22).

9 "Of course it is not a question of resorting to the same concept of writing and of simply inverting the dissymmetry that now has become problematical. It is a question, rather, of producing a new concept of writing. This concept can be called *gram* or *différance*" (P 26).

10 See also *Positions* 69.

11 "This lost certainty, this absence of divine writing, that is to say, first of all, the absence of the Jewish God (who himself writes, when necessary), does not solely and vaguely define something like "modernity." As the absence and haunting of the divine sign, it regulates all modern criticism and aesthetics. There is nothing astonishing about this. "Consciously or not, " says Georges Canguilhem, "the idea that man has of his poetic power corresponds to the idea he has about the creation of the world, and to the solution he gives to the problem of the radical origin of things" (WD 10).

12 Jacques Derrida, *Of Grammatology*, tr. by G. C. Spivak (Chicago, University of Chicago Press; 1976), p. 6.

13 See especially Foucault's essay, "What is an Author?" in Paul Rabinow, ed., *The Foucault Reader* (New York, Pantheon Books; 1984); and Barthes' essay, "The Death of the Author" in Roland Barthes, *Image – Music – Text* (New York, Hill and Wang; 1977).

14 I discuss in detail this and other points of disagreement with the standard

contemporary analysis of the phenomenon in my *Works and Worlds of Art* (Oxford, Clarendon Press; 1980), Part Three. On the point made in the text above: my own view is that composing or telling fiction is itself the performance of an illocutionary act. Not of course the act of asserting; rather, the act of *inviting imagining*. "Let the following be imagined" or "Let us imagine the following": that is the fictioneer's preface. Furthermore, the writer or teller of fiction often wishes to assert something by way of performing the discourse act of fictionalizing. The death of the author is mostly no more than a rumor! But this analysis of fiction is controversial; John Searle and Kendall Walton, for example, disagree. Searle thinks that to write or tell fiction is to *pretend* to perform illocutionary acts. Walton thinks that to write fiction is to compose a text for a society in which there are rules mandating imagining. Thus each, in his own way, concedes "the death of the author."

15 Though notice that on the standard analysis of fiction, which Barthes and Foucault accept, one will want to practice something *very much like* discourse interpretation; since the view is that the *narrator* performs acts of discourse.

16 Barthes, "Death of the Author," p. 148.

## 10 PERFORMANCE INTERPRETATION

1 I should observe that authorial-discourse interpretation, performance interpretation, and putative textual sense interpretation, by no means exhaust the activities which are regularly called "interpretation." In fact, a multiplicity of very diverse activities are regularly so-called – making talk about interpretation often completely bewildering. I am focusing all my attention here on those activities which might be described as trying to extract noematic and designative content from a text. But sometimes, the activity of using such noematic or designative content as a guide to what should be done in the present situation is called "interpretation"; thus, it is said that in rendering judgment on constitutional cases, the U.S. Supreme Court is "interpreting" the Constitution. Such interpretation was called "tropological" interpretation by the medievals; traditionally it was also called "*applicatio.*" Sermons, called *predicatio*, were traditionally understood as consisting mainly of interpretation of this sort. (On this last point, see G. R. Evans, *The Language and Logic of the Bible: The Earlier Middle Ages* (Cambridge, Cambridge University Press; 1984), pp. 8 ff. Sometimes the attempt to discover one and another thing about the genesis of the text is called "interpretation"; that is what goes on in some Freudian "interpretations." And sometimes what might, in my judgment, better be called "extrapolation" is called "interpretation." It's easiest to explain what I have in mind here by reference to authorial-discourse interpretation, though the point also pertains to performance interpretation. Consider the totality of the designative content of some piece of discourse; add to that designative content what is *suggested* by the discourser. Then

one can raise the question: what else would be the case if that designative
content were the case? Setting about answering that question would be to
engage in *extrapolation*. Often it is the case, especially in discussions of
fiction, that what I here call "extrapolation" is called "interpretation." I
discuss various issues about extrapolation in some detail in my *Works and
Worlds of Art*, Part Three, §3. What was traditionally called "typological"
interpretation is a species of extrapolation. (I will say a bit more about
this in Chapter 12.)

2  Mary Hesse, *Models and Analogies in Science* (New York, Sheed and Ward;
   1963).
3  See my *Works and Worlds of Art* (Oxford, Clarendon Press; 1980), Part Two.
4  I will be discussing these concepts in the next chapter.
5  In Frank McConnell, ed., *The Biblical and the Narrative Tradition* (New York,
   Oxford University Press; 1986).
6  In his book *Mimesis*, Kendall Walton develops what is essentially a
   performance theory of how fiction is to be understood and interpreted. I
   do not think that that theory will do in general; but, for the reasons
   indicated in the text, such a theory has far more plausibility for fiction
   than for most texts.

## 11 THE FIRST HERMENEUTIC

1  The best discussion of the workings of tropes is, in my judgment, Robert
   J. Fogelin, *Figuratively Speaking* (New Haven, Yale University Press; 1988).
2  John R. Searle, "Metaphor," in A. Ortony (ed.) *Metaphor and Thought*
   (Cambridge, Cambridge University Press; 1979). I will incorporate page
   references to this essay in my text. Donald Davidson, "What Metaphors
   Mean," in *Inquiries into Truth and Interpretation* (Oxford, Clarendon Press;
   1984).
3  Swinburne, *Revelation*, pp. 19–20.
4  He continues, "there are various other cues that we employ to spot
   metaphorical utterances. For example, when reading Romantic poets, we
   are on the lookout for metaphors, and some people we know are simply
   more prone to metaphorical utterances than others" (114). It's interesting
   to note that Augustine also took absurdity to be the clue to non-literal
   use: "When words taken literally give an absurd meaning, we ought
   forthwith to enquire whether they may not be used in this or that
   figurative sense which we are unacquainted with ... in this way many
   obscure passsages have had light thrown upon them" (*de doctrina Christiana*,
   III. xxix. 41).
5  Though I do agree with the thesis of Steven Knapp and Walter Benn
   Michaels, in their well-known article "Against Theory" (*Critical Inquiry*,
   Summer 1982), that even to classify something as *words* rather than mere
   *designs* is to assume an intention of a certain sort behind their production
   or presentation.

6  The best general discussion, with which I am acquainted, of the relevance of authorial intention to interpretation in the arts, is Noel Carroll, "Art, Intention, and Conversation" in G. Iseminger, ed., *Intention and Interpretation* (Philadelphia, Temple University Press; 1992). Since composing the account offered in the text of the relevance of authorial intentions to interpretation of texts, I have come across an account which is almost exactly the same by Gareth Evans in his *The Varieties of Reference* (Oxford, Clarendon Press; 1982), pp. 67 ff.

## 12  SECOND HERMENEUTIC

1  And beyond that, what the human writers said is worth attending to in its own right. As Charles M. Wood remarks, in *The Formation of Christian Understanding* (Philadelphia, Westminster Press; 1981), p. 74: "Whichever way this reinterpretation of texts within the canonical context is achieved, it undoubtedly involves some loss of the sharp individuality of the diverse voices which might be heard in scripture: their sacrifice, it may be thought, to the cause of a unitary reading of scripture. It would be not only unfortunate but theologically indefensible if these voices were to be silenced – outshouted by God, so to speak – and their reality denied, particularly now that critical-historical study has increased our awareness of the humanity of these authors and thus of our commonality with them, and has enabled us to be both profoundly challenged by and thoroughly critical of what they have to say."

2  Andrew Louth, *Discerning the Mystery* (Oxford, Clarendon Press; 1983), p. 129.

3  The best of the medieval theorists were clear on the fact that typological interpretation deals with, as they put it, the signification of things rather than the signification of words; see G. R. Evans, *The Language and Logic of the Bible: The Earlier Middle Ages*, §4, on "Words and Numbers and Things." I am myself skeptical about this notion of things signifying things; a good many of the high medievals were so as well. G. R. Evans, in *The Language and Logic of the Bible: The Road to Reformation*, p. 46 ff., cites, for example, William of Auvergne as holding that among things there are similitudes but not significations. That amounts to accepting what, in the text above, I called "simile interpretation," while rejecting typological interpretation.

4  Though the framework that the medievals used for thinking about these matters was somewhat different from the one which I am developing, the counterpart point within their framework eventually became commonplace among them. After centuries of confusion as to what was the *literal sense*, eventually there was a convergence around the conviction that it was what the human authors intended to say; thus the literal sense included figurative uses. See G. R. Evans, *The Language and Logic of the Bible: The Road to Reformation* (Cambridge, Cambridge University Press;

1985), §7, "The Literal Sense." A convergence also developed around the conviction that the literal sense is the basic sense; *cf.* Evans, Vol. I, p. 8, and vols. I and II, *passim*.

5 The point has been made in recent years by a number of other writers as well. See esp. Brevard Childs in the introductory sections of *The New Testament as Canon* (Philadelphia, Fortress Press; 1985). Childs offers this as an example: "When seen in an historical or literary isolation an enormous chasm separates Galatians from the Pastoral epistles. However, from within the New Testament canon the Pastorals have been assigned a particular function which is certainly neither to be identified with the early Pauline letters nor characterized as hopelessly contradictory" (30). David Kelsey and Charles M. Wood take the further step of arguing that it is analytic of the concept of *canon* that to say that the Bible is the *canon* of the Church implies that the Church ought to interpret the books of the Bible as sections of *one book*. *Cf.* Wood, in *The New Testament as Canon.*, p. 91 ff.; and David H. Kelsey, *The Use of Scripture in Recent Theology* (Philadelphia, Fortress Press; 1975). Kelsey makes an important point in this regard: "ascribing 'wholeness' to the canon is not identical with ascribing 'unity' to the canon. The canon's 'unity' would consist of a coherence or even consistency among its contents. It could only be demonstrated by exegetical study. The canon's 'unity,' if it has any, might be invoked to account for its effectiveness at accomplishing the end to which it is used. But it is not logically necessary that the canon actually exhibit such 'unity' in order for it to be construed as some kind of 'whole' "(106).

6 It is, says G. F. Evans, "a first principle of mediaeval exegesis that there can be nothing contradictory in Scripture" (*The Language and Logic of the Bible: The Earlier Middle Ages*, p. 126). See the entire Part III, on "*Disputatio*," in that volume.

7 It's true that God can only reveal what is actual or true; but that's also the case for you and me. It's analytic of the concept revelation that this is the case. But as for speaking, in contrast to revealing, I don't myself find it obvious that God should assert only what is true. Why should God not "accommodate" Godself to us by sometimes asserting what is helpful in our particular situation even though it is not strictly speaking true? Parents do this sort of thing all the time, and are praiseworthy for doing so. However, to introduce this consideration into the discussion in the text would complicate it enormously; so I have decided, with some reluctance, to conduct the discussion as if we knew that God would only assert what is true.

8 Pretty much the same results which I want to achieve by speaking of the author's way of making or developing a point, Swinburne (in *Revelation*) tries to achieve with his notion of *presupposition*. I have some difficulties with Swinburne's explanation of his concept – which is why I have chosen

a different tack. It's interesting, though, that sometimes, in his explanation of *presupposition,* Swinburne quite clearly has the very same distinction in mind that I do, between point, and way of making the point.

9  For a different opinion on this point, see the very interesting essay by Harold Fisch, "Song of Solomon: the Allegorical Imperative," in his collection *Poetry with a Purpose* (Bloomington, Indiana University Press; 1988).

10  Hans Frei, *Types of Christian Theology* (New Haven, Yale University Press; 1992), p. 5.

11  Hans Frei, "The 'Literal Reading' of the Biblical Narrative in the Christian Tradition: Does It Stretch or Will It Break?".

12  Swinburne, *Revelation,* p. 178. *Cf.* pp. 192–93: "since the books of the New Testament, as well as the Old, gain their status as canonical documents through the Church's recognition of their inspiration by God, they too must be interpreted in the light of central Christian doctrines proclaimed by the Church as codifying in precise and clear form the essence of the Christian revelation. Thus clearly some New Testament passages say or imply that Jesus Christ was God and had existed from all eternity: clearly the opening passage of St. John's Gospel for example carries this implication. Other New Testament passages do not seem to think of Christ in such exalted terms and seem to imply that his exalted status ... was only his subsequently to the Resurrection. Romans 1: 4 seems to have this lower Christology ... If we take St. John's Gospel and the Epistle to the Romans as two separate works written by two separate authors, the most plausible historical interpretation of the latter suggests that those authors had different views about the status of Christ. But if we think of them as having the same author, God, who also guided the Church to produce the creeds, the initially less natural interpretation of Romans must be the true one. These works have no authority for Christians unless they see them as deriving their authority from the Church's recognition of their inspiration by God, and in that case all the rules of textual interpretation force upon them, as their true meaning, a meaning compatible with central Christian doctrine, as formulated by the Church – which includes the divinity of Christ."

13  HAS SCRIPTURE BECOME A WAX NOSE?

1  Mircea Eliade, *The Myth of the Eternal Return* (Princeton, Princeton University Press; 1965), pp. 55–56.

2  G. W. Leibniz, *New Essays On Human Understanding,* tr. and ed. by P. Remnant and J. Bennett (Cambridge, Cambridge University Press; 1981), 444–45.

3  *On Christian Doctrine,* III, 10, 15

4  John Locke, *A Second Vindiction of the Reasonablenesss of Christianity,* in *Works*

(12th edition, 1824), Vol. 6, p. 295. The image of the wax nose had become traditional by Locke's time. Basil Hall, in his article "Biblical Scholarship: Editions and Commentaries" (*Cambridge History of the Bible*, Vol. III [Cambridge, Cambridge University Press; 1963]), p. 48, traces it back to Geiler of Kaiserberg: "the despairing conclusions of Geiler of Kaiserberg, who at the end of the fifteenth century said that Scripture was a 'nose of wax' to be turned in any way by the too frequent misuse of the allegorical method of interpretation." (I owe this reference to Kathryn Greene-McCreight.) Another traditional image for the same phenomenon was *gallus in campanili*: the weathercock in the church tower, blown about by every "wind of doctrine."

5 Frei, "Response to 'Narrative Theology: An Evangelical Appraisal'," in *Trinity Journal* 8 NS (1987), pp. 21–22.

6 See especially "The 'Literal Reading' of the Biblical Narrative in the Christian Tradition: Does It Stretch or Will It Break?" in Frank McConnell, ed., *The Bible and the Narrative Tradition* (New York, Oxford University Press; 1986).

7 Hans Frei, *Theology and Narrative*, ed. by G. Hunsinger and Wm. C. Placher (New York, Oxford University Press; 1993), p. 31.

8 Hugh of Amiens stated well the standard medieval position. I quote from G. R. Evans, *The Language and Logic of the Bible: The Earlier Middle Ages*, p. 35. "'our words' cannot impose upon the Deity itself (*ponunt in ipsam deitatem*) any of the ordinary things they mean: 'action' or 'passion' or 'variety'. Therefore take careful note that words and any sayings which are taken to signify God' are not to be classified in terms of 'the parts of speech which the grammarians lay down'."

9 G. W. Leibniz, *Essays on Human Understanding*, pp. 499–500.

## 14 ILLOCUTIONARY STANCE OF BIBLICAL NARRATIVE

1 Concerning Matthew's genealogy, this is what N. T. Wright concludes in *The New Testament and the People of God* (Minneapolis, Fortress Press; 1992): "The genealogy then says to Matthew's careful reader that the long story of Abraham's people will come to its fulfillment, its seventh seven, with a new David, who will rescue his people from their exile, that is, 'save their people from their sins'. When Matthew says precisely this in 1: 18–21 we should not be surprised" (386).

2 See Hans von Campenhausen, *The Formation of the Christian Bible* (Philadelphia, Fortress Press; 1972), pp. 170–71: "In theory there were three ways in which the Gospel literature could be standardized. The first was that adopted by Marcion: to select one single gospel, to revise it in accordance with one's own ideas, and then to declare this and this alone to be *the* Gospel ... Secondly, an attempt might be made to combine the trustworthy and useful elements in all texts into a single new gospel; or finally, one might select various gospels, and pronounce them valid in

combination, as a complex unity. Prevailing practice had prepared the way for the last-named of these three solutions; but it too had serious obstacles to overcome, since, as is well known, the gospels do not agree at every point, and indeed, if we include John, display very considerable differences of content. Nevertheless, it was this solution which in the end prevailed ..." (See also p. 211).

3  Another possibility is that the illocutionary stance which I will suggest, though not that of the human discourse of the Gospels, is nonetheless that of the divine discourse of which the human discourse is the instrument. Though I will not here explore this alternative possibility, it must definitely be kept in mind.

4  I develop these points about fiction much more elaborately in my *Works and Worlds of Art*, Part Three.

5  Thus I agree with the following vigorous words of Meir Sternberg in *The Poetics of Biblical Narrative* (Bloomington, Indiana University Press; 1985), p. 32: "Were the narrative written or read as fiction, then God would turn from the lord of history into a creature of the imagination, with the most disastrous results. The shape of time, the rationale of monotheism, the foundations of conduct, the national sense of identity, the very right to the land of Israel and the hope of deliverance to come: all hang in the generic balance. Hence the Bible's determination to sanctify and compel literal belief in the past."

6  Cambridge, Cambridge University Press; 1992.

7  Here is Sternberg's summary: "the biblical narrator also appeals to the privilege of omniscience – so that he no more speaks in the writer's ordinary voice than Jane Austen does in hers, but exactly as a persona raised high above him – with one crucial difference in convention. Omniscience in modern narrative attends and signals fictionality, while in the ancient tradition it not only accommodates but also guarantees authenticity.

As a rule of narrative communication, inspiration amounts to omniscience exercised on history: the tale's claim to truth rests on the teller's God-given knowledge. The prophet assumes this stance (or persona) explicitly, the storyteller implicitly but none the less authoritatively. And its assumption enables him to bring to bear on his world (and his audience) what would elsewhere count as the poetic license of invention without paying the price in truth claim. Herein lies one of the Bible's unique rules: under the aegis of ideology, convention transmutes even invention into the stuff of history, or rather obliterates the line dividing fact from fancy in communication. So every word is God's word. The product is neither fiction nor historicized fiction nor fictionalized history, but historiography pure and uncompromising" (34–35).

8  Sternberg himself often makes the confusion which he himself so sternly warns against. Let me cite one passage, from near the beginning of the book: "[This] is the Bible's original world view: unlike all pagan deities,

God is truly and exclusively all-knowing. Does this epistemological novelty in the sphere of world order extend to the epistemology and operation of point of view in the narrative? Does the monotheistic article of faith give a new bearing to the inherited rule of omniscience? Is it, for example, that the narrator assumes omniscience because he could not otherwise do justice to an infallible God and impress on the reader, by appropriate suppressions, his own fallibility? Since the Omniscient inspires his prophets, moreover, does the narrator implicitly appeal to the gift of prophecy, so as to speak with redoubled authority as divine historian?" (12). Sternberg eventually gives a decisive "Yes" answer to all these questions. But the (implied) narrator doesn't appeal to the gift of prophecy; it's the author who appeals to the gift of prophecy. And the narrator doesn't assume omniscience "because he could not otherwise do justice to an infallible God"; the narrator, on Sternberg's analysis, *is* God. But neither does the author assume omniscience. He claims to be inspired, indeed; but to claim or pretend to be omniscient would be to claim or pretend to be God. And that, the biblical authors did not do.

9　"We have already seen," says Sternberg, "how and why the biblical artist assumes an omniscience equal but subservient to God's" (119). Presumably this means that the biblical artist plays the role of an omniscient being. Would the theology of the ancient Hebrews – that very theology which Sternberg emphasizes – really have allowed anybody to play such a role?

10　That this is in fact what is happening is pretty clear from this passage: the conversation of the rabbis, quoted above, "draws notice to various aspects of what one would call today the biblical writer's omniscience: the ability to penetrate the mind of one character ... or more ... and to narrate simultaneous events wide apart in space ..." (59). The literary critic would indeed use his term of art "omniscient narrator" [n.b., *narrator*, not *writer*, as Sternberg says] to describe the point of view in question. But to be omniscient, in the real sense, one has to know an awful lot more than that! In a later passage, Sternberg says, "In the Esther passage, we recall, the rabbis postulate divine inspiration to account for [the narrator's] unlimited access to knowledge" (76). But the rabbis didn't account for the narrator's knowledge but for the author's! And they didn't account for the author's "unlimited access to knowledge," since they surely didn't believe that the author had unlimited access. They accounted for knowledge by the author which – as I have been putting it – goes beyond our normal human ken.

11　There's one passage in which Sternberg is clearly understanding the concept of an implied narrator along these lines: "The narrator ... is the figure chosen and devised by the author to perform the telling" (74).

12　Sternberg says in one passage: "To say that the biblical writer exercises or enjoys the license of invention (under whatever guise) is to say that he is omniscient; and to say that he is omniscient is to invest him with a storytelling privilege that the same writer would hardly lay claim to in his everyday life (least of all, if he indeed happens to double as a character, his life within the tale). On laying down the pen with which he had just been tracing the inmost mysteries of God and humanity, a Jehoshafat would no more presume to read his own wife's mind with any approach to certainty than the rest of us do" (68–69). But this is all confused. Within Sternberg's conceptuality, it's the *narrator* who is supposed to be omniscient, not the writer; whereas it's the *writer* who is supposed to be inspired, not the narrator. For God is supposed to be the narrator; and obviously God doesn't have to be inspired. The author has to be inspired, so as to know what God narrates by way of the words of the text. But that falls far short of inspiration making the writer omniscient. As Sternberg never tires of emphasizing, in the theology of the Hebrews, only God is omniscient.

13 "God speaking through an inspired medium," that, says Sternberg, is "what the rabbis literally affirm to be the narrative situation" (76). Perhaps some of them did. But all Sternberg cites evidence for, is that some of the rabbis attributed the author's knowledge of some items in the implied chronicle of his narration to inspiration.

14 I have been emphasizing that it is one thing for the authors of the biblical narratives to have known some of the things in the implied chronicles of their narratives by inspiration, and quite another thing for them to have tacitly prefaced their entire narration with the words, "Thus spoke the Lord." The question I am posing in the text above is, what is the evidence for the claim that they were doing the latter. But the evidence Sternberg cites for his claim that, at the time, they were regarded as inspired, is also exceedingly weak. See page 77 and following.

15 There is one additional passage which might perhaps be interpreted as containing an argument for the thesis: "It is inconceivable that a story-teller who keeps in closer touch with God's doings and sentiments than the very prophets who figure among his dramatis personae would operate as their inferior in divine sanction; or that his claim would be challenged by the only society that canonized its sacred writings because it pinned on them faith and hope alike" (79). Maybe so. But that's fully compatible with the author of narrative speaking in his own voice.

16 To be specific, in my *Works and Worlds of Art*, §§ x and xi of Part Three.

17 And discrepancies within the Hebrew Bible (Old Testament) as well; *cf.* the famous one between II Samuel 24: 1, where it says that *God* incited David to number the people, and I Chronicles 21: 1, where the chronicler attributes the incitement to *Satan*. Sternberg never explains how he would deal with such discrepancies, pleading that he is just interpreting. One surmises that he sees more at stake. If one concedes error in the implied chronicles, then something has to go in the background ideology that Sternberg attributes to ancient Israel; and Sternberg is exceedingly reluctant to concede that anything in that ideology has to go. None-theless, God wouldn't have said it, if it's false; and it would be very odd of

God to inspire the author so that he knows of things beyond his normal ken, and not inspire him to get right those things that fall within his normal ken.

18	Vidal calls *Burr* "a novel" on its title page (New York, Random House; 1973). But in an "Afterword," this is what he says about the book: "Why a historical novel and not a history? To me, the attraction of the historical novel is that one can be as meticulous (or as careless!) as the historian and yet reserve the right not only to rearrange events but, most important, to attribute motives – something the conscientious historian or biographer ought never to do./ I have spent a good many years preparing and writing *Burr* and I have tried to keep to the known facts. In three instances, I have moved people about ... Otherwise, the characters are in the right places, on the right dates, doing what they actually did. Obviously I have made up conversation, but whenever possible I have used actual phrases of the speaker ... Although the novel's viewpoint must be Burr's, the story told is history and not invention."

19	New York, Knopf; 1991.

20	Discussing the principles of interpretation proposed in the medieval *Glossa Ordinaria*, G. R. Evans in *The Logic and Language of the Bible: The Earlier Middle Ages*, p. 46, says this: "The reversal of chronological order in a historical narrative may, too, be a 'way of speaking' (*genus locutionis*)." Eusebius, in a well-known passage from his *Church History*, iii, 39, cites Papias as alluding to a tradition to the effect that Mark was just indifferent to issues of chronology: "the tradition which [Papias] gives in regard to Mark, the author of the Gospel. It is in these words: 'This also the presbyter said: Mark, having become the interpreter of Peter, wrote down accurately, though not indeed in order, whatsoever he remembered of the things said or done by Christ. For he neither heard the Lord nor followed him, but afterward, as I said, he followed Peter, who adapted his teaching to the needs of his hearers, but with no intention of giving a connected account of the Lord's discourses, so that Mark committed no error while he thus wrote some things as he remembered them. For he was careful of one thing, not to omit any of the things which he had heard, and not to state any of them falsely.'"

21	The superficial similarities between my suggestion, and the position developed by Paul Ricoeur in his essay, "Interpretative Narrative" (in Regina M. Schwartz, ed., *The Book and the Text* [Oxford, Blackwell; 1990]) might lead some readers to overlook the fundamental difference in our positions. Ricoeur speaks of the gospel writers as "narrativizing the kerygma." He sees each of the writers as having a christology that he wants to "illustrate" and "signify" and "communicate"; he speaks of the kerygma as "calling" for a narrative, and of the writers as "looking" for a narrative. He then goes on to consider whether the narratives "fit" the kerygma, whether there is a "homology." Mark's narrative "historicizes the kerygma of the risen Christ"; he has "placed all the resources of the narrative art for negativity and even obscurity at the service of his christology of a suffering and crucified Son of Man." My suggestion is not that the gospel writers have a christology (a "theologoumen") that they decide to express by composing narratives about Jesus, but that the gospel writers compose narratives of Jesus' life designed to illuminate who Jesus was and what God was doing in him. It was Schama's purpose to compose a "portrait" of Wolfe and the battle on the Plains of Abraham, one that would, while remaining a "portrait" of that historical figure and those historical events, also show something about the craft of history. It was not his purpose to compose a discourse about the role of uncertainty in the craft of history, deciding to use as means thereto the telling of some stories about Wolfe. Ricoeur suggests that his view resembles that of Hans Frei; but to the contrary, it is fundamentally different. Frei never tired of insisting that the gospels are not about christology, but about Jesus enacting the events whereby he became the Christ. The point of the narrative is the events in their christological pattern.

### 15 ARE WE ENTITLED?

1  Locke's theory of moral obligation is quite clearly a divine *command* theory, not just a divine *will* theory; so the notion of God speaking has not entirely disappeared from his thought. But his account of religious faith, for example, is not that it consists of believing what God says on God's say-so, but that it consists of "the assent to any proposition ... upon the credit of the proposer, as coming from God in some extraordinary way of communication" (*Essay*, IV, xviii, 2). In his late book, *The Reasonableness of Christianity*, Locke does now and then speak of "the word of God"; but he carefully explains that what he means by the word of God is just proclaiming Jesus to be the Messiah (§ 40). The word of God does not require a divine speaker!

2  Locke's thought on the matter is especially clear from the preface to his paraphrases of St. Paul's epistles, where he says that Paul "had the whole doctrine of the gospel from God, by immediate revelation; and was appointed to be the apostle of the Gentiles, for the propagating of it in the heathen world ... A large stock of jewish learning he had taken in, at the feet of Gamaliel; and for his information in christian knowledge, and the mysteries and depths of the dispensation of grace by Jesus Christ, God himself had condescended to be his instructor and teacher. The light of the gospel he had received from the Fountain and Father of light himself ... [H]e was full-stored with the knowledge of the things he treated of; for he had light from heaven, it was God himself furnished him ..." (Preface in *Works* (12th edition, 1824), pp.xiv–xv, xvii).

3  Might there not be cases in which God reveals something to someone without sending any confirming signs? Yes, there might. What must be added then is this: if the result of one's search for a confirming miracle

proves negative, one considers whether the content of the purported revelation is (in some rather strong sense) "consonant to" the content of already confirmed revelation. If so, one ought to accept this new content, on the ground that it is probably true; and since it is harmless to believe, in addition, that God revealed it to one, one is permitted so to believe. Locke, *Essay*, IV, xix, 16.

4  For a fine discussion of belief and the will, see William P. Alston, "The Deontological Conception of Epistemic Justification" in Alston, *Epistemic Justification* (Ithaca, Cornell University Press; 1989). I should say that the concept of a *doxastic practice* which I will develop in the text differs considerably from that which Alston develops in his *Perceiving God*. His doxastic practice is a "family" of belief-forming processes, each involving a certain input and a belief output, related by a certain "function." Mine are fundamentally ways of using such processes – ways of getting into a position for one or another of these to be activated.

5  See his *After Virtue* (Notre Dame, Notre Dame University Press; 1981).

6  An interesting blend of the two thoughts is this: "You ought to have known better than to believe that that was the meaning of 'serendipitous' without checking it out in a reputable dictionary." Here the thought is that he ought to have known something which, presumably, he did not know; and that what he should have known is that there is a better basis for his believing or disbelieving the proposition in question than the basis which his belief in fact has. In addition, the suggestion is clearly in the air that he should have secured that better basis.

## 16 AFTERWORD

1  And there remains the issue of how we get from the immediate conviction that *this passage before me* is a medium of divine discourse, to the conclusion that Scripture as a whole is the medium of divine discourse. I have interpreted Calvin as holding that the Holy Spirit produces convictions of the former sort; in fact, his discussion is somewhat ambiguous on the matter (see especially the opening of §5 of I vii). I suppose it's possible for someone to have read through all of Scripture and then, looking back over its totality, to have the conviction well up immediately within her that this totality – this passage which is the whole of Scripture – is a medium of divine discourse. I would suppose that experience to be much more rare than the others, however. And in any case, the arguments in the text against regarding such experiences as good reason for preferring the divine discourse construal of Scripture over its competitors, apply to this totalizing experience as well.

2  There might well be a plausible story of happenings in the early church which constitutes a good reason for the same conclusion, but which was not told *within* the early church. In his book *Revelation*, Richard Swinburne tells a story about happenings in the early church which supports the

conclusion that the Bible is a transmitter of divine revelation; he argues that the story goes beyond plausibility to probability. One might be able to adapt his story so that it yields the conclusion that the Bible is an instrument of divine discourse. Thus, several story lines may yield the same conclusion. I am interested in the story that the early church, by way of at least some of its members, told about itself.

3  Incidentally, every now and then one finds it said that the story told by the early church, of Christ commissioning the apostles to go into all nations as his witnesses, is myth in the service of power, the ground offered being that those same writings make it seem likely that some of the apostles never departed far from Jerusalem. This strikes me as an extraordinarily wooden way of reading the texts; one might as well object that there were some nations to whom no apostle went. Jesus is not recorded as saying to the twelve, "Each and every one of you must go out into all the nations." What he said is that *you twelve* must do so. And obviously the apostolate did go out into "all the nations". The fact that the apostles appear to have parcelled out the work seems to me to be the most natural thing in the world for them to have done. It may be added that the commissioning of the apostolate to go out into all the nations is compatible with failure on the part of some of the apostles to carry out their share of the commission.

4  "For I delivered to you as of first importance what I also received, that Christ died for our sins in accordance with the scriptures, that he was buried, that he was raised on the third day in accordance with the scriptures, and that he appeared to Cephas, then to the twelve. Then he appeared to more than five hundred brethren at one time, most of whom are still alive, though some have fallen asleep. Then he appeared to James, then to all the apostles. Last of all, as to one untimely born, he appeared also to me" (I Cor. 15: 3 ff.).

5  This is the picture from within the New Testament. For a judgment of the situation taking all the evidence into account, see Hans von Campenhausen, *The Formation of the Christian Bible* (Philadelphia, Fortress Press; 1972), p. 259: "The predominant importance of the apostles is, of course, disputed by no one. They are the first and most notable witnesses to Jesus, and possess outstanding authority and holiness. This status is already there in Irenaeus, and within the catholic church it is absolutely taken for granted."

6  "With personal encounter with the risen Lord, personal commissioning by Him seems to have been the only basis of the apostolate. That this commission was given primarily to the twelve is connected with their participation in the history of the earthly Jesus, who specifically prepared them to take up and continue His preaching, yet now as the proclamation of Jesus as the One who had come in fulfillment of OT prophecy. Materially, therefore, two elements are linked with the apostolate in the first community. By the commission of Jesus a number of men, especially

those who were closest to him during His life, became His representatives in the sense that they took His place and thus assumed an authoritative position in the little company of Christians. Yet the altered situation meant that they also became missionaries, and this form of their work was what really characterised their office ..." (Rengstorff, article on *apostolos* in *Kittel's Theological Word-Book of the New Testament*, pp. 431–32).

7   "The fact remains, however, that what is here (in the book of Revelation) explicitly stated, in keeping with the special character of the last book of the Bible, is indicative of a state of affairs that is of essential significance for the entire history of redemption of the New Testament. For it indicates that the authority of God is in nowise limited to his mighty works in Jesus Christ, but that it also extends to their proclamation in the words and writings of those who have been especially appointed as the authorized bearers and instruments of divine revelation. The written tradition established by the apostles, in analogy with the writings of the Old Testament, thereby acquires the significance of being the foundation and standard of the future church. The redemptive historical ground of the New Testament canon must, therefore, be sought in the apostolic power and tradition ..." (Herman Ridderbos, *The Authority of the New Testament Scriptures*), pp. 26–27.

8   *The Formation of the Christian Bible* (Philadelphia, Fortress Press; 1972).

9   A point made by Brevard Childs in the introductory parts of his *The New Testament as Canon* (Philadelphia, Fortress Press; 1985). "The shape which the canon has given the New Testament offers a peculiar construal of the Christian tradition which the early church provided." (pp. 39–40). "The *skandalon* of the canon is that the witness of Jesus Christ has been given its normative shape through an interpretive process of the post-apostolic age" (p. 28).

10  A point made in a number of his writings by James Barr. See, for example, Chapter I, "Before Scripture and After Scripture" in his *Holy Scripture: Canon, Authority, Criticism* (Philadelphia, Westminster Press; 1983).

11  von Campenhausen takes the majority of his predecessors to have held that the formation of the canon followed "the apostolic principle"; and he interprets this as the principle that for a book to be accepted into the canon, it must have come from the hand of an apostle. He then easily shows that the church did not follow this principle – by pointing, for example, to Luke. (See esp. pp. 204 ff. and 253 ff.) But surely the principle embraced by his predecessors was not that one, but rather some such principle as the one I indicate in the text above: for a book to be accepted into the canon, it had to be faithful to the apostolic tradition and come from an apostle or an intimate of an apostle. It "is theologically crucial to see that the church never claimed to have 'created' a canon, but it saw its task in discerning among competing claims what it recognized as apostolic" (B. Childs, *New Testament as Canon*, p. 44).

12  The point is made at various points in Childs, *New Testament as Canon*.

# Index